D0933946

Research Ideas
for the Classroom

Early Childhood Mathematics

T114

Research Ideas for the Classroom

Early Childhood Mathematics

ROBERT J. JENSEN, *Editor*

**National Council of Teachers of Mathematics
Research Interpretation Project**

SIGRID WAGNER, *Project Director*

MACMILLAN PUBLISHING COMPANY
NEW YORK

Maxwell Macmillan Canada
TORONTO

Maxwell Macmillan International
NEW YORK   OXFORD   SINGAPORE   SYDNEY

Macmillan Publishing Company
866 Third Avenue
New York, NY 10022

Maxwell Macmillan Canada, Inc.
1200 Eglinton Avenue East, Suite 200
Don Mills, Ontario M3C 3N1

Macmillan Publishing Company is part of the Maxwell Communication Group of Companies

Library of Congress Catalog Card Number: 92-5479

Printed in the United States of America

Printing number
4   5   6   7   8   9   10

Library of Congress Cataloging-in-Publication Data
Research ideas for the classroom. Early childhood mathematics /
   Robert J. Jensen, editor ; National Council of Teachers of
   Mathematics Research Interpretation Project, Sigrid Wagner, project
   director.
        p.   cm.
     ISBN 0-02-895791-1 — ISBN 0-02-895794-6 (pbk.)
     1. Mathematics—Study and teaching (Preschool) 2. Mathematics—
   Study and teaching (Primary) I. Jensen, Robert J. II. Wagner,
   Sigrid, 1942–   . III. National Council of Teachers of Mathematics.
   Research Interpretation Project.   IV. Title: Early childhood
   mathematics.
   QA135.5.R465   1992
   372.7'044—dc20   92-5479
                                                         CIP

The paper used in this publication meets minimum requirements of American National Standard for Information Sciences—Permanence of Paper for Printed Library Materials. ANSI Z39.48-1984. ⊚™

Contents

Series Foreword

*R*esearch Ideas for the Classroom (RIC) is a three-volume series of research interpretations for early childhood, middle grades, and high school mathematics classrooms. These books reflect the combined efforts of well over two hundred researchers and teachers to produce a comprehensive and current compilation of research implications in mathematics education. We hope these volumes will serve as a useful sequel to the popular *Research Within Reach* published a decade ago by the National Council of Teachers of Mathematics (NCTM). Much research activity has transpired in the past few years and whole new lines of inquiry have emerged, particularly in the area of technology. It is time to look again at what research has to offer in the way of ideas for the classroom.

The ultimate goal of research in mathematics education is to improve learning and teaching, and from this perspective the RIC volumes will serve as a valuable complement to the NCTM Research Agenda Project (RAP) monographs published in 1988 and 1989. The RAP monographs provide syntheses of several strands of existing research, as well as recommendations for future directions. The RIC volumes link the existing research to the classroom and provide ideas for teachers to explore with their own students.

From still another perspective, the RIC volumes should serve as an important supplement to the NCTM *Curriculum and Evaluation Standards* and *Professional Teaching Standards*. Chapter authors were asked to indicate where research supports recommendations in the *Standards* and where a research base is lacking. We hope these frequent citations will help guide implementation of the *Standards* and inform future recommendations.

A subtitle for the RIC volumes might be *Learning from Students*. Part of the value of research in mathematics education lies in the process itself, the process by which we learn from our students what they understand and how that understanding develops, how they feel about mathematics, and what factors affect those feelings. Any teacher who has ever asked a question or noticed an expression of puzzlement or delight has engaged in informal research. What we learn from students may cause us to question our assumptions, fortify our knowledge, investigate our reasoning, or rethink our methods of teaching.

Because research is a learning process, interpreting research becomes a multilayered process of construction in which objective phenomena are filtered through the subjective inferences of researchers, editors, and readers. Yet, as with most learning, this individual process of construction leads, over time, to shared systems of beliefs that influence our behavior in remarkably similar ways. We may tend to regard the key elements of these belief systems as "truths" even though we know that truth is a function of the times, context, and people involved.

The authors of the chapters in *Research Ideas for the Classroom* have attempted to convey the key points suggested by research in their areas of specialization. We hope that you, the reader, will be intrigued enough by ideas described in these pages to do two things: (a) go to the source of the authors' inspiration, the research reports listed at the end of each chapter (especially those marked with an *), and (b) go to the source of the researchers' inspiration, to students, and try some of these research activities yourself. By so doing, you can peel away several layers of subjective interpretation and come that much closer to learning the "truth" from your own students.

The NCTM Research Interpretation Project began in 1988 with a proposal to the National Science Foundation (NSF) to produce an updated and comprehensive set of research interpretations for the mathematics classroom. The project was funded under NSF Grant No. MDR-8850572. The editorial panel and advisory board met in the spring of 1989 to structure the volumes and identify chapter topics. To enhance communication between teachers and researchers, as well as insure the readability and practicality of the books, it was decided that chapters would be co-authored by a researcher and a teacher.

Without a doubt, the most crucial step in any writing project is picking the right authors. Researcher co-authors were chosen by the editorial panel for their knowledge of the research literature and their ability to interpret findings for the classroom. The researchers selected teacher co-authors for their expertise in teaching and the creativity of their ideas.

Authors agreed to an imposing array of requirements designed to guarantee comprehensive coverage, minimum overlap, and uniform format. They were given a long list of subtopics to be included in their chapters and then were told that they had to address all these topics in only twenty manuscript pages of text and five pages of references! They were asked to give some preference to easily accessible research reports, including research-based articles in *Mathematics Teacher*, *Arithmetic Teacher*, and *School Science and Mathematics*. They were asked to identify (*) articles that are especially rich in ideas for teaching.

Chapter development was a four-stage process. Editors and advisory board members reacted to chapter outlines and preliminary bibliographies from the standpoint of coverage and structure of the total volumes. First drafts of chapters were reviewed by researchers for breadth of coverage and balance of treatment within each chapter. Second drafts were reviewed by teachers for clarity of writing and practicality of suggestions for the classroom. Third drafts went to the publisher.

Each volume looks at research from the perspective of the learner, the content, and the teacher. Two chapters in each volume focus on the learner—one on cognition and one on affect. The content chapters vary according to the level, but each volume includes chapters on problem solving and technology. Four or five chapters in each volume focus on teaching—models of instruction, planning curriculum, classroom interaction, and evaluation. Each volume concludes with a chapter on teachers as researchers, which includes descriptions of research activities conducted by teachers within the constraints of the typical classroom environment.

The chapter structure makes each book easy to read selectively. References to accompanying chapters are included wherever appropriate, yet each chapter is quite comprehensible by itself. It is our sincere hope that most readers will enjoy an entire volume for its wealth of useful information and interesting ideas.

As comprehensive as the editors, authors, and reviewers have tried to be in a limited number of pages, the astute reader will surely note that some important themes are underrepresented. Some content topics (e.g., discrete mathematics, statistics, integers, inequalities), despite their importance in the mathematics curriculum, lack a substantial research base related to teaching and learning. Some themes, perhaps most notably that of gender and mathematics, have such a substantial research base that numerous books and monographs have been devoted to those single themes. Gender and mathematics is addressed in RIC in the chapters on affect, but we encourage the interested reader to consult other publications for further information. Other themes (e.g., multiculturalism or communication) have long histories of research but only recently within the field of mathematics education. We leave it to the next edition of NCTM research interpretations to report on these areas.

On behalf of the editorial panel, we thank the National Science Foundation, and especially Raymond J. Hannapel, for encouraging and supporting the project and for supplying copies of these books to mathematics supervisors across the country. We thank Lloyd Chilton for his help in launching the volumes and arranging for publication. We thank James D. Gates and Cynthia Rosso at NCTM and Philip Friedman and Michael Sander at Macmillan for helping in many ways throughout the project. We thank the advisory board—John A. Dossey, Mark J. Driscoll, Fernand J. Prevost, Judith T. Sowder, Douglas B. Super, and Marilyn N. Suydam—for their enthusiastic vision and willingness to share ideas. We thank the reviewers whose thoughtful comments and suggestions helped improve the quality of the final product. Most especially, we thank the authors for their considerable talents, their cheerful willingness to meet impossible constraints, and their patience in awaiting the final outcome.

I personally want to thank the volume editors—Robert J. Jensen, Douglas T. Owens, and Patricia S. Wilson—for the exceptional skills and tireless efforts they devoted to the project. It was an honor and a pleasure to work with them—they made a big job a lot of fun!

Sigrid Wagner

Introduction

Robert J. Jensen

This volume is the result of a collaboration among teachers—both elementary and university—with experience and expertise in the area of early childhood mathematics education. The co-authors of each chapter had the task of summarizing and synthesizing the research in a specific area of mathematics education and reporting these findings in a straightforward manner. In fact, they have done much more than that by also highlighting areas of continued concern and by raising questions for future research. As a further bonus, you will find many ideas and suggestions for ways in which classroom teachers can get directly involved in the research process by conducting small-scale investigations in their own classrooms.

Authors have been asked to provide, where possible, classroom implications based on their interpretation of the weight of the research findings in a specific area. Your interpretation of these same research findings will occasionally vary from those of the authors of this volume. As a classroom teacher you not only have a unique opportunity to "check it out" with your own students but are encouraged to do so. This book is not intended to be a methods text, so suggested activities are typically limited to prototypes or activities that themselves might form the basis for some classroom action research.

The Early Childhood Volume follows the *Research Ideas for the Classroom* Series format; placing chapters within separate sections broadly identified as "learning," "processes and content," "teaching," and "classroom research." I will begin by providing a brief lead-in to the individual chapters contained in these four sections. Then I will identify some common themes that recur across the volume, and finish with a closing comment of my own.

Learning

Ginsburg and Baron (Chapter 1) consider the broad issue of how children learn and what we can do as teachers to assist in this process. They provide us with evidence that young children come to school with a natural curiosity about quantitative events and some informal, yet powerful, problem-solving skills. These children have already constructed intuitive mathematical notions. We are challenged to make use of the child's physical and social environment as motivating arenas for further quantitative reasoning and problem solving. The research on children's cognition reveals the innate ability for all children to learn mathematics; it is up to us to guide their use of these informal skills to construct meaningful beginning notions of mathematics.

Renga and Dalla's (Chapter 2) review of affective issues in learning documents the importance of attitudes toward mathematics, and oneself as a learner of mathematics, to children's subsequent ability to reason mathematically and apply this reasoning to learn about the world around them. Evidence suggests that although attitudes are rather fluid in young children they are generally quite positive for most youngsters. Teacher feedback is critical at this juncture in a child's schooling and we are sensitized to each individual child's "right to be wrong." Learning from mistakes and initial misunderstandings is the natural mechanism for intellectual growth; not validating this process can unwittingly foster learned helplessness or mathematics anxiety.

Processes and Content

Research on developing early notions of number and numeration is the theme of Chapter 3, Payne and Huinker's lead into the Early Childhood volume's section on mathematical processes and content. There appears to be much more to a child's notion of number than is revealed by an ability to count rotely from 1 to 20 to 100 or even higher. The positive consequences of developing part–whole understanding for small numbers, the thinking of numbers in a variety of groupings as opposed to just a collection of single things, appears to aid children in accomplishing many diverse mathematical tasks. Trying some of the suggested activities would be a great way to begin your own classroom research, the results of which could be used to inform your own teaching in this critical area for young children's mathematical development.

Baroody and Standifer (Chapter 4) extend the theme of early numeration to examine what research reveals about the operations of addition and subtraction in the primary grades. The resulting synthesis provides a wealth of useful information for the classroom teacher with many implications for implementing effective arithmetic instruction. One message—that addition and subtraction should be introduced through word problems that children can solve with the use of developmentally appropriate manipulatives—comes through loud and clear.

Kouba and Franklin (Chapter 5) echo similar sentiments in their review of research on the operations of multiplication and division. They contend that mathematics is "making sense of situations." To develop rich, contextually meaningful notions of the basic operations they exhort us to expand the range of numbers, the language, and diversity of everyday situations that can be modeled by the operations of multiplication and division. Variety and flexibility in representing multiplicative situations includes experienced-based scripts, manipulative models, pictorial models, spoken language, and written symbols. We are warned, however, that only after ample experience with describing, representing, and exploring multiplication and division situations physically and pictorially, does it make sense to introduce writing and abstract number sentences.

Van de Walle and Watkins (Chapter 6) focus their review on the concept of "number sense." Children need an overall instructional program of high quality in this area, not quick fixes, since the individual facets of number sense are intricately connected and rely upon a strong conceptual development. The authors suggest that "number sense is more a way of teaching than a topic to be taught," and emphasize that it cannot be compartmentalized into a textbook chapter or instructional unit. Their recognition of the importance of open-ended verbal interactions in the classroom for teaching number sense lends further support to the significance of the NCTM standard on "mathematics as communication."

Hembree and Marsh (Chapter 7) review problem solving in the early childhood grades, synthesizing research knowledge across a wide range of related areas. They find evidence to support the claim that young children enter school already good problem solvers. These same children, however, are not necessarily adept in solving the more formalized word or story problems that are sometimes thought to be synonymous with problem solving in mathematics class.

Wilson and Rowland's (Chapter 8) review of research on measurement reveal it to be a topic that is both extremely useful and extremely complex. They provide us with an insightful research foundation from which to guide the development of children's ability to measure. The authors outline common problems students are likely to encounter, and some necessary prerequisites to be aware of in planning our instruction.

Fuys and Liebov (Chapter 9) had the task of synthesizing the research literature in the broad areas of geometry and spatial sense. Their research review provides us with perspectives for reflecting on the geometry learning environment in our classrooms today. They challenge us to provide a richer, more continuous activity-oriented program in geometry based on research-supported learning principles and classroom practices.

Langford and Sarullo (Chapter 10) discuss aspects of rational number concepts that are developmentally appropriate for children in the primary grades. Conceptual misunderstandings are well documented. The issue of language is a recurring theme with suggestive implications for both teaching practice and further research. More learning environments conducive to children's developing conceptual understanding of common and decimal fractions are needed—can we meet the challenge?

Teaching

The *Professional Teaching Standards* (NCTM, 1991) identifies four broad areas that become the focus of its standards for teaching mathematics: tasks, discourse, environment, and analysis. Each of the five chapters in the "teaching" section of this volume addresses all these teaching standards to a certain extent, but the following rough guideline for the partitioning of these pedagogical issues across the chapters may be helpful. Chapter 11, "Calculators and Computers," focuses primarily on tools for enhancing discourse (Std. 4) and worthwhile mathematical tasks (Std. 1); Chapter 12, "Classroom Organization and Models of Instruction," focuses primarily on the classroom learning environment (Std. 5) and the student's role in discourse (Std. 3); Chapter 13, "Curriculum: A Vision for Early Childhood Mathematics," focuses primarily on worthwhile mathematical tasks (Std. 1); Chapter 14, "The Teacher's Influence," focuses primarily on the teacher's role in discourse (Std. 2) and the learning environment (Std. 5); and Chapter 15, "Assessment and the Evaluation of Learning," focuses primarily on analysis of teaching and learning (Std. 6).

Campbell and Stewart (Chapter 11) look at the research concerning the use of calculators and computers to assist in the teaching of mathematics in the early grades. Our curriculum itself seems to be part of the research issue, as Campbell suggests "It's not a question of using technology to teach traditional primary math, it's 'what can primary math be, now that these tools are available?'"

Thornton and Wilson's chapter (Chapter 12) on classroom organization and models of instruction report research related to both teacher- and student-centered models of instruction. Research does not seem to support the popular current practice of leveling math classes according to abilities, suggesting that educational "common sense" can sometimes lead us astray. Mixed ability groupings, cooperative learning groups, teacher-centered versus student-centered strategies, are all discussed. Where do we go from here?

Dougherty and Scott (Chapter 13) present a vision for early childhood mathematics curriculum based on a synthesis of related research findings. Their stance is empowering to teachers, indicating that teachers make the final decisions about the mathematics curriculum they present to their students. We are led naturally to question how close our visions for mathematics overlap the mathematics we present to the students in our classes.

Bush and Kincer's chapter (Chapter 14) on teacher influences on the classroom environment has much to offer. We come almost full cycle from Chapter 2's emphasis on affect when we read here about how teacher actions, both conscious and unconscious, signal students on what a teacher values, and in turn can influence students' feeling toward mathematics.

Robinson and Bartlett (Chapter 15) had the difficult task of summarizing research in the area of assessment and evaluation of learning in the early childhood grades. There seem to be more open questions than answers in this area. One thing appears clear, no one method of assessment is best in all situations. We must develop awareness of, and skills in, a variety of assessment techniques if we are going to align more closely our means of assessment with the new content emphasis of the NCTM Curriculum Standards (1989).

Classroom Research

Margaret Ackerman (Chapter 16) reacts to the entire volume from the perspective of a reflective teacher. She shares her insights and reactions to various messages in the book. One way for readers to become involved in the act of becoming the reflective practitioner that she describes would be to consider what they might have said had they been given Margaret's task of reacting to the state of our research knowledge as presented in this volume. In that context, what unanswered questions would you raise for the early childhood mathematics education community? What are some things that you would like to experiment on in your own classroom?

Common Themes across Chapters

What I found perhaps most striking as I read the volume was the themes that recurred across diverse content areas. The following teaching implications seem to be suggestive of these themes:

- Build upon children's strengths and informal strategies; treat them as able, valuable members in a community of learning.
- Use a "good" question or problem to motivate interest in a particular topic or to introduce new concepts.
- Focus on language and communication of ideas in early childhood math classes, both in spoken and written formats.
- Encourage connections among the various content areas; much that is important in mathematics involves bridges among related knowledge fields.
- Use alternate assessment approaches for a truer picture of children's actual mathematical ability.
- Change classroom dynamics through cooperative groupings, classes of heterogeneous ability levels, and new technologies.
- Become involved in your own classroom action research.

Teachers, administrators, and others interested in mathematics education have been given a far-reaching set of curriculum and evaluation standards (NCTM, 1989) and a companion set of professional teaching standards (NCTM, 1991). Research in the teaching and learning of mathematics has reached a critical juncture in time. Never have we known so much but also never have we set our goals for a mathematically literate society so high. Much work remains, but it is helpful at this point to separate myth from knowledge in mathematics education. We all owe a great debt to the chapter authors of this volume for their efforts to present in so clear a fashion the "current state of our amassed wisdom" with respect to research in early childhood mathematics. We do know some things about the way children learn mathematics that can be of much assistance. Let us use this knowledge to improve mathematics instruction for all students.

References

1. NATIONAL COUNCIL OF TEACHERS OF MATHEMATICS (1989). *Curriculum and evaluation standards for school mathematics*. Reston, VA: The Council.
2. NATIONAL COUNCIL OF TEACHERS OF MATHEMATICS (1991). *Professional teaching standards*. Reston, VA: The Council.

Research Ideas
for the Classroom

Early Childhood
Mathematics

PART I

Learning

CHAPTER 1

Cognition: Young Children's Construction of Mathematics

Herbert P. Ginsburg and Joyce Baron

> *INTERVIEWER:* What are you doing in math?
> *SONYA (age 6):* Well, it gives me a lot to think about. I know how to do two plus two. I just gotta learn how to do math.

The goal of this paper is to give you a practical way of thinking about how young children learn mathematics and how you can teach it. We will show that during the preschool years children display a natural curiosity concerning quantitative events and spontaneously construct an informal mathematics. In the natural environment and without formal instruction, they actively develop notions such as more and less and addition and subtraction. Although imperfect and different from the adult's way of thinking, this informal mathematics is relatively powerful and indeed can serve as the foundation for the later learning of mathematics in school.

> Think of informal mathematics as analogous to the child's spontaneous speech. Just as everyone learns to talk, and spoken language is the foundation for reading, so everyone develops an informal mathematics that should be the foundation for the written mathematics learned in school.

On entrance to school, children encounter formal mathematics. At first, children are eager to learn it. But most children do not find the task easy, and many are not successful. Some children treat mathematics as an arbitrary, nonsensical system, a symbol game separate from the rest of life. Others attempt to connect the formalities of mathematics with comfortable intuitions and procedures. In both cases, children's approach to mathematics may differ in important ways from adults'.

"Unfortunately, as children become socialized by school and society, they begin to view mathematics as a rigid system of externally dictated rules governed by standards of accuracy, speed, and memory. Their view of mathematics shifts gradually from enthusiasm to apprehension, from confidence to fear." (National Research Council, 1989, p. 44)

How can the teacher help the child to master the mathematics taught in school? The teacher must first recognize that learning mathematics involves far more than memorizing facts, acquiring behaviors, or mastering basic skills. Mathematics cannot simply be written on the child's blank slate of a mind. Mathematics is not liquid to be poured into an empty vessel: for one thing, the vessel is not empty, and for another, the liquid in it changes the composition of what is poured in. Instead, the teacher needs to foster understanding—to help the child make meaningful connections between existing informal knowledge and the socially structured system of formal mathematics.

Connections. Aye, there's the rub. Fostering connections means treating students as individuals. Teaching addition to a student who tells you that 8 + 7 = 15 because 8 + 8 = 16 and 8 + 7 is one less than 8 + 8 must be approached differently than teaching the same operation to a student who solves 8 + 7 by counting to 8 and then on to 15.

We begin our account by describing how and what young children learn in the natural environment, and how this informal knowledge can be enhanced. Then we discuss how children construct formal mathematical concepts in school and how teachers can help. We conclude by debunking some common myths concerning children's learning of mathematics.

Learning in the Environment

What the Environment Has to Offer

Mind always develops in an environment, both physical and social. The quantitative environment is so pervasive and so fundamental that we are often oblivious to it. All children develop in an environment containing a multitude of quantitative phenomena and events. From infancy, children encounter small, discrete objects that can be manipulated, touched, and counted. All children view some sets that are more numerous than others. All children experience hunger, want something to eat, and then want more to eat.

Moreover, the physical environment of quantity appears to offer rich stimulation across widely diverse cultures. In what culture, however impoverished, does the child lack things to count? In what culture cannot one add to what one had before? Mathematical events and phenomena appear to be universal in the physical world.

Children also encounter a social environment affording important notions of quantity. Children hear adults counting. They see adults using numbers in shopping. They see numbers on telephones, buses, and houses. And they may even encounter "educational" television programs in which characters count and occasionally calculate.

These social environments vary considerably from culture to culture. Some cultures offer educational television; others do not. Some cultures are characterized by an everyday written mathematics—as on telephones or houses—and others are not. But almost all known cultures offer a fundamental mathematical system, namely the counting words. Moreover, in virtually all cultures studied, counting systems are highly elaborate, most often involving a base-ten system, and extend to rather large numbers (8). Furthermore, research has shown that some "primitive" cultures offer surprisingly rich mathematical environments. For example, the Zinacantan Indians of Mexico weave patterns rich in geometric complexity (17).

These quantitative features of physical and social reality are so fundamental that they are reflected in the child's earliest language. Among the baby's first words are "more" and "'nother" (4). Quantitative notions also play key roles in children's literature (33). The child encounters—and understands—the story of the three bears, small, larger, and largest, each with beds and bowls and chairs of appropriately graded size. The tale turns on the functional relation between the size of the bears and belongings in the environment. Cultures around the world offer folk tales and stories containing similarly elaborate quantitative notions.

In brief, throughout development, before and after entrance to school, children are normally exposed to physical and social environments rich in mathematical opportunities. Children encounter quantity in the physical world, counting numbers in the social world, and mathematical ideas in the literary world.

How the Child Learns

Although natural and social environments afford children many opportunities to learn quantitative notions, opportunities are not enough; children need to exploit them. According to Piaget (14), children have a biologically based propensity to learn from the environment. Children are natural learners. They accommodate to environmental demands; they assimilate what the environment has to offer. Piaget stresses the intrinsic motivation underlying children's learning. Children learn because their minds are made to learn. When they cannot fully assimilate new events, cognitive conflict is created and the acquisition of new knowledge reduces the disequilibrium. In the Piagetian view, children are naturally curious, learning in order to expand their knowledge.

> "Students need to experience genuine problems regularly. A genuine problem is a situation in which, for the individual or group concerned, one or more appropriate solutions have yet to be developed. The situation should be complex enough to offer challenge but not so complex as to be insoluble." (National Council of Teachers of Mathematics, 1989, p. 10)

But there is no doubt that other motives promote learning as well. Children often learn because knowledge can be of practical use. Thus, Africans in preliterate societies learn elaborate mental calculation because it helps them perform the tasks of commerce (15). And children learn also in order to gain the approval of parents and other adults. So in the everyday world—a world affording a rich quantitative environment—children have several strong motivations to learn.

What the Child Learns

The almost inevitable outcome is the construction of elementary forms of mathematical knowledge. Typically this informal knowledge is not directly taught but is instead substantially created by the child. Differing from the adult's knowledge, it may take distinctive forms. At the same time, the child's informal knowledge is relatively powerful and can serve as the foundation for later school learning.

> "It is clear that children's intellectual, social, and emotional development should guide the kind of mathematical experiences they should have in light of the overall goals for learning mathematics. The notion of a developmentally appropriate curriculum is an important one." (National Council of Teachers of Mathematics, 1989, p. 18)

One example of informal knowledge involves adding. As early as 2 or 3 years of age, children begin to develop an intuitive idea of adding. An ingenious series of experiments (11) has shown that most young children, from 2 to 4 years of age, develop an intuitive notion of things being added or taken away. In one of these studies, for example, young children were repeatedly shown a set of three objects. After the children learned to name the set with the arbitrary label "winner," the set was hidden and an object was surreptitiously added to it. Upon seeing the set again, the children declared that it was no longer the "winner" since something was added to it. Asked how the set could be "fixed," the children replied that something must be taken away. In this case, the children did not need to calculate in order to determine the exact number of the set, but clearly understood something about how addition and subtraction can alter quantities. Other investigators (5) have confirmed these results.

We must not confuse a child's adding of objects with readiness for written work. There is a crucial difference between counting three pennies and four pennies to discover that there are seven pennies and memorizing the answer to 3 + 4 on a worksheet.

By the age of 4 or so, children begin to calculate in concrete addition situations. One study (16) presented 4-year-old children with a task in which three objects displayed in one group were to be added to four objects shown in another group. Children at this age generally perform the calculation accurately by means of the strategy "counting all." This involves counting the members of both sets from the beginning. Even though the child already knows, because he or she has counted them, that one set contains four objects and the other three objects, the child counts: "One, two, three, four . . . five, six, seven."

The 4-year-old usually interprets addition as the act of combining and counting separate sets. Addition involves operating on sets in order to get a new set. The corollary of this notion is that addition is not defined as the equivalence between two quantities. The young child does not interpret three plus four as another name for or as equivalent to seven. Rather, seven is what you get when you do something to three plus four. As we shall see below, this "action interpretation" of addition is mathematically legitimate but at odds with what is usually taught in school.

Many 5- and 6-year-olds will tell you that writing 7 = 3 + 4 is not "allowed." When pressed for a reason why they will say that the 3 and the 4 should be on the other side of the equals sign. Try asking first graders if it is OK to write 7 = 7.

As time goes on, the child's approach to addition calculation evolves and matures. Children spontaneously develop efficient approaches to calculation (18). Eventually, children abandon "counting all" for a more advanced and easier approach, namely "counting on," usually from the larger number. It is as if they get bored with counting all and discover that it is easier simply to count on from the larger number. Thus, in the case of four plus three, children eventually perform the calculation by saying "four . . . five, six, seven."

"Sandy, make believe there are four peanuts and three peanuts. How many are there altogether? Seven? Tell me how you did it."

"There were four peanuts on this side," she said pointing to the right side of her forehead, "and three on the other side. And I just moved the three over to the four side and that made—four, five, six, seven—yeah, seven."

Eventually, concrete supports are no longer needed; the child calculates solely on a mental level. The child can now add four plus three "in his head." Often this is accomplished through the use of vivid mental imagery. The child pictures four objects and three objects in the mind, and counts the images, again usually from the larger number. Other children accomplish the calculation by means of spoken numbers only, without visualizations of the objects. Thus, four plus three is added simply by use of counting numbers, without reference to objects, mental or physical (for a review of early counting and calculation, see 10 [Ch. 8], 12).

We see then that young children begin with intuitive notions of adding and subtracting, and gradually develop means for calculation, at first involving concrete objects, and later, mental representations.

The Generality of Informal Knowledge

Cross-cultural research has shown that the development of addition shows a remarkably similar course of development in diverse cultures. The general finding (21) is that children from various cultures, literate and preliterate, rich and poor, of various racial backgrounds, all display a similar development of informal addition (and other aspects of informal mathematics, like systems for counting and enumeration). Thus, unschooled African children display strategies of addition similar to those of American children (15). In the course of commerce, largely unschooled street children in Brazil develop sophisticated and effective means for mental calculation (6). Within the United States there are few racial or social class differences in the development of basic aspects of preschool children's concrete addition and other key informal abilities (16).

Let us be clear on what the research demonstrates. It shows that the general course of development of informal mathematical abilities is similar across boundaries of culture, race, and class. All children seem to develop basic mathematical abilities of the type described. The research does not show, however, that children from these various groups are identical in their mathematical thinking. Within the United States, poor black children perform at a somewhat lower level on certain informal mathematical tasks than do more affluent white children (16, 31). But both of these groups display the same basic pattern of development. The general conclusion is not that mathematical thinking is identical across cultures, but that children from various backgrounds acquire the fundamentals of informal addition in a similar developmental progression.

Why is this? As we have seen, part of the explanation is that children are natural learners, and part is that all children develop in an environment, physical and social, in which opportunities for learning addition abound.

The Enhancement of Informal Mathematics

Consider first a general approach to mathematics education for young children and then some specific suggestions.

An Approach to Early Mathematics Education

The psychological research we have reviewed shows that two common views concerning early mathematics education are incorrect. One position maintains that the education of young children—in preschool and even kindergarten—should focus mainly on social–emotional development and should avoid such topics as mathematics and even reading, because young children are not "ready" for these subjects and will therefore be harmed by studying them. But as we have seen, young children are indeed "ready" for mathematics: They are interested in mathematical topics—like counting and which of two sets has "more"—and spontaneously develop a fairly complex set of informal ideas about quantity in the natural environment. Why deprive them of the opportunity to pursue an intellectual interest which they can enjoy and from which they can profit?

> "The child *invents* mathematical knowledge from her or his actions on objects, so direct, concrete experiences with many objects at the child's developmental level are crucial to the formation of accurate concepts." (Maxim, 1989, p. 36)

A second untenable position maintains that young children should be taught the same kind of formal, written mathematics that older children learn. In this view, it is important to help children learn the "basics" and the earlier this can be done, the better. Often proponents of this view, stressing the careful writing of numbers and the memorization of "number facts," place a heavy emphasis on workbooks designed to drill children in mastering these "basic" skills. This view is incorrect because it ignores children's informal mathematics and introduces written number in a meaningless way, inappropriate for children at any age.

> "Educators who use . . . direct approaches to mathematics teaching with children prior to the age of four or five are warned that their artificial structure and limitations serve only to lessen interest, exploration, and experimentation if those approaches are introduced before the child has experienced informal number activities. However, once the child has indicated an interest and need, and most will by the age of four or five, teachers can organize direct experiences with numbers that help children build desired concepts." (Maxim, 1989, p. 38)

The evidence leads us to maintain that young children are indeed interested in mathematics and ready to learn it. Of course, to say this does not mean that they should be taught the subject in an inappropriate fashion, through dull drill focusing on meaningless (for them) written symbols. No one should be taught in this way! Instead, a useful approach should involve stimulating young children's spontaneous mathematical interests and activities in the natural environment and helping them enrich and supplement their informal mathematics. Here are some ways to do this.

Enhancing the Environments of Quantity.

Children growing up in stimulating environments will almost certainly acquire some basic mathematical ideas. And as we have seen, many of these ideas are virtually universal across wide variations in culture. At the same time, we as educators and parents are eager to enrich children's environments, to provide children with further opportunities for learning. How should this be done? Here is an example of a class-room activity that capitalizes on the informal mathematical understandings of children ages 4 through 6 or 7 (for similar examples, see 30). The teacher can prepare daily or weekly graphs on which the children record various kinds of information. For example, one very rich source of math conversation is a week-long graph to record the number of buttons the children have on their school clothes. On Monday they may find that the class total is sixty. On Tuesday there may be only forty-three. By Wednesday many of the children will have remembered that they counted buttons on the previous two days and will insist that they be allowed to wear whatever clothes they own that have the most buttons. By Thursday there may be a decline as the clothing with the most buttons is likely to be in the laundry. But on Friday watch out! If there is a button box in the house you can be assured that some of the children will have discovered it and persuaded someone to sew extra buttons on shirts, pants, socks, and sneakers.

> Ideas for graphing projects include "How far do you live from school?" "How many of your relatives live in our city/town?" "How many baby teeth have you lost?" and "How many 'grown-up' teeth do you have?" Plot the last two together and you have a source of very rich math talk.

Once the class has collected the data over a period of a week, it is time to talk math. The children have certainly been exposed to many opportunities to observe and construct informal quantitative understandings during the time they have been collecting the data. Now the teacher's role is to provide an environment in which those informal, intuitive understandings can be extended and made more mathematically explicit. The graph that now contains the week's worth of button counting is full of mathematical questions just waiting to be asked.

> Connections are crucial. They are the bridges between informal and formal understandings. Some are formed through conversation, some through writing, some through drawing. All are formed by the mind of the learner, often with the guidance of the teacher.

- "Let's read the graph and see how many buttons we wore on each day of this week. How many on Monday? Tuesday? . . ."
- "On which day did we wear the most buttons?"
- "How many more buttons did we wear on Wednesday than on Monday?"
- "On which day did we wear the least number of buttons?"
- "Why do you think that Tuesday was the day we wore the least number of buttons?"

Mathematically aware teachers don't let these opportune moments go by. Yes, it takes time, attention, and genuine interest on the part of the adult to follow up on the child's question; but when the question is asked, adults can be sure that the child is truly engaged in thinking informally about quantity. This is the teachable moment, and the adult should seize the opportunity to help the child explore the mathematical ideas and make them more explicit.

The Introduction of Formal Mathematics

In most societies, the child, already equipped with a functioning mathematical mind, enters school somewhere around the age of 5 or 6. Schools are artificially created social institutions designed to pass on to children the accumulated social wisdom, one aspect of which is formal mathematics. In contrast to the child's informal system, formal mathematics is written, codified, a body of material conventionally defined and agreed upon, organized and explicit. Formal mathematics is what Vygotsky (38) calls a "scientific" system—coherent, explicit, organized, and logical. By contrast, the child's informal mathematics is a "spontaneous" system—intuitive, emotional, implicit, and tied to everyday life.

We adults want young children to learn formal mathematics because of its potential power and beauty. But we cannot assume that children will learn it in the form in which we present it. As we shall see, children construct—they must construct—their own understanding of school mathematics (19). As Piaget (29) put it, "To understand is to invent." Formal mathematics cannot simply be imposed on the child; the child must reinvent it to make it his or her own.

> Some children have extremely good memories. They can master math facts early through the brute force of memorization. But don't let their success fool you into believing that they really understand the material. Genuine understanding does not come easy; it has to be constructed by the child.

From this perspective, two key questions arise, one referring to learning and the other to teaching. First, what sense do children make of the formal mathematics presented to them? If children do not receive the school mathematics as transmitted, how do they construct an understanding of it? Second, how can the teacher promote learning? If teaching is not instruction—that is, the direct transmission of knowledge—what is the teacher's role? To what extent, and how, should the teacher attempt to influence the child's construction of knowledge? Let us consider these questions in the context of the learning and teaching of the "equals sign."

Learning the Equals Sign

Most typically, teachers introduce the equals sign as indicating equivalence. In their view, the equals sign is meant to signify that the arithmetic statement to the left of the sign is equivalent in number to the statement on its right. Thus in the case of

$3 + 4 = 7$, $3 + 4$ is defined as equivalent to, or even another name for 7. This is certainly a useful and valid view of $=$. It is a view that children should eventually come to understand. But in general, despite the teacher's best efforts, young children do not interpret $=$ in this way (3). Instead, children construct their own meaning for $=$.

When asked to explain the meaning of $=$, children often say that it refers to "all together" or to "adding" or "taking away" or in the immortal words of Tammy, a first grader, "It means that the end is coming up." What children mean is that for them a written statement like $3 + 4 =$ refers to a series of actions that are to be performed on the given numbers in order to get a result. The $+$ indicates that adding is required, and the $=$ indicates primarily that it is time to get the answer. This interpretation has little to do with the teacher's intended meaning for equivalence. Typically, children maintain that a sentence like $7 = 4 + 3$ is unacceptable because it is "written backwards." We see then that despite the teacher's instruction stressing $=$ as equivalence, children generally construct their own "action" interpretation of $=$: it indicates that a calculation has to be performed in order to obtain a result.

Why didn't the children learn what the teacher taught? On a general level, the answer is that children do not simply receive knowledge intact from adults; they must construct it or reinvent it for themselves. On a more specific level, there are two reasons for children's interpretation of $=$ as an action to be completed. One reason is that children's informal approach to addition involves acting on quantities in order to obtain a result. Thus mental addition involves such methods as counting on from the larger number; it does not involve equivalence in the sense teachers intend to convey. Given this fact, we should not find it surprising that children assimilate the written $+$ and $=$ signs into their informal approach to addition.

Worksheets should include equations like: $3 + 4 = 5 + \square$; $8 = 0 + \square$. They should present problems like: "Using two addends write as many number facts as you can that equal 9" and "Explain in your own words why we can say that $7 = 7$ and $7 = 3 + 4$."

Another reason for children's action interpretation is that the examples typically presented in class, in homework lessons, and in workbooks all stress addition as calculation. In class, children learn how to add $4 + 3$, perhaps using manipulatives like Unifix cubes. Children's actual written work in the classroom also has little to do with addition as equivalence; the fact is that written problems of the sort $3 + 4 =$ mainly require children to calculate in order to get a result and do not involve them in explicit consideration of the equivalence of the two sides of the statement. Despite the official presentation of $=$ as equivalence, both informal procedures and actual classroom experience lead children to the construction of the notion of $=$ as an indicator of activities to be performed. In this and in other areas, children do not simply learn what is taught, but construct their own interpretation of the mathematics.

How should teachers react to a situation in which children construct ideas diverging from conventional mathematical notions? There are several ways to respond. One possibility is to "shout louder." The teacher can repeat the equivalence explanation more loudly than before, ignoring the child's spontaneous construction. This is unlikely to succeed at any deep level. Although the children may repeat the teacher's words, they will no doubt continue to maintain their " = as activity" approach. Indeed, it has been observed that this type of approach persists into the study of algebra, even though teachers have by this time been shouting at a high volume for a number of years.

Another approach is to understand the children's constructions and to use them in a productive fashion. In the case of the = sign, the teacher might observe that the notion of = as a desired action is perfectly legitimate. For example, when we teach addition as movements on the number line, the = sign can be construed as indicating a movement to be performed in order to get to the final resting place: 3 + 4 = 7 means that you start on position 3 on the number line, move ahead 4 spaces, and finally come to rest on position 7. All this does not involve equivalence in the conventional sense. So one approach is to recognize that in this case, the child's interpretation is indeed a legitimate mathematical view and that one can use it to explain = in terms of familiar, and easily understood, models like the number line.

> Teaching in this way requires insight into the child's interpretation. Teachers must know what each child knows and doesn't know about each topic presented so that subsequent teaching can move the child from his present constructions to the next level of knowing. This is true not only for equivalence but for all math skills.

Teaching the Equals Sign (and Other Concepts)

At the same time, it is the teacher's responsibility to help the child advance beyond his or her initial construction. The teacher cannot leave the learning of mathematics entirely to the child and must instead intervene so as to lead the child to reinvent formal mathematics—to construct ideas and procedures that would not have arisen spontaneously in the mind of the child in the absence of adult help.

In the case of =, the child should be led to recognize that several interpretations are valuable, especially the view of = as equivalence. The teacher's goal is to have the child learn the formal mathematical idea that the two sides of the equation are equivalent in number—for example, that the quantity 4 + 3 is the "same as" 7. Given this notion, you can then legitimately say that 7 = 4 + 3.

But how should the adult help? One approach to teaching equivalence is to define it purely in terms of the formal system of written mathematics—to introduce explicit definitions, theorems, and the like. This may be how mathematicians eventually come to understand equivalence, but it is usually not a good way to teach it. Except for the most advanced students, definitions in formal terms are usually mere words with little meaning. Students may learn the words but often do not understand the concepts behind them.

A sounder approach is to attempt to connect formal mathematical concepts with informal intuitions. In the case of the = sign, the teacher helps the child to connect the formal notion of equivalence with informal ideas relevant to this topic. In the everyday environment, the child has had experiences with balancing, as on the teeter-totter or seesaw. Equivalence can be seen, at least initially, as a kind of balancing. This gives some experiential substance—some body—to an abstract idea.

> A potentially fascinating and informative area of investigation is an examination of how advanced mathematicians visualize the relationships they study. Even they find it hard to express their thinking in words most of us would understand: "Physics is just as abstract as math . . . but somehow physicists are better at finding images to convey their work to the public. . . . We mathematicians have much more trouble finding metaphors to describe what we do." (Lippsett, 1990, p. 30)

An even more effective way to teach equivalence is to introduce a "bridge" between the informal ideas and the formal definition. In the case of the = sign, the bridge might be the common balance beam approach to addition (see, for example, 32). The child might engage in such activities as placing sets of three and four objects on the left side of the balance and seven on the other; the child might then reverse the positions of the objects, now placing the sets of three and four on the right side and the set of seven on the left (see Fig. 1.1). Throughout these activities, the appropriate numerals and symbols are explicitly linked to the various objects.

Activities like these may lead the child to construct a new view of addition and of the equals sign, which can now be seen as indicating a kind of balancing, a phenomenon with which the child is already familiar on an informal level. The notion of

FIGURE 1.1   Balance beam apparatus for teaching addition

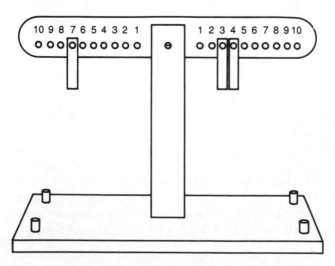

balance may also help the child to understand that 7 can be seen as a name for 3 + 4, and that 5 + 2 is equivalent to 4 + 3.

> A pan balance can be used for teaching addition, providing that the former is sensitive, accurate, and the weights are carefully calibrated so that three weights and four weights do equal the weight of one seven-weight as well as that of two weights and five weights.

Note that in this example, the balance beam is a bridge—an artificial and concrete device introduced by the teacher to teach a formal idea that the child has not spontaneously constructed. The bridge helps the child connect the formal idea and symbol to what is already known (the child's informal knowledge). The balance beam—called a "manipulative" because it is a real object that the child can work with and explore—serves the metaphorical function of relating the formal notion of equivalence to the informal idea of balancing. The manipulative is not useful if it fails to bridge these two areas. From the perspective of mathematics education, there is no point in having the the children work with the balance beam unless it helps them to understand the notion of equivalence.

> Careful and deliberate connections between manipulatives and the underlying concepts they are designed to illustrate are crucial to the construction of useful mathematical understanding. Some children become highly adept at moving the manipulatives but never make the mental leap to the corresponding numeric abstraction.

Such bridges exist for many areas of mathematics, not just the equals sign (a useful Japanese approach for teaching elementary mathematics is discussed in 20), and can help to produce an understanding which involves far more than the repetition of verbal statements or proofs provided by the teacher.

Assessment

To promote learning, the teacher must gain insight both into children's informal mathematics and into their construction of written mathematics. Thus, the teacher may find it helpful to recognize that a child performs addition mentally by counting on from the larger number. The teacher needs to recognize when the child construes = as "all together" and believes that it is incorrect to write $7 = 4 + 3$. In brief, good teaching requires that the teacher conduct sensitive assessments of children in the classroom.

> For many children "concrete manipulative objects" include fingers and other parts of the body.

The teacher can easily give achievement tests to discover how well students can add, subtract, multiply, divide, create equivalent fractions, and so on. But tests of this type usually do not reveal a great deal about the child's thinking. Other approaches can be more valuable: The teacher can gain insight into thinking by carefully observing the child's activities and written productions in the classroom and by taking the opportunity to "talk math" with students (see, for example, 22).

If a nontraditional approach to assessment seems overwhelming try it with just two children at first. Begin with two students who seem confused or who consistently rely on parroted explanations. Nonthreatening but probing questions will reveal areas of misunderstanding.

How can teachers be expected to conduct such assessments at the same time they are planning and implementing a required math curriculum? When there is barely time to cover the material that needs to be presented, how can teachers be asked to include even more? The answer is that it may not be necessary to include anything more: Sensitive assessment is part and parcel of good teaching. Teachers need to focus on and interpret the information they already have in order to obtain assessments that can be used to help the child construct meaningful understanding.

Examining Written Work

In checking a child's written work a teacher can take several approaches. The usual procedure is simply to mark the wrong answers and return the paper for corrections. But a useful alternative is for the teacher to look for patterns of errors in each child's work and spend a few moments with individual children as the papers are returned in order to unravel the erroneous thinking.

Here are five problems with errors in calculation. The answers are not random; they are instead the result of a systematic rule, consistently applied. Try to discover the rule the student used. Helping the student means spending the time to discover the rule and then spending more time re-teaching the concept that should underlie the calculation. Bear in mind that the child who is capable of creating an erroneous rule in the first place is probably a stronger student than the one who makes a series of seemingly unrelated errors.

The child who creates an erroneous rule is actively engaged in constructing his or her own reality. The child's wrong answer results from a kind of creativity.

$$
\begin{array}{ccccc}
77 & 84 & 53 & 24 & 33 \\
-58 & -22 & -19 & -8 & -22 \\
\hline
21 & 62 & 46 & 24 & 11
\end{array}
$$

When the teacher realizes that the rule this student was using is to subtract the smaller number from the larger number, then a powerful piece of information has been obtained (other such rules are described in 1 and 13). The information is powerful because it enables the teacher to help the student to understand the basis for the mistake, correct it, and, most important, to delve one step deeper into mastering the number system.

The child's written work includes not only numerals, but also pictures and English language statements—all of which can be informative. Several writers (for example, see 2) have proposed creative ways in which to encourage and examine children's written productions for evidence of mathematical thinking.

Talking Math

It is important for the teacher to keep track of each child's thinking as new topics are presented. While at first this may seem impossible to do, it is not as difficult as it appears. The teacher should listen critically to answers, probe for deep understanding, ask questions that demand explanations, not just factual answers, and encourage a classroom atmosphere supportive of both weak and strong students. And this can happen only when the teacher has created an environment of mutual trust. The teacher needs to trust the child to be honest about what he or she knows and does not know and can and cannot do, and the child needs to trust the teacher to be helpful, not punitive, when weaknesses are revealed.

According to Stigler (37), Japanese teachers spend more time than do American teachers in encouraging their students to produce comprehensive verbal explanations of mathematical concepts and algorithms. This may contribute to Japanese children's success in mathematics.

Here is an example. The teacher has presented the problem $26 \times 4 = $. She watches as Joey does the computation and asks questions from time to time.

"Joey, why did you put that little two above the two in twenty-six?"

"I don't know. I just learned that that's what you do. It's called carrying and you carry up the number that you didn't write down when you multiplied four times six."

"Why did you write down that four?"

"Because four times six is twenty-four. I put the four there and the two up there."

By this time the teacher knows that Joey has mastered arithmetic almost solely on the strength of his ability to memorize. Multiplication doesn't make sense; it is a sequential procedure to be followed. Work with manipulatives as well as a strong program in problem solving would be appropriate for Joey at this time.

Debunking Some Myths

We have seen that mathematical cognition begins with the informal and the intuitive and that formal mathematics must be constructed, not taught. We conclude by examining some common misconceptions concerning young children's knowledge of mathematics.

1. *Some children cannot learn math.* No doubt some individuals do not have the talent to pursue higher mathematics. But there is no reason why all normal children cannot learn elementary arithmetic. There is nothing very complicated about the arithmetic and geometry taught in the primary and elementary years. In fact, as Piaget pointed out, much of elementary school arithmetic is simply an elaboration of what children already know on an intuitive level. If mathematics were taught properly, all children should achieve a reasonable proficiency in it.

2. *Boys learn math better than girls.* At the primary and elementary school level, there are in fact very few differences between boys and girls in mathematics performance. Some differences do emerge beginning in about the seventh grade but these, the evidence suggests, are less a reflection of girls' lack of talent in mathematics than of our culture's view (perhaps now changing) that it is inappropriate for girls to do well in mathematics and other technical subjects. For interesting reviews of this controversial issue see (7) and (25).

3. *Poor children and minority children do not perform well in mathematics.* At the beginning of the primary years, poor children in general and minority children in particular are strongly motivated to perform well in school mathematics and other subjects (35). By around the third or fourth grade however, important differences in both motivation and achievement do indeed begin to emerge (9). The reason for this is not entirely clear. In our view, it is unlikely that the poor performance results from a lack of mathematical ability in poor and minority children. Instead, the failure is likely to result (28) from motivational difficulties ("Why should I learn math; it is unlikely to get me anything") or from teacher stereotypes ("These kids can't be very good in math"). As noted above, the evidence appears to suggest that all children, including the poor and minorities, have the potential to learn elementary school mathematics, at least when they are motivated and when the subject is adequately taught.

4. *American children have less mathematical ability than Asian children.* Research has shown that during the preschool years and at the kindergarten level, American and Asian children perform at roughly the same level (34); Asian children do not begin with a "head start." Differences between the groups emerge only after a year or two of schooling and have less to do with inequalities in ability than with differences in motivation and teaching. Asian children are taught that by being diligent and working hard they will be able to master even those areas of learning that they find very difficult (36). Success is attributed to hard work more than to innate ability. All children are expected to work hard and all children are expected to succeed. And generally they do.

5. *Mathematics learning disabilities are common.* They are not common. Many cases of "learning disabilities" are incorrect diagnoses. Virtually all children have the ability to learn elementary mathematics if it is presented properly. Most cases of "learning disabilities" involve children who have a poor understanding of mathematics but not an inability to learn it under stimulating conditions. In most cases the reason for the difficulty is not intellectual inadequacy but inappropriate teaching.

Were mathematics education improved, many apparent "learning disabilities" would disappear.

Conclusion

Children construct mathematics by assimilating what is taught into what they already know. Teachers should help the child to elaborate these constructions in meaningful directions. There is no reason why virtually all children should not achieve a reasonable level of proficiency in elementary mathematics.

Looking Ahead . . .

I hope that in the next ten years researchers will pay more attention to children's feelings about mathematics and their motivation to learn it. Researchers can't fully understand mathematics learning without considering personality, feelings, and motivation, and teachers can't teach well without sensitivity to these personal aspects. I hope too that researchers will emphasize problems of assessment, in particular the question of how to assess children's thinking in the everyday classroom context. To teach well, teachers need to understand their students' thinking as it occurs in the classroom; perhaps psychologists can help them to do this.

Herbert P. Ginsburg

"The main purpose of evaluation . . . is to help teachers better understand what students know and make meaningful instructional decisions." (National Council of Teachers of Mathematics, 1989, p. 189)

I'm still wondering about whether or not teachers will take up the call of the *Standards*, to find the time and make the effort to challenge their students to delve and think more deeply than ever before. Many of us were not taught as we now wish our students to be taught. We are lacking role models for how good math education should be conducted. Can we create an atmosphere that supports questioning? Can we focus on how the children learn rather than on how we teach? Can we be the teachers we never had? I'm still wondering . . .

Joyce Baron

About the Authors

Herbert P. Ginsburg is professor of psychology and mathematics education at Teachers College, Columbia University.

Joyce Baron is assistant principal at Fieldston Lower School, Riverdale, New York. The authors work together on issues of informal assessment in the classroom.

References

1. ASHLOCK, R. B. (1990). *Error patterns in computation* (5th ed.). Columbus, OH: Charles E. Merrill.

*2. AZZOLINO, A. (1990). Writing as a tool for teaching mathematics: the silent revolution. In T. J. Cooney & C. R. Hirsch (Eds.), *Teaching and learning mathematics in the 1990s: 1990 Yearbook*. Reston, VA: National Council of Teachers of Mathematics.

3. BAROODY, A. J., & GINSBURG, H. P. (1983). The effects of instruction on children's understanding of the "equals" sign. *The Elementary School Journal, 84*(2), 199–212.

4. BLOOM, L. (1970). *Language development: Form and function in emerging grammars.* Cambridge, MA: M.I.T. Press.

5. BRUSH, L. R. (1972). *Children's conceptions of addition and subtraction: The relation of formal and informal notions.* Unpublished doctoral dissertation, Cornell University.

6. CARRAHER, T. N., SCHLIEMANN, A. S., & CARRAHER, D. W. (1988). Mathematical concepts in everyday life. In G. B. Saxe & M. Gearhart (Eds.), *Children's mathematics. New Directions for Child Development, 41*, 89–111.

7. CHIPMAN, S. F., BRUSH, L. R., & WILSON, D. M. (1985). *Women and mathematics: Balancing the equation.* Hillsdale, NJ: Erlbaum.

8. DANTZIG, T. (1954). *Number: The language of science* (4th ed.). New York: Macmillan.

9. ENTWISLE, D., & HAYDUK, L. A. (1978). *Too great expectations.* Baltimore: Johns Hopkins University Press.

10. FUSON, K. C. (1988). *Children's counting and concepts of number.* NY: Springer-Verlag.

11. GELMAN, R., & GALLISTEL, C. S. (1978). *The child's understanding of number.* Cambridge, MA: Harvard University Press.

*12. GINSBURG, H. P. (1989). *Children's arithmetic: How they learn it and how you teach it.* (2nd edition). Austin, TX: Pro Ed.

13. GINSBURG, H. P., & MATHEWS, S. C. (1984). *Diagnostic Test of Arithmetic Strategies.* (DTAS). Austin, TX : PRO-ED.

14. GINSBURG, H. P., & OPPER, S. (1988). *Piaget's theory of intellectual development.* (3rd Ed.) Englewood Cliffs, NJ: Prentice-Hall.

15. GINSBURG, H. P., POSNER, J. K., & RUSSELL, R. L. (1981). The development of mental addition as a function of schooling and culture. *Journal of Cross-Cultural Psychology, 12*, 163–168.

16. GINSBURG, H. P., & RUSSELL, R. L. (May, 1981). Social class and racial influences on early mathematical thinking. *Monographs of the Society for Research in Child Development, 46*(6, Serial No. 193).

17. GREENFIELD, P. M. (1984) A theory of the teacher in the learning activities of everyday life. In B. Rogoff & J. Lave (Eds.), *Everyday cognition: Its development in social context.* Cambridge, MA: Harvard University Press, 95–116.

18. GROEN, G., & RESNICK, L. B. (1977). Can preschool children invent addition algorithms? *Journal of Educational Psychology, 69*, 645–652.

*19. KAMII, C. K. (1985). *Young children reinvent arithmetic: Implications of Piaget's theory.* New York: Teachers College Press.

*20. KAPLAN, R. G., YAMAMOTO, T. A., & GINSBURG, H. P. (1989). Teaching mathematics concepts. In L. B. Resnick & L. E. Klopfer (Eds.), *Toward the thinking curriculum: Current cognitive research. 1989 Yearbook of the Association for Supervision and Curriculum Development.*

21. KLEIN, A., & STARKEY, P. (1988). Universals in the development of early arithmetic cognition. In G.B. Saxe & M. Gearhart (Eds.), *Children's mathematics. New Directions for Child Development, 41*, 5–26.

22. LABINOWICZ, E. (1985). *Learning from children.* Menlo Park, CA: Addison-Wesley.

23. LIPPSETT, L. (1990). The Art of Math, *Columbia, 15*(3), 28–35.
*24. MAXIM, G. W. (1989). Developing preschool mathematical concepts. *Arithmetic Teacher, 37*(4), 36–41.
25. MEYER, M. R., & FENNEMA, E. (1988). Girls, boys, and mathematics. In T. R. Post (Ed.). *Teaching mathematics in grades K–8*. Boston: Allyn & Bacon, 406–425.
26. NATIONAL COUNCIL OF TEACHERS OF MATHEMATICS, COMMISSION ON STANDARDS FOR SCHOOL MATHEMATICS (1989). *Curriculum and evaluation standards for school mathematics*. Reston, VA: The Council.
27. NATIONAL RESEARCH COUNCIL (1989). *Everybody counts: A report to the nation on the future of mathematics education*. Washington, DC: National Academy Press.
28. OGBU, J. U. (1978). *Minority education and caste*. New York: Academic Press.
29. PIAGET, J. (1973). *To understand is to invent: The future of education*. New York: Grossman.
*30. RUSSELL, S. J., & FRIEL, S. N. (1989). Collecting and analyzing real data in the elementary school classroom. In P. R. Trafton & A. P. Shulte (Eds.), *New directions for elementary school mathematics: 1989 Yearbook*. Reston, VA: National Council of Teachers of Mathematics.
31. SAXE, G., GUBERMAN, S. R., & GEARHART, M. (1987). Social processes in early number development. *Monographs of the Society for Research in Child Development, 52*(2, Serial No. 216).
*32. SHOECRAFT, P. (1989). "Equals" means "Is the same as." *Arithmetic Teacher, 36*(8), 36–40.
*33. SMITH, N. J., & WENDELIN, K. H. (1981). Using children's books to teach mathematical concepts. *Arithmetic Teacher, 29*(3), 10–15.
34. SONG, M. J., & GINSBURG, H. P. (1987). The development of informal and formal mathematical thinking in Korean and American children. *Child Development, 58,* 1286–1296.
35. STEVENSON, H. W., CHEN, C., & UTTAL, D. H. (1990). Beliefs and achievement: A study of Black, White, and Hispanic children. *Child Development, 61,* 508–523.
36. STEVENSON, H. W., & LEE, S. (1990). Contexts of achievement. *Monographs of the Society for Research in Child Development, 55*(1–2, Serial No. 221).
*37. STIGLER, J. W. (1988). Research into practice: The use of verbal explanation in Japanese and American classrooms. *Arithmetic Teacher, 36*(2), 27–29.
38. VYGOTSKY, L. S. (1962). *Thought and language*. Cambridge, MA: MIT Press.

CHAPTER 2

Affect: A Critical Component of Mathematical Learning in Early Childhood

Sherry Renga and Lidwina Dalla

> CASE 1: *Nathan is a 6-year-old boy who has a great deal of difficulty in mathe-matics. He becomes easily frustrated and has decided, "I'm no good at math." He was referred to the school counselor when he wadded up his paper and began to cry after he received a poor test grade. . . .*
>
> CASE 2: *Nadine is a 7-year-old girl who has not been achieving well in the area of mathematics. Her positive attitude, however, has not been shaken by her poor grades. She continues to say, "Next time I will get all those right."*

Nathan's and Nadine's emotions, moods, and motivation were very different, yet they both received the same score on their papers. How Nathan and Nadine feel about themselves has an effect on and is affected by their learning of mathematics.

The interactions and influences between affective and cognitive development concern mathematics educators. The *Curriculum and Evaluation Standards* (6) lists "Learning to value mathematics" and "Becoming confident in one's own ability" as essential affective outcomes for the mathematical well-being of all students. This chapter summarizes research about primary students' attitudes toward and beliefs about mathematics and motivation.

Students' Attitudes

Attitude is the tendency to respond favorably or unfavorably to given circumstances or objects. Attitudes toward mathematics include liking fractions or geometry and not liking story problems or long division. When a child has experienced repeated failure in a given mathematical situation or on a mathematical topic, that child's response in a similar situation in the future may be, "I do not like fractions" or "I cannot solve story problems." These are attitudinal responses. Most educators view positive attitudes as an important goal of instruction both because they feel it is important that students enjoy mathematics and because they feel that positive attitudes facilitate learning.

Even though young children's attitudes change rapidly and it is difficult to measure them, it is important to study the formation of attitudes toward mathematics in the primary grades since attitudes generally develop over a period of time.

The fourth National Assessment of Educational Progress (NAEP) (4) found that most third graders have positive attitudes toward mathematics and indicate that they are willing to work hard on mathematics tasks. In grades 3 and 4, research data (14, 19) indicate a definite relationship between attitudes toward mathematics and other variables such as achievement, teacher quality, respect for the instructor, and students' perceptions of their ability. The relationship between mathematics attitude and achievement appears to be significantly stronger in boys than in girls in grades 3 and 4, especially late in the school year; further, attitudes are more closely related to achievement of computational skills than to achievement of conceptual skills (14). In one study (19) in grade 4, if students liked the type of feedback provided by the teacher and felt that the teacher was fair and was committed to students' learning, then they usually had a positive attitude toward mathematics; the correlations were higher for boys than for girls. On the other hand, students' attitudes were apparently not significantly affected by the student interaction and management–organization variables measured; these included enjoyment of classmates, school environment, class environment, difficulty of subject, competition, favoritism, formality, and disorganization.

How to Improve Students' Attitudes

Students' attitudes toward mathematics can be improved when teachers behave in the following ways:

- Show an enjoyment for mathematics.
- Make mathematics fun through the use of concrete models and discovery lessons.
- Show that mathematics is useful in everyday life as well as in careers. Children might discuss how they and their parents use math every day. For example, kindergarten children determine whether they have the same number of napkins as

plates when setting the table, and first- and second-grade children compute how much more money they need to buy a coveted item.

"To some extent, everybody is a mathematician and does mathematics consciously. To buy at the market, to measure a strip of wallpaper, or to decorate a ceramic pot with a regular pattern is doing mathematics. School mathematics must endow all students with a realization that doing mathematics is a common human activity." (6, p. 6)

- Consider students' interests when planning instruction. Nearly every concept taught in elementary mathematics can be approached through creative story situations or story books that address students' areas of interest.
- Establish short-term, obtainable goals. Have children keep individual folders in which they record basic facts they have learned or assignments they have completed.
- Provide mathematical experiences at which children can succeed. One way to do this is to adjust the difficulty level of tasks to the background and cognitive developmental level of students.
- Make mathematics understandable by effective and meaningful teaching methods (26).

School personnel should take action to improve attitudes toward mathematics— by routinely assessing mathematics attitudes and variables that appear to predict attitudes—and make changes in teaching, the learning environment, and the mathematics program to address results of the findings (19).

Attitudes can be improved by giving students the opportunity to communicate mathematics by discussing mathematical processes, procedures, alternatives, and algorithms as they work in cooperative small groups. Students who have trouble with computation can often be encouraged to verbalize or write descriptions of their approach to problems (6).

"Interacting with classmates helps children construct knowledge, learn other ways to think about ideas, and clarify their own thinking. Writing about mathematics, such as describing how a problem was solved, also helps students clarify their thinking and develop deeper understanding. Reading children's literature about mathematics, and eventually text material, also is an important aspect of communication that needs more emphasis in the K–4 curriculum." (6, p. 26)

Students' Beliefs

A primary goal of mathematics instruction is to assist children in developing the belief that they can do mathematics. Students' beliefs, feelings, and perceptions that appear to be related to the learning of mathematics are confidence in learning mathematics, mathematics anxiety, perceptions of the causes of success and failure in school, and learned helplessness.

> "For each individual, mathematical power involves the development of personal self-confidence." (6, p. 5)

Confidence in Learning Mathematics

Confidence in learning mathematics, mathematics self-concept, and self-efficacy in mathematics are closely related beliefs that pertain to whether students think that they can learn new mathematics concepts or ideas and achieve well in mathematics. For purposes of this chapter, we will consider the three topics mathematics self-concept, self-efficacy in mathematics, and confidence in learning mathematics together.

Students who are consistently labeled as low-ability, discipline problems, or behaviorally disordered learn to see themselves in those categories and behave accordingly. On the other hand, students who receive messages that indicate that they are capable, responsible, and well-behaved perceive themselves as possessing those attributes and demonstrate behaviors that verify their beliefs. Once a given self-concept is established, the student tends to accept feedback and experiences that fit into that concept of the self and to reject messages that indicate different expectations (12). Students' perceptions of themselves as learners influence their school learning in general and their learning of specific areas within subjects (20). Thus, students might believe that they can do well in mathematics in general but that they have difficulty with fractions; or they may feel that they are not capable in mathematics in general but that they do well on computation tasks. Since students' views of themselves as learners play a direct role in their performance in the mathematics classroom, teachers need to be able to ascertain how students perceive themselves as learners and help them develop confidence in their ability to learn mathematics.

> "The self-concepts of students are heavily influenced by those who treat them as able, valuable, and responsible—as well as by those who treat them as unable, worthless, and irresponsible. At some level of awareness each of us is always asking a very basic question: 'Who do you say I am?' The answer to this question influences how we behave and what we become." (12, p. 27)

Self-efficacy relates to beliefs that individuals have about their ability to perform in a given situation. Efficacy judgments result from inferences based on past and present performance and feedback relating to that performance and on comparison of one's own performance with that of others. Self-efficacy is important because it influences whether a person will attempt new tasks and how persistent and successful he or she will be.

"The curriculum must take seriously the goal of instilling in students a sense of confidence in their ability to think and communicate mathematically, to solve problems, to demonstrate flexibility in working with mathematical ideas and problems, to make appropriate decisions in selecting strategies and techniques, to recognize familiar mathematical structures in unfamiliar settings, to detect patterns, and to analyze data. The K–4 standards reflect the view that mathematics instruction should promote these abilities so that students understand that knowledge is empowering." (6, p. 18)

Studies on confidence in learning mathematics in grades K–4 have investigated the relationship between students' achievement and/or confidence and teacher feedback, providing them with information about the achievement of peers, giving them specific goals, and the use of peer models.

Teacher Feedback. Teacher feedback is positively related to children's assessment of their abilities by second and third grade. Young children modify their expectations as a result of failure experiences and teacher feedback regarding their performance less than older children do. These results may be due to a number of factors. Young children are quite egocentric and tend to lose this egocentrism at about age seven. Children at the preoperational stage may not remember and integrate information about past performance; they may judge their competence based on social reinforcement rather than on feedback about correctness of outcomes (24). We might question the implied premise that the teachers' expectations and assessment of children's abilities are realistic while the children's own estimates of their ability are unrealistic. Perhaps the appropriate conclusion here is that the children had realistic expectations until their expectations were lowered by constant negative feedback. "A growing body of research points to the teacher—his or her attentiveness, expectations, encouragements, attitudes, and evaluations—as the primary focus in influencing students' perceptions of themselves as learners" (12).

"Young children may attend more to social reinforcement—praise or criticism— than to objective, symbolic, or normative feedback directly related to their performance. Thus, a nice, socially reinforcing, or encouraging teacher is probably a more important factor in young children's achievement-related cognitions than is their actual performance on tasks." (1, p. 154)

Since teacher feedback is positively related to children's assessment of their mathematical abilities, teachers should provide feedback that focuses on what students do right, treats mistakes as a normal part of learning, shows them what both their skill and conceptual errors are, helps them understand why they made errors, provides them with the means for evaluating their own processes and solutions, gives suggestions for improvement, and makes them feel they are competent. Conferences between the teacher and the students are one viable means of providing this feedback.

Positive feedback may also take the form of assigning special projects to individual students, sending parents letters praising students' accomplishments, behaviors, or efforts, or just demonstrating interest in each child. Interest in the students can be shown by listening to them, making personal contacts with each student each day, sending written notes to students, and giving the same amount and type of attention to each student. Teacher feedback and the classroom climate should stress cooperation and self-improvement in relation to past performance rather than comparison and competition with peers.

"I do not believe that it is possible for an individual to live a cocooned life in which no failures, no mistakes, no slips will be encountered. These missteps in life (including mathematical learning) can be highly deleterious if totally unexpected; they are less interfering and less intense if their occurrence is a normal feature of life and, therefore, expected to occur at some time or another." (5, p. 15)

"The second graders have just finished working on addition and subtraction with regrouping. On a written test, many of them 'forget' to regroup when they need to in subtraction. Instead, they do this:

$$\begin{array}{r} 50 \\ -38 \\ \hline 28 \end{array}$$

"The teacher, Mr. Lewis, thinks they are being careless. He feels a little annoyed because this is something on which he has spent a lot of time. He decides, though, that he should sit down with the children one by one for a few minutes and have them talk through a couple of the problems and how they solved them. He thinks he may be able to tell what they are doing wrong this way.

"He chooses a couple of problems from the test and asks the children to justify their answers using bundles of Popsicle sticks. He discovers that most of them are not connecting the work they did in class with manipulatives to these written problems." (7, p. 65)

Providing Information about the Achievement of Peers and Goals. One source of self-efficacy information is the comparison of one's own performance with that of others, particularly of peers. Five- and 6-year-olds do observe their peers' progress, and second graders compare their performance to that of other children, but children do not consistently use the information gained from comparison to change their behavior or their view of themselves or to evaluate their own competence until about fourth grade. For example, kindergartners did not compete by increasing their pace when they observed that their peers were working faster than they were (13).

"Within the classroom, where success and failure are so prevalent, examination performance and social comparison provide constant and important inputs that in part determine self-worth and personal esteem . . . . Concern with the self lies at the core of human experience and therefore must play a role in any theoretical formulation in the field of human motivation, and is of particular importance in the study of student life." (1, p. 17)

In one study (15), low-achieving children in grades 4 and 5 were given information about how their peers had performed on the assigned task, and it was suggested that the students set a goal of working a given number of problems during each session. The children who received both goals and comparative information developed skills and confidence for solving problems. Children who received only goals developed confidence but did not attain the same level of skill development. The children may have assumed that if they were able to attain the goal of working a given number of problems they had mastered the task.

The Use of Peer Models. In one study (17), peer models were used to enhance self-efficacy and achievement in mathematical skills among remedial students from ages 8 to 10. Students developed higher self-efficacy for learning and achievement from observing peer models of the same age and sex as themselves receiving instruction and learning skills. "Coping" models demonstrated typical fears and deficiencies of students, were initially hesitant, made errors, reflected negative achievement beliefs but gradually improved their skills, and verbalized coping statements. "Mastery" models demonstrated faultless performance, reflected positive attitudes, emphasized their own ability and self-efficacy, and made tasks appear easy. In a follow-up study (18), children appeared to benefit more from observing coping models than mastery models; the mastery model was also effective when more than one model was used. Using more than one model may increase the likelihood that subjects will identify with at least one of the models observed and give credibility to the successful learning demonstrated by the models.

The finding that peer models can be used to enhance self-efficacy and achievement in mathematics suggests that students will benefit by working in cooperative groups that focus on and verbalize thinking processes as they work together to learn skills and solve problems.

Mathematics Anxiety

Mathematics anxiety may be defined as a fear or dislike of mathematics, as a negative attitude toward mathematics, or as a negative emotional reaction to mathematics. Studies done on mathematics anxiety have focused primarily on adults or students in grade levels above K–4; thus, teachers may need to conduct action research in their own classrooms to assess the mathematics anxiety of their students.

Preschool and first-grade children are generally positive about their ability to succeed on mathematical tasks (24). Their confidence is, in many instances, reinforced by the positive feedback that they receive from teachers whether or not the feedback is tied to social or cognitive goals (1). These findings may indicate that children do not develop math anxiety in the early elementary grades as long as they receive a great deal of positive feedback.

Preventing Mathematics Anxiety.   Even though mathematics anxiety may not be a widespread problem in grades K–4, it is important that teachers in these grades help prevent anxiety from developing. The mathematics classroom atmosphere should be relaxed, positive, and supportive. Students need to be given successful experiences so they will feel confident. Since children in the primary grades are in the concrete operations stage of cognitive development, one way to enhance success is to provide many experiences at the concrete level. Students need to have a good basis of well-developed concepts and skills at each stage of their mathematical development so they will have a foundation on which they can continue to build.

Teach the language and symbolism of mathematics.   Teachers should model problem-solving strategies rather than present a finished product; one way to do this is to let students present suggestions, try their ideas, and let them see why they do or do not work. Have students share their strategies and their thinking processes so they do not get the idea that some people can do mathematics while others cannot. Students need to have experiences with problems for which the solution or solution strategy is not immediately apparent so they develop techniques for attacking such problems and are willing to persist in finding a solution.

> "The development of a student's power to use mathematics involves learning the signs, symbols, and terms of mathematics. This is best accomplished in problem situations in which students have an opportunity to read, write, and discuss ideas in which the use of the language of mathematics becomes natural. As students communicate their ideas, they learn to clarify, refine, and consolidate their thinking." (6, p. 6)

> "Inability to handle frustration contributes to math anxiety. When a math-anxious person sees that a problem is not going to be easy to solve, he tends to quit right away, believing that no amount of time or rereading or reformulation of the problem will make it any clearer. Freezing and quitting may be as much the result of destructive self-talk as of unfamiliarity with the problem. If we think we have no strategy with which to begin work, we may never find one. But if we can talk ourselves into feeling comfortable and secure, we may let in a good idea." (27, p. 67)

Be aware that math anxiety may be confounded by or confused with test anxiety. Give positive feedback on tests, provide adequate time to perform mathematical tasks, and attempt to reduce the tension that is frequently associated with mathematics classes and testing situations.

If children are confident in their ability to do mathematics, they are not likely to develop math anxiety; thus, the ideas suggested earlier for developing children's self-confidence in their mathematical abilities would also help prevent the development of math anxiety in students.

Self-Perceptions of the Causes of Success or Failure

An important set of beliefs is one that deals with what a person perceives as causes of his or her success or failure in school. Individuals are said to have an "internal locus of control" when they attribute outcomes to their own ability or effort. Individuals are said to have an "external locus of control" when they attribute outcomes to factors outside themselves and beyond their control, such as difficulty or luck. Stable factors are seen as being invariant; they reside in the individual (ability) or the task (difficulty). Unstable factors depend on conditions at the time in the individual (effort) and the situation (luck) (28).

> "The guiding principle of attribution theory is that individuals search for understanding, seeking to discover why an event has occurred . . . . Search is most evident when there has been an unexpected outcome (e.g., failure when success was anticipated), and when a desire has not been fulfilled." (1, pp. 18, 19)

When an achievement outcome is observed, it will usually be explained by both teachers and students in predictable ways. Expected outcomes will be attributed to stable factors while unexpected outcomes will be attributed to unstable factors (29). If a student to whom high ability is attributed fails at a task, the failure will likely be attributed to a lack of effort. If a low-ability student fails, the failure will likely be attributed to low ability rather than to lack of effort. When low-ability students study hard but fail anyway, they may interpret the failure as proof that they are not capable and decide not to try rather than fail. Thus, an important effect of student attribution is its effect on persistence. If a child believes more effort will result in getting the correct answers, more effort is probable. If the child feels luck determines the outcome, persistence is not seen as relevant. A comparison of achievement of Chinese, Japanese, and American children (22) indicated that Japanese mothers believe that effort is the most important criterion in determining school achievement of children, while American mothers credit ability as being the most important factor. It is highly probable that these beliefs influence the amount of time and effort that children devote to their school work in these countries and their resulting level of achievement.

Several researchers (2, 9, 23) have noted that perceptions of ability become lower with increasing age and that there are qualitative differences among the types of attributions made by young children, older children, and adults. Due to developmental differences, young children may not have developed cognitive processing abilities to the point where they can remember, logically analyze, and use past successes and failures to interpret feedback, assess their performance, and compare their performance to that of others and to task difficulty to determine ability; thus, they view themselves as competent and capable of being successful (2).

"One of the more disturbing conclusions of recent studies of mathematics education is that the American public tends to assume that differences in accomplishment in school mathematics are due primarily to differences in innate ability rather than to differences in individual effort or in opportunity to learn. These beliefs surface in many ways—in studies of parents' views, in common self-deprecating remarks ("I never could do math"), and in public infatuation with early tracking as a strategy for mathematics education." (8, p. 9) "Other societies make the assumption that all students can learn mathematics and that learning is a matter of effort . . . . Our expectations have a great deal to do with how we respond to students and consequently to what students believe that they can do . . . . The two sets of *Standards* challenge us to create learning environments for students and for teachers in which the building of confidence in the learning and doing of mathematics is a primary goal." (7, p. 192)

Apparently, young children do not distinguish among ability, effort, and outcome. There appear to be four levels of reasoning involving the concepts of effort and ability among children ages 5 to 13 (9). Five- and 6-year-old children do not systematically distinguish among effort, ability, and outcome; these children believe that students who achieve more have more ability and better work habits than those who achieve less. From ages 7 to 9, effort is viewed as a cause of outcome, but children do not use ability to explain how equal scores can result in spite of unequal effort; these children believe that individuals who exert equal effort should achieve equal outcomes, and see failure as the result of faulty effort such as working too rapidly or too hard. From age 9 to age 12, children inconsistently use ability to reconcile differences between effort and outcomes. By age 11, children clearly differentiate ability from effort, and ability and effort are seen as interdependent causes of outcomes; these children believe that outcome is limited by level of ability (9).

"It is not surprising that children of elementary school age do not differentiate between effort, ability, and outcome. Teachers themselves do not always differentiate these dimensions in their feedback. . . . Praise is usually given more for social behavior or school-appropriate behavior than on the basis of the quality of children's products. A teacher's 'good' may refer to the child's good conduct (e.g., working alone quietly), effort, or the quality of his or her work, or all of these simultaneously. Many verbal comments do not clearly indicate on which of these dimensions the teacher is commenting." (1, p. 160)

Attributions that imply that the student is likely to be successful in the future and that failure can be overcome will likely result in students choosing similar tasks and extending effort and persisting on those tasks in the future. On the other hand, attributions that imply that the student is not likely to be successful in the future may cause the student to avoid the same or similar tasks in the future or to put little effort into the tasks; then failure can be attributed to lack of effort rather than to lack of ability. Attributing success to unstable external factors such as luck may inhibit effort. It is the individual's perception of the causes of success and failure that mediate future performance—not the success and failure per se (2).

Since children often do not understand task goals or evaluation and thus make inappropriate attributions for success and failure, teacher feedback must be related to lesson goals and must make clear the purposes of assignments and the criteria for grading. For example, the teacher must distinguish between the content and the form of completed assignments and between academic and behavioral feedback. Classroom practices should not exaggerate the importance of ability or comparative standards or make levels of performance salient.

Teachers' perceptions of students are indicated by their behaviors and influence students' attributions of their own ability. Teachers need to be familiar with attribution theory not only so they can help shape the attributions that students make but so they will make appropriate attributions resulting from an appraisal of a given outcome for a given individual based on the myriad of possible causes. For example, when a high-ability student fails, the failure may occur because the task is beyond the student's current cognitive developmental level rather than due to a lack of effort. If a low-ability student fails, the failure may not be due to a lack of ability but to a lack of effort or persistence on the task.

"It is important for teachers to work on developing positive perceptions of their students, themselves, and education if they wish to be a beneficial presence in the lives of students. Positive perceptions means viewing students as able, valuable, and responsible as well as seeing oneself and education in essentially favorable ways." (12, p. 37)

Learned Helplessness

Learned helplessness is the belief that the individual cannot control outcomes. Learned helplessness can be general or specific to a given subject area such as mathematics. It frequently develops as a result of an encounter with or repeated exposure to uncontrollable failure experiences. It usually includes feelings of incompetence, lack of motivation, and low self-esteem. Once individuals develop the belief that given circumstances are beyond their control, they retain that belief after the circumstances are altered so that they are under the individuals' control (3). Learned helplessness is related to attribution theory. Students who exhibit learned helplessness tend to attribute failure to uncontrollable external stable factors or to lack of ability and success to either task difficulty or luck (11).

Learned helplessness affects the motivational, cognitive, and emotional levels of behavior. When students have experienced what they view as uncontrollable failure in early encounters with new tasks, they will not be motivated to respond in succeeding situations because they have learned that they will fail regardless of their responses. They are unable to perceive that the learning situation has changed from one in which failure is beyond their control to a situation in which their responses could reverse the failure. The students experience a great deal of emotion in new situations. If they continue to fail while trying to succeed, they frequently demonstrate apathy or depression (3).

There have been few studies on learned helplessness in mathematics. Thus, this is an area in which teachers could conduct action research in their own classrooms. In one study (3) on learned helplessness, students were timed on each of five sheets of problems; when they finished each sheet, they were told that they had not completed as many problems as their classmates in the stipulated time; thus, the feedback was not contingent on the students' actual performance. This exposure to noncontingent failure had a debilitating effect on performance on subsequent problems of the same type, and the induced helplessness transferred across tasks.

Preventing the Development of Learned Helplessness.   To help prevent the development of learned helplessness in children, the teacher could do the following:

- Provide children with successful experiences early.
- Help children make appropriate attributions about effort, persistence, and strategy and de-emphasize attributions to ability.
- Teach frustration tolerance.
- Give feedback on both correct and incorrect work and suggest strategies for improvement.
- Point out patterns of errors and require students to correct errors.
- Be alert to symptoms of learned helplessness such as goofing off, not working up to capacity, turning in sloppy or unfinished work, and unwillingness to attempt mathematics tasks.
- Relate past learning to concepts currently being taught (3).

Persistence is related to previous successful experiences. To provide successful experiences, the teacher must pay close attention to the difficulty level of required tasks. It may be helpful to discuss which tasks are easy and which are difficult, why one concept is difficult while another one is not, and how various students deal with tasks they consider difficult. Such discussions would help make children aware that most students find some tasks difficult, provide them with strategies for dealing with difficult tasks, and give them a sense of control over the tasks by letting them express their feelings about the tasks.

Motivation

Some children love to come to school and work on mathematical activities; others appear anxious about school and lack enthusiasm for lessons in mathematics. Students must be motivated before they can be expected to learn. Usually individuals learn because they want to achieve particular goals.

"Throughout their school years, some students become more creative, some less so; some become excited about learning, some become bored and disillusioned; some become intellectually active, some less active. Some students fall in love with books, others learn to hate them. Some develop a passion for physical exercise, others learn to avoid it." (12, p. 38)

Goals that tend to motivate academic achievement behavior are frequently categorized as intrinsic or extrinsic. *Intrinsic goals* can be task-related goals such as understanding concepts or feeling good about solving a problem or ego-related goals such as performing better than others or showing more intelligence than others. *Extrinsic goals* may be social goals such as pleasing others or other rewards such as grades, stars, or praise (25).

Intrinsically motivated learners tend to be process oriented; they spend considerable time on problems because they enjoy finding relationships and learning concepts. The optimum form of intrinsic motivation appears to be task involvement. Children who are task-involved value learning and understanding, focus on the process of completing and mastering tasks, and choose tasks that offer a reasonable level of challenge. They endeavor to learn new skills rather than exhibiting skills or concealing a lack of skills (10). Teachers can induce and maintain task-involvement by focusing on concepts rather than on computation, providing a variety of tasks, discussing why tasks are assigned, modeling enthusiasm for learning, allowing students to evaluate themselves, focusing evaluation on increasing mastery of concepts and skills, providing assistance in a manner that allows students to feel responsible for successful outcomes, and choosing materials or allowing students to choose materials of an appropriate level of difficulty.

"A developmentally appropriate curriculum encourages the exploration of a wide variety of mathematical ideas in such a way that children retain their enjoyment of, and curiosity about, mathematics. It incorporates real-world contexts, children's experiences, and children's language in developing ideas." (6, p. 16)

Children who are motivated by ego-related goals are concerned with achieving external reinforcement or demonstrating competence rather than with learning and understanding. Children who are ego-involved and who perceive their ability as high select tasks offering a reasonable level of challenge so they can demonstrate their ability without making errors or showing confusion. Learners who are ego-involved and who perceive their ability as low attempt to avoid looking incompetent; thus, they may choose excessively difficult tasks on which they could not reasonably be expected to succeed, or they may choose very easy tasks so that success is assured. Ego-involvement may have some value in motivating learning, but it is clearly inferior to task-involvement and is counterproductive for students who view their ability as low (10). It appears that ego-involvement is fostered by teaching practices that emphasize competition and comparison of students' performance.

FIGURE 2.1   Numbers are beautiful.

It is difficult to motivate learning consistently through extrinsic rewards; indeed, the use of extrinsic incentives may impede learning, since students focus on obtaining rewards rather than upon the task itself (10).

Competition appears to have some motivational benefits when it is embedded in the context of cooperative small-group instruction conceptualized by Slavin (21). In this situation, students are expected to work together on academic tasks within each, usually heterogeneous, group to assist one another in learning concepts and skills so they can compete with other groups within the classroom. The group is usually rewarded on the basis of the achievement of all group members. The focus of group tasks is on discussing ideas and understanding processes; children are encouraged to look for relationships and solve problems as well as learn concepts. Cooperative learning appears to be more effective in promoting student achievement than traditional instruction when group rewards are given based on achievement of individual group members. High-quality peer interactions such as giving and receiving clear explanations are also important for cooperative strategies to be successful (21).

The effects of tangible, extrinsic rewards on remedial children from ages 8 to 11 were studied by Schunk (16). It was found that arithmetic skills and self-efficacy were enhanced by providing rewards that were contingent on performance, but that offering rewards for participation was no better than offering no rewards. Offering rewards for learning and making progress makes children feel that the learning is valued and that they are expected to learn. Offering rewards for simply completing a task regardless of the quality of the work may convey the impression that learning is not important or even that the teacher feels the students are unable to perform adequately.

Conclusion

Research on affect in mathematics education has made us aware that affective variables do influence students' progress in mathematics, but has not yet presented a cohesive picture of the role affect plays in the learning of mathematics. In this chapter, we have offered many suggestions for teachers for dealing with affective issues in the mathematics classroom; these ideas are based on implications that are suggested by available research rather than on definitive studies that have shown a clear relationship between teacher behaviors, student affect, and mathematics learning. We still need research on all aspects of affect as they relate to mathematics learning. Teachers could conduct action research in their own classrooms on topics such as the following:

- How affective variables vary for different types of learners, learning contexts, or instructional methods.
- When affective variables emerge, how tenaciously children cling to them, and under what conditions they are formed.
- Assessing the effects of cooperative learning on attitudes toward problem solving.
- Contrasting the effects of written comments (positive vs. neutral or negative) on student papers.
- Charting the effects of specific stress reduction techniques on student anxiety.

Looking Ahead . . .

To meet the NCTM goals that students "learn to value mathematics" and "become confident in their ability to do mathematics," research findings must be translated into classroom practices. Teachers and researchers must continue to seek answers to the questions of when and how affective variables develop, how they are demonstrated, how they influence learning, and how teachers can foster the development of positive attitudes and beliefs in mathematics. Teachers must also assess the attitudes and beliefs of the students in their classrooms and analyze their own teaching behaviors. They can then use this information to determine how instruction, assigned tasks, and the classroom structure and environment are influencing these attitudes and beliefs and design learning environments and tasks which encourage students to become positive, motivated, confident, and persevering learners of mathematics.

Sherry Renga

We have reviewed the relationship between affective variables and students' behavior in the mathematics classroom, but there are many areas that need more research. I still wonder how to best compile and use information on the affective characteristics of my own students. I now lean toward using personal journals and student conferences to give students the opportunity to verbalize their feelings about mathematics. Cooperative learning is also beneficial. Working together builds self-esteem and confidence in the students' ability to do math. Perhaps cooperative activities that involve students in real-world mathematics and concrete materials can be effective in improving my students' belief in their ability to do mathematics.

Lidwina Dalla

About the Authors

Sherry Renga is associate professor of mathematics at Eastern Washington University, Cheney, Washington. She teaches methods and content courses in mathematics for pre-service and in-service teachers. She is interested in the development of confidence, mathematical knowledge and concepts, and problem-solving skills in teachers and future teachers.

Lidwina Dalla teaches third- and fourth-grade mathematics at Hamblen Elementary School, a departmentalized, alternative school, in Spokane, Washington. She is interested in helping students develop connections between mathematics and other subject areas, in enhancing students' problem-solving skills, and in increasing students' belief in their ability to do mathematics.

References

1. AMES, R. E., & AMES, C. (Eds.). (1984). *Research on motivation in education (Vol. 1): Student motivation*. New York: Academic Press.

2. BLUMENFELD, P. C., PINTRICH, P. R., MEECE, J., & WESSELS, K. (1982). The formation and role of self perceptions of ability in elementary classrooms. *Elementary School Journal*, 82(5), 401–420.

3. GENTILE, J. R., & MONACO, N. M. (1986). Learned helplessness in mathematics: What educators should know. *Journal of Mathematical Behavior*, 5(2), 159–178.

4. KOUBA, V. L., BROWN, C. A., CARPENTER, T. P., LINDQUIST, M. M., SILVER, E. A., & SWAFFORD, J. O. (1988). Results of the fourth NAEP assessment of mathematics: Measurement, geometry, data interpretation, attitudes, and other topics. *Arithmetic Teacher*, 35(9), 10–16.

5. MCLEOD, D. B., & ADAMS, V. M. (Eds.). (1989). *Affect and mathematical problem solving*. New York: Springer-Verlag.

6. NATIONAL COUNCIL OF TEACHERS OF MATHEMATICS (1989). *Curriculum and evaluation standards for school mathematics*. Reston, VA: Author.

7. NATIONAL COUNCIL OF TEACHERS OF MATHEMATICS (1991). *Professional standards for teaching mathematics*. Reston, VA: Author.

8. NATIONAL RESEARCH COUNCIL. (1989). *Everybody counts: A report to the nation on the future of mathematics education*. Washington, DC: National Academy Press.

9. NICHOLLS, J. G. (1978). The development of the concepts of effort and ability, perception of academic attainment and the understanding that difficult tasks require more ability. *Child Development*, 49, 800–814.

10. NICHOLLS, J. G. (1983). Conceptions of ability and achievement motivation: A theory and its implications for education. In S. G. Paris, G. M. Olson, & H. W. Stevenson (Eds.), *Learning and motivation in the classroom* (pp. 211–237). Hillsdale, NJ: Erlbaum.

11. PARSONS, J. E., MEECE, J. L., ADLER, T. F., & KACZALA, C. M. (1982). Sex differences in attributions and learned helplessness. *Sex Roles*, 8(4), 421–432.

12. PURKEY, W. W., & NOVAK, J. M. (1984). *Inviting school success: A self-concept approach to teaching and learning*. Belmont, CA: Wadsworth.

13. RUBLE, D. N., BOGGIANO, A. K., FELDMAN, N. S., & LOEBL, J. H. (1980). Developmental analysis of the role of social comparison in self-evaluation. *Developmental Psychology*, 16, 105–115.

14. SCHOFIELD, H. L. (1982). Sex, grade level, and the relationship between mathematics attitude and achievement in children. *Journal of Educational Research*, 75(5), 280–284.

15. SCHUNK, D. H. (1983a). Developing children's self-efficacy and skills: The role of social comparative information and goal setting. *Contemporary Educational Psychology*, 8, 76–86.

16. SCHUNK, D. H. (1983b). Reward contingencies and the development of children's skills and self-efficacy. *Journal of Educational Psychology*, 75(4), 511–518.

17. SCHUNK, D. H., & HANSON, A. R. (1985). Peer models: Influence on children's self-efficacy and achievement. *Journal of Educational Psychology*, 77(3), 313–322.

18. SCHUNK, D. H., HANSON, A. R., & COX, P. D. (1987). Peer-model attributes and children's achievement behaviors. *Journal of Educational Psychology*, 79(1), 54–61.

19. SHAUGHNESSY, J., HALADYNA, T., & SHAUGHNESSY, J. M. (1983). Relations of student, teacher, and learning environment variables to attitude toward mathematics. *School Science and Mathematics*, 83(1), 21–37.

20. SHAVELSON, R. J., BOLUS, R., & KEESLING, W. J. (1980). Self-concept: Recent developments in theory and methods. *New Directions for Testing and Measurement, 7,* 25–43.
21. SLAVIN, R. E. (1987). Cooperative learning: Where behavioral and humanistic approaches to classroom motivation meet. *Elementary School Journal, 88*(1), 29–37.
22. STEVENSON, H. W., LEE, S. Y., & STIGLER, J. W. (1986). Mathematics achievement of Chinese, Japanese, and American children. *Science, 231,* 693–699.
23. STIPEK, D. (1981). Children's perceptions of their own and their classmates' ability. *Journal of Educational Psychology, 73*(3), 404–410.
24. STIPEK, D. J. (1984). Young children's performance expectations: Logical analysis or wishful thinking? In J. G. Nicholls (Ed.), *Advances in motivation and achievement* (Vol. 3, pp. 33–56). Greenwich, CT: JAI Press.
25. STIPEK, D. J. (1988). *Motivation to learn: From theory to practice.* Englewood Cliffs, NJ: Prentice-Hall.
26. SUYDAM, M. N. (1984). Research report: Attitudes toward mathematics. *Arithmetic Teacher, 32*(3), 12.
27. TOBIAS, S. (1978). *Over-coming math anxiety.* Boston: Houghton Mifflin.
28. WEINER, B. (1974). *Achievement motivation and attribution theory.* Morristown, NJ: General Learning Press.
29. WEINER, B., FRIEZE, I., KUKLA, A., REED, L., REST, S., & ROSENBAUM, R. M. (1971). *Perceiving the causes of success and failure.* New York: General Learning Press.

PART II

Processes and Content

CHAPTER 3

Early Number and Numeration

Joseph N. Payne and DeAnn M. Huinker

There are 5 children playing in the park and 8 more joined them. How many children were then playing in the park?
Here is how three children solved this problem.
TIM: Displayed 5 counters, and then 8 counters. He counted them by ones, "One, two, three . . . thirteen. So thirteen in all."
KELSEY: Thought for a moment and said, "Five and five make ten. Three more makes thirteen. So thirteen in all."
JANE: Displayed two fingers on one hand and three on the other. "Eight and two make ten. Three more makes thirteen. So thirteen."
Which children were thinking of numbers using groups? Which one was probably thinking of numbers only as made up of single things? What do these results mean for the kind of curriculum and instructional methods for numbers to be used with young children?

An overview of the K–4 curriculum for whole numbers is summarized in Standard 6 of the *Curriculum and Evaluations Standards for School Mathematics.* Students should be able to:

- Construct number meanings through real-world experiences and the use of physical materials.
- Understand our numeration system by relating counting, grouping, and place-value concepts.
- Develop number sense.
- Interpret the multiple uses of numbers encountered in the real world.

The extensive research literature shows how children develop number concepts and learn to count. There are some but not as many studies on place value and larger numbers. This chapter deals with these two aspects of number with the first part on meanings for early numbers and the second part on numeration. In both parts, there is consistent emphasis on children using concrete materials and performing actions on the materials to develop conceptual structures about number and numerosity, the cardinality of a set.

Meanings for Early Numbers

Understanding number requires much more than verbal counting. It also includes the ability to determine the total number of objects and reasoning about that numerosity using number relationships. Numerosity and reasoning are influenced by the size of the numbers and the ability to think using groups. Since numbers are used in a variety of ways and with a variety of symbols, context and symbols are added influences on children's understanding of number. These ideas are developed in this section under the headings: Using Numbers, Counting, Connecting Counting and Cardinality, Thinking in Groups, and Writing Numerals.

Using Numbers

As children encounter the many uses of numbers, they need to interpret the uses and make meaning of the numbers. Sarah will be 7 years old on the second of March. She invites six friends to a birthday party and uses numbers in different ways in her invitation (Fig. 3.1).

The uses of number can be summarized as sequence, counting, cardinal, measure, ordinal, and nonnumerical (10). When the number names are verbally recited in the standard sequence without referring to objects, they are being used in the *sequence* context, often called "rote counting," where children repeat the words much like they recite the alphabet. The *counting* context of number, also referred to as "rational counting," involves matching each object or event with a number name. Children may be able to count a set of objects, but still not realize that the last

FIGURE 3.1   Birthday party invitation
with many uses of number

Please come to my birthday party on
Tuesday March 2 at 4:00 p.m. I live
at 355 Third Avenue. I'll be 7 years old.

Sarah

number stated in the count sequence also names the cardinal value of the set, a crucial step in children's understanding of number. When children can use number names to tell "how many" objects or events are in the whole set, they are using number words in a *cardinal* context. The cardinal number quantifies or describes the numerosity of a set.

In a *measure* context numbers tell how many units there are along some continuous dimension. Children need to fill or cover objects with a specific unit, count the number of units, and then shift from the count meaning to the measure meaning. Children must understand the cardinal context first and the measure context later. Background for measure contexts is helped by using units in cardinal contexts. For example, "I see you have 4 cars" rather than "I see you have 4," emphasizes the use of numbers to describe and quantify something, which is helpful with measures such as 5 centimeters or 2 liters.

A number name that indicates the relative position of an object in an ordered set is used in an *ordinal* context. Children learn the initial ordinal words, first, second, and third, from everyday situations. They construct others from sequence, counting, and cardinal contexts. The production and understanding of ordinal numbers grow from but lag behind counting. Ninety-five percent of the 5-year-olds could produce the first eight number words but only 57 percent could produce the first five usual ordinal words (3). Only 25 percent of 727 children entering kindergarten could point to the third ball while 82 percent could produce a set of three objects (29).

Action research-ordinal use of numbers
Teach children the ordinal use of number with the names "number one, number two, number three, and so on." Compare results from this with the use of the names "first, second, third . . . "

Numbers used in a *nonnumerical* context are for identification purposes: telephone numbers, social security numbers, house numbers, bus numbers, athletes' jersey numbers, and UPC codes. Confusion can result, for example, when a child thinks that player number 36 is the thirty-sixth person on the team.

Much early counting is done to learn the conventional number sequence. It is important to develop other uses of numbers and to connect them to one another. Children need many opportunities to learn the number sequence, to count objects, to state the cardinal number, to measure objects by filling or covering, and to explain the ordinal and nonnumerical meaning of numbers.

Counting

Children's beginning number sequence generally consists of three portions. The first portion contains an accurate number–word sequence such as "one, two, three." This is followed by a stable incorrect portion such as "six, eight, five" which is consistently repeated on each count. The final nonstable incorrect portion changes with each count, for example a child counts "five, nine, twelve, ten" and on the next count says "five, thirteen, ten, twenty."

Children as young as 18 months of age begin to say the number sequence and most children can count by rote to 10 or 20 when they enter kindergarten (2, 10, 11), with ability strongly affected by opportunities to practice (9).

Learning the number sequence
Record the number sequence to 20 on an audiotape, repeating the sequence several times. Have a child or group count aloud as they listen to the tape.

Children's ability to produce an accurate number sequence is only a beginning in their understanding of number. The next step is to attach a quantitative meaning to the number words by gaining skill in rational counting. This involves coordinating the objects to be counted with the number sequence by using an indicating act, usually pointing. Most mistakes that children make while counting sets of objects are a result of faulty indicating acts or not attending to which objects have been counted and which still need to be counted (9). As children count sets of objects, they need to be observed to see if they can coordinate their verbal counting with their actions on the objects. Do they say one number name for each object they touch? Do they touch and count each object and only touch and count it once? Children often have trouble keeping track of the objects, may skip some of them, or may count an object more than once (10, 11). Do they have trouble starting or stopping their number sequence? Some children will point to the first object and say "one, two," while others will get to the last object but continue to say extra number names (11).

Children often need to develop a method of partitioning a set of objects into the items that have been counted from those that still need to be counted. When children count objects which can be moved around they are more accurate than when they

FIGURE 3.2   Mat for keeping track of counted objects

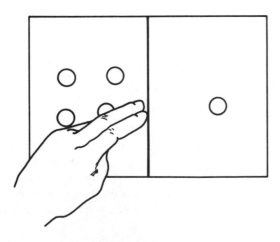

count a set of pictured objects (43). If the objects can be moved, it helps to have the children start with all the objects on one side of the line as shown in Figure 3.2 and then slide one object at a time to the other side as it is counted. If the objects cannot be moved, children should use some method of marking the objects that have been counted, such as covering or crossing off. Children's counting of pictured sets can be greatly improved when they are taught to cross off each pictured object as it is counted (18). Telling children to "try really hard" as they count the objects also increases their accuracy because as their effort is increased all kinds of errors are reduced, particularly the skipping of objects (9). The following activity can help children become more aware of how to count accurately.

Catch the mistake and make it right
Introduce the children to Mr. Mixup, a puppet who makes lots of counting mistakes. "Watch Mr. Mixup very carefully as he counts these blocks. If you catch a mistake, raise your hand right away, so we can help Mr. Mixup count these blocks correctly." Have Mr. Mixup make the following mistakes: (a) skip an object, (b) count the first or last object twice or another object more than once, (c) make errors in the number name sequence, or (d) report the cardinal value of the set as a number different than the last one spoken. When the children catch a mistake, ask, "What happened?" and "Can you explain to Mr. Mixup why it's a mistake and tell him how he can be more careful the next time he counts?" (6).

Action research–counting objects
Design a plan to help children improve in their counting of objects and pictures of objects. Arrange objects in a row first and then in a circle and have children move each object as it is counted. Provide pictures of objects in a row or regular arrangement, and also in a circular or random arrangement. Teach students to mark each object as it is counted. See if these strategies help children with counting tasks and how much practice it takes.

Connecting Counting and Cardinality

Children take an important step in their understanding of number when they connect counting to cardinality. This connection enables children to reason with numbers.

When a 2-year-old is asked to count a set of four cars and tell how many, the usual response is some number other than her/his last counted word (9). A 3-year-old on the same task is likely merely to count the set again, "one, two, three, four" with the "How many?" question interpreted as a request to count the objects (9, 10, 11).

Eventually, some event occurs that suggests to children that the last counted word might be the answer to the how-many question. They may have heard emphasis on the last word or were taught to say the last word again. Children as young as 2 and 3 years old can learn the last-word rule from a very brief teaching intervention. Using sets of six, five, and seven objects, children were told, "When you count, the last word you say tells you how many things there are. Watch me, one, two, three, four, five, six. Six. There are six blocks. Watch again . . . So the last word you say in counting tells you how many things you have" (9).

This last-word response is the first indication that children realize counting has a purpose beyond itself. While the initial last-word responses reflect that children have learned the rule, the last name may not in the child's mind actually refer to the cardinality of the whole set of objects. The last word may not even be the correct numerosity of the set if the child used an incorrect number sequence or counted inaccurately, say, by skipping an object. For example, Marketta counted a set of five pennies by saying "one, two, three, six, ten" and then responded "ten" when asked, "How many pennies are there?" Even if children are not making a cardinality reference, their ability to give a last-word response appears to be a first step in connecting their counting to the cardinal meaning of numbers.

The transition to understanding that the last counted word refers to the whole set requires a shift in children's thinking from a counting situation to a cardinal situation. For example, Ian first counts the set of five cars as separate objects, "one, two, three, four, five," and notes that five is said as the last object is counted. Then he shifts his thinking as he perceives that five refers to all of the objects as a group. This "integration" of separate objects into a single entity or group allows children to give cardinal meaning to numbers (9, 37). This transition is a key development in children's understanding of number because it allows children to integrate their counting knowledge with an understanding of groups.

Counting progresses from objects that can be seen to less concrete things such as spaces, finger points or number words, and at the most abstract level, to counting as an entity in itself without the counting being related to any other representation (37).

Piaget (1952) used a logical operations model, including classification, ordering, and conservation, to describe children's development of number concepts. Adherents to this position suggested strengthening these logical operations prior to work on number skills such as counting. Research results suggest a different conclusion. Practice on meaningful counting activities led to an improved performance not only on number skills but also on logical operations. Explicit readiness training in logical operations was seen as unnecessary (5).

Thinking in Groups

Once children begin making connections between counting and cardinality, they can begin to "think in groups" and make an important advance in their number concepts. By thinking in groups, children see relationships between numbers and are more flexible in dealing with quantities.

Children at a young age can learn to see groups of twos and threes (11, 16, 17). Children as young as 2 years old know that they have two cookies when they have one for each hand or that they have two shoes when they have one on each foot. This ability to identify quickly the number of objects in a set without counting has been labeled "subitizing." Subitizing is limited to small numbers, usually just two and three when dots are randomly arranged (16, 17). For sets with more, children and adults either count the set by ones, subitize small subgroups, or recognize special patterns within the set of objects (Fig. 3.3) and combine these to determine the whole amount.

A person successful in helping children think in groups said that we need to "start with learning to see twos and threes, seeing the group as a whole with one quick focus of the eyes" because once children can see them, they can think them (32).

Seeing twoness and threeness
Hide three pennies. Uncover the pennies and ask, "How many pennies are there?" Watch to see if the child counts by ones, or sees the group as a whole. Repeat with two pennies. Encourage a quick response. The goal is to tell how many in a one-second glance.

Making twos and threes
The objective is to see and make twos, not to see how many twos. Give each child 10 counters. Have them break the set into parts by making twos. Then put the whole set of objects back together and repeat until the twos are made quickly. Next start with 12 counters and make sets of three. Initially it may take a minute, but with practice in almost 10 seconds.

Recognizing groups of two and three helps in seeing numbers four through ten as made up of smaller groups. For example, children can see five as a three and a two or as two twos and a one. They could learn ten as two fives, a six and a four, two threes and a four, or three threes and a one. This thinking involves acquiring a part–whole understanding of number and is a major advancement in children's conceptual knowledge of number (30). Now children can develop many relationships among numbers because they can think of a number as both a whole amount and as being comprised of smaller groups or parts.

The value of using a part–whole approach with kindergarten children in contrast to the more traditional approach of just counting by ones has been demonstrated (7). Children first learned about zero, one, and two in six lessons. Then they learned each number from three through seven in three-lesson sequences. In the first lesson

FIGURE 3.3   Patterns for four, five, and six

of each sequence, the number was introduced using concrete and oral activities that focused on the whole amount and parts that could make the whole. For example, five was talked about as "two and two and one, three and two, one and four, and zero and five." The numeral was introduced in the second lesson and the children were asked to recognize it. In the third lesson, children wrote the numeral.

After twenty-five lessons on the numbers zero through seven, including some review lessons, the children using the part–whole approach scored significantly higher on number concepts, problem solving, and place value than the children who just counted by ones. The number concepts test included rote and rational counting, cardinal number, subitizing, one-to-one correspondence, conservation of number, inequality, ordinal number, and part–whole knowledge. Children in the part–whole approach scored significantly higher on cardinal number and part–whole components of the test.

One activity used in the kindergarten study to illustrate parts and wholes was "Hiding Hands." Give each child five sticks. "Put the sticks in your lap. Use all your sticks and put part of them in one hand and part of them in the other hand. Trevor, show us one hand. How many sticks are in Trevor's hand?" All the children look and say "three." "Trevor has three and . . . " Trevor now holds up his other hand and the children say "two" together. "Trevor has three sticks and two sticks. Help me remember. How many sticks did Trevor have to start with?" Repeat the demonstration with other children, focusing on the different ways parts of five can be shown. Include zero and five as legitimate parts. Repeat the activity for other numbers (7).

Coloring parts
Give each child an uncolored picture of a set of objects, such as seven balloons. Have each child decide and then color part of the balloons purple and the other part green and then tell how many of each color.

Activities with "Flash Math" also build number recognition and part–whole concepts. Prepare a set of paper plates, cards, or transparencies with groupings of two

FIGURE 3.4   Grouping of six dots
              for Flash Math

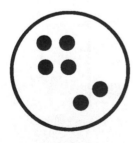

through ten dots in many different arrangements (see 39, 41). Then flash each group for one or two seconds. After each flash, ask, "How many dots did you see?" and "How did you see them?" For the group of dots in Figure 3.4, a child might say, "I saw a four and a two" and another child might say, "I saw three twos."

Ten-frames also work well for "Flash Math." Put counters on a ten-frame, always filling the top row first and the bottom row from left to right as in Figure 3.5. "How many dots are in the top row? in the bottom row? in both rows altogether?" Practice until the children can recognize the number in the ten-frame in one or two seconds.

Action research–recognizing groups
Use dice, dominoes, hand-drawn dot cards, or transparencies with patterned arrangements and ten-frame displays and practice recognizing groups over a period of several weeks. Allow three or four seconds for a response at first. Then decrease the time to one second as children improve in their ability to recognize the number. Display two patterns at the same time and have children tell the total on both. Do children see numbers as made up of easily recognized parts? Do they have a greater variety of ways in thinking about a number? Are they more willing to describe what they see? Are they more ready for addition and subtraction? After children recognize numbers six through ten easily on the ten-frame, play the games "Five and Something" and "Ten Less Something," for example, "Seven is five and two. Seven is ten less three."

Part–whole understanding of number provides a stronger conceptual base for addition and subtraction strategies. Some researchers think that interpreting addition and subtraction with this part–whole knowledge is a more complex and mature way of thinking about these operations and that children do not understand them until second or third grade (4, 31). The children in the kindergarten study, however, transferred their part–whole knowledge to the solution of simple addition and subtraction word problems, with twice as many problems solved than by children taught to count by ones. Learning about number through parts and wholes is a promising approach. It appears to lead naturally into a mature understanding of addition, subtraction, multiplication, and division as evidenced by studies on word problems in grades 3 and 4 (14, 28).

FIGURE 3.5 A ten-frame for seven

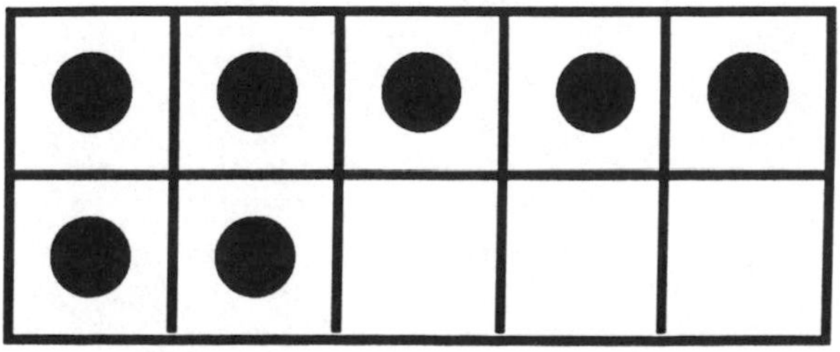

Initially children need to learn about parts and whole amounts with small numbers, zero through ten. The part–whole knowledge is extended and elaborated upon over the years as children learn to interpret numbers as composed of tens, hundreds, and thousands, enabling them to be flexible and inventive with mental computation, estimation and paper/pencil computation.

Writing Numerals

Children must learn to write numerals, just as they learn to write letters of the alphabet. Children can recognize and read one-digit and two-digit numerals before they are able to write them (1). When children have become successful at recognizing numerals and matching them to quantities, they can then be asked to write numerals. This pattern of instruction was followed in the kindergarten part–whole study.

Blocks up and blocks down
Give each child five blocks. Show a numeral (e.g., 4), and have students say its name. Then say, "Four blocks up." Each child pushes up four blocks. Repeat for other numbers, sometimes say its name and sometimes just point to it.

Being able to recognize a numeral requires having a mental image of it, whereas being able to write numerals requires muscle control and copying skills. Children who can recognize numerals may still write reversed or otherwise incorrect numerals, but these errors usually correct themselves as children move through school and should not cause undue concern. As children begin learning to write numerals, they need symbolic models of the numeral present to look at and copy. It is helpful to have the numeral and a picture of the quantity on each card to reinforce this connection, as in Figure 3.6. Dots should not be put on the numeral because this encourages counting by ones rather than thinking in groups.

Begin by having children describe in their own words what each numeral looks like to them (40). They might say that the numeral "8" looks like a snowman or two circles. Another child might say that the numeral "9" looks like a balloon on a stick or a circle with a line coming down on the right side. Numerals can be grouped with similar characteristics, such as those with all straight lines, those with loops, and

FIGURE 3.6   Numeral and number
             card for five

those with curves. One child thus discovered that he could make nines with an upside-down six with the circle on the other side of the stick

Motor plans can be developed for each numeral to indicate where to start, in which direction to go, and whether it is round or straight. Number nine might be "Like a balloon on a stick—go around and down." Children can begin learning motor plans for numerals by tracing their finger over felt or sandpaper numerals. Next, children can say the motor plan as they draw big numerals in a cake pan filled with a thin layer of sand or salt, draw on paper with fingerpaints, or write with chalk on the board. Then children can make smaller numerals on paper with their pencils or crayons while thinking of the writing plan. These motor plans help children guide their writing process.

Action research—writing numerals
Have children visualize and describe the numbers when they are first learning to write them. Which numbers have curves? Which have straight lines? Which curves are at the top? Which curves are at the bottom? Which ones face left? Which ones face right? Do activities like this for a few weeks and see the effect it has on the way children write numbers. Do they make fewer reversals? Are there fewer mistakes in making nines and sixes?

Summary

Children need to develop meanings for small numbers that will build a strong conceptual base for later work with place value, larger numbers, and operations of addition, subtraction, multiplication, and division. Children begin by learning the correct number sequence and developing methods for accurately counting sets of objects. Their understanding of numbers takes on new meaning when they connect counting with an understanding of quantity or cardinality.

Children make a major advance when they can see and think groups of twos and threes, providing the basis for developing part–whole ideas for numbers to ten. Thinking of numbers six to ten in relation to benchmarks of five and ten increases understanding. The part–whole meaning for small numbers is used and extended to larger numbers in which parts can be ten, hundred, or thousand, as described in the next section.

Recognizing numerals by their characteristics and developing motor plans for numerals helps children write them correctly. The overall goal is to relate concepts of number with oral language and written symbols.

Meaning for Larger Numbers–Numeration

Achievement results are unacceptably low on the meaning of place value and larger numbers. The 1988 NAEP results showed that less than half of third-grade students were successful with tasks involving place–value notions beyond tens, and difficulties with addition and subtraction algorithms were conjectured to be related to poor understanding of place value (19).

A status study of children's understanding of place value in grades 2 through 5 used a digit correspondence task (33, 34). A child is presented with twenty-five sticks. The child is asked to count the sticks and write down the number. The five is then circled and the child is asked, "Does this part have anything to do with how many sticks you have?" The question is repeated as "2" is circled. One-third of the fifth graders and one-half of the fourth graders did not know that the two represents twenty sticks, with much lower performance for second and third grade students. Other researchers document similar problems (15, 20).

Such poor results are by no means necessary. In a seminal study in 1972, children in grade 1 achieved near mastery on a wide variety of place–value tasks after a longer than usual instructional time—fifteen lessons (27). Concepts were found to be much more complex than expected, leading to the identification of three major aspects of place value called *base representation*, *oral name*, and *numeral*. Oral number names were especially difficult. While children knew more about number names when instruction began, they did not do as well on number–name tasks as on other types of tasks at the end of instruction.

The diagram in Figure 3.7 is a modification of one used earlier (25). It highlights the three major components of place value understanding for two-digit numbers, *quantities and base name, number name,* and *place–value numeral*.

FIGURE 3.7   Components of place–value understanding

Quantities and
base name

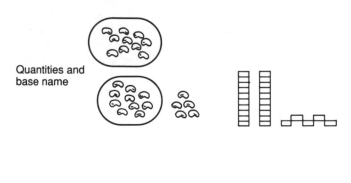

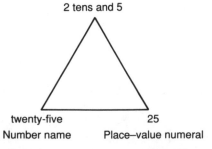

2 tens and 5

twenty-five   25
Number name   Place–value numeral

FIGURE 3.8 Making and counting tens

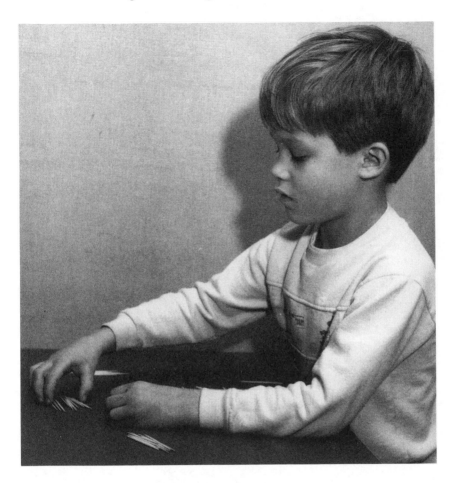

Counting by ones is a child's most trustworthy method of ascertaining the nume-rosity of a set. Consequently, counting should also be included as an important com-ponent of children's understanding of two-digit and larger numbers (38, 39).

Oriental cultures have a regular system for number names. For example the name for twelve is given as "ten two" and forty-seven as "four ten seven." The English names for decades do use "-ty" to mean "ten" but the prefixes "twen-," "thir-," and "fif-" hardly sound like "two," "three," or "five." To complicate matters further, the English names of teen numbers are reversed so that the ones digit is named first. It is no surprise then that children write 61 for "sixteen" or read 71 as "seventeen." Any instructional program in the early grades must give regular attention to number names, recognizing that number–name tasks will take longer to teach to mastery.

FIGURE 3.9   Using base-ten blocks

The Tens Structure–Numbers to 100

Children's initial concepts of smaller numbers depend on counting by ones, even though some of the numbers may be viewed in terms of smaller groups. There is a beginning of structure beyond counting by ones in the emergence of the tens-one structure (15, 30). Children recognize that the names "four, five, six . . ." are repeated for the teen numbers and for the twenties, thirties, and so on. In everyday activities, parents and teachers can further highlight the tens structure and help children attach deeper meaning to the number names when they count objects by ones to solve everyday problems. Children can begin to see that there are more efficient ways to determine numerosity than just counting by ones (Fig. 3.8).

The deliberate use of ten as a part of the structure in learning to count in grade 1 has proved quite successful compared with an approach emphasizing just counting by ones (13). Children who counted by tens using manipulative materials (Fig. 3.9) showed a decided advantage on transfer tasks for addition and subtraction (6 tens + 2 tens, "thirty-three plus twenty"), word problems (Jim has seventy toy cars and twenty trucks. How many cars and trucks does he have altogether?), and place value tasks (Show me *forty-six* using bundles of ten. How many tens are in *forty-six?*). Achievement was even more noticeable after a six-week retention period when children practiced counting using tens at least once a week. At the beginning of instruction, both groups could count to the 70s and after the two weeks of instruction both groups could count to the 90s.

In this grade 1 developmental sequence, children began by counting groups of ten orally and then wrote the numerals for tens. Next they counted tens and ones, first with up to nine singles and then with more than nine singles. Finally, they gave special attention to the teen numbers and to sequence with numerals. The following descriptions give the flavor of that sequence.

Counting Groups of Ten. Children's fingers are counted by tens using base names and the usual number names (Fig. 3.10). Clear enunciation is needed because *fifty* and *fifteen* are difficult to distinguish. Children can make ten dots on a card, which can also be used for counting by tens.

FIGURE 3.10   Using fingers to count by tens two ways

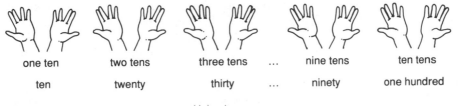

| one ten | two tens | three tens | ... | nine tens | ten tens |
| ten | twenty | thirty | ... | ninety | one hundred |

Using base
names and
number names

Numerals for Tens. The numerals for tens are related to bundles of ten and to oral names. As children count orally, they relate the numerals to the number of tens, for example, 30 with 3 tens. Games such as "Which Ten is Missing?" and "What Ten Comes Next?" provide interesting practice (Fig. 3.11).

FIGURE 3.11   Numerals for tens

Counting Tens and Ones Orally.   Children count groups of ten and singles, first with up to nine singles (Fig. 3.12) and then with more than nine singles. Bundles of sticks can be used or cups with ten objects each (42) (Fig. 3.13). The numerosity *forty-three* can be determined by counting by ones.

FIGURE 3.12   Counting groups of ten and single objects

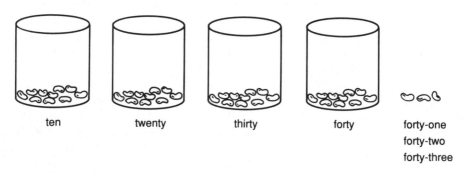

ten   twenty   thirty   forty   forty-one
                                                    forty-two
                                                    forty-three

Ten-frames are also useful to show tens and ones, as shown in Figure 3.14.

When children count by ones, they most often stop at a given "nine," unable to say the next decade (36). Using more than nine singles helps children see the next decade. For example, as one is added to fifty-nine, there are ten singles that can be made into another ten. Children can see that since **6** comes after **5**, **60** comes after **59**.

Teen Numbers.   The difficulty with teens needs special attention, both to the names and to the meaning of the numbers. Showing *seventeen* as a seven and a ten can be done with two ten-frames or with single objects (Fig. 3.15). Again, clear enunciation is needed to distinguish the *-teen* in seven*teen* from the *-ty* in seven*ty*.

Sequence with Numerals.   Numeral cards and a 100-chart can be used to help children recognize the sequence of numerals and relate this sequence to the oral names. Calculators with a constant function are also useful in counting by ones and by tens (Fig. 3.16).

Maintenance is needed, of course, and especially so over summer vacation as was demonstrated in a kindergarten pilot study (13).

Action research—using tens with early counting
Would teaching children to count using tens help children more when they are first learning to count in kindergarten? Begin using ten as a part of the structure in counting to thirty. Then, instead of concentrating on counting by ones to 100 as is usually done, teach children to count to find the number of groups of ten. Then teach the number names for groups of ten and count objects using tens and ones. Relate these to bundles of ten and to the numerals. See if this helps children learn to count, to solve problems, and begin the development of place value ideas.

FIGURE 3.13 Counting tens and ones

Extending Place Value Concepts for Two-Digit Numbers

The previous sequence of activities does not focus explicitly on the value of each of the digits in a numeral. A place–value chart is helpful in making more explicit the connection between the quantity (bundles of sticks or base-ten blocks) and the numeral as shown in Figure 3.17.

In digit-correspondence tasks, the two easiest tasks used nine or fewer single objects and the most difficult used ten or more single objects (33, 34). The task is illustrated in the first drawing in Figure 3.18.

More than Nine Singles. Write the numeral to show how many are in Figure 3.18. To write the numeral 52, ten singles must be grouped to make a ten. Then when asked about what the 5 has to do with the number of objects, the grouped ten must be combined with the four tens shown.

Counting by ones beginning with a given number of tens can focus on the need to regroup after getting ten singles (see Fig. 3.19).

FIGURE 3.14 Ten-frames for numbers

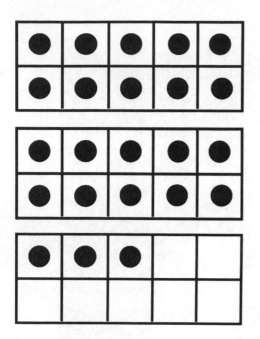

FIGURE 3.15 Seventeen as seven and ten

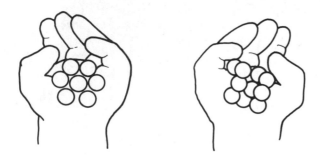

FIGURE 3.16 Skip-counting on a calculator

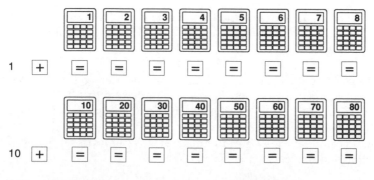

Counting and Regrouping.   Display two tens. Then add singles while counting by ones. After counting to *twenty-nine*, add one more single. See if students see the need to regroup and say *three tens* or *thirty*. Repeat for other decades.

Suggestions for extending place–value concepts are illustrated in the following activities (38, 42).

Regrouping.   Use the cups of beans shown previously. Put nine more beans with the singles, regroup and write the numeral 52, and show that the 5 means five tens. Then remove seven and tell the number remaining.

Children can develop a better sense of number while doing estimation (22). Children estimate parts, knowing the whole as suggested in the following activity.

Estimate the Number for this Point.   Use a meter stick and draw a segment 100 cm long, marking each end. Locate a point and mark it with an arrow. "What number do you estimate will go here?" Have each student write her or his estimate. Then check with the meter stick (Fig. 3.20).

Modify the activity by giving a number such as 78 and have students estimate its location. Allow five students to make a mark and write their initial by it. The winner is the one closest to the correct mark as determined by the meter stick.

Base-ten blocks can be used on the overhead projector to determine the number and to do mental computation (21).

Flash Math and Mental Computation.   Place four longs and five singles on the overhead projector. Flash it initially for about two seconds. "What number do you see?" Repeat with other numbers, reducing the time to one second. After students can easily tell the number displayed, do mental computation. "What number is two 10s more? [65] two 10s less? [25]" Initially, it may be necessary to illustrate with base-ten blocks.

Two numbers can be compared using the same technique, with one number demonstrated at the top with base-ten blocks and the other illustrated at the bottom.

The use of base-ten blocks in activities such as these reinforces place–value concepts and gives children an indication of the kind of mathematics they can be expected to do mentally.

FIGURE 3.17   A place-value chart for groups of ten

TENS	ONES
4	3

FIGURE 3.18   Numbers with more than nine singles

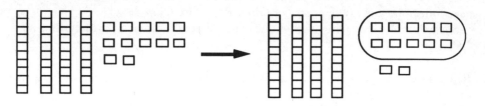

FIGURE 3.19   Counting and regrouping ones

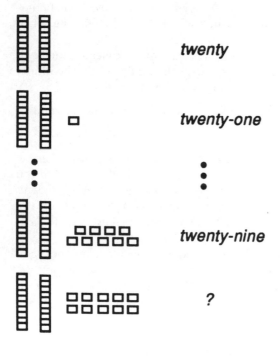

twenty

twenty-one

twenty-nine

?

FIGURE 3.20   Estimating with a meter stick

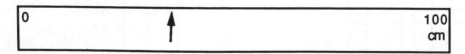

Estimate. What number goes here?

Diagnosing Place–Value Knowledge

Diagnosing what children know about place value should include a variety of tasks. Diagnosis is important especially in later grades to help determine what needs to be taught. The digit-correspondence tasks can provide initial information. To provide a more detailed assessment, tasks can be organized according to the three major relationships, oral names and numerals, oral names and quantities, and numerals and quantities. Beyond these three relationships, there is a need to see if children understand that counting by ones gives the same number as using tens and ones.

The results for a diagnostic assessment can show clearly needed emphases in instruction.

Oral Names—Numerals. This is the easiest of the three relationships. It should include special attention to teen numbers, reversals, and numbers in the twenties, thirties, and fifties, where mistakes occur more frequently.

1. "Can you read these numbers?" 17 39 50 56 71
2. "Circle numbers on this hundred chart as I read them."
   sixteen twenty-five forty-one sixty eighty-nine

Oral Names—Quantities. Display several bundles of ten and at least forty single sticks. Alternatively, use base-ten blocks.

3. "Can you show me forty sticks? forty-five sticks?" Note if the child uses bundles of ten or just single sticks.
4. Use the display of forty-five sticks. "If you count these sticks by ones, how many will you get?" Note whether the child has to count again by ones or is able to say the number directly. After the child says the answer, ask: "Do both ways give the same number?"
5. "Can you show me one hundred? How many tens is that?"
6. Display four 10s and thirteen single sticks. "How many sticks are here?" Note if the child makes a ten and then counts five 10s. "How many tens are there altogether? How many single sticks are left over?"
7. Which is larger, "thirty-nine" or "eighty-one"? Note if the child uses bundles of ten or if the child needs to count by ones.

Numerals—Quantities. 8–12. Use the same tasks as those for oral names-quantities but use numerals instead of oral names. For task 6 with numerals, use "four 10s and 13."

Larger Numbers

There is similarity between the goals for two-digit numbers and three-digit numbers. One major advantage for three-digit numbers is the regular way the numbers are named, assuming that the irregular two-digit names have been mastered. There is one task that is of considerably greater difficulty and that is developing number sense for these larger numbers.

In an early study, after two full weeks of instruction on place value in grade 3, children did not have a good sense of the numerosity of numbers beyond 200 or 300, even though they could read and write numbers in the thousands and millions (35). Depth of understanding can come only from experiences over a lengthy period of time.

It is easier to build the relationships between base-ten blocks, numerals, and oral names. Instruction can begin by naming hundreds orally, move to place–value charts where numbers are named using base values, and to regrouping activities.

Count Hundreds.   Use base-ten blocks or large bundles and count the number of hundreds. Then have children give the usual name orally, noting the ease by which it is done just by omitting the "s" (Fig. 3.21).

Place–Value Chart and Base Names.   Develop and use place–value charts (25, 38). Read the number in a chart using base names and the usual name (Fig. 3.22).

Do the reverse, giving the base name or usual name and have students give the other two. Practice the three relationships suggested by the triangular model used in Figure 3.23. Include examples such as "three hundred four" where a zero is needed and errors are likely to occur.

FIGURE 3.21   Counting the number of hundreds and using number names

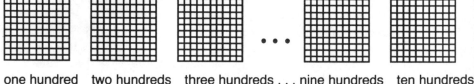

one hundred   two hundreds   three hundreds . . . nine hundreds   ten hundreds

one hundred   two hundred   three hundred . . . nine hundred   one thousand

FIGURE 3.22   A place-value chart with base names and number names

HUNDREDS	TENS	ONES
2	3	4

two hundreds   three tens   four ones

two hundred thirty four

FIGURE 3.23   Components of place–value

**Quantities
and
base name**

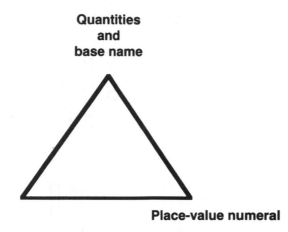

Number name   **Place-value numeral**

One More and Ten More.   Surprising results have come from interviews with third graders, indicating their poor grasp of place value (20). When they were asked to write the number that is one more than 342, half the students made mistakes. The errors were 453, 442, 452, 352, 1,342, and 5,342. When asked to write the number that is ten more than 243, about two-thirds of the students were incorrect, giving answers of 233, 353, 342, 251, 1,243, 121,413, 1,227, 1,244, and 2,530,687,413.

Beyond the informative results from interviews, there are many excellent suggestions for building place–value understanding (Fig. 3.24). When children were asked to use base-ten blocks, they changed their original perspectives and reorganized their ideas.

Regrouping.   Use tasks similar to the regrouping tasks for two-digit numbers (Fig. 3.25). Initially, keeping the ones digit as 0 makes the initial instruction easier because there is one less thing that students must keep in mind. "How many hundreds can you make and how many tens are left over?" (one more hundred and two tens left over) How many small blocks are there altogether? (three hundreds two tens, or three hundred twenty).

Count by Tens and by Ones.   Use the display from the previous activity. "How can you tell how many tens there are altogether? Can you find more than one way to tell how many?" (count by ten from one *ten* to *thirty-two tens* or use hundreds and count *ten, twenty, thirty, thirty-one, thirty-two*).

Count by ones to verify that the numerosity is three hundred thirty. It seems tedious to do but it begins to build number sense for these larger numbers.

Counting on the calculator is quicker and more fun, and especially so when there is a race to see who can do it the quickest. Have students determine the number of tens to count to 100, 500, and 1000.

FIGURE 3.24   Showing ten more with base-ten blocks

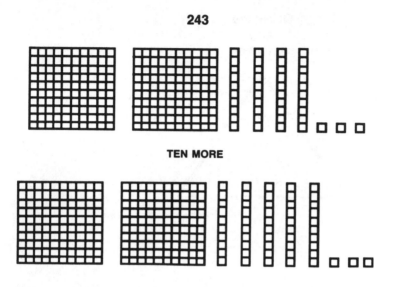

TEN MORE

FIGURE 3.25   Regrouping tens

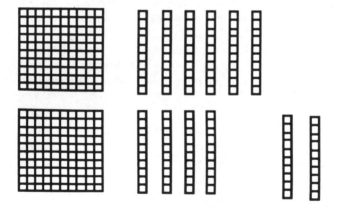

An in-depth analysis of place–value concepts gives special emphasis on relating base-ten blocks and base names (called "multiunit named value representations") (8). The researcher suggests that the use of colored chips, as in chip trading, may confuse children because it gives no support to quantitative meanings as relative size of the hundreds and thousands is not evident in the chips. Also, there is little value in expanded notation such as 300 + 40 + 2, because it is merely one symbol replacing another symbol, 342. There is strong support in using base-ten blocks with a variety of tasks, although little attention to the numerosity for larger numbers. An increased understanding is reported of the relationship between digits and the base-ten blocks that represent the digits as students use base-ten blocks while learning the addition and subtraction algorithms in grade 2. Base-ten blocks are used to extend the number names for numerals with more than three digits.

The varied activities for three-digit and larger numbers as suggested here require students to deepen their understanding of place value and numerosity. With continuing attention both to place value and to numerosity, students' understanding will continue to grow and develop.

Summary

To understand two-digit and larger numbers, children need to relate quantities and base names to number names and to place–value numerals. Concrete bundles of sticks or base-ten blocks are essential in achieving this understanding. Beyond such tasks that are associated with place value, the numerosity or sense of size needs to be developed by counting by ones and later counting by tens and by hundreds.

There must be a substantial increase in the amount of instructional time devoted to place value to achieve the kind of understanding essential for everyday use and for other mathematical topics such as addition and subtraction algorithms. The present status of students' understanding is poor, reflecting insufficient instructional time and inadequate developmental work. After initial instruction, regular maintenance is required and may enhance and deepen children's understanding.

Instruction and assessment need to move beyond the simpler tasks to ones that require more thinking and analysis. Higher order tasks include giving number names and place–value numerals when seeing more than nine singles, more than nine tens, and more than nine hundreds. These regrouping tasks help prevent conceptual development from remaining at an immature level, at the same time providing preparation for other mathematical topics.

For smaller numbers and for larger numbers, there is clear evidence of the value of instruction requiring higher order thinking that goes beyond merely counting by ones. Developing part–whole ideas for small numbers is surprisingly beneficial for other mathematical tasks. Using concrete objects, counting tens, and counting by tens when learning the numbers to 100 provide a welcome bonus in children's ability with problem solving, place value, addition, and subtraction. These promising ways to enhance children's understanding and use of number point to needed modifications in curriculum and instructional practice in the primary grades.

Looking Ahead . . .

In preschool and kindergarten children rarely do more than count by ones. What would be the result if part–whole ideas for small numbers were used consistently throughout preschool and kindergarten? What would be the result if there was consistent attention to the tens structure for numbers as children learn the numbers to 100? Most research studies are based on relatively short instructional periods. We need to know the effects for longer periods of time with a wider variety of instructional tasks. What would be the results if there were continuing instruction on place value and numerosity over several grade levels?

Joseph Payne

The ideas in this chapter are intended to strengthen children's understanding of numbers with part–whole meaning and connections among quantities, oral language, and symbols. Will this establish the foundation for further work with numbers and computation? Will they be more flexible in solving problems? Will they be more apt to recognize if an answer is reasonable? Will this help children become more confident in their use of numbers? I wonder if I will have enough time to help my students develop this deeper understanding of number and whether, for the sake of my students, I can afford not to take the time.

DeAnn Huinker

About the Authors

Joseph N. Payne is professor of mathematics education in the School of Education at the University of Michigan. He is editor of the NCTM professional book *Mathematics for the Young Child*. His interests include the development of children's concepts of fractions and decimals as well as place value for whole numbers.

DeAnn M. Huinker taught elementary school in Iowa and is now an assistant professor in the Department of Curriculum and Instruction at the University of Wisconsin–Milwaukee. She teaches mathematics education courses for preservice and in-service teachers. Her interests include the development of children's number sense and operation sense.

References

1. Baroody, A. J., Gannon, K. E., Berent, R., & Ginsburg, H. P. (1983). The development of basic formal math abilities. *Acta Paedologica, 1*(2), 133–151.
2. Baroody, A. J., & Price, J. (1983). The development of the number–word sequence in the counting of three-year-olds. *Journal for Research in Mathematics Education, 14*, 361–368.
3. Beilin, H. (1975). *Studies in the cognitive basis of language development.* New York: Academic Press.
4. Carpenter, T. P. (1986). Conceptual knowledge as a foundation for procedural knowledge: Implications from research on the initial learning of arithmetic. In J. Hiebert (Ed.), *Conceptual and procedural knowledge: The case of mathematics* (pp.113–132). Hillsdale, NJ: Erlbaum.
5. Clements, D. H. (1983). Training effects on the development and generalization of Piagetian logical operations and knowledge of number. *Journal of Educational Psychology, 76*, 766–776.
6. Clements, D. H., & Callahan, L. G. (1983). Number or prenumber foundational experiences for young children: Must we choose? *Arithmetic Teacher, 31*(3), 34–37.
7. Fischer, F. E. (1988). The development of number concept using two curricular approaches. Unpublished doctoral dissertation, University of Maryland.
8. Fuson, K. C. (1990) Conceptual structures for multidigit numbers: Implications for learning and teaching multidigit addition, subtraction, and place-value. *Cognition and Instruction, 7*(4), 343–403.

9. Fuson, K. C. (1988). *Children's counting and concepts of number.* New York: Springer-Verlag.

10. Fuson, K. C., & Hall, J. W. (1983). The acquisition of early number word meanings: A conceptual analysis and review. In H. P. Ginsburg (Ed.), *The development of mathematical thinking* (pp. 49–107). New York: Academic Press.

11. Gelman, R., & Gallistel, C. R. (1978). *The child's understanding of number.* Cambridge, MA: Harvard University Press.

*12. Gibb, E. G., & Castenada, A. M. (1975). Experiences for young children. In J. N. Payne (Ed.), *Mathematics learning in early childhood, Thirty-Seventh Yearbook* (pp. 95–124). Reston, VA: National Council of Teachers of Mathematics.

13. Hong, H. (1988). Effects of counting by tens on counting ability of kindergarten children and first graders. Unpublished doctoral dissertation, University of Michigan.

14. Huinker, D. M. (1990). Effects of instruction using part–whole concepts for one-step and multi-step word problems in grade four. Unpublished doctoral dissertation, University of Michigan.

15. Kamii, C. K. (1985). *Young children reinvent arithmetic: Implications of Piaget's theory.* New York: Teachers College Press.

16. Khlar, D., & Wallace, J. G. (1973). The role of quantification operators in the development of conservation of quantity. *Cognitive Psychology, 4,* 301–327.

17. Khlar, D., & Wallace, J. G. (1976). *Cognitive development: An information-processing view.* New York: Erlbaum.

*18. Kolnowski, L. W. (1984). The effects of the arrangement of objects and oral directions on success with counting tasks. Unpublished manuscript. Detroit Public Schools, Detroit, MI.

19. Kouba, V. L., Brown, C. A., Carpenter, T. P., Lindquist, M. M., Silver, E. A., & Swafford, J. O. (1988). Results of the fourth NAEP assessment of mathematics: Number, operations, and word problems. *Arithmetic Teacher, 35*(8), 14–19.

*20. Labinowicz, E. (1985). *Learning from children: New beginnings for teaching numerical thinking.* Menlo Park, CA: Addison-Wesley.

*21. Leutzinger, L. P., & Bertheau, M. (1989). Making sense of numbers. In P. R. Trafton (Ed.), *New directions for elementary school mathematics, 1989 Yearbook.* (pp. 111–122). Reston, VA: National Council of Teachers of Mathematics.

*22. Leutzinger, L. P., Rathmell, E. C., & Urbatsch, T. D. (1986). Developing estimation skills in the primary grades. In H. L. Shoen (Ed.), *Estimation and mental computation, 1986 Yearbook.* (pp. 82–92). Reston, VA: National Council of Teachers of Mathematics.

*23. Liedtke, W. (1978). Rational counting. *Arithmetic Teacher, 26*(2), 20–26.

24. National Council of Teachers of Mathematics. (1989). *Curriculum and evaluation standards for school mathematics.* Reston, VA: Author.

*25. Payne, J. N., & Rathmell, E. C. (1975). Number and numeration. In J. N. Payne (Ed.), *Mathematics learning in early childhood.* (pp. 125–160) Reston, VA: National Council of Teachers of Mathematics.

26. Piaget, J. (1952). *The child's conception of number* (C. Gattegno & F. M. Hodgson, Trans.). London: Routledge & Kegan Paul.

*27. Rathmell, E. C. (1972). The effects of multibase grouping and early or late introductions of base representations on the mastery learning of base and place–value numeration in grade one. Unpublished doctoral dissertation, University of Michigan.

*28. Rathmell, E. C., & Huinker, D. M. (1989). Using "part–whole" language to help children represent and solve word problems. In P. R. Trafton (Ed.), *New directions for* *elementary school mathematics* (pp. 99–110). Reston, VA: National Council of Teachers of Mathematics.

29. REA, R. E., & REYS, R. E. (1971). Competencies of entering kindergarteners in geometry, number, money, and measurement. *School Science and Mathematics*, 71, 389–402.

30. RESNICK, L. B. (1983). A developmental theory of number understanding. In H. P. Ginsburg (Ed.), *The development of mathematical thinking* (pp. 109–151). New York: Academic Press.

31. RILEY, M. S., GREENO, J. G., & HELLER, J. I. (1983). Development of children's problem-solving ability in arithmetic. In H. P. Ginsburg (Ed.), *The development of mathematical thinking* (pp. 154–196). New York: Academic Press.

*32. RISDEN, G. (1978). Words of wisdom of an 80-year-old tutor. *Education*, 99, 154–156.

33. ROSS, S. H. (1986, April). The development of children's place–value numeration concepts in grades two through five. Paper presented at the annual meeting of the American Educational Research Association, San Francisco, CA. (ERIC Document Reproduction Service No. 273 482)

*34. ROSS, S. H. (1989). Parts, wholes, and place value: A developmental view. *Arithmetic Teacher*, 36(6), 47–51.

35. SCRIVENS, R. W. (1968). A comparative study of different approaches to teaching the Hindu-Arabic numeration system to third graders. Unpublished doctoral dissertation, University of Michigan.

36. SIEGLER, R. S., & ROBINSON, M. (1982). The development of numerical understandings. In H. W. Reese and L. P. Lipsitt (Eds.), *Advances in child development and behavior* (Vol. 16). New York: Academic Press.

37. STEFFE, L. P., VON GLASERSFELD, F., RICHARDS, J., & COBB, P. (1983). *Children's counting types: Philosophy, theory, and application*. New York: Praeger.

*38. THOMPSON, C. (1990). Place value and larger numbers. In J. N. Payne (Ed.), *Mathematics for the young child* (pp. 88–104). Reston, VA: National Council of Teachers of Mathematics.

*39. VAN DE WALLE, J. (1988). The early development of number relations. *Arithmetic Teacher*, 35(6), 15–21.

*40. VAN DE WALLE, J. A. (1990). Developing concepts of number. In J. N. Payne (Ed.), *Mathematics for the young child* (pp. 62–87). Reston, VA: National Council of Teachers of Mathematics.

*41. VAN DE WALLE, J. A. (1990). *Elementary school mathematics, teaching developmentally*. White Plains, NY: Longman.

*42. VAN DE WALLE, J. A., & THOMPSON, C. S. (1985). Partitioning sets for number concepts, place value, and long division. *Arithmetic Teacher*, 32(5), 6–11.

43. WANG, M. C., RESNICK, L. B., & BOOZER, R. F. (1971). The sequence of development of some early mathematics behaviors. *Child Development*, 42, 1767–1778.

Counting by tens on a calculator

CHAPTER 4

Addition and Subtraction in the Primary Grades

Arthur J. Baroody and Dorothy J. Standifer

Alissa, a new first grader, was shown the expression 3 + 2 = ? and asked: "How much is three plus two?" She squirmed in her seat and finally confessed: "I haven't learned that yet." Asked how much three pennies and two more pennies are altogether, Alissa quickly put up three fingers on her left hand and two fingers on her right hand, counted the fingers, and responded cheerfully: "Five!"

Addition and subtraction have been and will continue to be a central focus of primary mathematics instruction (16). However, research indicates that we need to rethink how these topics are taught. It clearly shows that the traditional, textbook-based approach to instruction underestimates children's mathematical ability (23). Children—like Alissa—do not come to school as blank slates, devoid of arithmetic knowledge. Typically, they have a wealth of informal knowledge: intuitive knowledge gleaned from everyday experiences. Though she lacks formal knowledge, knowledge of the symbolic mathematical notation taught in school, Alissa clearly understood the problem about a real addition situation. Moreover, though she had not yet memorized the arithmetic fact 3 + 2 = 5, Alissa had invented her own counting-based strategy for determining sums.

Different Approaches to Arithmetic Instruction

Skills Approach. Traditionally, the primary aim of arithmetic instruction has been the mastery of arithmetic facts and computational procedures. A skills approach is based on the assumption that the most effective vehicle for fostering the acquisition of basic skills is direct instruction. This entails breaking a subject matter into small steps, explaining and demonstrating each step, providing guided practice, and assigning large amounts of practice to ensure mastery of each step. A skills approach, then, focuses on symbolic representations, paper-and-pencil work, and memorizing facts and procedures.

However, when symbolic representations are introduced too quickly and not related to children's existing informal knowledge, students are forced to memorize school mathematics by rote. Though most do learn to compute answers correctly, many cannot apply their school-learned arithmetic knowledge. For example, some children have difficulty deciding what operation to use when solving a problem. Completing numerous worksheet or workbook problems without any apparent purpose further reinforces the beliefs that mathematics is uninteresting and does not involve thinking.

A second-grade teacher interviewed her two *best* students at the end of the year. Though they could efficiently use the school-taught multidigit computational procedure to obtain the correct answers on their written assignments, the children had made no progress in their understanding of place value (58). Correct answers do *not* necessarily imply understanding.

Moreover, a gap between formal instruction and informal knowledge is a primary cause of learning difficulties (26, 29). Many children forget all or critical parts of what they have memorized. For example, in the solution below, the child has remembered all the steps of the renaming algorithm (step-by-step procedure) but one: reducing the tens place.

$$\begin{array}{r} \overset{1}{43} \\ -27 \\ \hline 26 \end{array}$$

Some children do not see any point in memorizing information that does not seem important or make sense to them. Others stop trying to memorize facts and procedures because they become fearful of failing. In brief, though a skills approach does foster mastery of basic arithmetic skills by many children, it often discourages thinking, promotes a negative disposition toward mathematics, and creates many learning difficulties, including math anxiety. Are there not less destructive ways of helping children master essential arithmetic skills?

Children often think school math and the real world are two different things. The extensive use of "worksheets" seems to perpetuate this belief. Children can get so caught up in computing answers that they do not see the beauty and patterns of mathematics. For many students, the focus is not on solving problems or justifying answers but on finishing assignments. They may think that understanding is not important or, at best, secondary to the correctness of their answers.

A New Direction.   According to the NCTM *Curriculum and Evaluation Standards* (37), mathematics instruction should focus on promoting understanding, problem solving, and a positive disposition toward mathematics. To do this, instruction must be developmentally appropriate. Research suggests that children actively construct arithmetic knowledge by interacting with their physical and social environments (33, 58). Understanding and thinking grow when children must reorganize existing knowledge to deal with real problems, surprises, and conflicting explanations.

According to the NCTM *Curriculum and Evaluation Standards* (37), students should be able to (a) model and discuss a variety of problem situations involving addition and subtraction; (b) relate formal language such as "plus" and symbols like + to problem situations and their own informal, counting-based knowledge; (c) recognize that formal symbolism such as $8 - 5 = 3$ can represent a variety of problem situations; (d) select and use computation techniques appropriate to specific problems; and (e) determine whether the results of computation are reasonable. Students should develop a reasonable proficiency with basic (single-digit) facts and multidigit algorithms.

Overview of the Chapter

To implement a developmentally appropriate approach, teachers must understand a child's current level of understanding or thinking and pose problems and questions just beyond it. This chapter summarizes recent research on the learning of single-digit and multidigit addition and subtraction and delineates implications for implementing developmentally appropriate arithmetic instruction. More specifically, it describes what research has discovered about children's informal arithmetic strengths and how informal knowledge can be extended and used as a basis for meaningful, thought-provoking, purposeful, and interesting formal arithmetic instruction.

To implement a developmental approach, teachers should give children the opportunity to use their existing knowledge to puzzle through a problem or question. They should listen carefully to children as they explain their ideas and solutions. Even confused or incorrect answers can be informative, because they reflect a child's current level of understanding. Moreover, it is important to encourage children to share their ideas and strategies with others (11, 33, 58). When adults and other students listen to them, it "tells" children that their ideas and strategies are important, which helps build confidence. It also helps them understand that what is really important in mathematics is thinking and communicating. Additionally, sharing strategies helps children to see that there is more than one way to solve problems. Getting students into the habit of justifying their answers further helps them to see that mathematics is something they are supposed to think about and comprehend.

Single-Digit Addition and Subtraction

Informal Concepts and Problem Solving

It is often assumed that solving word problems is a relatively difficult task and that word problems should be introduced after formal addition and subtraction skills. Research indicates, however, that many children can use their informal arithmetic knowledge to analyze and solve simple addition and subtraction word problems before they receive any formal arithmetic instruction (10). Indeed, children can often solve simple word problems before they comprehend formal expressions such as $5 + 2 = ?$ or $5 - 2 = ?$ (23, 26).

Types of Word Problems. A variety of addition and subtraction situations exist in the real world. Encountering a variety of problems can challenge children's thinking and help them construct a more complete understanding of addition and subtraction. Table 4.1 summarizes one way of classifying addition and subtraction word problems. For a more complete taxonomy, see Fuson (23).

Both Change-Add-To and Change-Take-Away involve beginning with a *single* collection and changing the initial collection by adding or removing something from it, which results in a larger or smaller collection. Part-Part-Whole, Equalize, and Compare problems all begin with *two* numbers, which are either added or subtracted, to find the whole or one of the parts.

Note that Change and Equalize problems cue action. Part-Part-Whole and Compare problems involve static situations that do not involve action. For example, Equalize problems imply that the difference between the two collections will be removed, while Compare problems imply that the difference will persist. For the latter, the operation (adding or subtracting) is done merely to determine the extent of the difference.

For each of the four main types of problems, the unknown can vary. For Change problems, the unknown can be the outcome of the change, how much the initial amount changed, or the initial amount. For Part-Part-Whole problems, the unknown can be the whole or one of the two parts. It may help to refer to the whole as "all," because children may more readily understand the latter term (23). For Equalize and Compare problems, the unknown can be the difference or one of the compared quantities.

Informal Arithmetic Concepts. A fundamental understanding of addition and subtraction evolves from children's early counting experiences (26). Preschoolers have numerous experiences that involve "change" situations: adding something to an existing collection to make it larger or removing items from a collection to make it smaller. Preschoolers also often notice the difference between two collections and sometimes, perhaps rather vocally, demand that the situation be rectified (e.g., "Mommie! You gave me two candies and Sis three. That's not fair; I need . . . one more"). Children can use their informal Change-Add-To view of addition, Change-Take-Away view of subtraction, and even their understanding of differences to comprehend and to solve simple word problems.

TABLE 4.1. A Taxonomy of Addition and Subtraction Word Problems

	. . . UNKNOWN OUTCOME	. . . UNKNOWN CHANGE	. . . UNKNOWN START
CHANGE-ADD-TO with	Alexi had 5 candies. Barb gave him 3 more. How many candies does he have altogether now?	Alexi had 5 candies. Barb gave him some more. Now he has 8 altogether. How many candies did Barb give him?	Alexi had some candies. Barb gave him 3 more. Now he has 8 altogether. How many candies did he start with?
	. . . UNKNOWN OUTCOME	. . . UNKNOWN CHANGE	. . . UNKNOWN START
CHANGE-TAKE-AWAY with	Alexi had 8 candies. He gave 5 to Barb. How many candies does he have left?	Alexi had 8 candies. He gave some to Barb. Now he has 3 left. How many candies did he give to Barb?	Alexi had some candies. He gave 5 to Barb. Now he has 3 left. How many candies did he start with?
	. . . UNKNOWN WHOLE	. . . UNKNOWN SECOND PART	. . . UNKNOWN FIRST PART
PART–PART–WHOLE with	Alexi had 5 fireballs and 3 lollipops. How much candy did he have altogether?	Alexi had 5 fireballs and some lollipops. He had 8 candies altogether. How many were lollipops?	Alexi had some fireballs and 3 lollipops. He had 8 candies altogether. How many were lollipops?

EQUALIZE with	. . . UNKNOWN DIFFERENCE	. . . UNKNOWN SECOND PART	. . . UNKNOWN FIRST PART
	Alexi had 8 candies. Barb had 5. How many more does Barb have to buy to have as many as Alexi?	Alexi had 8 candies. Barb had to get 3 more candies to have the same number as Alexi. How many candies did Barb start with?	Alexi had some candies. Barb, who had 5 candies, had to get 3 more to have the same number as Alexi. How many candies did Alexi have?
COMPARE with	. . . UNKNOWN DIFFERENCE	. . . UNKNOWN SECOND PART	. . . UNKNOWN FIRST PART
	Alexi had 8 candies. Barb had 5. How many more candies did Alexi have than Barb?	Alexi had 8 candies. He had 3 more than Barb. How many candies did Barb have?	Alexi had some candies. He had 3 more than Barb who had 5. How many candies did Alexi have?

Note. The examples shown above for EQUALIZE and COMPARE problems are the "more" versions. "Less" versions could also be written for each. For example, the less version of the EQUALIZE with UNKNOWN DIFFERENCE would read: Alexi had 8 candies. Barb had 5. How many does Alexi have to give up to have as many as Barb?

Direct Modeling. If allowed to use objects such as blocks or fingers or graphic representations such as pictures or tally marks, most first graders and many kinder- gartners can—with little or no help—solve problem in which the outcome, whole, or difference is unknown (45). Children initially model the meaning of such prob- lems directly (12, 17). That is, they try to imitate the action or situation detailed in the story (see Table 4.2). Because different types of problems imply different actions or situations, children's solution strategies typically vary from one type of problem to another.

Indirect Modeling. Without instruction or prompting, children—even those with learning difficulties—seem to monitor their behavior and spontaneously invent in-

TABLE 4.2. Concrete Strategies for Directly Modeling Various Types of Addition and Subtraction Word Problems

Type of Word Problem	Direct Modeling (Concrete Strategies)
Change-Add-To and Part-Part-Whole: Outcome or Whole Unknown	Concrete counting all: 1. Count out objects to represent the starting amount (one part); 2. produce objects to represent the amount added (the second part); 3. count all the objects put out to determine the outcome (the whole).
Change-Take-Away: Unknown Outcome	Concrete taking away: 1. Count out objects to represent the starting amount; 2. remove the number that the problem specifies were taken away; 3. count the remaining objects to determine the amount left.
Equalize: Difference Unknown	Adding on: 1. Create two parallel rows of objects to represent each set; 2. add objects to the smaller row until it is equal to the other row; 3. count the number of objects added to the smaller row.
Compare: Difference Unknown	Matching: 1. Create two parallel rows of objects to represent each set; 2. count the number of unmatched objects in the larger row.

creasingly efficient computing strategies (3, 43). For problems that involve finding a sum, many children invent a version of counting all, which entails counting up to the first term and then continuing the count while keeping track of (counting off) the second term. For three and five, for example, a child might say, "one, two, *three*; four [that's one more than three], five [that's two more], six [that's three more], seven [that's four more], eight [that's *five* more]—eight." Fingers put up successively are often used instead of the verbal keeping-track process indicated in the brackets above.

Children typically can simplify the keeping-track process by counting out the larger number first (3). For example, for three and five, it is easier to count up to five first and then count off three more numbers. In time, nearly all children shortcut this procedure further with the invention of a counting-on strategy: beginning with an addend instead of counting from one (e.g., three and five: "*five*; six [that's one more], seven [that's two more], eight [that's *three* more]—eight").

Children also devise verbal computing strategies for subtraction. For Change-Take-Away situations, many children eventually use a counting-down strategy. One such strategy entails starting with the number of the initial amount, counting backward a number of times equal to the amount taken away, and announcing the last number counted to indicate the amount left. For five take away three, for example, a child would start with five and count "four [that's one taken away], three [that's two taken away], two [that's three taken away]—two left."

For Equalize and Compare situations, children invent another verbal strategy: counting up. This procedure entails starting with the smaller number and counting forward until the larger number is reached—while keeping track of the number of steps in the forward count. For instance, to find the difference between five and three, a child might say: "Three; four [that's one more], five [that's two more]—the answer is two."

Relative Difficulty of Word Problems.   Modeling a problem in which the outcome, whole, or difference is unknown is relatively easy. Of these situations, Equalize and Compare problems may be more difficult to model than Change and Part-Part-Whole problems (12, 23, 33, 51). Because of their informal change-add-to and take-away views of addition and subtraction, it is even more difficult for children to model a problem in which the change or a part is unknown. Unknown start or unknown first-part problems may be especially confusing, because children are accustomed to knowing the starting amount.

Exposure to Problem Types.   Textbooks and teachers typically expose children to just a few problem situations, namely Change-Add-To and Take-Away Unknown-Outcome and Put-Together Unknown-Whole problems (23). Research suggests that exposure to a wide range of problem types from the beginning of school—as is done in the former Soviet Union—could significantly improve children's performance, even with more difficult problem types (50). Children can learn to distinguish among different types of addition and subtraction word problems and can learn to solve them (23). For example, teachers who participated in an in-service program called Cognitively Guided Instruction (CGI) were introduced to a relatively broad range of problem types and how children informally solve them (see 11). After a year, the

students of these teachers significantly outperformed control students on more difficult types of word problems.

The CGI program has four guiding principles:

1. Instruction should develop understanding, with problem solving serving as the organizing focus.
2. Instruction should facilitate students' active construction of knowledge.
3. Each student should be able to relate problems, concepts, or skills being learned to the knowledge that he or she already possesses.
4. Because instruction should be based on what each child knows, it is essential to assess continually whether a child could solve a particular problem and *how he or she solves it.*

Instructional Implications.   The arithmetic operations should be introduced in meaningful contexts and should build upon or build up children's informal strengths.

• **Exploit everyday situations to introduce and to discuss addition and subtraction.** Various situations in the classroom, playground, or home involve adding and subtracting (33). Games provide a natural and entertaining avenue for doing addition and subtraction (4, 30, 33, 59). Numerous children's stories entail addition and subtraction and can provide a basis for discussing these operations and predicting outcomes. For example, "One Elephant Balancing" by Edith Fowke (Harcourt Brace Jovanovich, 1989) involves repeatedly adding one item, and "Porwigles" by Julie Holder (in J. Foster [Ed.], *First poetry book*, Oxford University Press, 1979) involves repeatedly taking away one. With both, a teacher can ask children what the outcome of adding (or taking away) one more would be and then continue the story to check their answers. By taking advantage of such everyday opportunities, teachers can help children apply or extend their informal arithmetic knowledge in meaningful, purposeful, and interesting ways.

Talking about time is one real way to broach the topic of addition and subtraction (33). For example, a teacher might note that it is two weeks before a vacation. Young children commonly want to know what such a time frame is in more familiar terms: days. The teacher can then note that one week is seven days and ask, "How many days would two weeks be?"

• **Word problems should be used to *introduce* addition and subtraction.** Because word problems can be more meaningful to children than symbolic expressions, they should be an integral aspect of instruction from the start (see 19). Moreover, children should have ample experience solving problems before symbolic expressions are introduced.

• **Children should be encouraged to use objects, draw pictures, or use tallies when solving addition and subtraction problems.** Counting should be recognized as a highly useful means for computing sums and differences (21, 26). Initially, children should be encouraged to count on their fingers, make marks, or use manipulatives.

• **Use developmentally appropriate manipulatives.** Some manipulatives better match children's informal mathematical knowledge and thus are more useful for introducing arithmetic operations than other manipulatives. For example, interlocking cubes and number sticks (numbered sets made of interlocking cubes; see Fig. 4.1), are clearly composed of units, which children can easily count. They can be physically put together and disassembled to model addition and subtraction problems.

• **Introduce addition and subtraction with small numbers (1 to 5).** With such problems, it is easier for children to count if they use concrete procedures or to keep

FIGURE 4.1 Number sticks

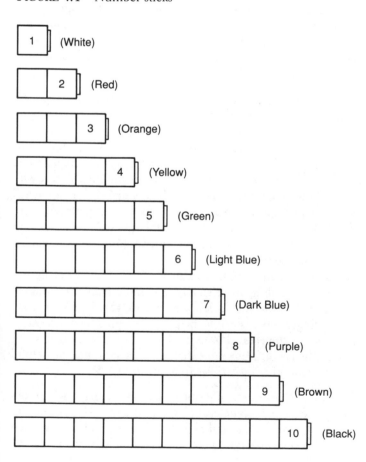

track if they use verbal counting procedures. Introduce problems with larger numbers *after* they have gained some proficiency with smaller numbers.

•   **Assess a child's readiness and informal arithmetic knowledge before beginning instruction.** To plan instruction effectively, it is important for a teacher to gauge *each* child's existing knowledge and to inventory his or her individual strengths and weaknesses (51). For example, can children count out a given number of items so that they can represent an addend? readily determine which of two numbers is more so that they have a basis for thinking about arithmetic? state the number after another so that they mentally add one and count on? easily count backwards so that they can count down to subtract? model or readily learn to model the meaning of simple word problems?

> Teachers can use word problems in a brief interview to assess children's informal mathematical understandings and strategies (see, e.g., 7).

•   **Provide arithmetic readiness experience for those who need it.** Children who come to school with relatively little informal experience need abundant, supervised counting experiences before beginning arithmetic instruction. These experiences can be extended by adding or subtracting one from a counted collection and asking how many items are now present.

•   **Foster the development of efficient computing strategies.** A useful approach for encouraging counting on is the hiding method (Fig. 4.2). This involves (a) presenting two collections and asking how many there are altogether, (b) hiding the first collection before a child has a chance to count from one, and (c) asking: How many am I hiding? So how many are there altogether? A second approach is to replace one of two dot dice with a numeral die (30, 59). This encourages children to start with the number on the numeral die and to count on using the dot die. A third approach is to help children master the prerequisite understandings for counting on (see 22 or 47). A fourth approach is to have children first determine the sum of $N + 1$ problems (such as six and one more) mentally. Once proficient with counting on one, adding two more can be introduced and so forth.

Encourage the learning of efficient keeping-track methods. This is especially important with problems involving adding on or taking away more than five. Mastery of finger patterns to 10, such as automatically knowing what seven fingers feel like, can be helpful. Chisenbop finger patterns can be helpful in keeping track (see 22).

Encourage the flexible use of strategies. For example, because counting down is difficult for many children when subtracting more than three or so, it may be helpful to encourage children to use counting up with such problems (3, 25).

•   **Instruction should use a wide variety of problem situations.** Begin with problems that are relatively easy to model—problems in which the outcome, whole, or difference is unknown. Begin with Change and Part-Part-Whole problems and then introduce Equalize and Compare problems. Later include problems in which the change, start, or part is unknown.

FIGURE 4.2   A hiding method for encouraging "counting on" and "counting back"

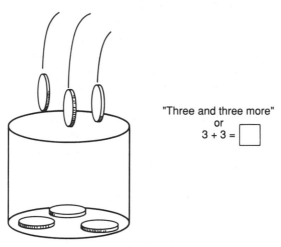

"Three and three more"
or
3 + 3 = ☐

The activity is also good for helping children "see" subtraction in an informal way of "counting back."

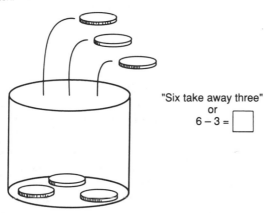

"Six take away three"
or
6 − 3 = ☐

The *Thinking Story Books* (Open Court, 1985) are a good source of various types of word problems.

An example of a problem that can occur in everyday school life is collecting permission slips (33). For example, a teacher can note that of the ten boys in the class, eight have returned their permission slips. The question can then be posed: How many more boys need to bring their permission slips in so that all the boys can go on the field trip?

Formal Concepts and Skills

Research suggests that instruction frequently overlooks children's need for a prolonged period of informal exploration (12). Physical models are often used only
briefly, if at all, to introduce addition and subtraction (23). Frequently, instruction
jumps quickly to drilling number combinations. Moreover, it is commonly assumed
that with sufficient practice, children can memorize the single-digit addition combinations like $9 + 6 = 15$ and their subtractive counterparts such as $15 - 9 = 6$
quickly—by the end of first grade. Children view addition and subtraction narrowly
from a single perspective (a change meaning), and this narrow conception is reinforced by instruction when it does not foster other interpretations for these operations
(40). Arithmetic principles and concepts are frequently introduced in an abstract
manner. For example, the idea of a missing part is often introduced symbolically as
a missing-addend number sentence such as $5 + \square = 8$.

Introducing Symbolic Arithmetic.   Informal arithmetic knowledge is the basis for
making sense of symbolic arithmetic (26, 29). More specifically, children interpret
formal addition expressions like $5 + 3 = ?$ in terms of their informal Change-Add-
To view of addition: How much are five things and three more altogether? Moreover,
children tend to interpret symbolic subtraction expressions such as $8 - 5 = ?$ in
terms of their informal Change-Take-Away concept: Eight things take away three
leaves what?

   If children do not see the connection between the formal symbolism and their
informal concepts and strategies, then they do not have a basis for understanding and
solving their written arithmetic work. These children may not comprehend formal
expressions like $5 + 3 = ?$ or $8 - 3 = ?$ and perform very poorly on written
arithmetic assignments. (Given verbally presented word problems with the identical
terms, these same children may well compute the correct answer to these problems.)

Mastery of the Basic Number Combinations.   Research indicates that memorizing
the single-digit addition and subtraction combinations is a drawn-out rather than a
quick process. Children proceed through three phases of development: (1) counting,
(2) reasoning, and (3) recall (49). Initially, children rely on concrete and verbal counting strategies to compute sums and differences. During this phase of informal calculation, children typically discover important patterns and relationships. They incorporate these discoveries into "thinking strategies," which can be used to reason out
unpracticed or unknown combinations. For example, children who know the addition doubles like $6 + 6$ may reason out near doubles like $7 + 6$ (e.g., if $6 + 6$ is
12 and 7 is one more than 6, then $7 + 6$ must be 1 more than 12, or 13).

   Research suggests that introducing drill before children understand symbolic arithmetic or before they devise their own ways to compute or reason out answers can
hinder mastery (51). Moreover, instruction that helps children focus on patterns and
relationships appears to be more effective than drill alone in fostering retention and
transfer to unpracticed problems (39, 51, 55). Practice, then, appears most effective
after a period of informal exploration and when done purposefully.

   Results of the CGI program (11) bear out this conclusion. Research suggests that
teachers are reluctant to sacrifice time devoted to teaching computational skills to

spend more time on developing understanding and solving problems. CGI teachers spent significantly more time on problem solving and significantly less time on drilling the basic combinations than did control teachers. Nevertheless, in year-end testing, children in CGI classes *recalled* significantly more combinations than those taught by control teachers who focused on drill and practice of arithmetic facts.

Addition and Subtraction Concepts. Children's informal knowledge about part–whole relationships is limited (23, 42). They do not recognize that a whole such as seven can be created by or decomposed into its component parts in various ways. More specifically, because of their informal Change-Add-To view of addition, many children do not realize that the operation is commutative: that the order of the addends does not affect the sum. For example, because they interpret 5 + 2 as five and *two more* and 2 + 5 as two and *five more* (as different situations), children naturally assume these combinations will have different sums (3). Moreover, they may assume that different-looking problems like 5 + 2, 6 + 1 and 4 + 3 also have different sums.

Children tend to interpret symbolic subtraction expression like 5 − 3 = ? exclusively in terms of a take-away meaning. They do not realize that such expressions can represent a difference (Equalize or Compare) meaning as well. Furthermore, initially, they do not understand the "complement principle"—recognize that subtraction combinations can be figured out by using their existing knowledge of the addition (3). For example, they do not recognize that the answer to 5 − 3 can be determined by thinking three plus what is five (3 + ? = 5) and recalling that 3 + 2 = 5 (33).

Missing-Addend Expressions. Children often have difficulty understanding missing-addend expressions such as 5 + ? = 8. A common answer is 13 (33). This problem often arises because the formal symbolism is not connected to real situations. When related to word problems, children can better understand and solve symbolic missing-addend expressions (13).

Instructional Implications. Formal addition and subtraction should be introduced in terms of children's informal knowledge. The emphasis of instruction should be on understanding the operation, accuracy, searching for patterns, and sharing ideas.

• **Link symbolic expressions such as 5 + 3 = ? or 8 − 5 = ? to concrete models and situations.** Not only is it important to begin with concrete experiences, it is important to ensure that children see the connection between symbolic arithmetic expressions and these informal experiences. Indeed, in *Mathematics Their Way* (2), "conceptual-level" activities are followed by a "linking-level" activity and only then are "symbolic-level" activities introduced. A linking-level activity can involve solving word problems concretely and then requesting children to record with symbols what they have done. Some teachers may first wish to have children devise and discuss their own recording systems and then introduce the conventional symbolism. Other techniques for linking informal and formal addition or subtraction are described in various sources (4, 18, 30, 57).

Irons and Irons (31) describe and illustrate four stages of representing word problems: (1) natural-language (children's) descriptions; (2) concrete or pictorial materials; (3) mathematical language; and (4) written symbols. The latter two stages are increasingly efficient ways of recording situations and should build upon—be linked to—the first two.

• **Reverse the process.** To foster and to check understanding, ask students to make word problems or concrete models for a formal expression like $7 + 3 = ?$ By sharing the word problems with one another, children may see that a formal expression can represent a wide variety of real-world situations. It also provides an interesting way of practicing arithmetic.

• **Practice with the basic number combinations should give children ample opportunity to use informal methods for determining sums and differences in purposeful and interesting contexts.** There is no doubt that practice is an important ingredient in mastering the basic number combinations. However, it should *not* be done at the expense of more important objectives, such as fostering a positive disposition toward learning mathematics. The use of informal calculational procedures should be encouraged as long as children need them. Computing sums and differences should be done for a reason—as a means to an end rather than an end itself. Moreover, it need not be dull. Solving word problems and playing games can provide ample practice for encouraging efficient strategies and fostering combination mastery in a challenging and entertaining manner (see, e.g., 1, 3, 4, 14, 21, 30, 33, 34, 38, 59). Dice games involving 0 to 5 dice can be used to practice sums up to 10. For sums to 18, use 5 to 9 dice. By judiciously picking dice, differences up to $18 - 9$ can also be practiced with such games. A deck of cards with arithmetic expressions can be substituted for dice.

Double War (33) is played like the card game War except that players draw two cards from their deck and sum their values. The player with the largest sum wins all the cards. Ties are broken by drawing another two cards and summing them.

Dice games can provide an incentive for inventing more efficient strategies as well as hours of interesting practice. As children become familiar with dice patterns, it may foster the invention of a transition strategy (e.g., a child may roll a four and two, recognize the pattern for four, and begin with "four" and count on "five, six" on the two die).

• **Instruction on the number combinations should focus on encouraging a search for and discussion of patterns and relationships (thinking strategies).** The basic addition and subtraction combinations provide a marvelous opportunity to explore for patterns. By using the patterns listed in Tables 4.3 and 4.4, children can greatly reduce the effort required to master the "basic facts" (see, e.g., 4, 6, 14, 21, 39, 54). Children can be guided to discover such patterns.

The ten-frame is a useful devise for helping children visualize sums between 6 and 10 in terms of patterns based on five (20). Children first explore the patterns for the numbers 1 to 10 (e.g., 6 fills up one column of the ten-frame and one cell of the second column). Next, children use the ten-frame to represent addition problems like $4 + 2 = ?$ (see Frame A of Fig. 4.3). By transforming $4 + 2$ into $5 + 1$, children can see that the sum is 6. In time, children can be encouraged to visualize what $4 + 2$ would look like on the ten-frame and to transform the problem mentally.

For sums greater than 10, a double ten-frame activity (see Frame B of Fig. 4.3) is especially helpful for teaching the recomposition-to-10 strategy for solving the relatively difficult plus-eight or -nine facts (4, 35, 53). Note that it also is useful for introducing the base-ten place–value idea that, say, 13 represents one group of ten and 3 ones, which is essential for multidigit mental computation later.

TABLE 4.3.   Some Thinking Strategies for Addition

1. *Zero rule:*	Addition involving zero does not change the other number. For example, $0+7=7$ and $9+0=9$.
2. *Number-after rule:*	The sum of, say, $6+1$ (or $1+6$) is the number after 6 in the count sequence. (This rule allows children to exploit their existing and automatic number-after knowledge.)
3. *Skip-next-number-rule:*	The sum of, say, $6+2$ (or $2+6$) is the number after the next number after 6 in the count sequence. (This rule allows children to exploit their mental representation of the counting sequence.)
4. *Commutativity:*	Addend order does not affect the sum. For example, both $6+3$ and $3+6=9$.
5. *Doubles plus (or minus) one:*	Combinations like $7+8$ can be thought of as the double $7+7$ plus one (or as the double $8+8$ less one).
6. *Doubles by recomposition:*	Combinations like $5+3$ can be converted into doubles by taking away one from the larger term and giving it to the smaller term $(5+3=[5-1]+[3+1]=4+4=8)$.
7. *Recomposition to 10:*	For combinations like $9+4$, the sum is $10+4$ less one because 9 is one less than 10.

TABLE 4.4.   Thinking Strategies for Subtraction

1. *Minus zero rule:*	Zero subtracted from a number leaves it unchanged. For example, $6 - 0 = 6$.
2. *Number-before rule:*	To subtract one from the number, state the number in the count sequence that comes before it. For example, for $7 - 1$, what number comes before 7 when I count? Six.
3. *Same-number rule:*	A number subtracted from itself leaves nothing. For example, $8 - 8 = 0$.
4. *The difference-of-one rule:*	Whenever neighbors in the sequence (e.g., 6 and 7) are subtracted, the difference is one ($7 - 6 = 1$).
5. *Complements:*	Any subtraction combination can be figured out by recalling its related or complementary addition combination. For instance, $8 - 5$ can be thought of as what do I need to add to five to make 8? Three (because $5 + 3 = 8$).
6. *Recomposition to 10:*	For combinations like $17 - 9$, the difference is $17 - 10$ plus one.

An approach that emphasizes thinking strategies can foster analytic thinking while making the learning of the basic combinations interesting and enjoyable. Such an approach is more likely to foster the beliefs that the essence of mathematics is searching for patterns and thinking, not the mindless memorization and recitation of facts. It is useful even for children with learning difficulties (56).

Research is less clear about how teachers should promote the learning of thinking strategies. Should teachers point them out directly, allow children to discover them, or have children who have invented strategies share them with others? Though it is more desirable to have children discover and share strategies, sometimes a more direct approach might be helpful and encourage children to find additional strategies.

• **Foster broad conceptions of addition and subtraction in meaningful contexts.** Word problems are an excellent way to introduce alternative meanings of addition and subtraction. By pointing out that symbolic subtraction expressions like $5 - 3 = ?$ can represent Equalize and Compare problems as well as Change-Take-Away problems, children can be helped to see that subtraction has difference meanings as well as a take-away meaning (22). Understanding that symbolic subtraction can have an equalize meaning may help children to recognize the complement principle, figure out differences, and master the basic subtraction combinations.

• **Foster the discovery of the commutativity principle and same-sum families.** These regularities are ideally suited for guided discovery learning. For example, children can be asked to solve word problems involving five and three more and three

FIGURE 4.3 Using ten-frames to visualize sums

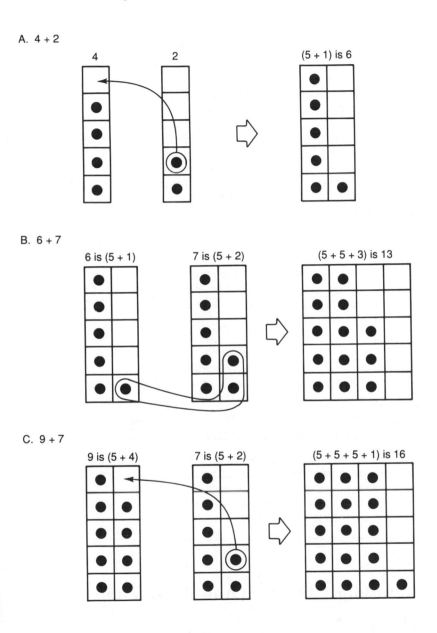

and five more and then asked to compare and discuss the results. Moreover, a variety of games and activities can be used to highlight the commutative principle and the same-sum concept (4). *Mathematics Their Way* (2) contains numerous decomposition activities for fostering part–whole understanding as well as commutative and same-sums concepts. These activities require children to produce a collection of a specified number and then subdivide the collection in various ways (e.g., four can be made with a group of four and a group containing none, none and four, three and one, one and three, or two and two).

The "Game of Ten" can be used to practice the various combinations summing to 10. The game is played with a regular deck of cards without face cards. The cards are placed face down in a pile, and the first card is turned over, by the dealer. The person to the left of the dealer turns over the next card and places it next to the first uncovered card. Play continues in this manner until a player uncovers a card equal to ten or a card that if combined with any previously uncovered card (or cards) equals ten. The player then announces his find and collects the card or cards. For example, if a player uncovers a three and a seven was uncovered earlier, the child would announce: "Seven plus three equals ten." The game ends when the deck of cards is exhausted. The winner is the person with the largest number of cards.

• **Introduce missing-addend expressions concretely and meaningfully.** To foster meaningful learning, relate missing-addend expressions to real situations such as word problems (13). An expression like $5 + ? = 8$ can be related to Change-Add-To Unknown-Change or Equalize Part-Unknown problems (see Table 4.1). Encourage children to solve such problems by using objects and, later, by counting up. Children can practice these solution strategies by playing games. In the Wynroth (59) Program, for example, children play a game called Supposed to Be in which they try to find the appropriate tiles (squares with dots) to fill in the blank of pictured collections like: $\boxed{\bullet} + \boxed{} = \boxed{\vcenter{\hbox{∴∴}}}$ Initially, children are encouraged to find the correct tile through a systematic trial-and-error process (first try a one, then a two, and so forth). Later, they can be encouraged to find the unknown by counting up.

Readiness for formal missing-addend instruction can be gauged by the following task: Tell a child how many counters you are holding in your hands; open one hand, keep the other closed and ask, "How many are in my closed hand?" Such an informal task is advocated in *Mathematics Their Way* (2) and can be done in an entertaining and nonthreatening manner.

Multidigit Addition and Subtraction

Informal Strategies

As with single-digit arithmetic, children can informally solve multidigit arithmetic problems before they can do so using written procedures.

Use of Existing Strategies. Typically, children initially try to compute multidigit sums and differences in the same way they computed single-digit answers. For a problem like 29 + 12, for example, many children would count on by ones: "29, 30, 31, 32, 33, 34, 35, 36, 37, 38, 39, 40, 41." It is remarkable that children get the right answer for such problems as often as they do. Clearly, though, such informal arithmetic strategies are not an efficient way to perform multidigit calculations and often children do make errors, if only by ±1.

Invented Strategies.   Given the opportunity, children can and do invent increasingly efficient mental-arithmetic procedures (see, e.g., 15, 34). Once children see a connection between their existing count-by-tens knowledge and addition by ten, they may solve a problem such as 29 + 10 by using the shortcut of stating the next decade after twenty and combining it with the ones digit: thirty + nine. In time, they may solve a problem like 29 + 12 by viewing it as 29 + (10 + 2) and count: "29; 39, 40, 41." Children also discover connections between their existing knowledge of basic combinations and multidigit combinations. For example, they may recognize that forty and thirty is seventy because four and three is seven. Children commonly invent a left–right procedure (e.g., 24 + 15: twenty and ten is thirty and four and five is nine—thirty nine), which has the advantage of generating the tens and ones terms in the order they must be stated for the answer (27). They can even invent procedures for mentally handling renaming situations such as 29 + 12 (34).

Moreover, given the opportunity, children can invent written arithmetic procedures. Pengelly (38) had first graders play a Wood-Trading game, using base-ten blocks to keep score (36). On their turn, children would throw dice, determine the sum, and collect that number of unit-blocks. When players collected 10 blocks, they traded them in for a long; 10 longs were traded in for a flat—100. (In a more advanced game children could trade 10 flats for a large cube [1,000].) They were asked to keep a written record of their score to 100. At first, children rather laboriously described how many units they collected on their turn and/or how they regrouped. Over the course of a year, though, children invented relatively efficient procedures for tallying and recording their scores. Some children basically invented the written renaming (carrying) procedure commonly taught in school.

Formal Multidigit Procedures

Unfortunately, many children do not have the opportunity to construct an understanding of base-ten, place–value concepts that serve as the underlying rationale for the written calculational algorithms (46). The result is often systematic errors such as subtracting the smaller digit from the larger regardless of its position (e.g., 36 − 29 = 13) (26).

The question of how and when multidigit written arithmetic can be introduced meaningfully remains unsettled (5). Research does indicate that the use of manipulative aids can significantly improve understanding of multidigit arithmetic (23, 51). Though certain models may be easily understood and used by some children, efforts to make instructions meaningful are more important than the particular materials used (51).

Research (46) shows that even when used, manipulatives do not guarantee understanding of the formal algorithms. Children frequently do not see the connection between a concrete model and written procedures (41). Instruction that links each step in a written algorithm to each step in a concrete procedure using base-ten blocks apparently can improve learning and transfer of algorithms (24) but does not ensure success (see 44).

Typically, multidigit arithmetic is done in a piecemeal fashion. Procedures without renaming are introduced before those involving renaming. Two-digit problems are introduced in second grade, three-digit in third, and four-digit in fourth. Research (e.g., 24) suggests that a meaningful approach makes such a drawn-out approach unnecessary. For example, when taught meaningfully, second graders were able to solve a ten-digit problem—a type of problem they had not previously practiced.

In terms of timing, many mathematics educators (3, 18, 34, 52, 59) recommend prolonged work with concrete models and mental arithmetic before introducing the written algorithms. To give children an opportunity to construct a deep understanding of the base-ten place–value concepts, some (16) even advocate delaying the introduction of the written algorithms until third or fourth grade. Some evidence (24) suggest, though, that second graders can benefit from instruction that introduces concrete models and the written algorithms together (23).

Instructional Implications

Multidigit addition and subtraction instruction should be done in a meaningful and interesting manner.

• **Instruction should be introduced to children in concrete ways and in conjunction with base-ten, place–value instruction.** The sequence of concrete embodiments (see column 1 of Fig. 4.4) is recommended by some (4, 18) to help children construct base-ten, place–value concepts underlying the written algorithm. Note that the first manipulative used is a proportional size embodiment: The object representing a 10 is 10 times larger than that representing 1. Moreover, it requires children to make a group of 10 themselves. This may help some children to view 10 simultaneously as a group (super-unit) and as something that can be unpacked into 10 ones (see 15, 46). The second manipulative illustrated is a pregrouped proportional size embodiment. For example, a long is a single rod hatched to show 10 units and is 10 times bigger than a unit-block. Such manipulatives are convenient to use especially when trading involves numbers larger than two digits. The third kind of manipulative, including colored chips or play money, introduces a relatively abstract 10-for-1 trading procedure (10 units are traded for one thing that represents, but does not resemble, a group of ten). Using a different-looking ten marker may help some children bridge the gap between highly concrete size embodiments and the relatively abstract model illustrated in row four. With this fourth manipulative, the only thing that distinguishes a ten from a one is the *position* of the marker. Note that the relatively abstract 10-for-1 trade *directly* models the formal procedure of writing a 1, not a 10 (100, 1,000, and so forth) above the tens (hundreds, thousands, or other) columns.

Not all mathematics educators believe all four steps illustrated in Figure 4.4 are necessary. Some, for example, recommend Steps 2 and 4 (23). Teachers will need to use their judgment as to what steps in the sequence are needed for a particular child.

FIGURE 4.4 A sequence of concrete and pictorial embodiments for teaching multidigit addition

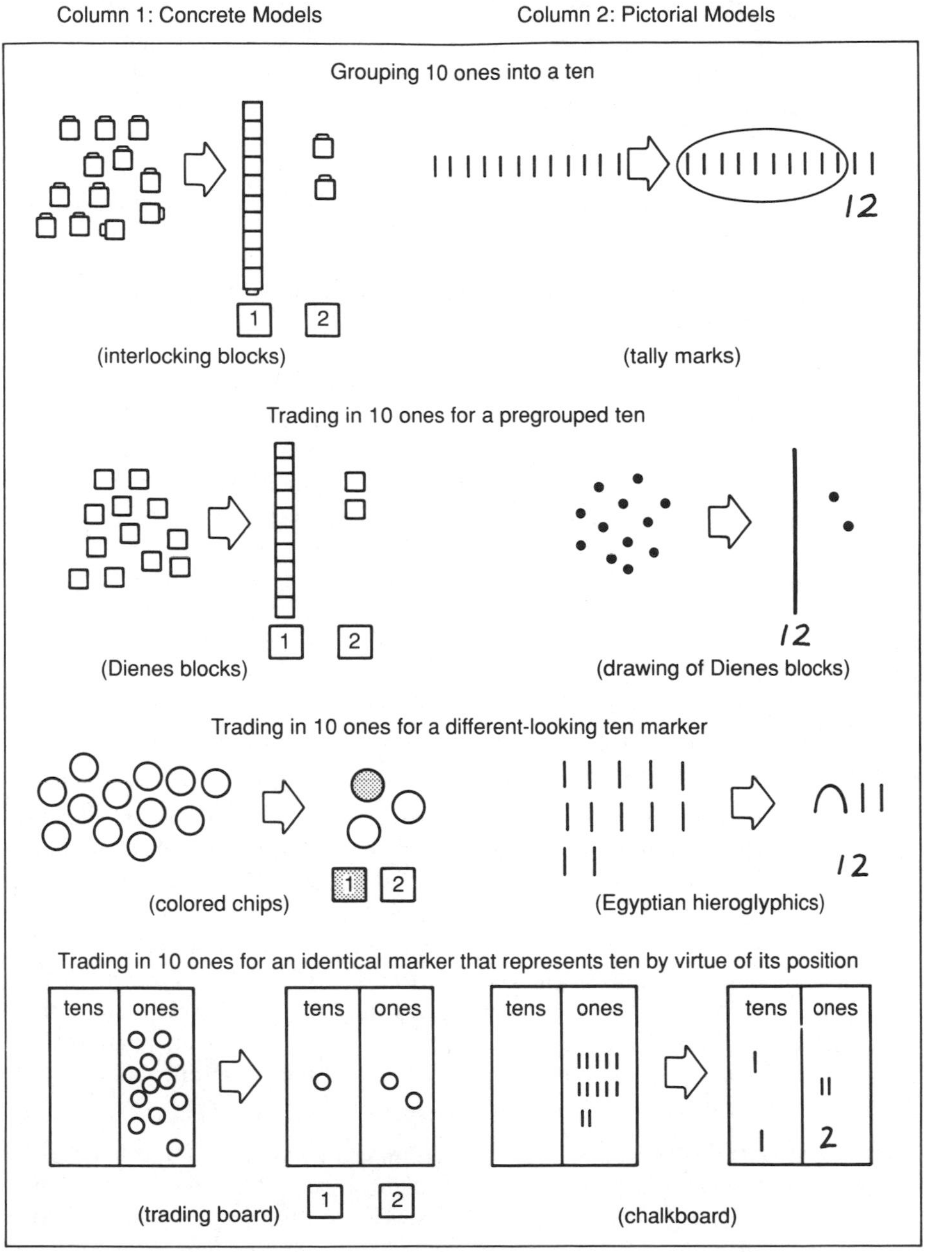
Column 1: Concrete Models
Column 2: Pictorial Models
Grouping 10 ones into a ten
1
2
(interlocking blocks)
12
(tally marks)
Trading in 10 ones for a pregrouped ten
1
2
(Dienes blocks)
12
(drawing of Dienes blocks)
Trading in 10 ones for a different-looking ten marker
1
2
(colored chips)
12
(Egyptian hieroglyphics)
Trading in 10 ones for an identical marker that represents ten by virtue of its position
tens
ones
tens
ones
1
2
(trading board)
tens
ones
tens
ones
1
2
(chalkboard)

Note: The concrete and pictorial models shown could be introduced without an accompanying numeral designation. This is probably unnecessary for many, perhaps most, children.

The use of pictorial models (see Column 2 of Fig. 4.4) may also be helpful. Some (e.g., 32) suggest that pictorial models are a necessary intermediary between concrete models and abstract, written arithmetic. Though it is not clear that this is the case (5), pictorial models can help provide a variety of models.

Though it is possible that using a variety of models may confuse some children, using a variety of concrete and pictorial models may have important advantages. It may help children to see that a procedure applies across a range of situations and may prevent some children from too narrowly identifying a procedure with one particular manipulative. Moreover, one manipulative may not have the same appeal or be equally meaningful to all children. Using a variety of models may make it more likely that something clicks with a particular child.

- **Instruction can be structured in various ways.** How instruction is structured depends, in part, on the goals of instruction:

1.   If the primary aim of a curriculum is to develop thinking and problem solving skills, an unguided-discovery approach could be used. For example, children could play a game such as Wood-Trading (36), described above. The children could be challenged to devise a way of keeping a written record of their scores so that the game could be continued after recess, the next day, after a weekend, or after a holiday. Children could be encouraged to discuss their recording system and to devise more efficient ones. With any luck, this will result in reinventing the highly efficient renaming algorithms. In essence, such an approach entails giving children the opportunity to invent and discuss their own mental and written procedures. It is thought that this will foster the autonomy, dispositions, and beliefs critical to self-regulated learning and problem solving (15, 34). Indeed, some suggest that children may not be ready to understand formally taught calculational procedures before they have invented their own procedures (8).

2.   A conceptual approach that is highly structured and teacher-directed can be used to teach the algorithms in a meaningful fashion. This approach might entail using base-ten blocks to provide a concrete model of the trading procedures; linking each step of the concrete procedure to each step of the written algorithm (see Fig. 4.5); and using block terms (e.g., "1 long and 2 small cubes"), base-ten place–value terms (e.g., "1 ten and 2 ones"), and counting terms (e.g., "twelve") interchangeably. Though children do not have the rich opportunity to invent and to share their own written procedures, this approach requires less class time than unguided discovery learning and prepares students for achievement tests in a timely fashion (23, 24).

3.   A guided-discovery approach combines these approaches and has some of the advantages of each. For example, a teacher might show children a concrete scoring procedure with base-ten blocks and with a written renaming algorithm and then encourage them to discover and discuss how the steps of a written renaming algorithm parallel a concrete procedure with blocks. This approach does not require a great deal of class time, yet provides some opportunity for children to discover connections.

• **Explicitly link the written algorithm to concrete models.** It is essential that teachers help children to see the connection between a written procedure and concrete embodiments. Some (22) suggest that a teacher point out the parallels between a written algorithm and a concrete model directly. A more child-centered approach might have students look for the parallels and discuss them in small groups or as a class.

> Burns (9) calls relating the concrete models to symbolic procedures the "Math Connection" and indicates that it is necessary whenever we use manipulatives as a means of teaching a concept.

> Children actively engaged in solving story problems through the use of "Story Mats," where they enact and orally solve a mathematical problem, can be then shown how to record the algorithm. Going from the enactment of the problem to the symbolic recording helps enhance understanding.

• **It is important that multidigit addition and subtraction instruction and practice be purposeful.** Solving story problems and keeping score for games are natural avenues for providing ample practice of concrete and written procedures in a personally important and entertaining manner. Small amounts of purposeful practice done on a regular basis is preferable to large doses of pointless worksheet drill (16).

> The "Roll Number Game" is used in *Real Math Level 2* (Open Court, 1985) and is a fantastic way to practice place–value skills. On paper or a chalkboard, a child or team of children draws a matrix:
>
>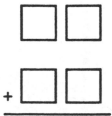
>
> The teacher randomly picks a digit 0 to 9. A player or team decides where they want to put the digit so as to make the largest sum possible. Once recorded, a digit may not be moved. This procedure is repeated three times. The sums are then computed and the player or team with the largest answer is given a point.

FIGURE 4.5 Linking the written algorithm with a concrete model

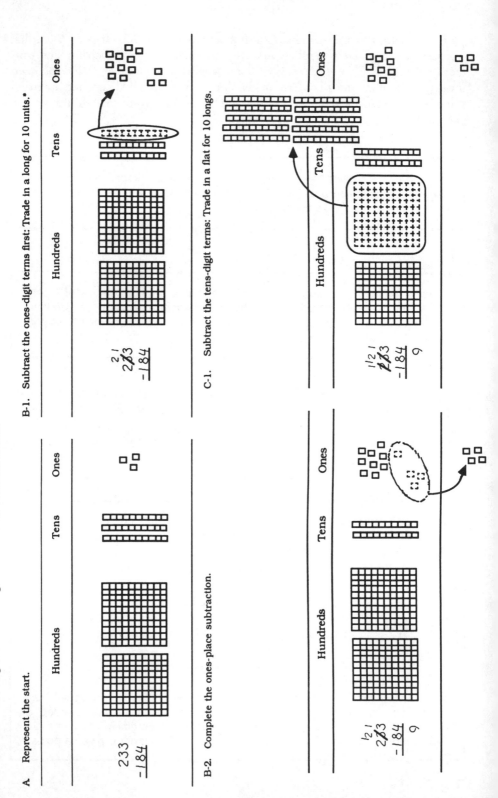

A. Represent the start.

B-1. Subtract the ones-digit terms first: Trade in a long for 10 units.*

B-2. Complete the ones-place subtraction.

C-1. Subtract the tens-digit terms: Trade in a flat for 10 longs.

C-2. Complete the tens-place subtraction.

D-1. Subtract the hundreds-digit terms, clear the subtrahend (the portion taken away), and answer the question posed by the problem.

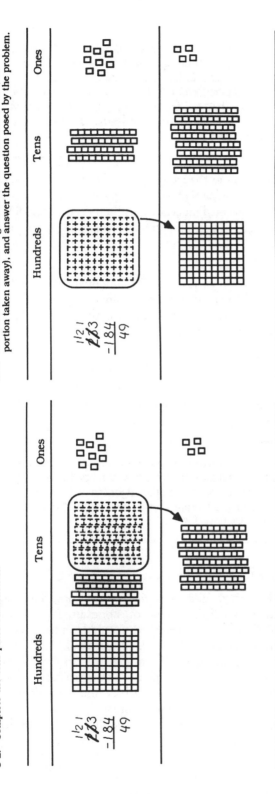

*Note that for some children, it may be easier to do *all the regrouping first* (e.g., Fuson, 1986), in which case, a child would then check the tens column subtraction. Seeing that it requires regrouping also, the child would then proceed to trade in a flat for 10 longs.

97

> The use of money in trading situations makes for a fine and meaningful method to underscore the more abstract concepts of our base-ten place–value system. Shopping games can be played where one of the rules is the exchange of ten $1 bills for one $10 bill, and ten $10 bills for one $100 bill whenever possible. With the children keeping their piles of bills separate, it's easy for them to count their money often and accurately, and provides practice in actual usage of counting money as a means of keeping score.

• **Underscore that there can be more than one correct procedure.** Children should realize that there are often various ways of calculating sums and differences. Encouraging children to share their invented procedures with others can help foster this belief. Some alternative procedures sidestep the difficult renaming process such as the expanded algorithm (see, e.g., 48) and the equal-addition for subtraction (e.g., $306 - 199 \rightarrow 307 - 200 = 107$) (28).

• **Underscore that errors are a vehicle for learning.** It is important that children appreciate that everyone can learn from their mistakes. If done in a constructive manner, discussing why a mistake was made can be instructive for everyone. Moreover, it can help children understand that making mistakes is a natural part of learning.

• **Reduce piecemeal instruction.** If done meaningfully, the written procedures with and without renaming can be introduced together. Problems with three digits and more can be introduced together. Fuson and Briars (24) even recommend introducing such problems at the same time as two-digit problems.

> The use of sets of problems that all require regrouping or no regrouping is an artificial device and encourages children to completely miss the point of regrouping "when necessary." It encourages the blind use of an algorithm without regard to its appropriateness. Children need to understand that borrowing is "just like at the bank . . . we only borrow when we have to!"

Looking Ahead . . .

Though researchers have learned much about the teaching and learning of addition and subtraction in recent years, there is still much to learn. For example, it is unclear whether concrete models of the renaming algorithms should be introduced well before the written algorithms in first grade or even kindergarten (2, 3, 18, 52, 59), or delayed until second grade and introduced in conjunction with the written algorithms (23, 24). Thus, though research can provide classroom teachers with invaluable guidance about teaching addition and subtraction, it cannot provide them definitive answers about all aspects of such instruction. Ultimately, classroom teachers must take the information available, experiment, and find what works best for their situation or for an individual child.

Art Baroody

Traditionally, mathematics has been a "silent subject" with children *quietly* listening to a teacher or completing written worksheet assignments. Research suggests that to foster arithmetic understanding and thinking, children need to be active. They need to be engaged in real and purposeful activities, to exchange ideas and strategies, and to defend their procedures and answers. Encouraging investigation and communication means breaking with the silent-subject tradition. I wonder if teachers, administrators, and parents will generally accept a more active and "noisy" approach.

Dot Standifer

About the Authors

Art Baroody is associate professor of curriculum and instruction at the College of Education at the University of Illinois, Champaign. His research focuses on the development of counting, number, and arithmetic skills and concepts.

Dot Standifer is a Chapter I Mathematics Teacher for the Paxton-Buckley-Loda Unit School District #10, Paxton, Illinois. She is currently a doctoral student at the University of Illinois and serves as a consultant and workshop presenter at the local and regional level.

References

*1. ASHLOCK, R. B., & WASHBON, C. A. (1978). Games: Practice activities for basic facts. In M. N. Suydam & R. E. Reys (Eds.), *Developing computational skills* (pp. 39–50). Reston, VA: National Council of Teachers of Mathematics.

*2. BARATTA-LORTON, M. (1976). *Mathematics their way*. Menlo Park, CA: Addison-Wesley.

*3. BAROODY, A. J. (1987). *Children's mathematical thinking: A developmental framework for preschool primary, and special education teachers*. New York: Teachers College Press.

*4. BAROODY, A. J. (1989). *A guide to teaching mathematics in the primary grades*. Boston: Allyn & Bacon.

5. BAROODY, A. J. (1990). How and when should place–value concepts and skills be taught? *Journal for Research in Mathematics Education, 21*(4), 281–286.

*6. BAROODY, A. J., & HANK, M. (1990). *Elementary mathematics activities: Teachers' guidebook*. Boston: Allyn & Bacon.

*7. BEBOUT, H. C., & CARPENTER, T. P. (1989). Assessing and building thinking strategies: Necessary bases for instruction. In P. R. Trafton & A. P. Shulte (Eds.), *New directions for elementary school mathematics* (pp. 59–69). Reston, VA: National Council of Teachers of Mathematics.

8. BIGGS, E. (1969). *Freedom to learn*. Reading, MA: Addison-Wesley.

*9. BURNS, M. (1984). *The math solution*. Sausalito, CA: Marilyn Burns Education Associates.

10. CARPENTER, T. P. (1986). Conceptual knowledge as a foundation for procedural knowledge: Implications from research on the initial learning of arithmetic. In J. Hiebert (Ed.), *Conceptual and procedural knowledge: The case of mathematics* (pp. 113–132). Hillsdale, NJ: Erlbaum.

11. CARPENTER, T. P., FENNEMA, E., PETERSON, P. L., CHIANG, C-P., & LOEF, M. (1989).

Using knowledge of children's mathematics thinking in classroom teaching: An experimental study. *American Educational Research Journal, 26,* 499–532.

12. CARPENTER, T. P., & MOSER, J. M. (1984). The acquisition of addition and subtraction concepts in grades one through three. *Journal for Research in Mathematics Education, 15,* 179–202.

13. CARPENTER, T. P., MOSER, J. M., & BEBOUT, H. C. (1988). Representation of addition and subtraction word problems. *Journal for Research in Mathematics Education, 19,* 345–357.

*14. COBB, P., & MERKEL, G. (1989). Thinking strategies: Teaching arithmetic through problem solving. In P. R. Trafton & A. P. Shulte (Eds.), *New directions for elementary school mathematics* (pp. 70–84). Reston, VA: National Council of Teachers of Mathematics.

15. COBB, P., & WHEATLEY, G. (1988). Children's initial understanding of ten. *Focus on Learning Problems in Mathematics, 10*(3), 1–28.

*16. COBURN, T. G. (1989). The role of computation in the changing mathematics curriculum. In P. R. Trafton & A. P. Shulte (Eds.), *New directions for elementary school mathematics* (pp. 43–58). Reston, VA: National Council of Teachers of Mathematics.

17. DECORTE, E., & VERSCHAFFEL, L. (1987). The effects of semantic structure on first graders' strategies for solving addition and subtraction word problems. *Journal for Research in Mathematics Education, 18,* 363–381.

*18. ENGELHARDT, J. M., ASHLOCK, R. B., & WIEBE, J. H. (1984). *Helping children understand and use numerals.* Boston: Allyn & Bacon.

*19. FEINBERG, M. M. (1988). *Solving word problems in the primary grades: Addition and subtraction.* Reston, VA: National Council of Teachers of Mathematics.

*20. FLEXER, R. J. (1986). The power of five: The step before the power of ten. *Arithmetic Teacher, 34*(3), 5–9.

*21. FOLSOM, M. (1975). Operations on whole number. In J. N. Payne (Ed.), *Mathematics learning in early childhood* (pp. 162–190). Reston, VA: National Council of Teachers of Mathematics.

22. FUSON, K. C. (1988). *Children's counting and concepts of number.* New York: Springer-Verlag.

23. FUSON, K. C. (1992). Research on whole number addition and subtraction. In D. Grouws (Ed.), *Handbook of research on mathematics teaching and learning* (pp. 243–275). New York: Macmillan.

24. FUSON, K. C., & BRIARS, D. J. (1990). Using a base-ten blocks learning/teaching approach for first- and second-grade place–value and multidigit addition and subtraction concepts. *Journal for Research in Mathematics Education, 21,* 180–206.

25. FUSON, K. C., & WILLIS, G. B. (1988). Subtracting by counting up: More evidence. *Journal for Research in Mathematics Education, 19,* 402–420.

26. GINSBURG, H. P. (1989). *Children's arithmetic* (2nd ed.). Austin, TX: Pro-Ed.

27. GINSBURG, H. P., POSNER, J. K., & RUSSELL, R. L. (1981). The development of mental addition as a function of schooling. *Journal of Cross-Cultural Psychology, 12,* 163–178.

*28. GROSSMAN, A. S. (1985). Subtraction algorithm: Upper grades. *Arithmetic Teacher, 32*(5), 44–47.

29. HIEBERT, J. (1984). Children's mathematics learning: The struggle to link form and understanding. *The Elementary School Journal, 84,* 497–513.

*30. HUGHES, M. (1986). *Children and number: Difficulties in learning mathematics.* New York: Basil Blackwell.

*31. IRONS, R. R., & IRONS, C. J. (1989). Language experiences: A base for problem solving. In P. R. Trafton & A. P. Shulte (Eds.), *New directions for elementary school mathematics* (pp. 85–98). Reston, VA: National Council of Teachers of Mathematics.

*32. JENCKS, S. M., & PECK, D. F. (1987). *Beneath rules.* Menlo Park, CA: Benjamin Cummings.

*33. KAMII, C. K. (1985). *Young children reinvent arithmetic.* New York: Teachers College Press.

*34. KAMII, C. K. (1989). *Young children continue to reinvent arithmetic—2nd grade.* New York: Teachers College Press.

*35. LABINOWICZ, E. (1985). *Learning from children: New beginnings for teaching numerical thinking.* Menlo Park, CA: Addison-Wesley.

*36. LAYCOCK, M. (1977). *Base-ten mathematics.* Hayward, CA: Activity Resources.

37. NATIONAL COUNCIL OF TEACHERS OF MATHEMATICS. (1989). *Curriculum and evaluation standards for school mathematics.* Reston, VA: Author.

38. PENGELLY, H. (1988, July–August). *Mathematical learning beyond the activity.* Paper presented at the International Conference on Mathematics Education (ICME 6), Budapest.

*39. RATHMELL, E. C. (1978). Using thinking strategies to teach basic facts. In M. N. Suydam & R. E. Reys (Eds.), *Developing computational skills* (pp. 13–50). Reston, VA: National Council of Teachers of Mathematics.

*40. RATHMELL E. C. HUINKER D. M. (1989) Using "part–whole" language to help children represent and solve word problems. In P. R. Trafton & A. P. Shulte (Eds.), *New directions for elementary school mathematics* (pp. 99–110). Reston, VA: National Council of Teachers of Mathematics.

41. RESNICK, L. B. (1982). Syntax and semantics in learning to subtract. In T. P. Carpenter, J. M. Moser, & T. A. Romberg (Eds.), *Addition and subtraction: A cognitive perspective* (pp. 136–155). Hillsdale, NJ: Erlbaum.

42. RESNICK, L. B. (1983). A developmental theory of numbers understanding. In H. P. Ginsburg (Ed.), *The development of mathematical thinking* (pp. 109–151). New York: Academic Press.

43. RESNICK, L. B., & FORD, W. W. (1981). *The psychology of mathematics for instruction.* Hillsdale, NJ: Erlbaum.

44. RESNICK, L. B., & OMANSON, S. F. (1987). Learning to understand arithmetic. In R. Glaser (Ed.), *Advances in instructional psychology* (Vol. 3, pp. 41–95). Hillsdale, NJ: Erlbaum.

45. RILEY, M. S., GREENO, J. G., & HELLER, J. I. (1983). Development of children's problem-solving activity in arithmetic. In H. P. Ginsburg (Ed.), *The development of mathematical thinking* (pp. 153–200). New York: Academic Press.

*46. ROSS, S. H. (1988). Parts, wholes, and place value: A developmental view. *Arithmetic Teacher, 36*(6), 47–51.

47. SECADA, W. G., FUSON, K. C., & HALL, J. (1983). The transition from counting-all to counting-on in addition. *Journal for Research in Mathematics Education, 14,* 47–57.

*48. STANIC, G. M. A., & McKILLIP, W. D. (1989). Developmental algorithms have a place in elementary school mathematics instruction. *Arithmetic Teacher, 36*(5), 14–16.

49. STEINBERG, R. M. (1985). Instruction on derived fact strategies in addition and subtraction. *Journal for Research in Mathematics Education, 16,* 337–355.

50. STIGLER, J. W., FUSON, K. C., HAM, M., & KIM, M. S. (1986). An analysis of addition and subtraction word problems in American and Soviet elementary mathematics textbooks. *Cognition and Instruction, 3,* 153–171.

*51. SUYDAM, M., & WEAVER, J. F. (1975). Research on mathematics learning. In J. N. Payne (Ed.), *Mathematics learning in early childhood* (37th Yearbook of the National Council of Teachers of Mathematics, pp. 43–67). Reston, VA: National Council of Teachers of Mathematics.

*52. THOMPSON, C., & VAN DE WALLE, J. (1980). Transition boards: Moving from materials to symbols in addition. *Arithmetic Teacher, 28*(4), 4–8.

*53. THOMPSON, C., & VAN DE WALLE, J. (1984). Let's do it: The power of 10. *Arithmetic Teacher, 32*(7), 6–11.

*54. THORNTON, C. A. (1990). Strategies for learning the basic facts. In J. Payne (Ed.), *Teaching and learning mathematics for the young child.* Reston, VA: National Council of Teachers of Mathematics.

*55. THORNTON, C. A., & SMITH, P. J. (1988). Action research: Strategies for learning subtraction facts. *Arithmetic Teacher, 35*(8), 8–12.

*56. THORNTON, C. A., & TOOHEY, M. A. (1985). Basic math facts: Guidelines for teaching and learning. *Learning Disabilities Focus, 1*(1), 44–57.

*57. VAN DE WALLE, J. (1990). *Elementary school mathematics: Teaching developmentally.* New York: Longman.

*58. WOOD, T., COBB, P., & YACKEL E. (1990). The contextual nature of teaching: Mathematics and reading instruction in one second-grade classroom. *Elementary School Journal, 90*(5), 497–513.

*59. WYNROTH, L. (1986). *Wynroth math program—The natural numbers sequence.* Ithaca, NY: Wynroth Math Program.

CHAPTER 5

Multiplication and Division: Sense Making and Meaning

Vicky L. Kouba and Kathy Franklin

When asked to find how many strawberries are needed for six cakes if three strawberries are put on each cake, one child carefully draws six cakes, then three strawberries on each cake and counts to find the total. Another child looks perplexed and asks, "Is it plus or minus?" Who is the more flexible thinker?

In a rush for abstraction and symbol manipulation, our mathematics curricula often move children rapidly through a conceptual understanding of multiplication and division. Unfortunately, children often lose their curiosity and understanding of mathematical relationships along the way. National and international (7, 15) studies show that our children perform as average, mechanical "whole-number calculators" rather than critical, involved thinkers.

> **Data from the 4th mathematics national assessment of educational progress**
> 77 percent of a sample of third graders correctly solved a symbolic division problem (12 divided by 3), but only 58 percent correctly solved the corresponding story problem. Similarly, 56 percent of those third graders were able to solve a symbolic multiplication problem (4 × 5) correctly, but only 32 percent solved the related story problem (15).

Thus, children behave in ways that indicate they believe the purpose of mathematics is quickly to identify operations and manipulate numbers rather than make sense of situations. This belief may have much to do with the documented (27) prevalence of the following immature strategies children use to solve word problems: (a) find the numbers and do an operation that has been done recently in class or that is comfortable; (b) just guess; (c) use the size of the numbers or some other superficial clue such as a "key word" to identify an operation; (d) try all the operations and choose the most reasonable answer; (e) base the operation on whether the answer should be larger or smaller than the numbers in the problem. These immature behaviors will persist until children's basic beliefs about mathematics change. Children need to see mathematics as making sense of situations.

Researchers and educators (5, 27) speculate that children's persistence in the use of immature strategies is inadvertently reinforced by three common characteristics of the typical mathematics classroom. First, the range of mathematical situations presented in classrooms and textbooks has been limited to a narrow set of simple, similarly structured story problems that seldom reflect daily life. Second, current mathematics education practices reward computing an answer rather than using the critical thinking processes of exploring, analyzing, interpreting, representing, hypothesizing, and verifying. Third, children have limited means for representing and solving situations. Recent research suggests ways teachers can counteract all three debilitating characteristics of mathematics classrooms.

Exposure to a Wider Range of Situations Is Needed

It is crucial that children in grades K–4 have experience with a wide range of multiplication and division situations. The range of situations should be expanded in the following ways.

Expand the Contexts of Situations

Teachers can help children develop greater facility with multiplication and division by routinely using situations from daily life and from other subject areas such as science, art, music, and social studies (8). Daily-life situations should include in-classroom and out-of-classroom situations. In the classroom children should help make decisions about sharing and distributing supplies, especially when many-to-one groupings or fractional partitionings need to be done. Many-to-one grouping experiences include deciding how many pairs of scissors are needed if three students share one pair, deciding on equal teams, or deciding how much money should be collected for a field trip if each person must pay $2.50. Fractional partitionings include deciding how the class should share five pizzas or three liters of soda, or deciding how to share the area for their desks fairly. Children may also organize objects into patterns and role-play buying and trading activities (see 31 for other examples).

Use daily applications
If ten children get five minutes each at the computer, how much time must we plan for? Will lunch time be long enough? What would happen if we used partners instead?

Experience with out-of-classroom situations help children see the connections between what they are learning about mathematics and how it is used. Children might keep a "journal" of how they see multiplication and division used. Entries might include personal or family experiences such as, "I needed seventy arcade tickets to get the two toys I wanted because thirty-five tickets were needed per toy;" or "It cost our family $23.20 to eat out because the buffet was $6.35 for each adult (two at $6.35) and $3.50 for each child (three at $3.50)." The journal also might include pictures or situations from magazines, newspapers, and catalogues depicting multiplication and division relationships, such as equal groupings or row-and-column arrays of objects.

Children should be encouraged to explore connections between multiplicative (multiplication and division) concepts and other subject areas (8). Examples include:

- In music, using beats per measure or "rhythm band" activities.
- In art, exploring the ratios of dabs of red to white paint in making different shades of red.
- In social studies, using map pins to show populations (one pin for every ten people), building scale models of neighborhoods, or finding out how many times taller than their houses or apartment buildings the Sears Tower is.
- In science, making or drawing proportional models of flowers, insects, or the like, exploring measurement relationships, or grouping data and making sampling predictions. (For example, "If we found 35 pieces of litter in one city block, how much litter covers our neighborhood?")

Expand the Range of Numbers from Whole to Fraction

Multiplication and division situations in grades K–4 are often limited just to whole number situations. This limitation does not reflect reality. It also leads children to conclude falsely that multiplication always makes the answer larger and division always makes the answer smaller (9). This, in turn, reinforces some of the immature strategies used by children (27). Children need hands-on experiences such as sharing three candy bars among six children or sharing two-and-a-half pizzas among nine children. These experiences emphasize the need to represent what is actually happening in a situation. They also give children the necessary background for visualizing and connecting symbolic sentences, (2 1/2 divided by 9) and (1/9 × 2 1/2), that appear in later grades.

Expand the Language

As part of a diverse experience, children also need to explore and develop the language used to describe and express multiplication and division situations. Many of the difficulties children have with multiplication and division relate to language (1).

Children often have difficulties with the language used in expressing many-to-one groupings in multiplication (33). Children who understand the statement "eight crayons in a box" may not understand "eight *per* box." Children need help in linking the various ways of describing multiplication and division to the interpretations and representations that make sense to them. *Per* is a particularly difficult term. Use a variety of terms as you and the children present and explain situations. Encourage the children to explain relationships in their own words and provide opportunities for them to practice the use of multiplicative language (group work, explanations of their thinking, presentations of projects to the whole class, etc.).

This does not mean using "key words" as a means for making sense of situations Using key words is a limiting, detrimental, strategy (27). Instead, model, encourage, and value (5):

- reflective reading and listening as a means of understanding the language of a situation
- use of thorough representation (physical, pictorial, and abstract)
- checking for reasonableness of each step in the interpretation, representation, and calculation related to a situation

---

The language of basic operations, such as the terms *factor, multiple, product,* and *quotient,* should be introduced and used informally in work with operations. Children can find the factors of a number using tiles or graph paper. This can lead to an investigation of numbers that have only two factors (prime numbers) and numbers with two equal factors (square numbers). (8, p. 42)

Expand the "Types" of Situations

Recent research (6, 23) has shown that teachers can provide a wider and better-sequenced range of situations if they have knowledge of the distinctions among situations and knowledge of some of the difficulties that arise related to the different situations. Many different ways of categorizing multiplication and division situations have been described in the mathematics education literature (21, 32). However, recent consensus points to organizing multiplication and division situations under two broad categories (4): "asymmetrical situations" and "symmetrical situations." The distinction between the two lies in the roles that the numbers play in the situation and the resulting division problems within each category.

Asymmetrical Situations.   These situations are called *asymmetric* because the numbers that are the factors have different labels and play different roles from each other. There are three types of asymmetric problems: grouping, rate, and scalar (see Fig. 5.1).

Grouping and rate situations have one number that states the number of elements in a set or establishes a unit ratio (for example, eight crayons per box, a pencil costs four cents). The other number or factor in grouping and rate problems states "how many sets" there are (eleven boxes, seven pencils in Fig. 5.1) and functions as the multiplier. The roles of the numbers are not interchangeable. Two boxes with eight crayons in each box is not the same as eight boxes with two crayons in each box.

FIGURE 5.1   Asymmetric situations

GROUPING PROBLEM:
Tara has 11 boxes of crayons. There are 8 in each box. How many crayons does she have in all?

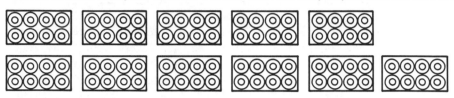

RATE PROBLEM:
Jerry bought 7 pencils that cost 4 cents apiece. How much did he pay (before taxes)?

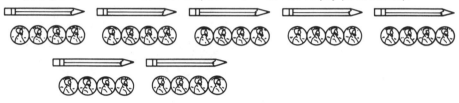

SCALAR PROBLEM:
Cory has 3 times as many sea shells as Sheila. Cory has 12 shells. How many sea shells does Sheila have?

In many grouping situations there is a word that implies a group, such as "boxes" in "eight crayons per box" and "plates" and "teams" in the following problems:

> I have 6 plates. Each plate has 7 cookies on it. How many cookies do I have in all?

> Five teams are playing in the tournament. Each team has 10 players. How many players are involved in the tournament?

Because we know crayons are placed in a box, we know we are relating *many* crayons to *one* box, not relating many boxes to one crayon.

The language in rate situations is not as clear as in grouping situations (14, 21). For example, consider:

> In our class there are 3 boys for every girl. If there are 9 girls in the class, how many boys are there?

Many children have trouble deciding whether the problem is represented as "many boys to one girl" or "many girls to one boy." There is no grouping word to provide a contextual clue.

Children who are successful at solving rate situations similar to the boy–girl problem rely on a matching representation rather than a grouping representation. They draw a picture or use objects to match three objects (boys) to one object (girls) (13). Thus, children may benefit from making and discussing many kinds of physical and pictorial representations for many-to-one relationships.

Because their factors are not interchangeable, scalar situations also are asymmetric. One factor states the number in a set (Sheila has twelve pencils), while the other is the number of sets (three times as many) and functions as the multiplier. Most children solve this problem by adding three twelves. Although researchers have not looked at scalar situations in depth, it is clear that understanding how to represent the situation is as important as with other situations. Children need a great deal of physical experience and guidance in understanding and modeling scalar problems, because they don't have a clear idea of what the statement "Corey had three times as many as Sheila" means. Listening to and observing children seems to be the best approach to identifying the guidance and experiences they need to make connections. For example, children who have difficulty with "five times as many" can physically trace their height along a hallway five times as a way to represent the problem "How tall is a giant that is five times as tall as you?" (for more on scalar situations see 10).

Because the factors in grouping, rate, and scalar situations are not interchangeable in function, two types of division problems are possible: measurement division, when the unknown is the number of groups (the multiplier); and partitive division when the unknown is the number of elements in each group or rate.

Young children are competent and creative at modeling both division situations. However, they represent measurement division problems differently from partitive division problems (14). To solve the measurement division problem of eighty-eight crayons grouped eight crayons to a box, many young children will count out eighty-eight crayons and then make groups of eight until the pool of eighty-eight crayons is used up. To solve the partitive division problem of 88 crayons placed equally into 11 boxes about half the children will use a Systematic Trial-and-Error Strategy (Fig. 5.2). They will count out the eighty-eight crayons, guess at the number that would go into a box and see if grouping by that guess results in eleven groups. If the result isn't eleven groups, they will try a reasonable second guess, and so on. The other half of the children will try a Dealing-Out Strategy (Fig. 5.3). They will deal out the eighty-eight crayons one-by-one to eleven groups and count the number in one group to calculate the answer.

Some children may use a building-up approach in conjunction with either the Systematic Trial-and-Error or the Dealing-Out Strategy (14). They do not begin by forming a set of eighty-eight, but decide on a grouping to test or deal out, and perform that action while keeping a running count of the total objects put into groups or dealt out. They stop when the count reaches eighty-eight. This strategy is quite close in structure to strategies used when making sense of multiplication and may be used to advantage in linking division to multiplication. Children should be encouraged to use the strategies that make sense to them, but also to share and try to understand other children's approaches.

FIGURE 5.2   Systematic Trial-and-Error Strategy for partitive division (88 crayons put equally into 11 boxes—how many in one box?)

FIGURE 5.3   Dealing-Out Strategy for partitive division (88 crayons put equally into 11 boxes—how many are in one box?)

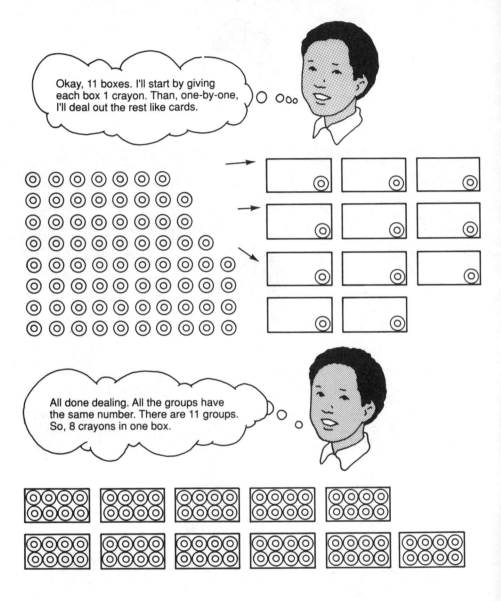

"When I've encouraged children to use the process that works for them, I don't see as much frustration, but rather a group of children who feel good about themselves enjoying math."

—K. Franklin

Symmetrical Situations. Symmetrical situations are those having factors with interchangeable roles. That is, it doesn't matter within the context of the situation which factor is the multiplier. The most common examples of symmetric situations are area and cross-product:

> (Area story problem). Alvinia's desk is 5 decimeters by 6 decimeters. What is the area of Alvinia's desk in square decimeters?

> (Cross-product). A deli that sells sandwiches made with one slice of meat and one slice of cheese has 3 kinds of meat (ham, turkey, and beef) and 2 kinds of cheese (Swiss and provolone). How many different meat and cheese sandwiches can the deli sell?

Because symmetric situations have no factor that is clearly the multiplier, they have only one type of division, a "missing factor" division. Symmetric situations make sense when they are represented by area models, arrays, rows-and-columns, or similar chart-type relationships.

Thus, children should have experience with sets, measurements, arrays, charts, pairings, tree diagrams, simple number lines, simple area models, number rods (Cuisenaire Rods), and many-to-one matching representations. Research indicates (13) that children function best when they experience a variety of representations for all multiplication and division situations and can model and explain the relationships among those representations.

Reward for Critical Thinking Is Needed

Our current mathematics education practices reward computations and answers, not exploring, analyzing, interpreting, representing, hypothesizing, and verifying. What children see happening in the mathematics classroom is what they think mathematics is (16). If multiplication and division are taught and tested as facts and algorithms to be unquestioningly memorized and used rapidly to produce a numerical answer (27), what incentive do children have for engaging in critical thinking? Research offers some suggestions for change.

Build from the Children's Knowledge

One key to getting children to think critically is getting them to value their own thinking and knowledge base. Thus, teachers must acknowledge and build instruction upon the knowledge base that children have. Children can and do use different, although limited, levels of representations to make sense of multiplication and division situations. They are able to do this before they have been formally introduced to multiplication and division, before they have memorized any multiplication facts, and before they know the words or formal symbols for multiplication (3, 14, and 30).

FIGURE 5.4   Multiplication is the inverse of division

Multiplication
There are 4 boxes with 3 hats in each. How many hats altogether?

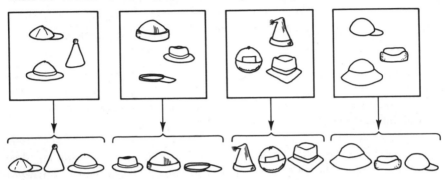

Division
You have 12 hats to put in boxes. If you put 3 hats in each box, how many boxes do you need?

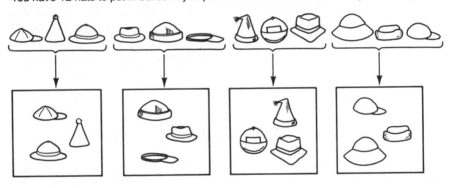

Strong evidence suggests that conceptual approaches to computation instruction result in good achievement, good retention, and a reduction in the amount of time children need to master computational skills. (8, p. 44)

Not all children in a classroom will be ready or able to represent and solve multiplication and division problems in the same way at the same time. Nor will all children follow the same developmental sequence in making sense of multiplication and division. However, research (1, 3, 14) suggests that teachers can make use of the following hypothesized developmental progress of thinking strategies.

Thinking Strategies.   Many children first make sense of multiplication and division situations by using representations related to counting, addition, and subtraction. They begin by physically modeling what is occurring in the situation (1, 3, 14). For example, for the situation, "If there are eight plates with four cookies on each plate, how many cookies are there in all?" children set out eight plates and put four cookies (or objects to represent cookies) on each plate. Then they count the total number of cookies. Many children progress to being able to make eight groups of four without having to use separate objects for the eight plates. Next, they are able to make one group of four and count it repeatedly eight times. When doing so they keep track of how many groups they have counted by using their fingers or some other memory device (such as nodding the head, seeing or writing tally marks, or rhythmic counting).

The physical modeling done at these progressively more sophisticated levels of representation provide a concrete basis for beginning to explore the relationships between multiplication and division. The final arrangement of the physical materials usually is the same for multiplication and division situations (that is, in equal groups). The teacher may ask why that is so or may ask the children to explore a related division situation immediately after working with a multiplication situation (Fig. 5.4).

More advanced levels of representation include counting by fours, counting on when they can't recall the next multiple (four, eight, . . . nine, ten, eleven, twelve, etc.), adding fours, and using derived facts such as "four groups of four are sixteen and sixteen plus sixteen is thirty-two." Although not all children advance through all stages, an examination of how a child solves a specific situation can give the teacher some idea of that child's level of sophistication in solving and whether he or she may be ready for a more advanced level. Advancement may be achieved by having the child compare his or her approach with someone's at the next level, by a well-planned question or sequence of questions prepared by the teacher, or by suggesting a useful strategy such as skip counting. The teacher might challenge the child to find a different way to solve the problem by providing a well-planned series of "discovery" activities or by having the child analyze a teacher demonstration (23).

Importance of Skip Counting.   Being able to use counting sequences other than counting by ones appears to be one of the keys in moving from one level of representation to another. Thus, in second and third grade, children may benefit from practice in counting forwards and backwards by multiples of numbers (skip counting). They usually have "picked-up," through classroom instruction or experiences at home, counting by twos and by fives. Practice in learning to count by threes, fours, and sixes also may prove useful when learning multiplication facts. Children may practice skip counting as a natural outgrowth of exploring and coloring patterns on the hundred chart, which has the numbers from 1 to 100 arrayed. Research (26) indicates that activities with the hundred chart not only intrigue children, but later help them to remember the answers to multiplication facts (Fig. 5.5).

Also, the calculator can be employed effectively to help learn skip counting (26). Repeated addition or counting by multiples is easy to perform using a calculator. For example, entering 5, +, 5, =, =, =, =, . . . generates a display of the multiples of five. Similarly, the writing of simple computer programs to print out multiples not only gives children another perspective on multiples, but also can be used by children for investigating patterns and exploring multiples of numbers other than whole numbers (1).

FIGURE 5.5   Using a hundred chart
             to explore multiples of
             four

1	2	3	■	5	6	7	■	9	10
11	■	13	14	15	■	17	18	19	■
21	22	23	■	25	26	27	■	29	30
31	■	33	34	35	■	37	38	39	■
41	42	43	■	45	46	47	■	49	50
51	■	53	54	55	■	57	58	59	■
61	62	63	■	65	66	67	■	69	70
71	■	73	74	75	■	77	78	79	■
81	82	83	■	85	86	87	■	89	90
91	■	93	94	95	■	97	98	99	■

1 TO 100 CHART _____

Emphasize Active Involvement

If children are to be critical thinkers, then they need to be actively involved in the learning of multiplication and division. The use of "hands-on" materials to develop concepts has been stressed for decades and remains important. However, other means for involving children have also proved successful.

> "It's exciting as a teacher to watch children use manipulative materials to develop their own algorithms. It's even more exciting to see the variety of different algorithms children discover when allowed and encouraged to be creative."
> —K. Franklin

Student-Written Problems.   The NCTM *Curriculum and Evaluation Standards for School Mathematics* (8) recommends emphasizing mathematics as a means for communication. Children benefit from making up (telling and writing) their own stories that can be modeled by the operations of multiplication and division situations. These activities reinforce the importance of knowing the multiplication and division facts and help establish links between operations and their applications (12, 22).

Student-Derived Algorithms.   Children should be actively involved in devising their own algorithms for solving multiplication and division problems. Research indicates that no single algorithm is the "right" algorithm to teach. In fact, recent research on addition and subtraction indicates that having children create their own large-number computational algorithms may be most advisable (6). This holds true for multiplication and division as well (17, 18).

The research also shows that to understand any two-digit multiplication or division algorithm children should have knowledge and understanding of place value, the

FIGURE 5.6   Measurement division developmental algorithm

"$220 was raised by a scout troop to buy tickets to a professional baseball game. If tickets cost $7 each, how many tickets could be purchased?"

. . . If 1 ticket costs $7 then 10 tickets cost $70 so . . .

```
  $220
- $ 70   . . . that's 10 tickets
  $150
- $ 70   . . . and 10 more
  $ 80
- $ 70   . . . and 10 more
  $ 10
- $  7   . . . and 1 more
  $  3   . . . so 31 tickets with $3 left over for snacks at the game
```

patterns resulting from multiplying by 10 and 100, and the basic multiplication facts, their meanings, and their properties (1).

> "We unintentionally err as teachers by not helping children develop links between physical, pictorial, and symbolic representations. Now that I do more of this, it's exciting to help children put the physical model and symbolic notation together and hear them say, 'I got it!'"
>
> —K. Franklin

Several researchers (1, 17, and 29) recommend the use of "developmental algorithms" (Fig. 5.6) that children build for themselves from their understanding and use of estimation, place value, multiplication by 10 and by 100, and the decomposition of numbers (for example, seeing 46 as four 10s and one 6 or as two 20s and six 1s). As with any algorithms, the children should be able to explain what they are doing. They should be able to demonstrate the validity of their algorithms by manipulating physical or pictorial objects. The physical materials that appear most effective in helping children make sense of multiplication and division algorithms are base-ten blocks (or similar manipulatives) and arrays (rows and columns) of objects (1). Finally, children should be able to link any symbolic notation directly to representations (26). An example is given in Figure 5.7. The combined use of the physical and pictorial models with the developmental algorithms should extend for more than just a few examples or exercises.

FIGURE 5.7   Connecting a solution using base 10 blocks with a developmental algorithm for multiplication

"Maria's class collected 69 pounds of aluminum cans on each of the first three days of their recycling drive. How many pounds of aluminum does this amount to?"

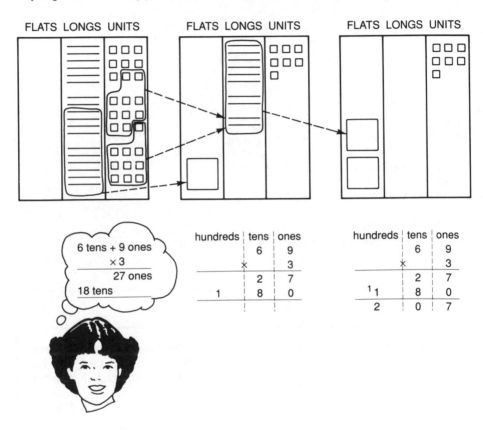

Using developmental or informal algorithms does take time. However, spending more time on developmental algorithms pays off in the long run by saving time on the practice of rules and by increasing children's understanding and motivation (18).

Assess More Than a Numerical Answer

Assessment must involve more than checking whether children have the correct answer, because children can get a "right" answer without understanding procedures (29). A more reliable check is whether they can explain, in their own words, why and how the procedure works. The use of children's explanations as an assessment measure is consistent with current recommendations for assessing children's problem solving skills (5). Children should be encouraged to look at why something works the way it does in mathematics, especially when examining patterns in number facts and in algorithms (31). The physical and pictorial work that children do to give meaning to the operations should provide the basis for their explanations of why algorithms work. Thus, the children should have some way physically and pictorially to model whichever multiplication algorithm they use. They also should be able to explain how the models match both the symbolic form of the algorithm and the conceptual knowledge they already have (11, 25).

> Children need more time to explore and to invent alternative strategies for computing mentally. Both mental computation and estimation should be ongoing emphases that are integrated throughout all computational work and assessment. (8, p. 45)

Assessment alternatives such as observations, interviews, and questions requiring children to explain the "whys" of their actions are being tried, with success, in some programs (6, 23). Other alternatives such as student portfolios including writing samples, open-ended questions, and student self-assessment have been successfully piloted by other teachers (2). Use of these methods requires careful planning by the teacher and cooperation by the administration on issues of testing.

Variety and Flexibility of Representations Is Needed

Often children persist in the use of immature strategies because they have insufficient means for representing situations (27). They may rely on too narrow a set of representations rather than working from a large, flexible structure across the usual five systems of representation, which are (20):

1. experienced-based scripts in which knowledge is organized around real world events that serve as general contexts for interpreting related and unrelated situations
2. manipulative models in which knowledge is organized around actions with physical materials
3. pictorial or figural models in which knowledge is organized around diagrams or images
4. spoken language
5. written symbols.

Building a repertoire of systems of representation takes time and careful planning. Children need experience with a variety of situations, knowledge of the nature of those situations, and ways of thinking that link representations across situations and operations. Research offers some suggestions for doing so.

Expand Experiences with Situations

At the same time that teachers increase the variety of multiplication and division situations children encounter, they must also insure that many of the situations are easily associated with different physical and pictorial representations (4, 6, 19, 23, 24). Suggested situations and their related representation are given in Figure 5.8.

Discourse activities, activities that employ student-to-student talk and student-dominated student-to-teacher talk, help children build knowledge about and links between situations and representations (17, 19). One successful approach (19) in-

FIGURE 5.8 Situations and pictorial representations

ARRAYS
A jumbo case of bottles has 8 rows of 6 bottle each. How many bottles does the case hold?

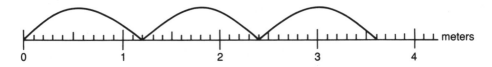

NUMBER LINES
Joan made 3 hops of 1.2 meters each. How far did she hop?

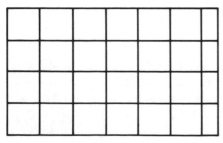

AREA
A patio of 4 meters by 6.5 meters has an area of how many square meters?

FIGURE 5.8 *(Continued)*

CHARTS
How many animal costumes, real or strange, could you make from 3 fronts and 3 backs?

BACKS	FRONTS		
	ele	par	po
phant	elephant	parphant	pophant
rot	elerot	parrot	porot
ny	eleny	parny	pony

PAIRINGS
I have 2 different balls and 3 different bats. How many different ball-bat pairs can I make?

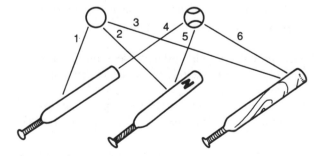

volved a series of activities. In essence, the children solved situations and then, in small groups, discussed their actions, the results of their actions, and the reasons for their actions. Next, they used the results of those discussions to reevaluate their bases for deciding how best to make sense of situations. Likewise, student-dominated, large-group discussion approaches were successful (17). The large-group discussions centered on children's responses to situations such as "Using only two kinds of coins, make $1.00 using 19 coins" (17, p. 316).

The keys to success with these kinds of discourse activities, appear to be:

- Discourse is centered on child-generated actions and ideas and the children are the main participants.
- Discourse is facilitated by the teacher so that all ideas, even incorrect ones are critically examined by all participants.
- Emphasis is on the structure of the situations (many-to-one groupings, relationships of numbers to labels, kinds of groupings or partitionings, reasonableness and use of answers especially for division situations involving remainders).
- Discourse is linked to previous experiences with physical and pictorial models as consensus is negotiated (17, 25).
- Attention is paid to the language associated with a fairly well-defined range of multiplication and division situations (19).

"It is my experience that children often learn more from discussion of incorrect responses than from correct ones."

—K. Franklin

Be Cautious with Symbolic Representations

Only after children have had ample experience with describing, representing, and exploring multiplication and division situations (physically and pictorially) does it make sense to introduce the writing of abstract number sentences. Research on children-generated story problems indicates that they don't have a clear understanding of how the numbers in a symbolic sentence are related to the objects in a situation (13, 24). The teacher must help the children make these connections. An example of how to move from pictorial representation to symbolic representation is given in Figure 5.9.

An important instructional practice that can help children link symbols to physical, pictorial, and language representations is to include the labels for the objects as part of the symbolic sentence (13), as was done in Figure 5.9.

Children's understanding of the relationships between pictorial representations and symbolic representations can be reinforced by exploring commutative relationships, as in Figure 5.10.

Understanding may also be reinforced by exploring examples that, on the surface, do not appear to be multiplicative in nature. For example, as shown in Figure 5.11,

FIGURE 5.9 Moving from pictorial to symbolic representations

PROBLEM
3 clowns each have 5 balloons. How many balloons are there in all?

Representing problem with a picture

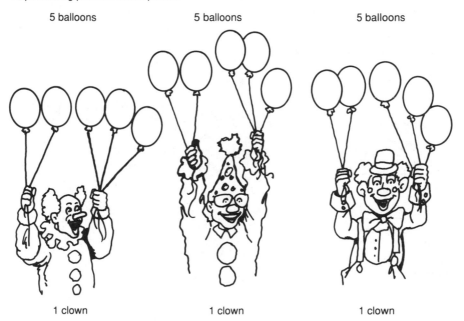

REPLACING PICTURE WITH LABELS AND ADDITION SYMBOLS

5 balloons + 5 balloons + 5 balloons = 3 groups of 5 balloons or 15 balloons

1 clown + 1 clown + 1 clown = 3 clowns each with 5 balloons

DESCRIBING IN "GROUPING" LANGUAGE
3 clowns each with 5 balloons is 15 balloons in all.

DESCRIBING IN WORDS USING MULTIPLICATION SYMBOLS
3 clowns × balloons per clown = balloons.

the picture of four clowns with unequal numbers of balloons may be represented by an addition sentence and by a more complex sentence using multiplication and addition. This type of flexibility in reasoning is possible if children have learned to examine and analyze situations carefully. Success also depends on having had practice in representing situations in as many ways as possible.

FIGURE 5.10   Examples of commutativity in multiplication

If 3 boxes have 5 bulbs each, how many bulbs in all?

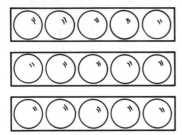

If 5 boxes have 3 bulbs each, how many bulbs in all?

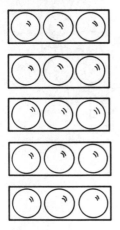

There are 5½ sacks of flour with 2 pounds in each sack. How many pounds of flour in all?

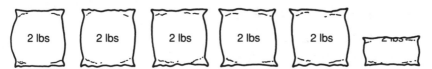

There are 2 sacks of flour with 5½ pounds in each sack. How many pounds of flour in all?

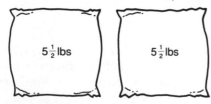

FIGURE 5.11 Flexibility in analyzing and representing a situation

"Look at the clowns. How many balloons in all?" Express with symbols.

One approach uses addition:

3 balloons + 5 balloons + 3 balloons + 4 balloons = 15 balloons

An inciteful reanalysis results in a multiplicative approach:

3 balloons + (3 balloons and 2 balloons) + 3 balloons + (3 balloons and 1 balloon) = 15 balloons
    WHICH IS:
(4 groups of 3 balloons) + 2 balloons + 1 balloon
    OR
(4 × 3) + 2 + 1 = 15

Conclusion

Overall, the research results imply that at grades K–4 the emphasis within the arithmetic strand of mathematics instruction should be on helping children develop a sound and varied conceptual basis for giving meaning to multiplication and division situations, rather than on either rushing into the memorization of multiplication facts or using those facts to solve symbolic problems in narrowly prescribed ways (one- and two-digit multiplication and division standard algorithms). As we provide an environment for this development of understanding, we need (a) to give children a rich communicative experience with a variety of multiplication and division situations, (b) to evaluate and reward more than just producing an answer quickly in a prescribed way, and (c) to help children build from their own experiences and understandings a variety of ways to represent and model multiplication and division situations.

Looking Ahead . . .

Researchers will need to sort out further which combinations of situations, experiences, representations, and models for multiplication and division will enable K–4 children to better avoid misconceptions about operations with rational numbers and direct and inverse proportions. Research should help identify which instructional experiences enable children to see that the focal point or reason for learning mathematics is not to be able to answer the question, "Is it plus, minus, times, or divide?" but to provide a mathematical means for exploring, elaborating on, and building meaning within the real world and the children's imaginations.

Vicky L. Kouba

Will teachers be motivated to change their instructional strategies to encourage students' creativity and critical thinking as long as school districts continue to administer standardized tests that primarily assess our students' ability to compute? Do colleges recognize the need to update their teacher education programs? Do school district administrators recognize the need for staff development and inservice education in elementary school mathematics in order that our teachers are knowledgeable and understand the most current mathematical research?

Kathy Franklin

About the Authors

Vicky Kouba is assistant professor in mathematics education at the State University of New York—Albany. Her research interests include children's acquisition of concepts and beliefs about mathematics.

Kathy Franklin is an elementary mathematics specialist who teaches at Shenendehowa Central Schools, Clifton Park, New York. Her interests include the effective use of manipulatives in mathematics.

References

*1. ANGHILERI, J., & JOHNSON, D. C. (1988). Arithmetic operations on whole numbers: Multiplication and division. In T. R. Post (Ed.), *Teaching mathematics in grades K–8: Research based methods* (pp. 146–189). Boston: Allyn & Bacon.

2. ASSESSMENT ALTERNATIVES IN MATHEMATICS (1989). Berkeley, CA: Project EQUALS and the Assessment Committee of the California Mathematics Council.

*3. BAROODY, A. J. (1987). *Children's mathematical thinking.* New York: Teachers College, Columbia University.

4. BELL, A., GREER, B., GRIMSON, L., & MANGAN, C. (1989). Children's performance on multiplicative word problems: Elements of a descriptive theory. *Journal for Research in Mathematics Education, 20*(5), 434–449.

5. CHARLES, R. I., & SILVER, E. A. (1988). *The teaching and assessing of mathematical problem solving.* Reston, VA: NCTM & Lawrence Erlbaum.

6. COBB, P., YACKEL, E., & WOOD, T. (1988). Curriculum and teacher development: Psychological and anthropological perspectives. In E. Fennema, T. P. Carpenter, & S.

J. Lamon (Eds.), *Integrating research on teaching and learning mathematics* (pp. 92–130). Madison: Wisconsin Center for Education Research.

7. CROSSWHITE, F. J., DOSSEY, J. A., SWAFFORD, J. O., McKNIGHT, C. C., & COONEY, T. J., (1985). *Second International Mathematics Study summary report for the United States.* Champaign, IL: Stipes.

*8. CURRICULUM AND EVALUATION STANDARDS FOR SCHOOL MATHEMATICS (1989). Reston, VA: National Council of Teachers of Mathematics.

9. GREER, B. (1988). Nonconservation of multiplication and division: Analysis of a symptom. *Journal of Mathematical Behavior,* 7(3), 281–298.

*10. HENDRICKSON, A. D. (1986). Verbal multiplication and division problems: Some difficulties and some solutions. *Arithmetic Teacher,* 33(8), 26–33.

11. HIEBERT, J. (1989). The struggle to link written symbols with understandings: An update *Arithmetic Teacher,* 36(7), 38–44.

*12. HOSMER, P. C. (1986) Students can write their own problems. *Arithmetic Teacher,* 34(4) 10–11.

13. KAPUT, J. J. (1989). Supporting concrete visual thinking in multiplicative reasoning: Difficulties and opportunities. *Focus on Learning Problems in Mathematics,* 11(1), 35–47.

14. KOUBA, V. L. (1989). Children's solution strategies for equivalent set multiplication and division word problems. *Journal for Research in Mathematics Education,* 20(2), 147–158.

15. KOUBA, V.L., BROWN, C. A., CARPENTER, T. P., LINDQUIST, M. M., SILVER, E. A., & SWAFFORD, J. O. (1988). Results of the fourth NAEP assessment of mathematics: Number, operations, and word problems. *Arithmetic Teacher,* 35(8), 10–16.

16. KOUBA, V. L., & McDONALD, J. L. (1987). Students' perceptions of mathematics as a domain. In J. C. Bergeron, N. Herscovics, & C. Kieran (Eds.), *Psychology of Mathematics Education, PME-XI,* Vol. 1 (pp. 106–112). Montreal: University of Montreal.

17. LAMPERT, M. (1986). Knowing, doing, and teaching multiplication. *Cognition and Instruction,* 3(4), 305–342.

*18. LAMPERT, M. (1989) Research into practice: Arithmetic as problem solving. *Arithmetic Teacher* 36(7) 34–36.

19. LEMOYNE, G., & TREMBLAY, C. (1986). Addition and multiplication: Problem solving and interpretation of relevant data. *Educational Studies in Mathematics,* 17, 97–123.

20. LESH, R., POST, T., & BEHR, M. (1987). Representations and translations among representations in mathematics learning and problem solving. In C. Janvier (Ed.) *Problems of representation in teaching and learning of mathematics* (pp. 33–40). Hillsdale, NJ: Erlbaum.

21. NESHER, P. (1988). Multiplicative school word problems: Theoretical Approaches and empirical findings. In J. Hiebert & M. Behr (Eds.), *Number concepts and operations in the middle grades* (pp. 19–40). Reston, VA: National Council of Teachers of Mathematics and Erlbaum.

22. PELED, I., & NESHER, P. (1988). What children tell us about multiplication word problems. *Journal of Mathematical Behavior,* 7(3), 239–262.

23. PETERSON, P. L., CARPENTER, T. P., & FENNEMA, E. (1989). Teachers' knowledge of students' knowledge in mathematics problem solving. *Journal of Educational Psychology,* 81(4), 558–569.

*24. QUINTERO, A. H. (1986). Children's conceptual understanding of situations involving multiplication. *Arithmetic Teacher,* 33(5), 34–37.

25. RESNICK, L. B., & FORD, W. W. (1981). *The psychology of mathematics instruction.* Hillsdale, NJ: Erlbaum.

*26. SCHULTZ, K. A., COLARUSSO, R. P., & STRAWDERMAN, V. W. (1989) *Mathematics for every young child*. Columbus OH: Merrill.

27. SOWDER, L. (1988) Children's solutions of story problems. *Journal of Mathematical Behavior*, 7(3), 227–238.

*28. SPIKER, J., & KURTZ, R.. (1987). Teaching primary-grade mathematics skills with calculators. *Arithmetic Teacher*, 34(6), 24–27.

*29. STANIC, G. M. A., & McKILLIP, W. D. (1989). Developmental algorithms have a place in elementary school mathematics instruction. *Arithmetic Teacher*, 36(5), 14–16.

30. STEFFE, L. P. (1988). Children's construction of number sequences and multiplying schemes. In J. Hiebert & M. Behr (Eds.), *Number concepts and operations in the middle grades* (pp. 119–140). Reston, VA: National Council of Teachers of Mathematics and Erlbaum.

*31. WHITIN, D. J. (1989). Number sense and the importance of asking "why?" *Arithmetic Teacher*, 36(6), 26–29.

*32. USISKIN, Z., & BELL, M. (1983). *Applying Arithmetic: A Handbook of Applications of Arithmetic*. Chicago, The University of Chicago.

*33. ZWENG, M. J. (1984). Division problems and the concept of rate. *Arithmetic Teacher*, 11, 547–556.

CHAPTER 6

Early Development of Number Sense

John A. Van de Walle and Karen Bowman Watkins

Number sense can be described as good intuition about numbers and their relationships. It develops gradually as a result of exploring numbers, visualizing them in a variety of contexts, and relating them in ways that are not limited by traditional algorithms. . . . No substitute exists for a skillful teacher and an environment that fosters curiosity and exploration at all grade levels (21, p.11).

An "intuition about numbers" is something that we recognize in students who seem to be especially clever with mental computation or who exhibit a comfort with numbers in real world contexts. This intuition is recognizable yet difficult to pinpoint exactly. The NCTM *Standards* document defines *number sense* as an intuition about numbers that involves five interrelated components: (1) number meanings, (2) number relationships, (3) relative magnitude of numbers, (4) relative effect of operations on numbers, and (5) meaningful referents for numbers and quantities (12).

> Number sense—
>   is nonalgorithmic
>   tends to be complex
>   often yields multiple solutions, each with costs and benefits, rather than unique
>   solutions
>   involves nuanced judgment and interpretation
>   involves the application of multiple criteria
>   often involves uncertainty
>   invoves self-regulation of the thinking process
>   involves imposing meaning
>   is effortful (36, p. 37)

While the *Standards* definition is useful for describing number sense, neither the curriculum nor the research literature is organized around these five components. The first section in this chapter explores several aspects of early number relationships that seem to contribute to the "intuition about numbers" described by the *Standards*. The second section examines the value of children discussing their invented ideas about numbers and operations. The final two sections consider the limited research related to mental computation and computational estimation in the early childhood years. These two related skills are not only dependent on a rich understanding of numbers, but seem to contribute to that understanding as numbers are combined and separated in flexible ways (43).

Early Number Relationships

Most children come to kindergarten with some counting skills, and many can count sets of up to ten objects (1). The traditional curriculum has tended to refine these mechanical counting skills, moving almost immediately to addition and subtraction activities. This early attention to addition and subtraction skills could profitably be delayed. In the early years, children require time with activities designed to help them construct a variety of number relationships. These relationships, the essence of number sense at this level, provide an important foundation for mastery of basic facts, mental computation, and a general facility with numbers.

More-than/Less-than Relationships

Children who know without recourse to counting that seven is two less than nine and one more than six, possess a powerful idea useful in many situations with numbers. If a group of seven objects has been counted and then one is removed, the one-less-than relationship indicates the number remaining without the need to count again. Counting, within the right types of games and activities, can help children focus on the important ideas of one- or two-more-than (or less-than). The same relationship proves useful in relating 5 + 5 to 5 + 6 (27). In a card game called "Double War" each player turns up two cards instead of one as in the familiar version of "War." Children initially count all of the marks on both cards to determine the winner, but soon begin to focus on comparisons among the cards. If a 2 and a 7 are turned up against a 4 and a 6, they may notice that the 6 is only one less than 7 while the 4 is two more than 2. Children begin to look for these and similar relationships rather than simply count all of the marks to compare totals (23).

For a variety of activities and games in which children learn relationships between numbers through counting activities (see 21, 28, and 51). Many of these suggestions use counters in constructing sets that are one or two more than or less than a given set. In the process of constructing these sets children not only count but make repeated comparisons between the given and the new amount. Each comparison and adjustment of the set being constructed provides another opportunity for the child to reflect on the more/less relationships between two quantities (23).

Relationships to Five and Ten

There is evidence indicating that it is useful to think about numbers in terms of five and ten (11, 45). We have five fingers on our hands and two sets of five make ten, the base of our number system. The idea is to think of seven as five and two more and also as three less than ten. For example, when adding 9 + 6, it is useful to think, "9 and 1 more is 10 and that leaves 5 more." Japanese children have been observed to use thought processes like this more frequently than American children do, and do so more spontaneously without specific instruction in the strategy (17, 26). One plausible explanation for this is that the Japanese rely heavily on a set of tiles consisting of bars and squares as a model for numbers (Fig. 6.1). Each bar is as long as five squares. The number 8 is shown with a bar and three squares. The tiles clearly show that eight is two away from ten and three more than five. Activities with pictures of these tiles and with the tiles themselves can be found in (23) and (51).

Mathematics educators (48, 51, 52) have had considerable success with ten-frames as a model for numbers. The ten-frame helps children construct the same type of relationship as the Japanese tiles. When two frames are used with counters, children are able to model addition and subtraction combinations and capitalize on the five and ten anchors as described earlier (Fig. 6.2).

Relationships to Real Quantities

Another type of "feel" for numbers is the ability to judge or estimate a quantity. Is a randomly arranged set of fourteen objects closer to ten or to twenty-five? Given a set of objects, about how many are there? Very little research has been done concerning how well children make these estimates or how we might help them develop an ability to estimate. One study with 4 and 5 year olds indicates that children can begin to judge if a set of objects is more or less than a specific reference number such as 5, 10, or 20 (2). Children do need help estimating set sizes (Fig. 6.3). Kindergarten children should begin with sets of four to twelve items, and then these amounts

FIGURE 6.1   Japanese number tiles

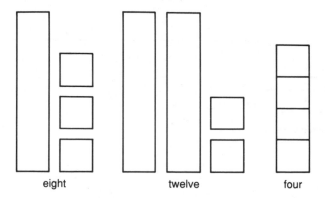

eight   twelve   four

FIGURE 6.2   Ten-frames

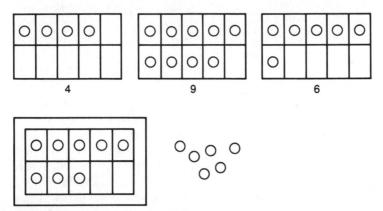

Counters on constuction paper ten-frame

should then be extended into the twenties or thirties. Kindergarten children can also begin to judge which of two displayed sets was closer to a given number (42).

Research suggests that the use of one or two reference points ("Is this more or less than ten? Is this less than ten, between ten and twenty, or more than twenty?") is quite useful in helping children develop and refine their number sense. Asking children to provide their own estimate of a quantity requires that they judge the quantity

FIGURE 6.3   Two early estimation activities

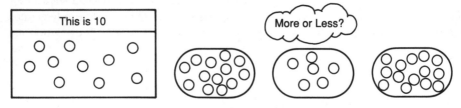

Caption: Show each set briefly on the overhead next to the reference set.

Ask if the new set is more or less than 10.

This stick is 10 cm long.

Estimate these lengths. Use the rod to help.
  (a) elbow to finger tip
  (b) around the flower pot
  (c) height of the door knob
  (d) distance between your eyes

and also decide on an approximate representation to offer as an estimate. Activities without reference points provide children no guidance concerning the types of numbers that are useful approximations for a particular quantity.

> "We see what we understand rather than understand what we see." (28)

For numbers above fifty, children have very few reference points upon which to base numeric estimates. In helping children make estimates of quantities, guide them toward making comparisons to other familiar quantities and measurements. The number of students in a classroom can be compared to the number attending the school play. The height of an adult can be used to estimate the height of a desk or of a flagpole. Benchmarks for numbers such as one thousand, ten thousand, or even one million are also important but difficult to find. Children can discuss how long is one thousand (or one million) seconds, how tall is a stack of ten thousand pennies, and other fun "big number" counts (see Chapter 3). Having number concepts tied to realistic reference points can help draw attention to the reasonableness of results in problem solving situations and in making estimations in real contexts.

Relative Magnitude Relationships

Relative magnitude relationships refer to the notion that a given number like 31 may be large with respect to 4, about the same as 28 or 35, and yet quite small in comparison to 525. Virtually no research has been done to assess children's knowledge of this type of relationship and very few activities exist in the curriculum to address it; yet a feel for the relative size of numbers is certainly part of the desired "intuition about numbers." Second graders can decide if 32 is closer to 28 or 68, and fourth graders are able to select whether $25.35 is closer to $30 or to $20 (42).

> Make your calculator "count."
>   Example: Count by threes. Press [+], 3, [=],[=],[=], . . .
>
> • How many presses to get to 20? to 50? to 100?
> • How long will it take to count to 1000? What if you count by nine's?
> • What patterns can you find? Are they always the same?
> • How are the patterns different if you start someplace other than 0?
>
>   Example: Press 4, [+], 3, [=],[=],[=], . . .

The following activity can help with relative magnitude relationships. On the board draw a long, blank number line and label the ends 0 and 1000. Other endpoints could also be used. Select numbers within this interval and ask students "about" where they think the numbers belong. After several numbers are established, ask children to suggest a number that they believe is "small" or "large" or "about the same" in comparison to a number already placed on the line. A new number that is judged to be large in one comparison can then be seen as small or about the same when compared to others on the line.

The relative magnitude relationship is also at the heart of understanding relative error in measurement. A 1 cm error in 345 cm is small but a 1 cm error in a measure of 7 cm is large. More research and new instructional ideas are clearly needed in this area.

Part-Part-Whole Relationships

Counting a set of seven objects by ones fails in helping children recognize that the same set of seven can be composed of three and four or of two and five (35). In counting the entire set there is no opportunity to reflect on the size of parts of the set or even that the set can actually be made of two or more parts. A part-part-whole understanding of number is an important breakthrough in children's mathematical development (14, 28).

"Probably the major conceptual achievement of the early school years is the interpretation of numbers in terms of part and whole relationships. With the application of a Part-Whole schema to quantity, it becomes possible for children to think about numbers as compositions of other numbers. This enrichment of number understanding permits forms of mathematical problem solving and interpretation that are not available to younger children." (35, p. 114)

Kindergarten children in a short, twenty-five-day study counted sets as usual but also separated the sets into subparts and counted these (14). Comparisons of different children's displays of subsets were made and discussed. This part-part-whole experience not only improved students' number concepts but also their problem-solving skills and early place value concepts—two areas not specifically addressed in this instructional treatment.

Make your calculator into a "Parts-of-Fifteen" machine.
   Here's how:
   Press 15 [−] 15 [=]
   Now you can practice naming the other part of 15 when you know one of the parts.
   Press 9. What goes with 9 to make 15?
   Press [=] to check. (ignore the −)
   Press any number between 0 and 15. What is the other part? Press [=] to check.

The Japanese curriculum consistently encourages flexibility in thinking about numbers in terms of subparts. At every grade level, as new numeration systems are introduced (whole numbers, fractions, decimals), there is an emphasis on how to compose and decompose numbers (26). Making bars of seven connecting cubes using two colors and then "reading" the bars (e.g., "five and two make seven") is a simple example of composition. Breaking a set of seven into two or more parts and reading the parts (e.g., "six and one make seven") is a related example of decomposition (51). These and similar part-part-whole activities consider only one number at a time and focus attention on various ways to construct the number in terms of subparts (Fig. 6.4).

Helping children make a part-part-whole analysis of one-step word problems for all four operations has been demonstrated to be an effective problem-solving method for third graders (22, 34). Counters are placed in set/subset relationships that model the structure of the problems. Children use the words "part" and "whole" to describe the quantities. The successes attributable to the part-part-whole approach suggests a strong connection between flexible number concepts and an understanding of the meanings of the operations (Fig. 6.5).

Fraction Relationships

Children's understanding of fractions is initially tied to pictures or physical models for fractions rather than developed from counting experiences as are whole number concepts (Fig. 6.6). After first developing an understanding of fractional parts and unit fractions (e.g., 1/2, 1/5, or 1/12), meaning for nonunit fractions can then be explored through counting. For example, five thirds is 1/3 and 1/3 and 1/3 (that's one whole) and 1/3 and 1/3 (3, 33).

Number sense with fractions seems heavily dependent on these understandings as well as on the knowledge of the relative sizes of fractions. For young children, the idea that eighths are smaller than fifths is bewildering since the number 8 is more than 5. Young children need opportunities to select the larger of two fractions (33).

FIGURE 6.4   While individuals may see a particular design differently, children can construct one or more part-part-whole relationships from their own designs. They use their own interpretation to "read" the designs.

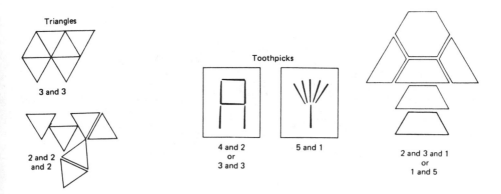

Triangles

3 and 3

2 and 2 and 2

Toothpicks

4 and 2 or 3 and 3

5 and 1

2 and 3 and 1 or 1 and 5

FIGURE 6.5   Small dot cards like these can be used in many early activities.

- Find pairs of cards with 10 dots in all. Find triples with 10 dots.
- Pick a card. Find one that shows one more. Two less.
- Make pairs that total 8. Turn one down in each pair.
  What number is turned down?

Reasoning processes will be different depending on the fractions being compared (e.g., comparison of 3/5 and 4/5 leads to a different relationship than a comparison of 2/3 and 3/4 or 2/3 and 3/8). Children should discuss and share different strategies for deciding which of two fractions is larger.

Concepts of fractions are discussed more thoroughly in Chapter 10 of this volume. It is important to realize, however, that children may likely not have number sense with fractions, even though their intuitions about whole numbers may be quite rich.

FIGURE 6.6   About how much is shaded?

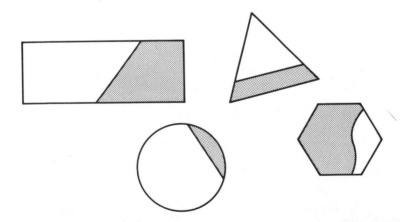

Instructional Approaches

In much of the literature surrounding number sense, examples of teaching almost always involve a high level of teacher–student and student–student interaction. Children create relationships about numbers, devise methods of solving problems, and share strategies for mental computations all within an environment of open-ended discussions. In the NCTM *Standards* (12), the K–4 *Standard* on communication notes: "Communication plays an important role in helping children construct links between their informal, intuitive notions and the abstract language and symbolism of mathematics."

Verbal Interaction and Concepts

Effective instruction has a strong component of student–student and student–teacher interaction (23, 24, 25). Within the context of the number development games noted earlier, children have a reason for doing mathematics. The feedback for their ideas comes from their discussions with their peers rather than through a one-way channel from a teacher. As a result, children are more likely to reflect on their own ideas and thus to create mathematical relationships. In teacher-initiated discussions, children who have never been exposed to standard computational procedures share and develop their own methods for doing multidigit computations. The use of place–value concepts and the flexibility of thought in these discussions are clearly in accord with the goals of good number sense development.

"Make mathematics exciting.
"Chinese and Japanese teachers create many opportunities during the class period and in homework assignments for children to participate in the intellectual quest that makes mathematics a potentially exciting subject. They do this by presenting problems that stimulate children to produce their own solutions instead of mimicking solutions that have been developed for them." (46, p. 31)

A "problem-centered approach" can be used to help children construct their own mathematical concepts. In a study with second graders, students worked on tasks through teacher-directed discussions or in small groups, subsequently sharing the results (11, 53). These findings demonstrate that discussion of problem solutions in a trusting environment leads to opportunities for conceptual development and alternative thinking strategies. Furthermore, this environment has been shown to be conducive to students' development of positive beliefs about mathematics and their abilities to solve problems. (See 5 and 6 for a collection of problem-solving, discussion-oriented activities for grades 1—6.)

The value of increased student verbal interaction is also supported by a comparison of Japanese and Chinese methods of instruction with those in American schools (47). It apparently is quite typical in an Asian primary classroom for children to consider only one or two simple problems such as $11 - 3 = 8$ for an entire class period. The problems are discussed in terms of different methods of solution, relationships involved, ways that they can be modeled with manipulatives, and related word problems. By contrast, in American schools the tendency is to spend a brief time on a teacher-directed explanation of a problem followed by children solving many similar problems with quickness and accuracy.

Formal versus Informal Mathematics

When students are in school situations they tend to use memorized rules and computational methods involving written symbolism. There is ample evidence that they frequently do these things with little or no understanding of either the rules or the symbolism. In out-of-school settings many children ignore the procedures that they are practicing in school. Instead, they use oral and mental methods instead of symbolism, and they rely almost entirely on ideas and strategies that make sense to them (19).

> Do 47 + 26 + 18 − 26 in your head.
> The height of a 10-year-old boy is 5 feet. What do you think his height will be when he is 20? (31, p. 79)

In most instances, informal, student-invented methods are quite different from pencil-and-paper methods but closely approximate the mental strategies used by those who are good at mental computation and estimation. The following are examples of mental computations done by Brazilian third graders (8).

- In a word problem the computation was $200 − 35$. "If it were thirty, then the result would be seventy. But it is thirty-five. So it's sixty-five; one hundred sixty-five."
- In a store situation the computation was $243 − 75$. "You just give me the two hundred [he meant 100]. I'll give you twenty-five back. Plus the forty-three that you have, the hundred and forty-three, that's one hundred and sixty-eight" (8, pp. 91–92).

These unusual but powerful methods were certainly not taught in school but they illustrate insights into computation and number that children may possess informally.

> Children seem to be overly bound, at times, to the tedious routines of pencil and paper computation.

$$
\begin{array}{r}
\overset{2}{4}\overset{\prime}{8}16 \\
2957 \\
+\ 314 \\
\hline
8087
\end{array}
$$

$$
\begin{array}{r}
2987 \\
\times\ 645 \\
\hline
14935 \\
11948 \\
17922 \\
\hline
1926615
\end{array}
$$

$$
48\overline{)3729} \quad 65\ R9
$$

Unfortunately, narrowly guided school learning can actually interfere with the cre-. ative and more useful informal methods that children are quite capable of. When asked to add 14 + 12 without pencil and paper, most fourth graders tend to add the 4 and the 2 first as they would on paper (15). However, at the seventh and tenth grade, where students are more removed from this type of activity in school, about a third of the students added ten to fourteen and then added two more or added the tens first. In contrast, at the first grade, prior to mastery of these rules, a majority of students use an add-tens-first approach (25).

Tell me the first thing that comes to your mind when I say "twenty-four."

A First Grade:
(Immediate responses)

- two dimes and four pennies
- (picked up) two base-ten rods and four unit cubes
- two dozen eggs
- four nickels and four pennies
- take six pennies from three dimes
- "My uncle was 24 on Saturday."
  "My mother was 24 last year."
  "I'll be 24 in 19 years."
- the day before Christmas
- when the hand (on a scale) is almost in the middle of 20 and 30.
- "My brother got a cut this long and it took 17 stitches to sew it up. That's almost 24."

A Third Grade:
(No spontaneous reaction)

- traced "24" in the air
- found "24" on the calendar
- "Twenty-four is on my watch once every hour." (21)

The traditional push to computational skill mastery has a tendency to narrow and compartmentalize children's numeric thinking rather than to integrate it and make it flexible (10).

Informal Mathematics in the Classroom

What specific activities can be structured to promote informal thinking and discussion in the classroom? How do we encourage students to be thinkers instead of robots mastering routines? Research provides some insights but it is important to recognize that children really can and do invent their own powerful methods of working with numbers.

Some evidence derived from studies of unschooled African children suggests that an understanding of numbers, especially the structure of the place–value system, is related to informal, student-invented computational procedures (41). In studies of grades 1 to 3, a close connection between understanding of numbers and operations with inventions of nonstandard procedures has been observed (7). These findings suggest that our instruction should focus more on number meanings than on drill of pencil-and-paper algorithms, and that more opportunities should be provided for children within the classroom to invent their own strategies (Fig. 6.7).

The use of physical models is especially important in the primary years, an idea that is certainly not new. However, rather than use models to explain the traditional procedures of pencil-and-paper operations, consider shifting the emphasis to using

FIGURE 6.7 *"Incredible Equations" from a second grade classroom, Louisville, Kentucky*

Each day in the "Incredible Equations" activity students generate equations to express the day of the month.

[Handwritten example of incredible equations generated by second graders.]

$$(50 \times 2) - 25 - 25 - 25 - 1 = 24$$

$$12 + 12 = 24$$

$$13 + 3 + 1 + 1 + 2 + 4 = 24$$

$$\begin{array}{r} 24 \\ \times\ 1 \\ \hline 24 \end{array}$$

$$(5 \times 5) - 1 = 24$$

$$24 - 0 = 24$$

$$\begin{array}{r} 1,000 \\ -\ 976 \\ \hline 24 \end{array}$$

$$\begin{array}{r} 20 \\ +\ 4 \\ \hline 24 \end{array}$$

$$16 + 4 + 4 = 24$$

$$14 + 10 = 24$$

$$\begin{array}{r} 500 \\ -476 \\ \hline 24 \end{array}$$

$$\begin{array}{r} 2,000 \\ -1,976 \\ \hline 24 \end{array}$$

$$17 + 3 + 4 = 24$$

models as thinking tools. In one school, children were exposed to wooden base-ten blocks beginning in the first grade (30). They were asked to solve problems involving all four of the operations but were not instructed in any standard pencil-and-paper methods until late in the third grade. Given free use of the base-ten blocks, the children invented a variety of different methods that turned out to be quite useful for mental computation. Children's natural tendency with base ten blocks is to work with the tens or hundreds pieces first as is done with mental procedures. This, of course, is the exact opposite of the approach used in pencil and paper methods.

When using models, simply present children with problems and let them determine methods of solution (Fig. 6.8). If children are allowed to talk to one another in cooperative groups to ease personal anxieties and increase the exchange of ideas, they will invent a variety of useful approaches. Cobb and Merkel (11) report at least five different ways that second-grade students added 39 + 53 without pencil and paper, and prior to any instruction in two-digit addition. Two of these solutions are described here:

> Anna: "Fifty plus 30 is 80, then 9 plus one more would be 90, plus 2 more would be 92."
>
> Mark (after a hint about 39 + 10): "Thirty-nine plus 10 is 49, and so you used up ten one time [puts up one finger], then you use up 10 again and that would make 59 [puts up a second finger], then 69, then 79, then 89 [sequentially puts up three more fingers] and that makes 50, then you put . . . so you add 39 and all these tens together and that makes . . . 39 . . . 49, 59, 69, 79, 89, then you add this in and that makes . . . 92." (11, pp. 79–80)

As children invent strategies that make sense to them, they develop increasingly powerful arithmetical concepts that they can build on in subsequent learning.

Models can also be used in a more directed manner (29). For example, present children with three bundles of ten and six single sticks on an overhead projector and ask, "How many?" Then add or remove one, two, or three bundles or one, two, or three sticks. With each change of the display, ask the children to explain how they know what the new display shows. Later, the change in the display can be a mental activity. Show four tens and seven ones and ask, "What if we add two more tens?" or "Let's take away 15. How much will be left?" Similar activities can be done with coins (Fig. 6.9).

Question: How much is 42 divided by 7?
Solution: 40 divided by 10 is 4; 3 and 3 and 3 and 3 is 12;
         12 plus 2 is 14; 14 divided by 2 is 7; 2 plus 4
         is 6.
         The answer is 6.
The solution of a second grader! (16)

The concern that a tens-first approach will interfere with ones-first, pencil-and-paper methods, is not well founded, especially if the informal, mental, tens-first methods are presented first (24). Pencil-and-paper methods should be taught as an alternative form of computation, not as "the" method of computation.

FIGURE 6.8   How would you find these totals?

FIGURE 6.9 What strategies would second graders use? Let them share their solutions. Adapted from (53).

Kamau has this much money:

He buys a pencil for 7 cents and a candy bar for 35 cents. How much money does he have left?

Mental Computation

As seen in the last section, children with a good sense of numbers are quite able to invent their own mental procedures. Flexible and efficient mental computation requires a knowledge of number relationships, a facility with basic facts, an understanding of the arithmetic operations, and possession of base-ten place value concepts. All require number sense.

Basic Fact Mastery

More research has been done in the area of helping children master basic facts than any topic discussed in this chapter. The focus of this research has been on the value of developing strategies for deriving the answer to a basic fact as opposed to repetitive drill techniques (1, 13, 28, 45, 49). For example, is it more effective to teach children to use a "bridge ten" technique for 5 + 9 (9 and 1 more is 10 and 4 more makes 14) than to drill this fact or even to encourage counting techniques? It is safe to say that while the discussion continues, most researchers favor the strategy approach.

Tammy figured out that when adding, if you add something to one number and subtract it from another, you will get the same result.

7 + 9 is the same as 6 + 10 or 5 + 11
Does it work for multiplication?
No. 6 × 7 is not the same as 5 × 8
Why?
Is there a rule or a pattern?

While a more complete discussion of basic fact mastery can be found in Chapter 4, the following points are appropriate here: (1) The evidence indicates that as children learn strategies for basic facts they do in fact learn their basic facts; (2) the strategies used for fact mastery may be an end in themselves as they incorporate the network of relationships we are calling number sense; (3) mastery of basic facts is essential to effective mental computation and estimation.

One important caveat: Many children who are explicitly taught fact strategies occasionally use them incorrectly. For example, in using a doubles strategy for 8 + 6 some children will double the 8 and add 2. In the domain of number facts and in other forms of mental computation, a mental algorithm or procedure can be drilled mindlessly (and hence used incorrectly) in much the same way as traditional pencil-and-paper methods. Thinking strategies for basic facts and other forms of mental computation must build directly on children's understanding of number and not be taught as mindless procedures.

Early Mental Computation

The suggestions already made for fostering informal computation methods, especially with the use of base-ten models, are among the few things that we know from research about mental computation in the primary grades. Some specific mental computation strategies can be isolated and developed and then practiced even as early as the second grade. For example, a *higher-decade addition fact* refers to the sum of a two-digit number and a one-digit number. Children can be helped to see how the same thinking that is used for 8 + 5 can help them know 78 + 5: 78 and 2 more is 80 and 3 more is 83. Next, this thinking can be expanded to help children add two-digit numbers. To compute 38 + 45, children can be helped with the use of models and discussion to add 38 and four 10s (or 40) to get 78, and then add 5 more as before. Here the strategies for basic facts and two different types of addition problems are connected. Similar approaches can be developed for higher-decade subtraction such as 63 − 7 and then 63 − 27.

> Number sense is a way of thinking rather than a body of knowledge and skills.

The hundreds board can be a useful model for helping children see how higher-decade addition and subtraction facts are related. The sum 8 + 7 on the hundreds board begins at 8 and ends in the next row at 15. Similarly, the sums 38 + 7, 48 + 7, . . . 88 + 7 all begin and end in the same columns. These and other pattern searches on the hundreds board can be quite useful in motivating children to develop patterns and see relationships (5).

Characteristics of Mental Computation

Several characteristics of mental computation techniques illustrate differences they have with pencil-and-paper methods. Mental computation procedures are:

• Variable and flexible. Given any one computation there are usually many different and effective methods to do the computation. Even with the same operation, different strategies may be used. For example, it is not likely that 83 − 79 would be computed the same as 83 − 51, or 83 − 7.

A first-grade child's solution to 246 + 178:
"Well, 2 plus 1 is 3, so I know it's 200 and 100, so now it's somewhere in the three hundreds. And then you have to add the tens on. And the tens are 4 and 7. . . . Well, um. If you started at 70, 80, 90, 100. Right? And that's four hundreds. So now you're already in the three hundreds because of the [100 + 200], but now you're in the four hundreds because of the [40 + 70]. But you've still got one more ten. So if you're doing it 300 plus 40 plus 70, you'd have 410. But you're not doing that. So what you need to do then is add 6 more onto 10, which is 16. And then 8 more: 17, 18, 19, 20, 21, 22, 23, 24. So that's 124. I mean 424." (7, p. 90)

- Active. The individual can select his or her own method.
- Holistic. The tendency is to work with complete numbers rather than single digits as in paper methods.
- Constructive. Frequently pieces of a computation will be done and then other parts added or subtracted. For example, one way to do 36 + 28 is 36, 46, 56, 66, then take off 2, 64.

(41)

Help students look before leaping. (20)
 1. Which of the following can you do without pencil and paper?
    7 × 3000   123 × 69   12 × 15   8 × 4.5
 2. Explain how the problem 156 − 100 can be used to figure the calculation 156 − 99.
 3. If 15 feet = 180 inches, how many inches are in 14 feet? in 16 feet? in 30 feet? in 45 feet?
 4. Without computing, select the pairs of calculations that have the same answers:
    (8 × 45,   4 × 90)
    1.8 × 3.5,   18 × 0.35)
    (88 × 87,   90 × 85)

Another observation about mental computation is that the context plays a strong role in how students solve problems (8, 18). Problems involving money and prices, figuring how many children there are in various settings such as on buses or at ballgames, and other real-world quantities seem to keep children's attention focused on number meanings in a problem. This is true for both the meanings of the quantities, such as dollars or cars, and the ones, tens, and hundreds meanings within the quantities. When students resort to pencil-and-paper methods, as they do frequently in typical classroom settings, they tend to focus more on individual digits and lose the meanings involved in the computation. This strongly suggests that real contexts should be used frequently in presenting mental computation tasks to children.

Virtually no research has been done on effective teaching strategies to develop mental computational skills in the early grades. The discussion here indicates that we are beginning to understand some of the characteristics of mental computation and the complex way it is tied to an understanding of number and number relationships.

Computational Estimation

In the last decade, computational estimation has received more and more attention in the curriculum. We now know from numerous studies that computational estimation is highly dependent on an understanding of the operations, knowledge of basic facts, place value concepts, and the ability to work with powers of ten (35, 38, 40, 44, 50). Mental computation and the ability to make comparisons between numbers are skills intimately connected with computational estimation (41). Since computational estimation is so heavily dependent on a strong network of concepts, it has generally not been introduced until about the third or fourth grade and most of the research efforts have been at the middle school level or higher.

> When estimating the product of 26 and 37, traditional front-end rounding suggests an estimate of 30 × 40, or 1,200. Good estimators, however, often take advantage of specific numbers. In this case, perhaps rounding 26 to 25 and 37 to 40 and reasoning since 4 twenty-fives is 100, 40 twenty-fives or 1,000 is a reasonable estimate. (43)

A study of children in grades 3, 5, 7, and 9 attempted to analyze the concept and skill components related to estimation (44). Findings showed that computational estimation is a highly complex process. It seems important that efforts to develop this process begin in the early grades. Early skills of "finding numbers close to a given value, recognizing which of two numbers is closer to a third, computing mentally, [and] recognizing when a problem does not demand an exact answer" (p. 145) are suggested as topics worthy of more attention. Several of these issues have already been addressed in this chapter.

Accepting Different Approximate Results

Children learn very quickly in school to believe there are single correct answers to questions involving numbers (9). As children move to the upper grades they can accept an approximate result, but have a strong tendency to believe that only one such result is acceptable (44). In an estimation exercise, these older students will compute an exact answer and then round the result using mechanical methods learned in school, confirming their belief in only one answer, albeit approximate.

Students in grades 5 and 7 have been found to be reluctant to round 267 to 250 when estimating 267 + 519 even though 250 plus 500 gives an easy estimate. Similarly, third graders resist rounding 27 to 25. Students seem tied to the mechanical methods of rounding to the nearest ten or nearest hundred and are not able to accept different close or rounded numbers for different situations.

A suggestion that is useful at all grade levels is to emphasize realistic situations where it is clear that no single answer exists (9, 50). Discussions of "How many bees are in the hive?" or "About how long will it take to read the story?" or "How tall will the plant grow?" may help children realize that many different answers might be equally reasonable.

By third or fourth grade, when computational estimation begins, different estimates should be discussed. Answer keys that provide a range of answers should be shared with students. Have children discuss why a range of acceptable responses in one situation might be narrower than in another. Let them decide on acceptable ranges for different computations.

Computational Estimation Strategies

Prior to the third grade, children are probably not ready to learn specific strategies for computational estimation. At these early levels time is more profitably spent on number meanings, mental computation, and on estimations of measurements and real quantities (38). Work with strategies such as using only the *front-end* digits, *rounding*, or the use of *special numbers* (tens, hundreds, half, fourth, etc.) can begin at the third or fourth grade. Most research efforts, however, have focused on children at the fifth grade and higher.

The front-end strategy is a good place to begin with younger students because it is easy and clearly illustrates the approximate nature of estimation. In a problem involving 276 + 45 + 317, students using the front-end strategy recognize that the two and the three are the front digits, temporarily ignoring the forty-five. They then think, "200 plus 300 is 500." As they become more proficient, adjustments can be made. "When I look at the rest of the numbers, seven plus four plus one is twelve or about one hundred and twenty more. About six hundred and twenty." Later, processes of rounding and adjusting an initial estimate can be introduced as refinements. Using rounding to estimate 37 x 46 students might think, "forty times fifty is two thousand. Since I rounded both numbers up, I know the answer is less than two thousand." In this illustration, products with powers of ten were used (special numbers) and an adjustment was made in the final result.

One teacher who had earlier taught certain estimation strategies to her fourth grade class was giving a test on traditional computation skills. She suggested estimating the answers first and then comparing the estimates with those they computed to at least check on the reasonableness of their answers. Fewer careless errors resulted. In a follow-up discussion, students commented that they had never done this before, simply because it had never been suggested (4). Others have also reported successful efforts at teaching estimation in the fourth grade. The reader is encouraged to look to 32, 37, 38, and 40 for more detailed descriptions of estimation strategies and teaching suggestions.

Conclusion

One overwhelming message comes through in all of the research: The individual facets of number sense are intricately connected and rely upon a strong conceptual development. This interconnected, multifaceted, and highly-conceptual nature of number sense suggests that it cannot be compartmentalized into textbook chapters or instructional units. Number sense is more of a *way of teaching* than a topic to be taught.

A major ingredient in a number-sense way of teaching is a high degree of open-ended verbal interaction in the classroom. Encouraging children to talk and share their ideas helps them make connections among these ideas both for themselves and their peers.

> "There is no way to build a standardized test—one in which the answers are prescribed in advance and in which only the results of reasoning, not its process or justification, are examined—that can give us a reasonable judgment of people's number sense. This is because number sense is a form of reasoning and thinking in the number domain." (36, p. 37)

As is true with all higher-order skills, the development of good number sense takes time and begins at the earliest level. As teachers, we can never say, "My children have mastered number sense." We can only say, "My children are developing a better number sense." It is a topic for every day, at every grade, with the most important foundation laid in the earliest years.

Looking Ahead . . .

The early childhood curriculum has long been dominated by pencil-and-paper computation and neatly compartmentalized in individual textbook chapters, with each chapter's topic relatively easy to assess. For number sense to be a valued goal, number concepts and relationships must be fully integrated into a broadened view of computation that includes mental computation and estimation. Research is needed to determine the effect of early number concept development and later mental processes. Of at least equal importance is a need to find methods to evaluate number sense. Benchmarks need to be established against which teachers can compare students' growth in their "intuition about numbers and relationships." Teaching can and must become much more active, verbal, interactive, group oriented, and dynamic than is typical today.

John A. Van de Walle

As I look around my classroom, how will I recognize the various levels of number sense my children possess? Can I expect all students to have number sense? How will I know when my children are approaching "proficiency" in number sense and thinking? Certainly, identifying component skills will not enable me to assess the possession of the interconnected ideas and thinking processes that make up number sense. I would like to see studies conducted over several years exploring the effects of exposing children to curricula rich in number-sense activities. While these issues are yet to be addressed, I find teaching mathematics from a number-sense perspective an exciting opportunity.

Karen Bowman Watkins

About the Authors

John A. Van de Walle is associate professor of education at Virginia Commonwealth University where he teaches classes for elementary and middle school teachers. He has been particularly interested in children's conceptual development and more recently in teachers' views of what it means to know mathematics.

Karen Bowman Watkins currently teaches fourth grade at Grange Hall Elementary School in Chesterfield County, Virginia. She has taught for ten years and has long held a special interest in the teaching of mathematics.

References

1. BAROODY, A. J. (1987). *Children's mathematical thinking: A developmental framework for preschool, primary, and special education teachers.* New York: Teachers College Press.
2. BAROODY, A. J., & GATZKE, M. R. (1991). The estimate of set size by potentially gifted kindergarten-age children. *Journal for Research in Mathematics Education*, 22(1), 59–68.
3. BOWMAN, K. (1987). Estimation strategies program. Unpublished manuscript, Virginia Commonwealth University, Richmond.
4. BEHR, M. J., WACHSMUTH, I., POST, T. R., & LESH, R. (1984). Order and equivalence of rational numbers: A clinical teaching experiment. *Journal for Research in Mathematics Education*, 15(5), 323–341.
* 5. BURNS, M. (1987). *A collection of math lessons from grades 3 through 6.* The Math Solution Publications. New Rochelle, NY: Cuisenaire Corporation.
* 6. BURNS, M., & TANK, B. (1988). *collection of math lessons from grades 1 through 3.* The Math Solution Publications. New Rochelle, NY: Cuisenaire Corporation.
7. CARPENTER, T. P. (1989). Number sense and other nonsense. In J. T. Sowder & B. P. Schappelle (Eds.), *Establishing foundations for research on number sense and related topics: Report of a conference* (pp. 89–91). San Diego State University, Center for Research in Mathematics and Science Education.
8. CARRAHER, T. N., CARRAHER, D. W., & SCHLIEMANN, A. D. (1987). Written and oral mathematics. *Journal for Research in Mathematics Education*, 18(2), 83–97.
9. CARTER, H. L. (1986). Linking estimation to psychological variables in the early years. In H. L. Schoen (Ed.), *Estimation and mental computation* (pp. 74–81). Reston, VA: National Council of Teachers of Mathematics.
10. CASE, R. (1989). Fostering the development of children's number sense: Reflections on the conference. In J. T. Sowder & B. P. Schappelle (Eds.), *Establishing foundations for research on number sense and related topics: Report of a conference* (pp. 89–91). San Diego State University, Center for Research in Mathematics and Science Education.
11. COBB, P., & MERKEL, G. (1989). Thinking strategies: Teaching arithmetic through problem solving. In P. R. Trafton (Ed.), *New directions for elementary school mathematics* (pp. 70–81). Reston, VA: National Council of Teachers of Mathematics.

*12. Commission on standards for school mathematics (1989). *Curriculum and evaluation standards for school mathematics.* Reston, VA: National Council of Teachers of Mathematics.

13. COOK, C. J., & DOSSEY, J. A. (1982). Basic fact thinking strategies for multiplication—revisited. *Journal for Research in Mathematics Education, 13*(3), 163–171.

14. FISCHER, F. E. (1990). A part-part-whole curriculum for teaching number in the kindergarten. *Journal for Research in Mathematics Education, 21*(3), 207–215.

15. HAMANN, M. S., & ASHCRAFT, M. H. (1985). Simple and complex mental addition across development. *Journal of Experimental Child Psychology, 40,* 49–72.

16. HAREL, G., & BEHR, M. (1991). Ed's strategy for solving division problems. *Arithmetic Teacher, 39*(3), 38–40.

17. HATANO, G. (1982). Learning to add and subtract: A Japanese perspective. In T. P. Carpenter, J. M. Moser, & T. A. Romberg (Eds.), *Addition and subtraction: A cognitive perspective* (pp. 211–223. Hillsdale, NJ: Erlbaum.

*18. HAZEKAMP, D. W. (1986). Components of mental multiplying. In H. L. Schoen (Ed.), *Estimation and mental computation* (pp. 116–126). Reston, VA: National Council of Teachers of Mathematics.

*19. HIEBERT, J. (1989). The struggle to link written symbols with understandings: An update. *Arithmetic Teacher, 36*(7), 38–44.

*20. HOPE, J. A.(1989). Promoting number sense in school. *Arithmetic Teacher, 36*(6), 12–16.

*21. HOWDEN, H. (1989). Teaching number sense. *Arithmetic Teacher, 36*(6), 6–11.

*22. HUINKER, D. (1989). Multiplication and division word problems: Improving students' understanding. *Arithmetic Teacher, 37*(2), 8–12.

*23. KAMII, C. (1985). *Young children reinvent arithmetic.* New York: Teachers College Press.

*24. KAMII, C. (1989). *Young children continue to reinvent arithmetic, 2nd grade.* New York: Teachers College Press.

*25. KAMII, C. (1990). Constructivism and beginning arithmetic (K-2). In T. J. Cooney (Ed.), *Teaching and learning mathematics in the 1990's* (pp. 22–30). Reston, VA: National Council of Teachers of Mathematics.

26. KROLL, D. L., & YABE, T. (1987). A Japanese educator's perspective on teaching mathematics in the elementary school. *Arithmetic Teacher, 35*(2), 36–43.

27. KULM, G. (1985). Counting and early arithmetic learning: Strategies and activities. Learning activities and implications from recent research. Washington, DC: National Institute of Education. (ERIC Document Reproduction Service No. ED 270 332)

*28. LABINOWICZ, E. (1985). *Learning from children: New beginnings for teaching numerical thinking.* Menlo Park, CA: Addison-Wesley.

*29. LEUTZINGER, L. P., RATHMELL, E. C., & URBATSCH, T. D. (1986). Developing estimation skills in the primary grades. In H. Schoen (Ed.), *Estimation and mental computation* (pp. 82–92). Reston, VA: National Council of Teachers of Mathematics.

*30. MADELL, R. (1985). Children's natural processes. *Arithmetic Teacher, 32*(7), 20–22.

31. MARKOVITS, Z. (1989). Reactions to the number sense conference In J. T. Sowder & B. P. Schappelle (Eds.), *Establishing foundations for research on number sense and related topics: Report of a conference* (pp.78–81). San Diego State University, Center for Research in Mathematics and Science Education.

32. NELSON, N. Z. (1967). The effect of teaching of estimation on arithmetic achievement in the fourth and sixth grades (Doctoral dissertation, University of Pittsburgh, 1966). *Dissertation Abstracts, 27,* 4127A.

33. POST, T. R., WACHSMUTH, I., LESH, R., & BEHR, M. J. (1985). Order and equivalence of rational numbers: A cognitive analysis. *Journal for Research in Mathematics Education, 16,* 18–36.

*34. RATHMELL, E. C., & HUINKER, D. M. (1989). Using "part–whole" language to help children represent and solve word problems. In P. R. Trafton (Ed.), *New directions for elementary school mathematics* (pp. 99–110). Reston, VA: National Council of Teachers of Mathematics.

35. RESNICK, L. B. (1983). A developmental theory of number understanding. In H. P. Ginsburg (Ed.), *The development of mathematical thinking* (pp. 109–151). New York: Academic Press.

36. RESNICK, L. B. (1989). Defining, assessing, and teaching number sense. In J. T. Sowder & B. P. Schappelle (Eds.), *Establishing foundations for research on number sense and related topics: Report of a conference* (pp. 35–39). San Diego State University, Center for Research in Mathematics and Science Education.

*37. REYS, B. (1986). Teaching computational estimation: Concepts and strategies. In H. Schoen (Ed.), *Estimation and mental computation* (pp. 31–44). Reston, VA: National Council of Teachers of Mathematics.

38. REYS, B. (1988). Estimation. In T. R. Post (Ed.), *Teaching mathematics in grades K–8: Research based methods.* Boston: Allyn & Bacon.

39. REYS, R. E. (1984). Mental computation and estimation: Past, present, and future. *Elementary School Journal, 84,* 547–557.

40. SCHOEN, H. L., FRIESEN, C. D., JARRETT, J. A., & URBATSCH, T. D. (1981). Instruction in estmating solution of whole number computations. *Journal for Research in Mathematics Education, 12*(3), 165–178.

41. SOWDER, J. T. (1988). Mental computation and number comparison: Their roles in the development of number sense and computational estimation. In J. Hiebert & M. Behr (Eds.), *Number concepts and operations in the middle grades* (pp. 182–197). Reston, VA: National Council of Teachers of Mathematics.

42. SOWDER, J. T. (1989). Research into practice: Developing understanding of computational estimation. *Arithmetic Teacher, 36*(5), 25–27.

43. SOWDER, J. T. & SCHAPPELLE, B. P. (Eds.). (1989). *Establishing foundations for research on number sense and related topics: Report of a conference* (pp. 89–91). San Diego State University, Center for Research in Mathematics and Science Education.

44. SOWDER, J. T., & WHEELER, M. M. (1989). The development of concepts and strategies used in computational estimation. *Journal for Research in Mathematics Education, 20*(2), 130–146.

45. STEINBERG, R. M. (1985). Instruction on derived facts strategies in addition and subtraction. *Journal for Research in Mathematics Education. 16*(5), 337–355.

46. STEVENSON, H. W., LUMMIS, M., LEE, S., & STIGLER, J. W. (1990). *Making the grade in mathematics: Elementary school mathematics in the United States, Taiwan, and Japan.* Reston, VA: National Council of Teachers of Mathematics.

47. STIGLER, J. W., & PERRY, M. (1989). Cross cultural studies of mathematics teaching and learning: Recent findings and new directions. In D. A. Grouws & T. J. Cooney (Eds.), *Perspectives on research on effective mathematics teaching, Vol. 1* (pp. 194–223). Reston, VA: National Council of Teachers of Mathematics.

48. THOMPSON, C. S., & VAN DE WALLE, J. A. (1984). The power of ten. *Arithmetic Teacher, 32*(3), 6–11.

49. THORNTON, C. A. (1978). Emphasizing thinking strategies in basic fact instruction. *Journal for Research in Mathematics Education, 9*(3), 213–227.

*50. TRAFTON, P. R. (1986). Teaching computational estimation: Establishing an estimation mind-set. In H. L. Schoen (Ed.), *Estimation and mental computation* (pp. 16–30). Reston, VA: National Council of Teachers of Mathematics.

*51. VAN DE WALLE, J. A. (1990). Concepts of number. In J. N. Payne (Ed.), *Mathematics* *for the young child.* (pp. 63–87) Reston, VA: National Council of Teachers of Mathematics.

52. WIRTZ, R. (1974). *Mathematics for everyone.* Washington, DC: Curriculum Development Associates.

*53. YACKEL, E., COBB, P., WOOD, T. WHEATLEY, G., & MERKEL, G. (1990). The importance of social interaction in children's construction of mathematical knowledge. In T. J. Cooney (Ed.), *Teaching and learning mathematics in the 1990's* (pp. 12–21). Reston, VA: National Council of Teachers of Mathematics.

CHAPTER 7

Problem Solving in Early Childhood: Building Foundations

Ray Hembree and Harold Marsh

Most curricular programs apparently assume that word problems are difficult for children of all ages, and that children must master symbolic addition and subtraction operations before they will be able to solve even simple word problems. We believe, however, that young children are good problem solvers. (22)

During most of the twentieth century, studies of ways to teach problem solving have claimed special time and attention. Much of the study has taken place in the middle grades and junior and senior high school, in line with beliefs that pupils who succeed at problem solving must first have developed a goodly amount of maturity in arithmetic. Nonetheless, a large group of studies has focused expressly on grades K–4, in expectation that problem solving can be an important element in developing that maturity. These aspirations were formalized when NCTM named problem solving to head its agenda for the 1980s, not only regarding grade 5 and beyond but all grade levels (23). A central position for problem solving is reaffirmed and extended in the current *Curriculum and Evaluation Standards*.

> Problem solving should be the central focus of the mathematics curriculum. As such, it is a primary goal of all mathematics instruction and an integral part of all mathematical activity. Problem solving is not a distinct topic but a process that should permeate the entire program and provide the context in which concepts and skills can be learned. (*Curriculum and Evaluation Standards*, NCTM, 1989, p. 23)

In light of the prospect for greater attention to problem solving in K–4, it may be instructive to see what research has already learned about young problem solvers. Is creative thinking, for instance, an essential factor in problem solving? Are boys innately better than girls at the process? Is outstanding skill at reading required? What conditions of problem construction will make problems simpler or harder? Is there a "method" of problem solving that ought to be taught in grades K–4?

To answer such questions, we turned to a project whose purpose had been to collect and integrate all the research that could be found on problem solving in mathematics. Hundreds of studies existed, mostly performed by traditional methods—experimentation and correlation—but partly by less formal methods such as observation. Results of the total collection and synthesis are found in a formal report of research (14). You will be reading a survey extracted and summarized for grades K–4. After this survey has been presented, the first-named author will offer suggestions for classroom practice based on the findings. The second-named author will then react from the view of a teacher on whom the recommendations will fall.

Definition of "Problem"

Early in this century, a mathematics problem was taken to be a task or question stated in words wherein the person attempting its answer must select the operations (see 21). If the procedures were given beforehand, the task was an "example" or, in modern terms, an "exercise."

Morton's definition was broadly applied. However, a weakness was noted, the lack of requirement for effort or delay on the part of the solver in selecting operations and arriving at a solution. Brownell seems among the first to stress the need for "blockage" in the problem-solving process (6). Polya echoed this need, declaring: "To have a problem means: *to search consciously for some action appropriate to attain a clearly conceived, but not immediately attainable, aim*" (27, p. 117). Distinguishing "exercises" from "problems," the survey considered the presence of blockage a standard requirement. Two kinds of problems were found to predominate in the research: *standard* (word or story) problems requiring translation of verbal statements into mathematical operations; and *process* or open-search problems for which the solvers possess no routine procedures for finding an answer.

Standard Problem: A train car has seats for 50 people. If 23 men and 19 women are seated in the car, how many seats are empty?

Process Problem: I have some pennies, nickels, and dimes in my pocket. I put three of the coins in my hand. How much money do you think I have in my hand? (*Curriculum and Evaluation Standards*, NCTM, 1989, p. 24)

Relational and Experimental Outcomes

Studies of problem solving by traditional formal methods fell into four broad categories: (1) characteristics of young problem solvers; (2) conditions for harder and easier problems; (3) effects of different instructional methods on problem-solving performance; and, (4) effects of classroom conditions on problem-solving performance. The following sections present the findings within each classification. Because the number of studies is large, only representative items will be cited herein as references.

Characteristics of Young Problem Solvers

The first results of the survey consider the link between measures of solving performance and each descriptor in a broad field of pupil characteristics (see the listing in Table 7.1).

Performance Measures.   Students excelling in one field of study are often proficient in others, so a large amount of research has probed for links between skill with problems and achievement in other skill areas. The following measures were studied: IQ, language skills, basic skills in mathematics, and problem-solving subskills and behaviors (32, 36).

Mathematical skills, especially concepts, were linked the most strongly with solving performance. Language skills and performance with problems were bound to each other at moderate levels. Native IQ was least connected to solving performance. Regarding subskills and behaviors, good problem solvers could "see" problems better and choose correct operations more often. They often drew pictures to aid comprehension. In judging whether problems were alike or unrelated, they used mathematical structure as the basis for their decisions. Poorer solvers seemed prone to judge problems according to context and surface details.

Mental Attributes.   Investigators over the years have examined the bonds between solving performance and a structure of intellectual skills: creativity, memory, general reasoning, and spatial abilities (20, 35). Strong relationships were found between skill with problems and general reasoning. Spatial skills and solving performance seemed less than powerfully bonded. Memory skills and problem solving were also modestly connected, supporting an observation that memory power in problem solving is more a matter of "what kind" than "how much" material is retained (18). Creative thinking connected the least with solving performance.

Personality Factors.   Relations were studied between solving performance and the following personality factors: attitude toward problem solving, conceptual tempo, field independence, and mental development (20, 35, 36). Researchers have noted that it would be wrong to diagnose student abilities on the basis of inclination or attitude (18); students with skill in mathematics may show the discipline little affection, and willingness may be found without much talent. The survey supported these observations; the linkage was small between attitude toward and performance at prob-

TABLE 7.1.   Pupil
             Characteristics

Performance measures:

IQ
Language skills
     Reading
     Vocabulary
Mathematical skills
     Computation
     Concepts
     Reasoning
Problem solving
     Subskills
     Behaviors

Mental attributes:

Creativity
Memory
Reasoning (general)
Spatial abilities

Personality factors:

Attitude toward
     problem solving
Conceptual tempo
Field independence
Mental development

Personal descriptors:

Gender
Grade level
Socioeconomic status

---

lem solving. *Conceptual tempo* regards the speed at which children make and act on decisions, conceived and measured along a scale from "reflective" for thoughtful children to "impulsive" for those who are rash. Though the bonds were not powerful, reflective students tended toward better performance with problems. *Field independence* is said to be present when children perceive individual items discretely from an embedding field. In contrast, field dependent children view the field in global fashion, preserving and conforming to its nature as a whole. Field independence appeared more related than field dependence to good problem solving.

Of all personality aspects, the factors most linked with good problem solving related to children's mental development. Conservers performed substantially better than children still in preoperations. A similar difference appeared *within* the concrete stage of mental development; children possessing high levels of skill in conservation and class inclusion scored well above children low in these skills. The more that students developed in the concrete stage of thinking, the greater their skill with problems.

According to Piagetian theory, kindergarten and first-grade children are just emerging from *preoperations*. They know that objects have permanence, but they struggle with the facts that an object can change in shape and weight and still remain the same object, that a number of objects can be rearranged and still remain the same number. In Piaget's terms, they cannot "conserve." As children learn how to conserve, they enter the stage of *concrete thinking*, which starts near ages 6 or 7 and continues through ages 11 or 12 (or later in some children). Here they grasp the notions of sets and subsets and use inclusion by classes to construct hierarchies of subsets. However, activities must pertain to real situations and objects, that is, to conditions they can directly perceive.

Personal Descriptors.   A number of studies set out to discover how students differ in solving performance regarding such personal characteristics as gender, grade level in school, and socioeconomic status (SES) (31, 35). In grades K–4, the girls and boys were equally good problem solvers. To study between-grade differences in problem-solving performance, pupils in adjacent grades were given the same problems test. The largest between-grade difference occurred for grades K versus 1 and 1 versus 2, after which the advantage of higher grade level declined. Advantaged children scored well above pupils embedded in low SES.

Conditions for Harder and Easier Problems

Comparison subtraction problems are typically hard for young children to solve (28). To make its solution path more apparent, the problem's question may be revised. Effects were examined as follows (16): Pupils at early grade levels were shown a picture of a group of birds and a smaller number of worms. The children were asked the traditional question: *How many more birds than worms are there?* Responses were collected. Then the children were told and asked: *Suppose the birds all race over and each tries to get a worm! Will every bird get a worm? . . . How many birds won't get a worm?* The differences in answers were striking, as you can see in Table 7.2.

This example highlights how the wording of a problem may determine the ease with which students can solve it. Small changes in setting and sequence of data— indeed in a host of characteristics—may change in major fashion the actions that students take toward solution. A mass of problem-solving research has sought to describe these characteristics, under the general theory that they impact comprehension and thus influence performance with problems. The integrated findings are presented

TABLE 7.2.   Percents of Correct Responses
             When a Problem's Question
             Is Asked Two Ways

School setting	How many more birds?	How many won't get?
Nursery school	17%	83%
Kindergarten	25%	96%
First grade	64%	100%

in this section, regarding three groups of characteristics: context, mechanics, and format.

Context.   Whenever two problems involve the same numbers and same mathematical relations but one deals, for example, with chickens and pigs in a barnyard and the other with boats on a river, the problems differ in "context." This feature thus delineates the non-mathematical setting of the problem situation. The following variations were studied (7, 38): abstract (using symbolic or intangible subjects or objects); concrete (involving a real situation and objects); factual (simply describing); hypothetical (not only describing but using if-then statements to contemplate possible changes); and, personalized (using the solver's own interests and characteristics to set up the problem). Children scored somewhat higher for problems with concrete settings compared with an abstract condition. Performance did not seem especially changed by the use of personalized problems or from factual as opposed to hypothetical situations.

Abstract: There is a certain given number. Three more than twice this given number is equal to 15. What is the number?

Concrete: Billy has 9 gumdrops. Josh has 2 less than twice as many gumdrops as Billy has. How many gumdrops does Josh have?

Factual: Susan has some dolls. Jane has 5 more than twice as many, so she has 17 dolls. How many dolls does Susan have?

Hypothetical: Susan has some dolls. If she had 4 more than twice as many, she would have 14 dolls. How many dolls does Susan have? (7)

Personalized: { Mary's cat / John's dog / Debby's rabbit }   got into the   { fishbowl / chickens / garden }   and ate 1/3 of the 18   { fish / chickens / carrots }.

How many   { fish / chickens / carrots }   did the   { cat / dog / rabbit }   eat? (38)

Mechanics.   This term applies to grammatical structure and how the problem's data are provided and arranged. The following variations were studied (3, 5, 25, 29): problem length, readability, action ("static" if the problem contained no change or movement, "dynamic" if elements were added to or taken from a given set), placement of question (first or last), order of data ("proper" if data appeared in the order needed to solve the problem, otherwise "mixed"), extraneous data, familiar versus unfamiliar terminology (say, "miles" as opposed to "kilometers"), and common versus variable set names ("dogs, dogs, dogs" instead of "dogs, animals, pets"). No advantage to solving performance appeared with regard to problem length, readability, or placing the question. The very young pupils scored better where the problems were dynamic and where common names for sets were used throughout the problem. Better performance was also found for data arranged in proper order and problems using familiar terms. Effects of extraneous data had been studied in grade 4 only. (Teachers at earlier levels may wish to examine effects of extraneous data in their own classes.) Using such data depressed performance.

Format.   The manner by which a problem is presented to the solvers is called "format." (It may, for instance, be written or oral. It may or may not involve the manipulation of some apparatus.) A paragraph of prose for silent reading by the solver constitutes the *standard* format. Two common variations included (a) the *telegraphic* format, which removed noncritical elements and provided essentials in terms of short phrases and (b) the *drawn* format, which presented problem items by way of a picture (diagram or figure) labeled with minimum verbal phrasing (17, 35). Figure 7.1 pro-

FIGURE 7.1   Problem presented in three different formats

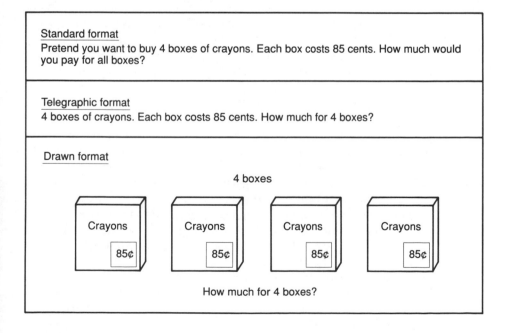

vides a problem in all three formats. Other variations included a picture along with the full problem statement; standard format with instructions for the solver to draw a picture; standard format with vocalization (where solvers considered the problem in silence while someone else read the problem aloud); and standard format with adjunct provisions (manipulatives, steps for the solver to follow, or a set of subquestions to help solvers analyze the problem). Dramatic performance improvements resulted from pictures provided with full problem statements. With lesser impact, drawn formats also tended toward better performance, especially for slower pupils. No benefits were found regarding the telegraphic format or the standard format with vocalization. Substantial solving improvements were found from allowing the uses of physical objects and sets of subquestions. However, pupils directed to follow step-by-step procedures performed less well than free-lance solvers.

Two cautions in using pictures ought to be noted:

1.   The pictures needed to be provided. In the absence of previous diagram training, instructions for solvers to draw a picture had no apparent effect on performance.

2.   The pictures needed to be presented directly on sheets where the pupils were working. Drawn formats projected onto a screen had little effect on performance.

Effects of Different Instructional Methods

Most research on teaching and learning has fallen into three classes: (1) instruction in using a "method" of solving; (2) instruction to develop subskills; and, (3) instruction in related fields. The following sections compare the effects of different instructional programs on problem-solving performance.

Instruction in Problem-Solving Methods.   Three approaches to teaching and learning have proved the most popular over the years: practice, algorithmic methods, and heuristics (34). Practice without explicit direction contains a simple instructional program—immerse the students in problems and help them devise their own solutions. Algorithmic methods have tried to establish rules and procedures which lead without fail to problem solutions. (The method of wanted-givens, for instance, asks pupils to answer the following questions: "What does the problem ask for?" "What facts are given?" "How should these facts be used to get the answer?" and "What is the answer?") Heuristics reject such a hard-and-fast strategy, treating the process of solving like mathematics in the making, governed less by fixed procedures than techniques of discovery and invention. In the typical case, heuristics were taught within Polya's guidelines (26): Understand the problem, plan toward its solution, carry out the plan, and examine the solution obtained.

Research has studied these various methods by giving the pupils instruction (a "treatment") and then comparing their scores with groups instructed by different methods (37). Across all lengths of treatment and all methods of instruction, pupils improved their solving performance from having instruction (whatever its form) as opposed to having no contact with problems. However, instruction in using a method produced performance that seemed no better than scores achieved through teacher-supervised practice.

Training in Problem-Solving Subskills.   The previous methods were typically taught as a complete approach to problem solving. In contrast, a number of studies have taken a "focused" view of the process, training the pupil in just one skill (11, 15, 39). The solving performance that followed such treatments could then be compared with achievements of pupils exposed to similar contact with problems but missing the specialized training. Such training included diagramming or picturing problems, translation from words to mathematics, composing original problems, and special mathematics instruction in reading and vocabulary.

Developing skill with diagrams gave the most pronounced effects on solving performance. Explicit training appeared essential; practice without direct instruction did not produce improvement. More modest gains in achievement resulted from training in writing original problems and training to strengthen mathematical vocabulary. Little effect was found to derive from special instruction in reading mathematics.

It needs to be noted that diagram training produced dramatic performance improvements not only in grades of early childhood but on into high school and college (14). In Grade 4 onward, training in the translation of words to mathematical symbols provided improvement almost as high as the gain provided by diagram training.

Instruction in Related Fields.   Researchers have looked at various disciplines for possible transfer effects on problem solving (15). Fourth grade pupils who had been trained in *general problem solving* were able to solve mathematics problems no better than pupils without special training. In the earlier grades, *computer training* provided no advance in skill at problem solving. When pupils received special training in *reading*, their subsequent problem-solving scores displayed no advantage over their peers who received no such training.

Effects of Classroom Conditions

The final group of research examined effects of classroom conditions on solving performance. Variations were studied as follows (11, 19): extent of attention to problems, homework, small-group study, and uses of programmed lessons, calculators, and computer assisted instruction. Moderate benefits were derived from studying problems intensively (that is, with more instructional time and more practice), parental help with homework, and computer assisted instruction. A use of calculators with problems also provided a moderate lift, the apparent result of greater accuracy and speed in computation. The pupils found little performance improvement in homework assignments they worked by themselves or programmed lessons especially crafted for step-by-step learning. Problem solutions from small-group study surpassed individual efforts. However, in subsequent testing on an individual basis, the pupils who had studied in groups appeared to fare no better than the pupils who studied alone.

Summary of Findings

So far, this review has considered (1) conditions and factors that seem *related* to problem-solving performance; and (2) conditions and factors that stand to *affect* problem-solving performance.

The first group of findings had been produced by studies of correlation. Possessing the same numerical base (the "correlation coefficient"), these findings may be compared by ranking. Listed below are the conditions of study from those most linked with solving performance to those least highly related. Because of statistical variability, the list should not be considered absolute but rather an indication of trends.

Conditions related to problem solving

- Knowledge of mathematical concepts
- Skill at computation
- Skill at mathematical reasoning
- Skill at general reasoning
- Use of structure in judging
  similar problems
- Use of a picture to help work
  problems
- Language skills
    Reading
    Vocabulary
- Spatial abilities
- Field independence
- IQ
- Memory
- Reflective conceptual tempo
- Creativity
- Attitude toward problem solving

The second group of findings (opposite page) emerged from experimentation and other comparative studies. These findings reflect integrative techniques which transformed all the outcomes to a common numerical base ("effect size"). Thus, the findings, like correlations, may be compared by ranking. The next bulleted list groups conditions of study by their perceived effects on problem-solving performance. The upper group shows conditions that may elevate performance, listed in terms of decreasing effect. The middle group lists conditions that appear to have little or no effect; thus, these conditions are alphabetized. The lower group ranks conditions whose presence appears to depress performance. (Please keep in mind the previous caution regarding statistical variability.)

Observational Findings

All of the previous findings resulted from integration of outcomes from correlations, experiments, and other comparative efforts. Aside from these studies, research exists derived from the observation of children engaged in problem solving. Discussions

Conditions that elevate performance

- Diagram training
- Picture with full problem statement
- Translation training
- Training in solving compared with no contact with problems
- School grade level
- Provision of manipulatives
- Level of conservation
- Intensive attention to problems
- Provision of subquestions
- Drawn problem format
- High versus low SES
- Parental help with problems
- Proper order of data in problems
- Common versus variable set names
- Training in composing problems
- Training in math vocabulary
- Use of calculators
- Dynamic action in problems
- Computer assisted instruction
- Familiar terms in problems
- Concrete versus abstract context

Neutral conditions

- Drawn format via transparency
- Factual/hypothetical contexts
- Gender
- Homework done by pupils
- Instruction in:
    General problem solving
    General reading
    Reading mathematics
- Instructions to draw a picture
- Personalized context
- Placement of question
- Practice without training in diagrams
- Problem length
- Problem readability
- Programmed materials
- Small-group instruction
- Telegraphic problem format
- Training in a "method"
- Vocalization of problem

Conditions that depress performance

- Extraneous data
- Use of fixed procedures

that follow will represent the observational style of research, with entries selected to help interpret the previous findings of formal research.

Importance of Problem Representation.   Of all the different instructional methods, instruction in drawing a figure or sketch has provided the greatest advantage to problem-solving performance. Providing physical objects for the children to use in modeling problems also developed large gains in performance. A number of observational studies supports the importance of taking time to "represent" the problem as the initial behavior toward its solution (12,17). At first, the representation is mental, developed by the words of the problem. Converting this mental image to the visible form of physical objects, diagrams, or pictures apparently helps the solver to "see" the problem better and to better flesh out its mathematical structure. This visual representation is then manipulated to arrive at a solution or develop an equation.

   Despite their value, researchers have cautioned against a nonjudicious use of such aids; "manipulatives don't come with guarantees" (2). Rather, they need to be used in ways that connect with the children's existing knowledge and in ways that require reflection and thought by the pupils.

Importance of Skill at Translation.   A major objective of the curriculum is skill with number sentences as an approach to solving problems (8). This is a task of abstraction, converting words to mathematical symbols; it therefore conflicts with demands for concreteness by K–4 pupils. A number of studies indicates that before young children may generate a number sentence to represent the elements of a problem, they first must be able to solve the problem without using a number sentence. Children seem readily able to learn how to write "canonical" sentences (in the forms $a + b = ?$ and $a - b = ?$). The task becomes much more difficult where the unknown set is an addend, minuend, or subtrahend in noncanonical sentences (4).

Is Learning a "Method" Important?   Outcomes of formal research have suggested that instruction in using a method of solving was no more effective at early grade levels than teacher-supervised practice. Indeed, requirements to use fixed procedures may serve to depress instead of improve problem-solving performance. These results may seem surprising until they are examined in light of observational findings. A group of studies has demonstrated that small children, without instruction, are able to solve simple problems in addition and subtraction, inventing approaches which they can apply to problem solutions (9). Imposing a method or set of procedures appears to run counter to natural instincts.

Children's Natural Inclinations.   The early strategies children bring to problem-solving activities include (1) creating models with fingers or manipulatives; (2) using counting methods (such as counting on from first addend, counting on from larger addend, counting backward, and counting unmatched elements from the construction of a one-to-one correspondence); and (3) a use of recalled number facts (1, 13, 33). Counting approaches are more efficient than models with fingers or physical objects; they also demand more advanced counting skills. Using number facts is a sophisticated strategy. Advancing children toward more efficient mathematical operations is an on-going goal of instruction. However, some children continue to use their early primitive strategies (such as counting on their fingers) even after several years of formal instruction. Thus, teachers may find it difficult to distinguish between children whose understanding, while clear, is expressed by primitive methods and children whose understanding itself may be primitive (10). There is value to probing below surface level to better discern true abilities in the children's concept-related and problem-solving activities.

Trends in the Study of Problem Solving. The hallmark of past research has been its orientation toward "product" as the measure of problem-solving performance. In recent years, the attention has shifted from *product* (solutions) to *process* (the path to solutions). According to Polya, this path is comprised of a set of mental behaviors: understand, plan, execute, and look back. The view of problem solving as behaviors performed in sequence suggests a need for the mind to possess a higher-level process that can oversee the behaviors and purposely regulate shifts from one to another. This higher process is *metacognition*, concerned with planning what to do and what is being done. Researchers of cognitive processes consider skill at metacognition a primary factor in good problem solving; indeed, a number of papers exist on the topic (30). However, little research has been done on how and when to develop this skill in the field of mathematics.

Implications for Classroom Practice

Our presentation of findings is finished. Along the way, we hope you have gathered a number of implications that pertain to your classroom activities. From our perspective, the following seem to merit your thought and reflection.

On Basic Skills. Continued stress on concepts and reasoning seem needed to build a foundation for good problem solving. There is also a need for special stress on the vocabulary of mathematics.

On Mistaken Beliefs. IQ, memory, and creativity seem only mildly related to solving performance. These results may be used to dispel beliefs that only the very bright students can be successful at problem solving.

Boys do not seem innately better than girls at solving problems. Differences in teachers' interactions and expectations across gender could account for much of the differences that emerge in later years.

The belief should be challenged that trouble with problems is basically trouble with reading. Some skill at reading is clearly required. Nonetheless, programs of special instruction in reading mathematics and general reading do not seem to offer improvement in solving; neither do moderate changes in problem readability levels. High skill at reading does not seem demanded for good problem solving.

On Problem Posing.   Factors of context, mechanics, and format relate to harder
and easier problems. Thus, they relate to problem *posing*, where teachers make up
their own problems in teaching and for assignment to pupils. These factors may be
especially helpful in dealing with pupil ability levels; using conditions toward easier
problems may help slower children make progress, while variations may be applied
to offer bright pupils more challenge. Below a problem is shown two ways: first with
the data in "proper" order and then with the data more scrambled, thereby providing
an easier and a more difficult version. Such variations in problem assignments can
help assure that *all* of the children solve *some* of the problems at each learning
session.

It also seems helpful to offer the children chances to pose their own problems.

Problem in Proper Order: Bob collected 60 pounds of paper to sell. He wrapped
the paper in 10-pound bundles. If he gets 20 cents per bundle, how much money
will Bob receive for the paper?

Problem in Mixed Order: Bob collected paper to sell in 10-pound bundles. He
gets 20 cents per bundle. If he collected 60 pounds, how much money will Bob
receive for the paper?

On Methods and Problem Representations.   The study of problems has taken for
granted that children should learn a "method" of solving. Even heuristics, the least
prescriptive, assign a set of procedures that the solver should consciously follow. Ob-
ligations to learn a method are called into question by past research findings.

1.   When they first enter school, young children can solve simple problems.
Moreover, their intuitive skills improve in spontaneous fashion as the pupils advance
from grade to grade.

2.   Attempts to ingrain a method of solving have failed to lift the children's performance beyond the levels achieved through practice with teacher oversight. Indeed, those pupils instructed to use a list of fixed procedures are usually found to
score below children left to their own devices.

These findings suggest that children possess a built-in method of problem solving,
complete with all the behaviors needed for working toward problem solutions. It
follows that classroom instruction ought to build upon and enrich their natural instincts. Past research supports this suggestion; the greatest advances in problem solving resulted from focused instruction. Training in diagram drawing provided the
highest improvement in solving (see box on page 160). Look also at the relative gains
provided by the use of physical objects and by having pictures provided with full
problem statements. Perhaps the early childhood grades should focus on problem
representation rather than striving to master a method. Consider this scenario:

• In the earliest grades, provide an abundance of physical objects for children to use
in problem solving.

- As the children mature, use pictures and figures to move them away from dependence on physical objects.
- When children are ready, give training in diagrams, asking that they provide their own pictorial representations.

It ought to be stressed that skill with diagrams needs to be nurtured, with training provided. Telling the students to "draw a picture" does not seem sufficient. Neither does offering practice in drawing but no direct intervention.

We hope to be clear: No suggestion is made that pupils ought to use physical objects or pictures to solve every problem. Some of the children may seldom need aids, and few should require them at each opportunity. What seems important for all the pupils is getting the habit of taking time to understand the problem before they plunge toward its solution. Specific training in representation will offer them tools for use on demand.

On Skill with Number Sentences.   Diagram drawing and sentence construction are kindred activities. Both involve problem representations, diagrams in a visual format and sentences in symbolic form. It stands to reason that pupils' trouble with number sentences ought to be eased if they are taught to use diagrams as an intermediate representation. The visual form can help them arrive at the higher abstraction of symbolization.

On Strategies and Concepts.   As researchers have noted, young children possess informal ways to add and subtract. A goal of instruction is moving the pupils to more and more efficient approaches, from modeling to counting methods and then to using number facts. In this regard, problem-solving activities can help identify pupils' bents in adding and subtracting and move them away from primitive methods. The use of more efficient approaches should help the pupils bring into balance their understanding of concepts and their abilities to express that understanding.

On Problem-Solving Assessment.   A focus on skill in representation implies a similar focus on that behavior during testing. Judgments of skill in representation, of course, should measure correctness. They also should offer the children great latitude for individual expression. (Chapter 15 provides a more detailed discussion of assessment.)

Synopsis

Suggestions emerging from past research provide for stressing basic skills, heading off mistaken beliefs, accounting for different ability levels, instructing in problem representation, and blending instruction in number sentences with stress on representation.

All these suggestions are made with an eye to the natural limits imposed on the children in tasks of abstraction. These limits are set by the level of thinking typical in grades K–4, the concrete stage of mental development. Research for the higher grade levels shows that the greatest advances in problem solving occur in middle school and high school, where students are able to deal with abstractions, consciously separate mental behaviors, generalize problem solutions, and apply Polya's guidelines for solving (14). Grades K–4 may thus be assigned the crucial role of *preparation for good problem solving*. They are the years for building foundations.

A Teacher Reacts

Teachers sometimes view research with skepticism, a large grain of salt. We may tend to deny its validity on the basis of our own experience, and perhaps we imagine sundry conditions that stand to prevent the application of its findings. My response to the present research departs from this tradition; I react to its implications with enthusiasm. The findings are practical, they are timely, and their broad resource base makes them credible. Let's consider several points from the classroom teacher's perspective.

1. In the synopsis, we are reminded that abstract thought is not ordinarily characteristic of the students with whom we deal in grades K–4. Obviously then, our students—even those highly motivated—will encounter developmental obstacles in attempting to reason logically, deductively, and symbolically. To overcome these limitations, we simply must rely on concrete representations of problems. The pupils may then manipulate the physical model to conceptualize and resolve the problem. As the pupil's mental development progresses, a semi-concrete approach with pictures and diagrams can complement and supplement the use of purely concrete representations.

Undoubtedly, there will be teachers who envision challenges to classroom management when counters and cubes and rubber bands and other throwable objects are used in modeling problems. However, my experience shows that stressful scenarios need not set the tone for problem solving. When the study of problems has been habitually accompanied by concrete and semi-concrete representations, management troubles tend to be minimal. Manipulatives used in the context of cooperative learning may also help to decrease their misuse in problem solving.

2. The research indicates that special attention to mathematical vocabulary can help promote success with problems. I would add the caution that the vocabulary needs to parallel the child's experience level. Effective K–4 teachers develop a repertoire of alternative descriptions for mathematics terms and symbols to increase their pupils' understanding. The danger then exists that these substitutions will continue to be used when no longer needed. Care should be taken to teach correct terms as soon as the child can manage those terms.

3. The research suggests strongly that students' skill with diagrams and pictures can provide understandings that may lead to problem solutions. The drawing of a picture is a natural extension of "acting out" a version of the problem. With a little practice and continued assurance that the goals are practical instead of artistic, most of my students are able to sketch a diagram that correctly relates the critical data of a

dramatized problem. The trick is to get the student to initiate the diagram independently. Teacher reliance on published material that already contains illustrations and diagrams probably contributes to the students' disinclination to draw their own. This condition could perhaps be remedied by using problems composed by the teacher along with those supplied by a publisher.

4.   Research implications involving translation also invite some commentary. Relatively minor attention seems given to this skill in grades K–4, probably because of requirements for abstract thinking not yet developed in most pupils of that age. Integration of translation training with problem representation through diagrams offers hope of easing the difficulty, not only for number sentences in equation form but also for statements involving inequalities. Asking the students to translate the sentence back into words after sentence construction may also be useful in helping them determine whether or not the statement is reasonable.

Looking Ahead . . .

Past research shows the value of pictures but has not revealed techniques of instruction for broad application. Numerous other questions remain: How to enter problem solving in scope-and-sequence charting; how and when to train children in metacognition; how to weave such findings into teacher training programs. As long-term goals, problem-solving researchers will need to study these questions. In the near term, however, they have to be answered by you creative teachers there in your classes.

Ray Hembree

How great it would be if implementing all the suggestions of this report could guarantee that K–4 pupils may solve all the problems they ever encounter. Such guarantees being impossible, will we all as teachers strive to assure that pupils leave our classes with enough interest and optimism to approach their future problems productively? I believe this assurance may be provided by building supports in the K–4 years that will help to develop higher skills in all the grades that follow.

Harold Marsh

About the Authors

Ray Hembree teaches mathematics and performs educational research in mathematics at Adrian College, Adrian, Michigan.

Harold Marsh is a teacher and mathematics coordinator for Adrian elementary schools, Adrian, Michigan.

References

1. BAROODY, A. (1984). Children's difficulties in subtraction: Some causes and questions. *Journal for Research in Mathematics Education, 15*, 203–213.

*2. BAROODY, A. (1989). Manipulatives don't come with guarantees. *Arithmetic Teacher, 37*(3), 4–5.

3. BEARDSLEE, E., & JERMAN, M. (1973). *Linguistic variables in verbal arithmetic problems*. University Park: Pennsylvania State University. (ERIC Document Reproduction Service No. ED 073 926)

*4. BEBOUT, H. (1990). Children's symbolic representations of addition and subtraction word problems. *Journal for Research in Mathematics Education, 21*, 123–131.

5. BILSKY, L., & JUDD, T. (1986). Sources of difficulty in the solution of verbal arithmetic problems by mentally retarded and nonretarded individuals. *American Journal of Mental Deficiency, 90*, 395–402.

6. BROWNELL, W. (1942). Problem solving. In N. Henry (Ed.), *The psychology of learning*. 41st yearbook of the National Society for the Study of Education. Part II (pp. 415–443). Chicago: University of Chicago Press.

*7. CALDWELL, J., & GOLDIN, G. (1979). Variables affecting word problem difficulty in elementary school mathematics. *Journal for Research in Mathematics Education, 10*, 323–336.

*8. CARPENTER, T. (1985). Learning to add and subtract: An exercise in problem solving. In E. Silver (Ed.), *Teaching and learning mathematical problem solving: Multiple research perspectives* (pp. 17–40). Hillsdale, NJ: Erlbaum.

9. CARPENTER, T., HIEBERT, J., & MOSER, J. (1981). Problem structure and first-grade children's initial solution processes for simple addition and subtraction problems. *Journal for Research in Mathematics Education, 12*, 27–39.

10. COBB, P. (1986). Concrete can be abstract: A case study. *Educational Studies in Mathematics, 17*, 37–48.

11. DARCH, C., CARNINE, D., & GERSTEN, R. (1984). Explicit instruction in mathematics problem solving. *Journal of Educational Research, 77*, 351–359.

*12. DE CORTE, E., VERSCHAFFEL, L., & DE WIN, L. (1985). Influence of rewording verbal problems on children's problem representations and solutions. *Journal of Educational Psychology, 77*, 460–470.

*13. FUSON, K. (1982). An analysis of the counting-on solution procedure in addition. In T. Carpenter, J. Moser, & T. Romberg (Eds.), *Addition and subtraction: A cognitive perspective* (pp. 67–81). Hillsdale, NJ: Erlbaum.

*14. HEMBREE, R. (1991). Experiments and relational studies in problem solving: A meta-analysis. *Journal for Research in Mathematics Education, 23*, 242–273.

*15. HENNEY, M. (1970, May). *Improving mathematics verbal problem solving ability through reading instruction*. Paper presented at the conference of the International Reading Association, Anaheim, CA. (ERIC Document Reproduction Service No. ED 044 243)

*16. HUDSON, T. (1980). Young children's difficulty with "How many more _____ than . . . are there?" (Doctoral dissertation, Indiana University). *Dissertation Abstracts International, 41*, 377B.

17. IBARRA, C., & LINDVALL, C. (1982). Factors associated with the ability of kindergarten children to solve simple arithmetic story problems. *Journal of Educational Research, 75*, 149–155.

*18. KRUTETSKII, V. (1976). *The psychology of mathematical abilities in schoolchildren*. Chicago: University of Chicago Press.

19. MAERTENS, N., & JOHNSTON, J. (1972). Effects of arithmetic homework upon the attitudes and achievement of fourth, fifth and sixth grade pupils. *School Science and Mathematics, 72,* 117–126.

20. MEYER, R. (1978). Mathematical problem-solving performance and intellectual abilities of fourth-grade children. *Journal for Research in Mathematics Education, 9,* 334–348.

21. MORTON, R. (1927). *Teaching arithmetic in the intermediate grades.* New York: Silver, Burdett.

*22. MOSER, J., & CARPENTER, T. (1982). Young children are good problem solvers. *Arithmetic Teacher, 30*(3), 24–26.

*23. NATIONAL COUNCIL OF TEACHERS OF MATHEMATICS. (1980). *An agenda for action: Recommendations for school mathematics of the 1980s.* Reston, VA: National Council of Teachers of Mathematics.

*24. NATIONAL COUNCIL OF TEACHERS OF MATHEMATICS. (1989). *Curriculum and evaluation standards for school mathematics.* Reston, VA: National Council of Teachers of Mathematics.

25. PAUL, D., NIBBELINK, W., & HOOVER, H. (1986). The effects of adjusting readability on the difficulty of mathematics story problems. *Journal for Research in Mathematics Education, 17,* 163–172.

*26. POLYA, G. (1945). *How to solve it.* Princeton, NJ: Princeton University Press.

*27. POLYA, G. (1962). *Mathematical discovery.* Volume I. New York: Wiley.

28. RILEY, M., GREENO, J., & HELLER, J. (1983). Development of children's problem-solving ability in arithmetic. In H. Ginsburg (Ed.), *The development of mathematical thinking* (pp. 153–196). New York: Academic Press.

*29. ROSENTHAL, D., & RESNICK, L. (1974). Children's solution processes in arithmetic word problems. *Journal of Educational Psychology, 66,* 817–825.

30. SCHOENFELD, A. (1987). Cognitive science and mathematics education: An overview. In A. Schoenfeld (Ed.), *Cognitive science and mathematics education* (pp. 1–31). Hillsdale, NJ: Erlbaum.

31. SCOTT, R., & LIGHTHALL, F. (1967). Relationship between content, sex, grade, and degree of disadvantage in arithmetic problem solving. *Journal of School Psychology, 6,* 61–67.

32. SILVER, E. (1979). Student perceptions of relatedness among mathematical verbal problems. *Journal for Research in Mathematics Education, 10,* 195–210.

*33. STEFFE, L., THOMPSON, P., & RICHARDS, J. (1982). Children's counting in arithmetical problem solving. In T. Carpenter, J. Moser, & T. Romberg (Eds.), *Addition and subtraction: A cognitive perspective* (pp. 83–97). Hillsdale, NJ: Erlbaum.

*34. SUYDAM, M. (1980). Untangling clues from research on problem solving. In S. Krulik & R. Reys (Eds.), *Problem solving in school mathematics* (pp. 34–50). Reston, VA: National Council of Teachers of Mathematics.

35. THREADGILL-SOWDER, J., SOWDER, L., MOYER, J., & MOYER, M. (1985). Cognitive variables and performance on mathematical story problems. *Journal of Experimental Education, 54*(1), 56–62.

36. WHITAKER, D. (1980). Relationships between selected noncognitive factors and the problem solving performance of fourth-grade children. In J. Harvey & T. Romberg (Eds.), *Problem-solving studies in mathematics.* Madison: University of Wisconsin, Research and Development Center for Individualized Schooling. (ERIC Document Reproduction Service No. ED 197 962)

37. WILSON, J. (1967). The role of structure in verbal problem solving. *Arithmetic Teacher, 14,* 486–497.

38. WRIGHT, J., & WRIGHT, C. (1986). Personalized verbal problems: An application of the language experience approach. *Journal of Educational Research, 79,* 358–362.

*39. YANCEY, A., THOMPSON, C., & YANCEY, J. (1989). Children must learn to draw diagrams. *Arithmetic Teacher, 36*(7), 15–19.

CHAPTER 8

Teaching Measurement

Patricia S. Wilson and Ruth Rowland

Rinnnggggg . . . it's 6 o'clock. After your shower, you realize that the water pressure seemed much lower than yesterday. You will have to look into it next week! Mechanically, you take the six-ounce orange juice can from the freezer and mix it with three cans of water. You pour your favorite cereal into a bowl and add milk. Sliding into your chair, you read the cereal box claiming that a three-ounce serving has ninety calories. Your bowl looks like it holds 1 cup and you wonder how many ounces of cereal you ate. No time to ponder. You ease your car into twenty-miles-per-hour traffic. At the corner you pull into the gas station, wondering why this four-person, economy-sized car, which was advertised to get thirty miles per gallon, is always out of gas. You put in eight gallons and you're on your way again. Your five-mile trip took half an hour! Oh well, there's still time to grab enough construction paper from the supply room to cover the bulletin board. Trying to decide how many sheets you need, you picture the bulletin board. It's about six desks long and maybe one third as high. That probably means about twenty-four pieces of paper. You hurry back to the room and just finish covering the bulletin board in time to see your thirty students of all shapes and shoe sizes trip into the room. A new twenty-four hours begins!

Measurement is an integral part of our lives, but we rarely notice the variety of measurements we use. In the normal course of a day, we use relatively few precise measures (e.g., six ounces of orange juice, three ounces of cereal, eight gallons of gas) but we do estimate constantly (twenty-miles-per-hour traffic, five-mile trip, half-hour trip, one-cup cereal bowl, about twenty-four sheets of paper). We frequently use nonstandard units such as three cans, six desks, or four-person car. We use several measurements that are comparative, such as lower pressure and economy-sized car. We use average measurements such as thirty miles per gallon even though we know there is some variance depending on conditions. Some measures are rates such as miles per hour or miles per gallon. We use a variety of different units of measure including two different units with the same name, ounces that measure capacity and ounces that measure weight.

Teaching needs to take advantage of these daily situations in measurement, but our current practices and curriculum do not incorporate enough real-world applications (17). Students need to be actively involved in measuring and need to encounter the associated problems such as choosing a unit or dealing with fractional units.

There are many opportunities during a typical day to address measurement concepts. I learned to notice applications in areas such as Social Studies, Science, and even in Language Arts.

- We estimated the area needed for the baby chicks we kept in the classroom.
- Each day we estimated their weights and then measured and recorded the actual weight.

—Ruth Rowland

It is easy to recall everyday measurement situations that are familiar to students, but think for a moment how frequently measurement concepts are used in learning mathematics. Measurement is an important foundation for most of what we do in elementary school mathematics. Counting is closely related to measuring. When we say there are five blocks in a pile, we are measuring the quantity of blocks. Teaching geometry involves numerous measurement concepts such as perimeter, area, angle measure, side length, and distance. We ask children to sort objects according to measurement properties such as length, volume, or weight. Fractions are often modeled using circles or rectangles. We assume that students are thinking about area and that they notice that the figure has been divided into three congruent parts, but we know that many students confuse length and area (18). Some students focus on only one dimension such as width. Students might incorrectly picture one-third as a circle divided into three parts where the width of each piece is equal as shown in Figure 8.1. Often confusion about measurement concepts contributes to misunderstandings in counting, geometry, mathematical properties, and fraction models.

FIGURE 8.1   Incorrect model of 1/3

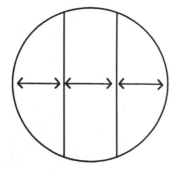

As adults, we have acquired our knowledge of measure over an extended time. Learning about one measurement system has helped us to learn about other systems (40). For example, knowing length is additive should help us to understand that other measurement systems such as area and time are additive.

Additive measures
The area of the living room and dining room is the sum of the areas of each room. If I worked one hour before lunch and two hours after lunch, I know I have worked 1 + 2 hours, or 3 hours.

However, we must know enough about each measurement systems' unique characteristics to avoid over-generalization. For example, rates and volume are not always additive.

Nonadditive measures
If I averaged 50 miles per hour on the first part of my trip and 40 miles per hour on the second part of my trip, I definitely did *not* average 40 + 50 or 90 miles per hour for the entire trip!

A cup of sugar stirred into 2 cups of water does not create 3 cups of solution.

Measurement is, at the same time, extremely useful and extremely complex. How can we help children learn to measure? What problems are students likely to encounter? Is some knowledge prerequisite for other knowledge? Research offers a foundation for addressing these questions and making tough teaching decisions.

Learning to Measure

Much of the research related to learning to measure is based on the pioneer work of Jean Piaget and his colleagues done in Switzerland in the late 1940s (26, 27, 35). Psychologists conducted extensive interviews with children in a laboratory situation to track the development of children's ideas of space and measure. In the following sections, we discuss some of the research findings that help us to understand how children learn to measure.

Perception and Representation

Piaget and Inhelder (26) claimed that children developed their spatial concepts at two distinct levels, perceptual and representational. Perceptual ideas were developed as a result of direct contact with objects. As students hold boxes, pace off distances, lift baskets of apples or trace over triangles with their fingers, they are developing perceptual knowledge about the associated objects. In contrast, students develop representational ideas by reference to objects that are not directly perceived. Students must use their imagination and memory to represent ideas. If a student is given a picture of a square and asked to reproduce the drawing, the task is measuring motor development and perception. If a child is asked to draw a square without an example, the task is measuring the ability to represent the perception. The two levels, perceptual and representational, work together to help the child create ideas about space. As students try to represent ideas, their perceptions change and as students' perceptions change, they are better able to represent ideas. Soviet researchers (42) were interested in promoting the growth of spatial thinking. They claimed students need to visualize mental objects and should practice rotating, sliding, and reflecting objects in their minds. They suggested activities where students observe objects and then draw the objects from different viewpoints.

Try this!
Place a pyramid on a table with children seated around the edge.

1. Ask students to draw the object without touching it. (Perceptual)
2. Remove the pyramid from sight, and ask the children to draw the pyramid. (Representational)

Action research
Set a chair, desk, or bicycle in front of the class. Ask third and fourth graders to draw the object from a top view, side view, and a front view.

1. Allow students to move around the object looking at it from different perspectives as they draw. (Perceptual)
2. Repeat the assignment with a different object, but ask the students to draw the different views while they remain in their desks. (Representational)
   Record the differences between the perceptual and representational drawings for each student.

Piaget and Inhelder (26) found young children's first representations of space ignored measure, proportions, and any sense of perspective. At ages 3 and 4, children are more attentive to ideas such as closeness, separation, order, and enclosure. By the time children are 6 years old, they can differentiate shapes according to their angles and even their dimensions, but there is a slight gap between recognizing and drawing shapes. By 7 years, students show more thought about the relationship of sides and angles. Before 7 years, children pay little attention to orientation.

Recent studies (4, 20, 30) have challenged Piaget's findings and have shown that children can achieve measurement concepts at a much younger age than previously suggested. Piaget and his colleagues have provided a valuable framework for studying the abilities of young children, but we must be cautious not to limit our expectations of young students. Recent research suggests that we still have much to learn about how young children perceive space and construct measurement concepts.

You may wish to design some tasks that would give you insight into when your students are working at the perceptual level or the representational level and to what degree they are attending to special characteristics of objects. Have students copy figures, draw objects that they can see, and draw objects from memory. How do the drawings differ? What characteristics of the objects seem important to students? Do the drawings reflect the original orientation, shape, and size? Does number seem to be more important than size and shape?

Activity, Construction, and Reflection

Students need to construct measurement concepts for themselves. Being actively involved in measuring helps students to construct ideas but we must not let the process end there. Our goal is to help students eventually develop abstract ideas such as unit, perimeter, area, and rate. The process of construction followed by reflection makes abstraction possible (26). After constructing ideas, children need to reflect on their ideas by discussing their activities or writing about them. The *Curriculum and Evaluation Standards* (22) emphasizes the importance of including opportunities for students to communicate mathematics in grades K–4. Intuition of space is not developed by collecting properties of a concept, but intuition requires that students actively construct and communicate ideas. It is tempting to teach and test for a collection of properties such as "there are three feet in a yard" or "every square has four sides of equal length," but it is not enough to listen to the teacher explain or list important ideas. If students construct ideas for themselves instead of just memorizing properties, they will be able to discuss these ideas and move beyond physical reality to abstract representations and relationships between properties. They will be able to operate with their new ideas.

Consider how this process might apply to learning the concept of perimeter. A child could begin constructing the concept with concrete materials such as string or sticks. They could create closed figures and show the paths around the figures. They could walk around a figure drawn with chalk on the floor. They could take two pieces of string with equal length and create two different figures, showing that different figures can have the same perimeter. These are ways for the student actively to construct ideas. Next, students need to reflect on their activities by telling what they did and what they discovered. The class should take this opportunity to question, probe, and challenge. This is in sharp contrast to reading a definition of perimeter from a book or watching the teacher demonstrate several examples of perimeter on the chalkboard. An active approach provides the child with a foundation for moving toward abstract generalizations about perimeter such as every closed figure has a perimeter, different figures can have the same perimeter, and the perimeter of a figure can be stretched out and measured like a line.

Counting and Measuring

The experience of learning to count and learning number concepts has many similarities with the experience of learning to measure and learning measurement concepts (27, 31). When students learn to count they work with discrete or separate objects assigning numbers in a one-to-one correspondence to represent the continuing string of objects. The major difference between counting and measuring is found in the actions. We count discrete or separate objects and we measure continuous properties such as length, area, or volume.

Despite the complexity of measurement concepts, the basic idea of measure is beautiful in its simplicity. A continuous property such as area, length, or density must be subdivided into discrete parts so they can be counted. First you choose a unit. Second, you repeat the unit covering the object. This process of iterating the unit divides the object into equal subdivisions with perhaps a fraction of a unit left over. Finally, the units are counted to produce a measure of the object. For example, if you wanted to measure the surface on the top of your desk, you would focus on the continuous property of area. You might choose a unit such as a square floor tile, a rectangular piece of paper, or a square foot. You would then iterate the unit covering the top of the desk by placing the tiles so there is no overlap and no spaces. If there is a region smaller than a unit remaining, you would decide how you want to account for this area (e.g., rounding, ignoring, using a different unit).

Try this!
Using a string or thin rope, define an irregular closed figure. Use square units to cover the area. Decide how to count the fractional parts of a unit.

Finally, you count the units and you have a measurement of the area of your desk. The process of measuring parallels the process of counting since it involves a similar attention to countable objects (choosing and placing square units on the desk) and inclusion (an area of two square units is part of an area of three square units).

Conservation, Transitivity, and Unit

The process of measuring is based on three fundamental components of measure: conservation, transitivity, and unit. A lack of understanding of any of these three components can cause problems in learning to measure.

Conservation.   Underlying all measurement is the idea that an object maintains the same shape and size if it is moved or subdivided into parts. If a child operates with this understanding, we say that he or she conserves.

Piaget tested the idea of conservation of length by presenting students with two rods of equal length. After the students agreed that the lengths of the two rods were equal, one rod was pushed ahead of the other rod. If a child claimed the moved rods were different lengths, the child was considered not to conserve length. To test conservation of area, students were shown two congruent rectangles. One of the rectangles was cut along the diagonal and the two pieces were rearranged to form a triangle.

Children who were able to conserve area recognized that the the two figures had the same area. Piaget (27) claimed that conservation of length and area were accomplished in parallel stages that were completed in the age range of 7 to 9 years old.

Conserving volume appears to come in two parts. Piaget found that by the time children were about 8 years old they could conserve volume in the sense that the quantity did not change. If a ball of clay was stretched into a long sausage shape, the students recognized that they were the same. However, students did not conserve volume in the sense of occupying space until they were about 11 years old. Younger students would claim that the sausage-shaped clay would displace more water than the ball of clay when put in a bowl of water.

Try this!
Test conservation of volume using cubes such as building blocks. Arrange a specific number of blocks in a tower, and then reconstruct the tower into a different shape using the same number of blocks. If the children recognize that the two buildings have the same volume, they conserve volume in the sense of occupying space.

Action research
Videotape students from several grade levels doing this activity, and compare the results across grade levels. Ask students to explain their thinking and illustrate their ideas using the blocks.

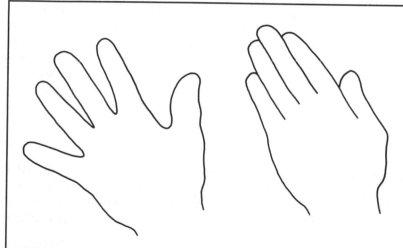

Try this!
Have each child trace around a closed hand and an open hand. Ask which has the most area? The class discussion is always interesting and you can actually see when a student realizes that the areas must be the same.

In 1984, Kathleen Hart (10) conducted some measurement experiments in England with 12–15-year-old students. Her findings were consistent with Piaget's findings for a majority of her students since 72 percent of her students conserved both length and area. However 70 percent of the students who could not conserve length could conserve area, and 70 percent of those who could not conserve area could conserve length. She also found that 29 percent of the students who could successfully complete a volume conservation task could not conserve length and area. These findings remind us that individual students do differ and we should use research findings as guidelines rather than dictates of what children can and cannot do.

Try some of the conservation tasks with your students and determine which students conserve length, area, or volume. This information will help you understand student errors, ask useful questions, and interpret their actions. Do not restrict your measurement activities because some of your students do not conserve; students will learn to conserve by participating and reflecting (12, 13).

Transitivity.   If you want to compare the length of two pencils, you would probably set them next to each other, align their erasers, and easily decide which was longer. A problem occurs if you want to compare two items that cannot be aligned and compared directly. If you want to compare the height of your work table to the height of a table in the library, you would want to use a stick or rod to mark off the height of your table, then carry the stick to the library, and compare length marked on the stick with the height of the library table. This process uses the idea of transitivity. If length a is less than length b and length b is less than length c, then length a is less than length c. This is the same process that you would use to compare the distance around your head with the length of your arm. You would wrap a string around your head, and then compare the length of the string to the length from your shoulder to your wrist. By comparing the length of the strings, you can compare the distances. Smedslund claimed that transitive reasoning was developed by the time students were 8 years old (34). Research findings vary on when to expect students to use transitivity. Most students will develop transitive reasoning by eight years old (13, 34), but it may occur as early as 4 years old (3).

Unit.   To understand the role of a unit of measurement, the student must understand what attribute is being measured. For example, if you are measuring area, you need a two dimensional unit such as square, triangle, or parallelogram to cover the surface. If you are measuring an angle, you need a unit such as a wedge or degree that will describe the turn or sweep between the rays.

Students must also understand how the chosen unit influences the number of units. A distance could be correctly reported as 72 inches or 6 feet illustrating that it takes more inches than feet to cover a given distance. This inverse relationship between size of the unit and number of units required is difficult for children (4, 13, 10).

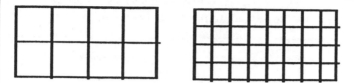

How many 1 cm squares?
How many square 1/2 cm squares?

While 87 percent of the British students (12 to 15 years) tested could figure out how many 1-cm squares were needed to cover a 4 x 2 cm rectangle, 60 percent doubled the answer to find how many 1/2 cm square tiles were needed. (The test problem did not show the grid.)

Action research

After covering rectangles with different square units, ask third- or fourth-grade students to cover a given rectangle (4 x 2) with 1 cm squares. Ask students to estimate how many 1/2 cm squares (show a 1/2 cm square) would cover the same area.

In one task, first- and second-grade students agreed that two strips were the same length. When one strip was covered with small units and the other was covered with fewer large units, students claimed that the strip with small units was longer because, numerically, it had more units (6). The numerical cue was more powerful than their perceptual cues about unit size. This study reminds us that measurement activities alone are not sufficient for making the point. It is helpful for students to cover distances with different units, but we cannot expect young children to focus on both dimensions, number of units, and sizes of units, without assistance from the teacher.

The National Assessment of Educational Progress (NAEP) reported that third- and seventh-grade students continue to have some difficulty with understanding units of measure (18). Students were shown a picture of three boxes of equal size. They were told that each box was to be filled with one of the following pictured objects: marbles, tennis balls, or softballs. Almost two-thirds of the national sample of third-grade students correctly reported that the softball box would have the fewest objects. However in a related task, students were told the number of sheets of paper that each person used to measure the height of a door and were asked who had the longest length of paper. Ninety-two percent of the third graders answered incorrectly and over half responded that the student who used the most sheets had the longest sheet of paper. In this problem the inverse relationship between size of unit and number of units was not clear. The picture format of the first problem may have cued the students to focus on the size of the units and to see an inverse relationship between the size of units and the number of units. In contrast, the second problem focused the students' attention on the number of units and they did not recognize the inverse relationship.

Some students focus intensely on number at the expense of all other considerations necessary in measuring. We know that the development of number ideas is closely associated with learning to measure, but early experiences where the answer is always a number encourages students to rely on numbers too much (10).

Measuring requires students to make decisions along several dimensions at the same time:

What is being measured?
(length, angle, weight)
What is a good unit?
(inches, square inches, ounces, floor tiles)
What is an appropriate procedure?
(iterating, covering, counting)
Which instrument is needed to count the units?
(ruler, protractor, thermometer)

Student Difficulties

Based on research about children's knowledge of measuring, most student difficulties can be attributed to one or more of the following problems:

1. lack of understanding about the properties being measured
2. underdeveloped perceptions and representations
3. lack of understanding of conservation and transitivity
4. lack of understanding about units
5. overemphasis on numerical cues

The next four sections provide examples of student difficulties as they occur in traditional measurement topics that you may be teaching in your classroom. Consider how these problems might be affecting your students as they investigate area, perimeter, ruler use, angles, volume, or any problem involving measurement.

Area and Perimeter

In comparing areas of rectangles, 5- and 6-year-old students tended to focus on the one-dimensional length of the rectangle, rather than the two-dimensional space enclosed (26). In Figure 8.2, rectangle A has an area of 5 square units and rectangle B has an area of 9 square units, but some students would claim the area of rectangle A is greater than rectangle B because rectangle A is longer. In this case, students seem to lack an understanding of the property of area.

Some students developed strategies for finding area that did involve both width and height. When asked to compare the areas of two rectangles, some students compared the sums of the height and width (2, 14, 32), and others compared the lengths of the diagonals of the rectangles (19). These strategies do not work in all cases, but they are useful for many common cases. These limited strategies may be an artifact of the narrow range of rectangles that students see (33). Since most rectangles used in classroom demonstrations are approximately the same shape, comparing the sum of the

FIGURE 8.2   Rectangles

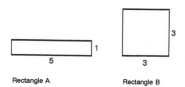

height and width works quite well! Students need to explore pairs of rectangles like those in Figure 8.2 in order to realize that their strategies may not work on all rectangles. Teachers need to vary their examples of rectangles and other polygons.

Distinguishing between area and perimeter continues to be difficult for students (15, 37). NAEP (18) reported that third graders showed little skill or knowledge about area and perimeter. This lack of understanding continued to cause problems in the upper grades (10, 18, 41). The poor performance at upper grade levels suggests a need for establishing a conceptual base at the elementary level. We need to focus on the properties of area and perimeter, appropriate units, and counting strategies. Formulas should follow the conceptual development and should not be emphasized in the K–4 mathematics curriculum.

Using a Ruler

NAEP reports that students worked well with instruments when they were in a familiar situation. Third graders were able to read and interpret correctly a thermometer, scale, and digital watch. However, most third graders and half of the seventh graders were unable to measure a line segment with a pictured ruler where the end of the ruler was not aligned with the end of the line segment. Students focused on one end of the line and read the number off the ruler in the same manner that you would read a thermometer.

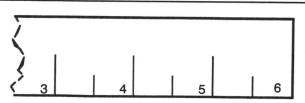

Try this!
Can your students measure a line segment with a broken ruler? You can make broken rulers out of strips of paper and allow them to measure small items in the room.

Action research
Ask students to explain how they used their broken ruler to measure. List several popular strategies (correct and incorrect) and record how many students used each strategy.

Students missed the importance of the starting place in positioning the ruler (13). We need to emphasize the role of the ruler as an aid for counting units. If you begin at 0, the number on the ruler coincides with the count of units, but it is just as important to realize that you can begin anywhere and use the scale on the ruler to help count the number of units in the length (36). Students' problems could also be related to not understanding transitivity, linear units, the property of length, or simply looking for numerical cues (numbers on the ruler) without even measuring.

Angles

Elementary children need to think of angle measure as an amount of turn. The traditional definition of angle as an intersection of two rays does little to help young children fit angle into their experiences. Elementary students are familiar with turns and being able to compare and measure turns is useful. This experience also provides an important foundation for a more formal approach to angle in secondary school. Due to a lack of attention or too formal an approach, both students and adults have difficulty measuring angles.

Learners are often misled by cues from the way an angle is represented, indicating that students do not understand the property being measured. They may focus on the length of the sides of the angle or the size of the arc drawn between the rays (8). In Figure 8.3 all of the angles have the same measure, but students often think that the measure of Angle B is greater than the measure of Angle A, because Angle B has longer sides or the measure of Angle D is greater than the measure of Angle C because the arc is longer in the drawing of Angle D. Orientation can also present problems for students. Since we frequently draw angles with one horizontal ray, students do not recognize angles in different positions. Students have referred to some right angles as left angles because they open to the left (29)!

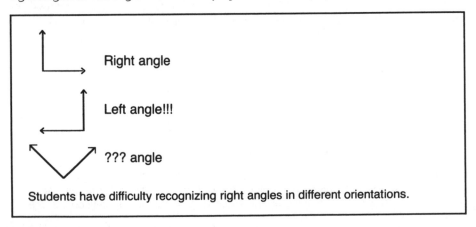

Right angle

Left angle!!!

??? angle

Students have difficulty recognizing right angles in different orientations.

Some students realize that they are measuring the amount of opening or the turn, but they want to measure the distance between the rays with the familiar ruler. Figure 8.4 illustrates that this strategy would be unsuitable because you would produce different measures depending on where and how you placed your ruler.

FIGURE 8.3 Comparing angles

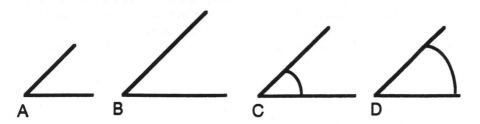

It is important to help students focus on what is being measured before we begin talking about units such as degrees or instruments such as protractors. Early elementary experiences focusing on an angle as a turn are critical in developing a concept of angle (39).

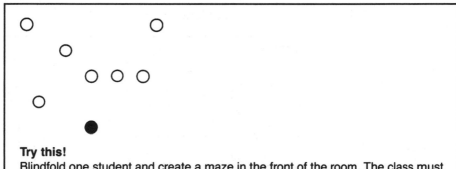

Try this!
Blindfold one student and create a maze in the front of the room. The class must give step and turn commands to guide the blindfolded student through the maze. They might begin with "step forward 2 steps, turn left 45 degrees or half of a quarter turn."

FIGURE 8.4 Common error in measuring angles

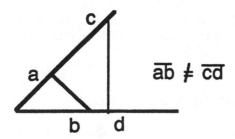

Computer activities can also help students develop the idea of angle as a turn. Elementary school children in England who studied the programming language Logo were taught to create graphics using commands such as forward fifteen steps and right turn forty degrees. These students were much better at comparing angles and ignoring irrelevant attributes such as orientation and length of rays than their counterparts who had not studied Logo, (24).

Volume

Volume is often perceived in two ways, capacity of containers, and space occupied by objects. Since children think of them separately, they are often confused when we try to talk about volume.

Primary students progress through gradual stages of conserving volume (21). The progress from no conservation of volume to a logical argument for conservation requires time. Sixty percent of interviewed kindergarten students predicted that if water were poured from one container into a wider container, the height of the water would be the same in both containers. In the third grade at the same school, 90 percent of the students predicted that the water would be lower in the wider container.

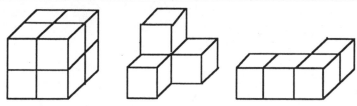

Try this!
Let your students make these buildings. After predicting how many blocks in each building, have the students take the buildings apart counting each block.

Give students 16 blocks and ask them to make two different buildings that each contain 8 blocks.

Elementary students have difficulty finding the volume of a cube made of sixty-four smaller cubes, because they only count the cubes they can see—omitting the cubes inside the larger cube. Elementary students should build different arrangements with the same number of blocks to help them see that different shapes can have the same volume. They also need to take apart buildings or composite cubes to see the blocks hidden from view. These activities help students build their perception and representations. They learn about the property of volume, and learn why a cube is a convenient unit of measure for rectangular solids.

Research-based Teaching Sequence

Research supports a logical teaching sequence that involves students in actively measuring (5, 7, 13, 14, 16, 40). Learning to measure is not something that can be done through listening or paper and pencil activities. Although elementary students are still developing foundational skills such a perception, representation, conservation, transitivity, and unit iteration, it is important to begin measurement activities early in the primary grades. These foundational skills are developed over an extended time by being involved (9, 11).

The process of learning to measure in a particular system can be divided into five sequential steps designed to span grades K through 5. In steps 2 through 4, estimation skills should be developed along with the measurement process. Students should go through the same steps for learning to measure length, area, volume, density, angles, time, or any other system of measurement. The basic steps are:

1. Identify the property to be measured.
2. Make comparisons.
3. Establish an appropriate unit and process for measuring.
4. Move to a standard unit of measurement.
5. Create formulas to help count units.

It is important to note that not only does each step prepare the learner for the next step, but each step sheds light on the previous steps. In addition to learning about a specific measuring system, this teaching sequence helps students compare measurement systems (25, 28). Students need to understand that the process used to count squares covering a flat rectangular surface (e.g., a checkerboard) can be modified to count cubes filling a three-dimensional rectangular space (e.g., a shoe box). Each measurement concept that is mastered serves as a foundation for new measurement concepts.

"I was often surprised at what students could or could not do. Some fourth graders worked on creating a formula for the perimeter of a rectangle (step 5), while others struggled with idea of comparing perimeters (step 2). Since it's difficult to predict what students can do, we need to use a variety of activities so we can engage students at different levels. I learned a great deal about each student's ability as I watched them try different activities."

—Ruth Rowland

Action research
Keep a log recording student achievements that surprise you. Try to identify measurement concepts that are present or missing.

Early grades should focus on the first two steps, while the upper grades need to review and proceed at the level of their students. Although many fourth and fifth grade students can create their own formulas (step 5), most formal work should be saved for middle school. Clearly, it is more important to complete a few steps thoroughly than to rush through all five steps. Resources for activities that fit easily into this instructional sequence are starred in the References. *Children Learn to Measure* (9) has sixty-four excellent activities that fit the suggested sequence.

Step 1: Identify the Property to Be Measured

Often objects we measure have several attributes including : area, capacity, density, distance, length, pressure, volume, weight, speed, temperature (7). Since each attribute has a nature of its own we should not overgeneralize properties. For example, the attribute of volume can be either additive (as with building blocks) or nonadditive (as with salt in water).

Time
By seven years of age, students use a variety of counting strategies to measure time and they may use the additive property of time to combine times. (38)

Rate
Young students learn the direct relationship between rate and distance before they can understand the indirect relationship between of rate and time for a given distance. By fourth grade, most students understand the relationship between rate, time, and distance (1).

Some problem situations involve more than one attribute and require that children's attention be focused on identifying these attributes and their properties. Figure 8.5 (p. 188) shows a parallelogram that was partitioned and recombined to form a rectangle. The area is conserved but perimeter is not. The properties of area and perimeter are best examined through hands-on activities (23).

Although attributes such as length or area can be measured directly, other attributes, such as temperature, must be measured indirectly by measuring the height of mercury in a thermometer. Usually volume can be measured directly, but often it is more convenient to measure it indirectly. The watermelon activity provides for both direct and indirect measurement.

Try this!
A watermelon makes an excellent object to use to help students focus on different attributes.

Indirect measure
To measure the volume of a watermelon, submerge the watermelon in a bucket full of water sitting in a larger tub. By measuring the displaced water, you will know the volume of the watermelon.

Direct measure
When measuring around the watermelon with a string, you are measuring a linear distance. When you measure the surface, you are measuring area, and when you measure the heaviness, you are measuring weight or mass.

Step 2: Make Comparisons

Often a comparison is a sufficient measure for a task. If you want to know which of two students is taller, you simply stand them side by side and compare heights. This measurement is number free. The number of centimeters or inches is irrelevant for your purpose. If you want to compare two angles, you need to line up the initial sides of each angle, and place the vertex of one angle on the vertex of the other angle. You do not need to know the number of degrees in either angle. Number-free comparison activities not only help the learner focus on attributes being measured (8), but they are appropriate for use with young children (22).

When comparing two angles, the angle with the greater opening is the larger angle regardless of the length of the rays. By comparing angles, the student must reflect on what attribute (opening) is being measured.

Try this!
Compare the area of different leaves.

Easy comparison
An easy way to compare areas is to see whether one region fits within another region.

Clearly, the small leaf has a smaller area.

Problem comparison
The comparison is more difficult if you want to compare the areas of a short, fat leaf and a tall, skinny leaf.

If you want to know *how much* larger one leaf is than the other leaf, you need to know the number of units in each area. This activity motivates the use of units.

FIGURE 8.5 Same area and different perimeters

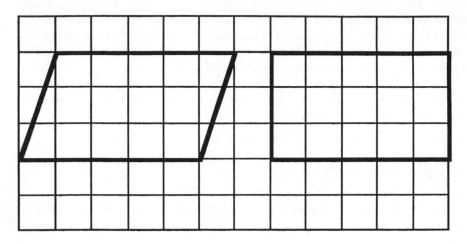

If you want to know *how much* taller one child is compared to another, a number-free comparison is not sufficient. This situation motivates a need for units to help in the comparison.

Step 3: Establish an Appropriate Unit for Measuring

Since the unit must fit the attribute being measured, developing appropriate units helps students focus on the attribute being measured. A triangle, a parallelogram, the palm of a hand, the face of a block, and a square tile are convenient nonstandard units for measuring area (17). For length, students might use paper clips, toothpicks, or a narrow strip of paper. Once students have chosen a unit, they still have two major difficulties.

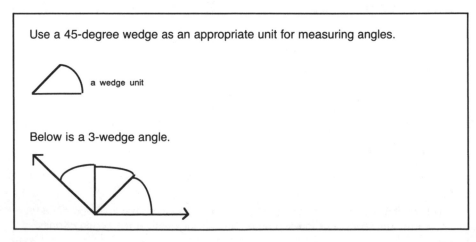

First, they may not know how to position the units to avoid overlaps and gaps. Since one unit is hard to manipulate, give students multiple units and allow them to place the units so they "cover" (extend, fill, complete) the attribute. For example, use paper clips to measure length, square tiles to measure area, wedges to measure angles, or cubes to measure capacity. The process of covering the length, area, volume, or angle helps students learn about the attribute being measured, the unit being used, and the process for covering.

The second problem students have is counting units and particularly partial units (10). If you are measuring common items around the classroom, you will naturally encounter measurements that do not include a whole number of units.

Try this!
Using grid paper or geoboards helps students learn to count units and fractional units when measuring area or length.

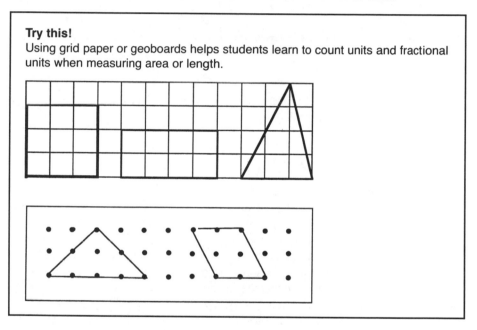

Allow students to decide on a strategy and question them about the implications for the strategy. They might decide not to count any fractional units, and then the measurement would be less than a more precise measurement. They may decide to group several fractional units to create whole units, making the measurement more precise.

Once you have units to use, relationships such as similarity and congruence can be explored (23). Notice that triangles A and B in Figure 8.6 are similar—having the same shape but different sizes. Triangle B is twice as wide and twice as tall as triangle A. How do the areas compare? This is also an appropriate time to help students focus on the relationship of the size of a unit and the number of units.

As students become familiar with the attribute they are measuring and appropriate units to measure that attribute, they will develop a need for instruments to help them count their units. Grid paper is an instrument that helps students count square units in a specific area. A tape measure is an instrument that counts units of length, and a protractor helps students count units of opening in an angle. By making their own

FIGURE 8.6   Comparison of areas of similar triangles

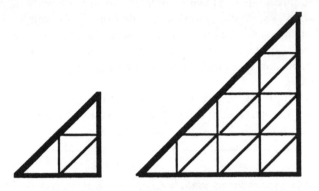

instruments, students begin to understand the purpose of standard instruments and the convenience of standard units.

Step 4: Move to a Standard Unit of Measurement

Standard units refer to conventional units that are used in commerce and daily tasks. They may be drawn from the old English system (inches, feet, pounds, acres, cubic yards, ounces, cups) or the metric system (centimeters, meters, square meters, grams, kilograms, liters). It is important for students to feel comfortable in both systems, but it is not necessary to spend time on conversions between systems (22). Standard units are necessary for communication between people and they correspond to available instruments such as a foot ruler marked in inches, a meter stick marked in centi-meters, a spring scale marked in pounds, or a protractor marked in degrees.

The curriculum related to using standard units should include work in choosing appropriate units, estimating measurements, using standard instruments, and inves-tigating error in measurement. Lessons should continue to involve students in mak-ing decisions, actually measuring, and reflecting on the process.

Step 5: Create Formulas to Help Count Units

Throughout the measuring process teachers should encourage students to develop shortcuts or special strategies for counting units, but emphasis on using formulas should be reserved for upper elementary school and middle school. In grades K–4, the study of measurement should build a foundation for the later development of formulas. Formulas should evolve out of measuring experiences and knowledge about geometry.

Formulas will only make sense to students after they understand the attribute being measured, the nature of the appropriate unit, and how to iterate that unit. When students confuse the formulas for area and perimeter, it indicates that they do not understand the vast differences between the properties of area and length, the appropriate units, and the measurement processes.

Try this!

Let students make up their own rules (formulas) for perimeter.

The formula for the perimeter of a rectangle should be seen as a quick or easy way to find the distance all the way around a rectangle.

1. Since the opposite sides of a rectangle must be equal, adding one length to one width and doubling the sum to find the total distance makes sense. This a rule for the formula $P = 2 \times (l + w)$.
2. Since a rectangle has two pairs of congruent sides, you can double the length, double the width and add the measures together. This is a rule for the formula $P = (2 \times l) + (2 \times w)$.
3. Since a rectangle has two pairs of congruent sides, double the length of the long sides and then count on all the units from the other sides. For example, the area of a 5 by 7 rectangle would be figured by: 7 doubled is 14, then count on 15,16,17,18, 19 (first width), 20, 21, 22, 23, 24 (second width). (rule proposed by a fourth-grade student)

If students persist in counting all the units or adding all four lengths of sides, they are not ready for the formula. The rule has to fit the way they think about finding the distance around the rectangle.

Final Thoughts

As you plan to teach measure, remember the diverse settings where we use measurement as we teach mathematical topics in elementary school and where we use measurement in our daily lives. We know that students gain useful measurement concepts through actively measuring and then reflecting on the experience. Fundamental components such as perception, representation, conservation, and transitivity contribute to a student's understanding of the measurement process, but these same abilities are developed through measuring. This dilemma suggests that we proceed with measurement activities and yet remain sensitive to student difficulties (9). The research-based teaching sequence described in this chapter will help students focus on the major measurement concepts that can be used across measurement systems such as length, area, volume, angle, temperature, and time. The *Curriculum Standards* reminds us that our goal at the elementary level is to build a "firm foundation in the basic underlying concepts and skills of measurement" (22). We want students to understand the attributes to be measured, to choose appropriate units, to estimate, to develop useful processes, and to use instruments and student-created formulas to facilitate their work. To reach our goals, we must begin teaching measurement concepts in kindergarten and involve students in actively measuring throughout their school experience.

Looking Ahead . . .

Since previous research suggests that students learn to measure by actually measuring, researchers are looking at how to implement activity-based lessons in the typical classroom as well as changes needed to support active student involvement. What do teachers need to know in order to guide students in measurement explorations? What kinds of management techniques encourage activity and at the same time prevent chaos? What kinds of social arrangements and materials facilitate exploration and reflection? We should explore a variety of sequences for instruction in measurement. Since children live in a three-dimensional world, is the one-dimensional concept of length *more* abstract than the three-dimensional concept of volume? We need to investigate learning measurement in the context of applications and especially in conjunction with geometry. How can we take advantage of computer activities and simulation capabilities to help students learn the fundamental concepts of measurement?

Patricia Wilson

Activity-based measurement lessons are used in my classroom. I wonder how much growth the students would have if given more opportunities to solve problems in all areas of the curriculum. How can I use problem solving more frequently, include the passive learner, and ensure that a common core of knowledge is learned? I wonder how I can help the students enrich their learning on the computer, especially with Logo and Geometric Presupposer. I wonder what happens to the student from an activity-oriented classroom who is later assigned to a classroom with a more traditional, textbook-dominated style of learning measurement.

Ruth Rowland

About the Authors

Patricia S. Wilson is associate professor of mathematics education at the University of Georgia. She has written and piloted geometry and measurement activities for grades K–5 as part of a National Science Foundation project, and currently is investigating cultural influence on mathematics.

Ruth Rowland is a fourth-grade teacher at South Jackson Elementary School in Georgia. She has taught elementary school for nine years, and uses geometry and measurement activities in her classroom frequently.

References

1. ACREDOLO, C., ADAMS, A., & SCHMID, J. (1984). On the understanding of the relationships between speed, duration, and distance. *Child Development, 55,* 2151–2159.
2. ANDERSON, N. H., & CUNEO, D. O. (1978). The height and width rule in children's judgments of quantity. *Journal of Experimental Psychology, 107,* 335–378.
3. BAILEY, J. H. (1971). The concept of transitivity in children. *Dissertation Abstracts International, 31B,* 7618.

4. CARPENTER, T. (1975). Measurement concepts of first- and second-grade students. *Journal for Research in Mathematics Education, 6* (1), 3–13.

5. CARPENTER, T. (1976). Analysis and synthesis of existing research on measurement. In R. A. Lesh (Ed.), *Number and measurement: Papers from a research workshop.* Columbus, OH: ERIC Clearinghouse for Science, Math, and Environmental Education.

6. CARPENTER, T., & LEWIS, R. (1976). The development of the concept of a standard unit of measure in young children. *Journal for Research in Mathematics Education, 7,* 53–58.

*7. DRISCOLL, M. J. (1981). Measurement in elementary school mathematics. In *Research within reach* (pp. 29–36). CEMREL, Inc. Reston, VA: National Institute of Education, National Council of Teachers of Mathematics.

8. FOXMAN, D., & RUDDOCK, G. (1984). Concepts and skills: Line symmetry and angle. *Mathematics in School, 13,* 9–13.

*9. GLENN, J. (Ed.) (1980). *Children learn to measure.* The Mathematical Education Trust, London: Harper & Row.

*10. HART, K. (1984). Which comes first—length, area, or volume? *Arithmetic Teacher, 31,* 16–18, 26–27.

*11. HIEBERT, J. (1981a). Cognitive development and learning linear measurement. *Journal for Research in Mathematics Education, 12,* 197–211.

12. HIEBERT, J. (1981b). Units of measure: Results and implications from national assessment. *Arithmetic Teacher, 28,* 38–43.

13. HIEBERT, J. (1984). Why do some children have trouble learning measurement concepts? *Arithmetic Teacher, 31,* 19–24.

*14. HILDRETH, D. (1983). The use of strategies in estimating measurement. *Arithmetic Teacher, 30,* 50–54.

15. HIRSTEIN, J., LAMB, C., & OSBORNE, A. (1978). Student misconceptions about area measure. *Arithmetic Teacher, 25,* 10–16.

*16. INSKEEP, J. (1976). Teaching measurement to elementary school children. In D. Nelson & R. Reys (Eds.), *Measurement in school mathematic* (1976 Yearbook) (pp. 60–86). Reston, VA: National Council of Teachers of Mathematics.

*17. KASTNER, B. (1989). Number sense: The role of measurement applications. *Arithmetic Teacher. 36* (6). 40–46.

*18. KOUBA, V., BROWN, C., CARPENTER, T., LINDQUIST, M., SILVER, E. A., & J. O., SWAFFORD. (1988). Results of the fourth NAEP assessment of mathematics: Measurement, geometry, data interpretation, attitudes and other topics. *Arithmetic Teacher, 35* (9), 10–16.

19. LEON, M. (1982). Extent, multiply, and proportionality in children's judgments of area. *Journal of Experimental Child Psychology, 33,* 124–141.

20. LIGHT, P., & GILMOUR, A. (1983). Conservation or conversation? Contextual facilitation of inappropriate conservation judgments. *Journal of Experimental Child Psychology, 36,* 356–363.

21. LINDSAY D. S., & CREEDON, C. F. (1985). Magic revisited: Children's responses to apparent violations of conservation. *Journal of Experimental Psychology, 40,* 338–349.

*22. NATIONAL COUNCIL OF TEACHERS OF MATHEMATICS (1989) *Curriculum and evaluation standards for school mathematics.* Reston, VA: Author.

*23. NEUFELD, K. (1989). Body measurement. *Arithmetic Teacher, 36* (9), 12–15.

24. NOSS, R. (1987). Children's learning of geometrical concepts through Logo. *Journal for Research in Mathematics Education, 18,* 343–362.

25. OSBORNE, A. R. (1975). The arithmetical and psychological foundations of measure. In

R. S. Lesh (Ed.), *Number and measurement: Papers from a research workshop.* Columbus, OH: ERIC Clearinghouse of Science, Math, and Environmental Education.

26. PIAGET, J., & INHELDER, B. (1967). *The child's conception of space.* p. 490. (F. J. Langdon & J. L. Lunzer, Trans.). New York: Norton.

27. PIAGET, J., INHELDER, B., & SZEMINSKA, A. (1960). *The child's conception of geometry.* p. 411. (E. A. Lurnzer, Trans.). New York: Basic Books.

28. SAXE, G., MOYLAN, T. (1982). The development of measurement operations among the Oksapmin of Papua New Guinea. *Child Development, 53,* 1242–1248.

29. SCALLY, S. (1990). The impact of experience in a Logo learning environment on adolescents' understanding of angle: A van Hiele based clinical assessment. Doctoral dissertation, Emory University.

30. SCHIFF, W. (1983). Conservation of length redux: A perceptual-linquistic phenomenon. *Child Development, 54,* 1497–1506.

31. SINCLAIR, H. (1971). Number and measurement. In M., Rosskopf, L., Steffe, & S., Taback, (Eds.), *Piagetian Cognitive-Development Research and Mathematical Education.* (pp. 149–159). Reston, VA: National Council of Teachers of Mathematics.

32. SILVERMAN, I., & PASKEWITZ, S. (1988). Devlopmental and individual differences in children's area judgment rules. *Journal of Experimental Child Psychology, 46,* 74–87.

33. SILVERMAN, I., YORK, K., & ZUIDEMA, N. (1984). Area-matching strategies used by young children. *Journal of Experimental Child Psychology, 38,* 464–474.

34. SMEDSLUND, J. (1963). Development of concrete transitivity of length. *Child Development, 34,* 389–405.

35. STEFFE, L., & HIRSTEIN, J. (1976). Children's thinking in measurement situations. In D. Nelson & R. Reys (Eds.), *Measurement in school mathematics* (1976 Yearbook) (pp. 35–39). Reston, VA: National Council of Teachers of Mathematics.

*36. THOMPSON, C., & VAN DE WALLE, J. (1985). Learning about rulers and measuring. *Arithmetic Teacher, 32* (8), 8–12.

37. WALTER, M. (1970). A common misconception about area. *Arithmetic Teacher, 17* (9), 286–289.

38. WILKENING, F., LEVIN, I., & DRUYAN, S. (1987). Children's counting strategies for time quantification and integration. *Developmental Psychology, 23* (6), 823–831.

*39. WILSON, P. S., & ADAMS, V. (1992). A dynamic way of teaching angle. *Arithmetic Teacher, 39*(5), 6–13.

*40. WILSON, P. S., & OSBORNE, A.R. (1988) Fundamental ideas in teaching about measure. In T. R. Post (Ed.), *Teaching mathematics in grades K–8: Research based methods* (pp. 384–405). Newton, MA: Allyn & Bacon.

41. WOODWARD, E., & BYRD, F. (1983). Area: Included topic, neglected concept. *School Science and Mathematics, 83,* 343–347.

42. YAKIMANASKYA, I. S. (1991) *The development of spatial thinking in school children* (P. Wilson, & J. Davis , Eds.; R. Silverman, Trans.). *Soviet studies in mathematics education, vol. 3.* Reston, VA: National Council of Teachers of Mathematics.

CHAPTER 9

Geometry and Spatial Sense

David J. Fuys and Amy K. Liebov

Spatial understandings are necessary for interpreting, understanding, and appreciating our inherently geometric world (28).

What comes to mind when you think of "geometry"? What might your students think? Responses would reflect the respective geometry learning experiences of both you and your students. This chapter is intended to familiarize you with current research on learning and teaching geometry in the primary grades and to help you use research-based ideas to enrich your students' geometry experiences. Before reading on, think about the geometry learning environment in your classroom. What geometry is taught, and how do you present it? What geometric understandings and spatial abilities do youngsters bring to the classroom, and how does your instruction enhance your students' geometric thinking? We will review related research to provide some perspectives for addressing these and other questions about learning and teaching geometry.

Geometry in K–4: Goals and Content

Is geometry an important part of your students' mathematics program? National, state, and local K–12 curriculum guidelines recommend that geometry play a prominent role in school mathematics. NCTM's *Curriculum and Evaluation Standards for School Mathematics (Standards)* (28) states that for grades K–4: "the mathematics curriculum should include two- and three-dimensional geometry so that students can—

- describe, model, draw, and classify shapes;
- investigate and predict the results of combining, subdividing, and changing shapes;

- develop spatial sense;
- relate geometric ideas to number and measurement ideas;
- recognize and appreciate geometry in their world." (28, p. 48)

The K–4 mathematics curriculum contains a host of geometry topics. We may recognize some topics as ones we learned in elementary school. Others may be less familiar: line of symmetry; topological ideas (open/closed curves); motion geometry such as slides, flips, turns; coordinates (see Fig. 9.1); and Logo geometry. Geometry also plays an important role in many nongeometric topics. Children can represent multiplication as repeated addition on a number line, or by an array of squares that connects it with area. They can use the geometry of familiar shapes to build an understanding of fractions (3, 4, 14) and notions of probability. In bar graphs children use their understanding of size to communicate about number. Inadequate geometric understanding can adversely affect learning of these other topics.

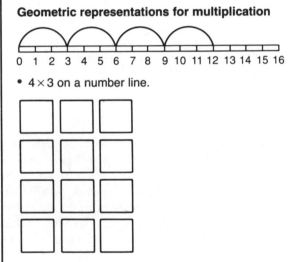

Geometric representations for multiplication

- 4 × 3 on a number line.

- 4 × 3 as an array of tiles. How many did you use?
- Make other rectangle arrays with the 12 tiles, and write a multiplication sentence for each.
- Explore: What rectangle arrays could you make with 11 tiles? 24?
- *Research idea:* Investigate how your students use geometric representations to explain thinking strategies for facts and to solve problems.

Geometry also provides a rich context for the early development of mathematical thinking, from lower-order thinking processes such as identifying shapes to higher-order processes such as discovering properties of shapes, creating geometric patterns, and solving geometric puzzles and problems in different ways (5, 11, 14, 43). Thus we can use geometry to implement the four NCTM standards related to process: *mathematics as problems solving, mathematics as communication, mathematics as*

FIGURE 9.1 Coordinate geometry and paths (5, 38)

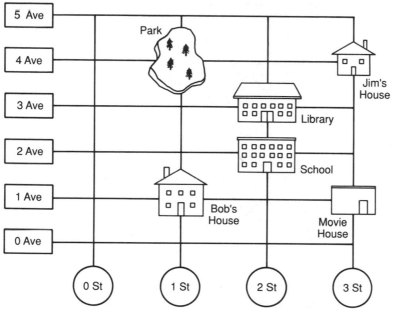

- What are the coordinates of Bob's house? Jim's house? the park?
- Find one way to go from Bob's house past the library to the park. How many blocks long was this path?

Explore: Find other paths. Are they all the same length? What are the shortest?

reasoning, and *mathematical connections*. We need to craft activities that feature several processes and interrelate geometry with other areas (Fig. 9.2). Geometry topics should not be taught in isolated units, but rather should be a natural and an integral part of the entire curriculum.

Although recommendations call for a rich geometry program in K–4, research indicates that, regrettably, little geometry is taught in the elementary grades, and that what is taught is often feeble in content and quality (5, 13, 31). When taught, geometry was the topic most frequently identified as being merely taught for "exposure," that is, given only brief, cursory coverage (31). Now, as implementation of the *Standards* goes forward, we need to examine what geometry we actually teach and take steps to close any gap between the recommended geometry curriculum and the one we provide our students.

We now examine five research perspectives that can help us implement an enriched geometry curriculum in the primary grades. The first two focus on how young children develop spatial thinking, the third on levels at which children can reason in geometry, and the fourth on concept learning. The fifth perspective involves more general research in early childhood education. Activities and suggestions are provided throughout the chapter to illustrate how we can apply knowledge gained from re-

FIGURE 9.2   Problem solving with tangrams

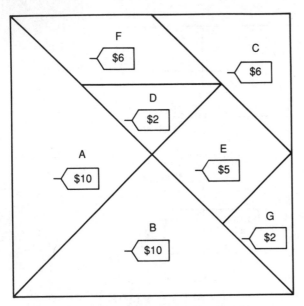

Cut out the tangram pieces and solve these problems.
• Use D and ___ to make a $4 triangle. Can you make a $4 square with them?
• Use ___, ___, and ___ to make a $10 rectangle. What other shapes can you make for $10?
• Make a square. How much did it cost?
Explore: Make other squares. What do they cost?
• Make a $20 polygon. How many sides? angles?
Explore: How many different $20 polygons can you make?

search in our teaching and also how we too can undertake "action research" in our classrooms.

A Piagetian Perspective

How do young children perform on such tasks as copying a triangle, identifying cutout shapes, or drawing how a cardboard box would look if we opened it up and laid it flat on a table? Insights into how children at different ages approach such spatial tasks are provided by the research of Jean Piaget and others. Piaget investigated children's spatial thinking through clinical tasks, such as those below, which involved mental "representation" of objects.

Touch and Draw/Identify.   Present the child with real objects or cardboard cutouts; let him or her touch and feel around each without being allowed to see it (Fig. 9.3). Then ask the child to name, draw, or point to it from a collection of visible objects (30, p. 18).

FIGURE 9.3   Shapes for Piagetian touch and draw/identify task

Look/Trace and Draw/Construct.   Show drawn figures; let the child trace them with a finger or even guide his or her motions. Without being able to look at the pieces, have the child draw them or copy rectilinear figures, using sticks (30, p. 53).

Look and Draw a Shadow.   Show how a light casts a shadow of an object on a screen when the object is placed between a light and the screen. Present objects and have the child predict and draw what its shadow on the screen would look like (30, p. 195).

Piaget found that children's performance on such tasks was developmental in nature, that is, they gradually develop spatial and geometric ideas in a spontaneous, independent, and age-related manner. Moreover, children first deal with *topological* aspects of shapes such as inside/outside, closed/open, then *projective* aspects such as curved/straight-sidedness, and finally *Euclidean* or "size" aspects such as length, angle size, and area. For example, on the touch and draw/identify task above, a young child (ages 3–4), when given a ⊚ , identified it or another shape that is topologically the same (such as ⌐), but did not discriminate curvilinear shapes from rectilinear ones, perhaps identifying an oval or ⬮ when given a square. Children (roughly ages 4–6) were more active in exploring shapes tactilely, and now distinguished shapes according to projective aspects but did not distinguish among shapes using Euclidean aspects, perhaps picking a rectangle or triangle when given a diamond. Finally, older children (about ages 6–8) explored shapes methodically, using Euclidean notions, and distinguished among complex forms.

Similar results on other spatial tasks supported the contention that "topological relations universally take priority over Euclidean relations" (30). This progression of spatial thinking from topological to projective and then to the Euclidean, known as the "topological primacy thesis," is the opposite of the one used in most primary school programs, which typically begin with measurement aspects of geometry. Some educators have used this thesis as a rationale for providing "developmentally appropriate" topological and projective experiences before Euclidean ones. They suggest that we give children qualitative activities before quantitive measurement tasks (33, 36) and provide environments that include building blocks (9, 35, 36), shadow-geometry (22, 36), and explorations of shapes drawn on balloons or made with Cuisenaire rods or modeling clay (9, 29, 36).

The topological primacy thesis is not uniformly supported by all the research. Some topological concepts such as "inside/outside" were found to develop earlier than others such as order and continuity (23). A study involving over 600 first graders in a program that included topological activities indicated that without studying topology, children could correctly answer about 70 percent of the topology questions posed, and that with instruction there was little improvement (37). Also, children learned Euclidean concepts without instruction on topological ideas. The investigator concluded that early programs in geometry that first deal with topology or that stress "knowledge" of content are not warranted. Rather, teachers should provide activities that sharpen youngsters' geometric thinking. Topological primacy thesis aside, this recommendation is in the spirit of Piaget's constructivist view that children develop spatial concepts by acting on objects and reflecting on their actions, not simply by looking at the objects. In our classes, we can use modifications of Piagetian-type tasks to investigate children's spatial thinking ourselves and also to provide informal instruction that nurtures spatial thinking. Youngsters can try a "feel and tell" grab-bag activity with familiar objects and geometric shapes (9), create block constructions and share what they did with their teacher and classmates (15, 35), or sit in a circle around an object, draw it, and compare drawings. Older children might draw an object showing different perspectives, perhaps as part of their study of modern art and cubism.

"The first task at the primary school level should not be to give a 'foundation of topological concepts' nor a 'preparation for symmetry' nor [is it] to convey 'knowledge of plane and three-dimensional basic shapes.' Instead an early program of geometry should make use of geometrical activities, mediate a readiness to experiment with paper, scissors, glue, strings, wood, etc., [encourage] a willingness to make sketches and exact drawings, and lead to *thinking* about these activities. In short, a program should initiate geometrical actions, drawing, and thinking." (37, pp. 295–296)

Spatial Sense

How would boys and girls do on spatial tasks such as finding triangles in a design, solving Tangram puzzles, completing a symmetric figure, or replicating a 3-D sculpture made with Cuisenaire rods? (See Fig. 9.4.) Tasks like these involve various aspects of spatial sense such as interpretation of visual information, visual memory, and visual processing such as rotating objects mentally (spatial visualization) and recognizing relationships between various parts of a configuration. Spatial abilities

FIGURE 9.4   Spatial thinking tasks

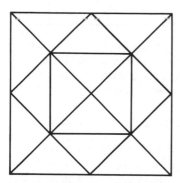

How many triangles can you find?
How did you find them?

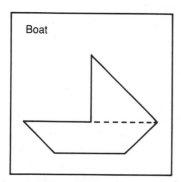

Use tangrams. Can you make this in two different ways?

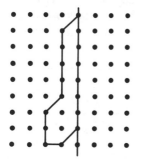

Complete this rocket ship.

and visual imagery play a vital role in mathematical thinking and are important for technical-scientific occupations (7, 12).

"Spatial sense is an intuitive feel for one's surroundings and the objects in them. To develop spatial sense, children must have many experiences that focus on geometric relationships: the direction, orientation, and perspectives of objects in space, the relative shape and sizes of figures and objects, and how a change in shape relates to a change in size." (28, p. 49)

The development of "spatial sense" in grades K–4 is a clear mandate in the *Standards* (28). This early attention to spatial thinking is supported by research of psychologists such as Piaget, art educators, and mathematics educators who identified developmental stages in children's drawings and other areas of spatial thinking and by research on spatial training for boys and girls. A recent comprehensive summary of the research on gender differences in mathematics and science revealed that, up to the mid-1970s, males outperformed females on many spatial tasks, but since then gender differences in spatial abilities are declining and the differences that remain are responsive to training (21). A close look at such tasks as mentally rotating a figure showed that no gender differences existed on accuracy but some on speed were evident favoring males. However, training reduced these differences. Research now suggests that we should accept spatial abilities as malleable and explore what instructional interventions and experiences can ameliorate performance. This recommendation is further supported by spatial training studies in primary grades using tangrams (45) and via a unit the geometry of slides, flips, and turns (12). Children in primary schools where the use of manipulatives predominated tended to perform better on spatial tasks than children in "material-free" schools (4). Collectively these studies tell us to provide hands-on spatial activities in grades K–4 and to assess their effectiveness for strengthening the spatial thinking of boys and girls. Since both boys and girls were found to vary considerably in accuracy and speed on spatial tasks, we need to be sensitive to time constraints and difficulty of tasks—perhaps presenting activities in a learning center where children can work at their own pace and choose tasks at different levels of complexity.

Figure–ground tasks

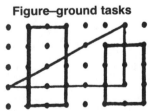

- How many rectangles can you find? How many triangles?
- On your geoboard make overlapping rectangles and triangles that make more triangles and rectangles.
  Record this on geoboard dot paper.

One research-based suggestion for the classroom is to stress children's use of manipulatives in activities that are designed to foster aspects of spatial perception (5, 12) such as *figure-ground* (identifying a specific figure in a picture or complex configuration) and *spatial relationships* (relating the position of two or more objects) (Fig. 9.5).

Another suggestion is to show children shapes, have them construct or draw what they see, and then respond to related questioning ("How did you see this? What did you copy first? Next? Could you copy it another way?"), which further stimulates spatial thinking (45). Second graders who used tangrams or drew diagrams to re-create visual images briefly shown on an overhead projector and then answered related questions showed "dramatic improvements in their spatial imagery over the course of a year" (45, p. 58). Moreover, this helped students "develop geometry concepts and learn geometric vocabulary, find geometric shapes in complex drawings, and develop such spatial operations as rotating images . . . They began to think about visually presented images in more than one way and to elaborate on and extend their own ideas " (45, p. 54).

A variation on the copy-a-shape task is to have children copy designs that encourage them to think about designs both holistically and in terms of its parts (24). Children might outline or color the designs on dot or grid paper (5, 14, 24). Also, a child can make a sculpture with color cubes or Cuisenaire rods and then tell a partner, who cannot see it, how to make it, which also fosters communication via spatial vocabulary. Free play, and lots of it, in spatial environments such as the "block corner" develops spatial thinking and promotes the use of spatial language (2, 15, 35). It also provides a setting for informal assessment of visual-perceptual strengths and weaknesses (12). Other ideas (24) include the use of two- and three-dimensional puzzles, construction of solids with commercial or everyday materials (toothpicks, small marshmallows), math-art projects, and position-in-space games (2) such as Simon Says. For further ideas see the February 1990 *Arithmetic Teacher*, which focuses on spatial sense.

Imagine "happiness." Perhaps the image you have is of an event, a color, or "a happy shape." Spatial thinking can be thought of as a visual form of general "imag-

FIGURE 9.5   Spatial relationships task

Use cubes to make a building like the one shown. (12, p.17)

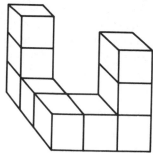

Figure 9.6   An imaging activity

Ask children to imagine being a circle. What could you do? How might you feel? Think of a "circular experience." Have children express their ideas by drawing, oral or written stories, or dramatizations.

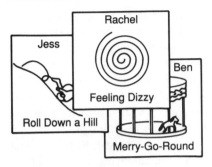

ing" (Fig. 9.6). The need for instruction on imagery is suggested by a recently developed body of research on imagery and its role in learning, memory, creativity, and problem solving (38). Use of visual imagery has proved effective in solving mathematics problems. Rather than make immediate use of numerical data in word problems, children were asked to close their eyes and imagine the problem situation, draw a picture of it, and then add relevant numerical data to the picture. This approach generated new enthusiasm for mathematics and improved problem-solving performance, especially for children with low reasoning ability (26). Using geometry in this way should be part of every student's repertoire for representing and solving problems and for communicating mathematically.

The van Hiele Model of Geometric Thinking

How does the geometric thinking experienced by students in the primary grades relate to their geometric thinking in the middle grades or even later when they study geometry in high school? This question was explored by two Dutch educators, Dina van Hiele-Geldof and Pierre van Hiele, who were concerned about difficulties many of their students encountered in secondary school geometry. They believed that secondary geometry, which emphasizes deductive reasoning and proof, requires a "high" level of thinking and that their students did not have sufficient prerequisite experiences in thinking at lower levels during the elementary grades. They formulated a model of five "levels of thinking" and proposed instructional "phases" to promote students' progress from one level to the next (44).

The van Hiele Model: Levels and Instructional Phases

According to the van Hieles, the learner, assisted by appropriate instruction, passes through levels of thinking, from visual recognition of shapes by their appearance as a whole (level 0) to analysis and description of shapes in terms of their properties (level 1) to three higher "theoretical" levels involving informal deduction (level 2), then formal deduction involving axioms and theorems (level 3), and finally work with abstract geometric systems (level 4).

Geometry in grades K–4 involves thinking mainly at levels 0 and 1. At level 0 (the *visual* level) a child judges shapes by their appearance as a whole. A square is identified because it "looks like one." P. M. van Hiele says, "There is no why. One just sees it" (44, p. 83). Young children need experiences that develop their global understanding of geometric objects such as constructing and drawing shapes, fitting 2- or 3-D shapes together, and looking for shapes in their home and school environments.

At level 1 (the *descriptive-analytic* level) children think about shapes in terms of their parts and properties involving the parts. Through experimentation (measuring, folding, drawing, or working with models), they discover properties of shapes such as squares have "four sides," "all equal sides," "all right angles." They also use the language of properties to describe shapes and to explain solutions for geometric problems. However, they do not yet deduce certain properties from others or consider which properties are necessary and sufficient for defining a shape. This occurs at level 2 (*informal deduction*) when children begin to use deductive reasoning to establish "why," such as explaining why all squares are rectangles but not all rectangles are squares. (See 10 and 13 for detailed descriptions of the levels and related activities for children.)

The van Hieles ascribed characteristics to the levels—such as being discontinuous and hierarchical with performance at one level requiring success at lower levels. Each level has its own language; for example, "square" on level 0 means a shape that "looks like one," while on level 1 it conveys a shape with certain properties, and on level 2 it is specified by a definition. The van Hieles assert that many failures in teaching geometry result from a communication gap between teacher and students, who have different meanings for geometric language and hence are talking on different levels. Finally, progress within a level and to the next level depends more on instruction than maturation or age.

The van Hieles (7, 10, 14, 44) also proposed five instructional phases to guide students' progression from one level to the next on a topic: (a) *information* (two-way conversation between teacher and pupils to acquaint them with the topic and to help the teacher see what they already think about it); (b) *directed orientation* (sequence of activities to engage students actively in exploring the topic); (c) *explicitation* (students become explicitly aware the topic and learn related geometric terminology); (d) *free orientation* (problem solving that requires use and synthesis of the topic); (e) *integration* (students build a summary of the topic and relate this to what they previously learned). Children can cycle through the phases for various topics before attaining the next level of thinking.

Research on the van Hiele Levels

Research on the van Hiele model in primary grades has focused on the usefulness of the levels for characterizing children's thinking and on the impact of instruction on fostering higher levels of thinking (Fig. 9.7). By using clinical interviews involving tasks such as drawing, sorting, and describing shapes, researchers found that young-sters think mainly at the visual level (6, 7, 17). Results confirmed the hierarchical aspect of the levels, but did not uniformly support discontinuity between levels since some children appeared to be in transition between levels 0 and 1, sometimes dealing with shapes visually, and other times in terms of properties (6, 7). Youngsters exhib-ited difficulties such as (a) recognizing shapes only in standard orientations; (b) in-correct concepts (saying a rectangle has two sides, the vertical ones, and referring to the other two as the "top" and "bottom"); (c) incomplete concepts (not identifying a triangle because it is "too skinny"); (d) imprecise terminology ("even" for parallel). Similar results and difficulties were found for students in grades 5–9, and their levels of thinking varied across different geometric topics (6, 7, 13). Causes for the low level of thinking included lack of instruction on geometry topics and emphasis on the visual level, indicating that we need to assess the amount and quality of the geometry instruction in our classes. Also, the research points out the need to examine closely students' explanations, not just the correctness of their answers, to gain insight into the quality of their thinking and their difficulties.

A brighter picture of how primary students can think is seen in several geometry "teaching experiments." Findings of twenty coordinated studies of geometry learning in grades 2–9 provided "overwhelming evidence . . . that children can learn geo-

FIGURE 9.7   Assessing students' level of thinking

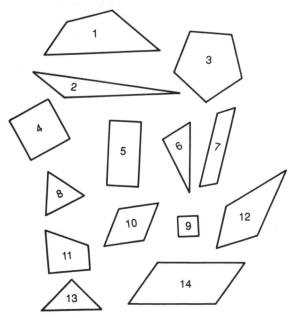

Investigate how your students think about shapes. Show a page of geometric figures or cutout shapes and ask, "which are triangles? . . . rectangles? . . . squares?" Then ask "why" and "how would you tell someone what to look for if he had to pick out all the triangles . . . ." You might repeat such questioning after your instruction to see if your students' thinking has changed.

metrical ideas if they are presented in an appropriate manner" (25, p. 26). Greatest gains were achieved in grades 3–5 when instruction emphasized children's making shapes, finding examples in the environment, and examining shapes in terms of their properties. Attainment of the descriptive-analytic level was reported for Soviet pupils in grades 1–4 (corresponding to our grades 3–6) in a curriculum experiment during the 1960s. The Soviet primary program had been revised to reflect the van Hiele levels and to provide a more diversified, continuous treatment of geometry (33).

Progress toward the descriptive-analytic level has been reported for younger children (grade 1) in a teaching experiment on quadrilaterals (17). Lessons involved only a little work at the visual level and instead stressed relationships between parts of shapes and properties of shapes. Important factors in the instruction included children's use of models; activities with guiding questions to stimulate thinking ("Let's play detective with these clues . . . what could it be? . . . draw the shape in your mind"); repetition and review, in particular of language for parts of shapes and properties; and a general-to-specific sequence of topics (quadrilaterals to rectangle-quadrilaterals to square-quadrilaterals) to help children think about subclass relationships between shapes.

"Logo" is a programming language that can be taught to young children. One aspect of Logo involves creating directions for moving a graphic turtle that leaves a trail of its path on the computer screen. Working with Logo on activities designed to foster thinking about shapes enhanced third and fourth graders' understanding of geometric concepts and also helped them make a transition from the visual level to the descriptive-analytic level (7, 8, 19, 20). Creating a Logo procedure to draw a shape requires children to analyze a shape in terms of its parts (angles, sides) and to reflect on how they can be put together. Children come to view shapes in terms of actions (90-degree turns) to construct them, and as a result, become explicitly aware of those action-based conceptualizations. Children also establish relationships between shapes—for example, realizing that "squares are special rectangles" by observing that their Logo procedure for rectangle (with sides set equal) can make squares. Features of these Logo environments included carefully crafted Logo activities that were coordinated with the math curriculum, cooperative problem solving, and use of multiple representations of concepts (drawings, list of properties, figures on the screen, Logo procedures), which students were encouraged to interrelate (20). This line of research promises to generate exciting developments in the future, such as enriched Logo-based geometry curricula (1) and software designed to guide children to explore topics and to develop more expert understandings (20).

These instructional successes in the primary grades and others in grades 5–9 (7, 13, 25) demonstrate the effectiveness of instruction designed to foster transition to higher levels of thinking. Although additional research is needed, especially teaching experiments that embody the van Hiele phases, the research offers many ideas for classroom practice (Fig. 9.8). First, assessment tasks and instructional activities from these studies can be adapted for use with our students.

- **Sorting Shapes.** Ask children to put cutout shapes into "families" such as the Right Family (all right angles) or the Four-Siders. Encourage them to find different ways to do this, to invent appropriate family names, and to use informal language of properties.

Drawing shapes with LOGO
Forward 100
Right 90
Forward 50
Right 90
Forward 100
Right 90
Forward 50
Right 90

- How might a student modify these commands for a rectangle to draw a square?
- What commands might the student change to draw a rectangle twice as large?

- **Shape Detective.** Turn over property cards one at a time and ask children to draw what shape the clues specify at each stage and tell when they are sure they can identify the shape (Fig. 9.9). At the end, you might ask which clues were necessary. Also, ask students to create clue puzzles for "geometry sleuth" classmates.
- **Shape Paths.** Children use Logo-like directions to tell how to draw a shape or walk a path to certain locations (To Library: ahead 10 steps, turn right, ahead 60 steps . . .).

Recommendations regarding the development of geometric language, particularly at the descriptive-analytic level, include: (a) relate unfamiliar new words to similar familiar ones (**triangle**, **tricycle**), (b) show explicitly that a term (face, side) has a different meaning in mathematics than it does in everyday usage; (c) use cooperative learning, which promotes both receptive and expressive use of language; and (d) pe-

FIGURE 9.8   Uncover-the-shape task

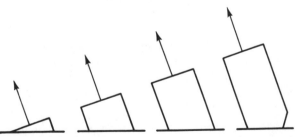

Uncover the **Mystery Shape** in stages. Ask what shape it could be and could not be and "why" at each stage.

FIGURE 9.9   Uncovering-property-clue-cards activity

What do I look
like? Who am I?

#1   for angles

#2   four angles

#3   one obtuse angle

#4   two right angles

Clue #5

Four clue cards have been turned over so far.
Can we tell what shape it is?
Do we need all the clues 1-4? Explain.
What could clue 5 be?
Such questions can foster desciptive-analytic thinking about shapes and also lead to the next level of informal deduction.

riodically review concepts and related terminology. Attention should also be given to logical and metacognitive language (13). Encourage careful use of quantifiers (all, some, none) and phrases for generalizations ("*a* square has . . . " to mean "*all* squares have . . . "). Words like "look at" and "identify" usually convey the visual level, while "property," "discover," and "explain" connote higher levels. Thoughtful use of such metacognitive words by you and your students can help them to realize the kind of thinking that is expected and to monitor their thinking relative to the expectations.

Recommendations can also be derived from research that analyzed geometry curricula in terms of the van Hiele model (13, 33). An analysis of the geometry material in three major USA text series (K–8) indicated that the K–4 geometry lessons (aim, expository material, exercises, test questions) dealt almost exclusively with the visual level (13). The cumulative effect of such low level curricula is to limit, or even impede, the development of children's geometric thinking during grades K–4. Little wonder that many students encounter difficulty in middle school and secondary school geometry, which presumes a sound apprenticeship in visual and descriptive-analytic thinking during primary grades. Clearly, we should not rely on textbooks alone for geometry instruction. We need to:

• Analyze the expository and exercise material and related suggestions in the teacher's guide before doing lessons and "fill in" gaps, such as reminding students to "explain why" when doing exercises in the text.

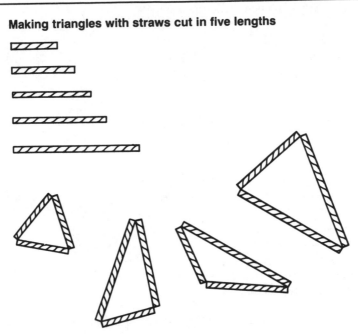

Making triangles with straws cut in five lengths

Imagine children working in groups to make triangles and investigating questions such as:

- Can we make a triangle with any three straws? Make a conjecture about when three straws will not work.
- How are two triangles alike? different?
- How can we sort the triangles?
- Where in our environment do we find these different types of triangles?
- Such purposeful questions stimulate thinking at the analytic-descriptive level. What other questions might we pose?

- Implement "purposeful" activities that provide a natural transition toward a higher level.
- Spiral activities on geometry topics thoughout the curriculum to provide a more continuous experience with those topics.
- Include questions during class discussions and on tests to assess thinking above the visual level. We probably will need to talk to children to assess the quality of their thinking, especially youngsters who cannot adequately express their ideas in writing.

Concept Learning in Geometry

How well do primary students understand such geometric concepts as angle, rectangle, cube? How might your students show they understand them? These are important questions since the geometry strand for K–4 programs contains a host of concepts involving two- and three-dimensional shapes. More generally, the *Standards* states that "the K–4 curriculum should be conceptually oriented" (28, p. 17). However, NAEP testing (18) indicates that many students demonstrate a lack of understanding of underlying concepts in mathematics. Surveys of classroom practice show "a heavy emphasis on skill development and slight attention to concepts" (31, p.11). Also, children exhibit various types of misconceptions such as under-generalization, which can occur because they included irrelevant characteristics; over-generalization, which can occur because some key properties are omitted; and languange-related misconceptions ("diagonal" means slanty). Research on concept learning sheds some light on how children form concepts (and misconceptions) with implications for ways to teach geometric concepts and also concepts in other areas of mathematics (even/odd, factor) and in other subjects.

One way children form a concept is to begin with a few cases and by averaging their features develop an "average representation" or prototype, which they use for categorizing new examples (34). Children may form prototypes that include extraneous or even erroneous features that can lead to misconceptions (7, 13, 41) such as thinking of a shape only in terms of cases in standard orientation, as usually found in the everyday world. However, beginning with "best examples," that is, "clear cases demonstrating the variation of the concept's attributes" (41, p. 281), can help develop correct concepts (Fig. 9.10). We need to provide "best examples" that are rich in imagery of familiar everyday objects and manipulative models that children have worked with. Research (20) indicates that children should develop multiple representations of concepts (everyday objects, manipulatives, diagrams, verbal definitions). Some children encode information better in a verbal format than visual, others vice-versa. Also, they should link representations for a concept, such as by drawing examples and giving a list of properties.

Primary pupils are better able to learn geometry concepts when they handle models and use diagrams (7, 25, 32). They should experience both region/surface models and side/edge models (Fig. 9.11). Children may find some aspects of shapes easier to grasp with one type of model than another. Here too they can connect representations for a concept—for example, interrelating angle as a "wedge," made with two fastened straws that open, a turn of their body, or a Logo turtle turn.

It is important to present both examples and nonexamples of a concept (7, 28, 41) as in the concept card (Fig. 9.12). Nonexamples have proved more effective than examples for "difficult" concepts and when familiar prototypes for a concept frequently have irrelevant features. Nonexamples should vary all irrelevant features. Carefully chosen nonexamples help children eliminate irrelevant features and identify critical ones.

The concept-card approach helps children learn how to formulate a correct definition. Initally children can use their own language for definitions, although it will be imprecise at times, and then through class discussion formulate a working verbalization using geometric terms. Youngsters may need to touch parts of shapes or concrete models when explaining verbally. Children sometimes memorize verbal definitions and can spout them with ease, so we are cautioned not to rely solely on verbal definitions to see if children understand a concept. Ask them to draw examples and nonexamples, or explain which cases are or are not examples and why.

FIGURE 9.10   Best examples

There are many examples of **regular polygons**.
Here are some best examples.

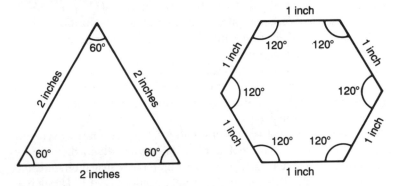

Fourth graders used these best examples to learn about regular polygons (41, p. L82). What other examples could we have used? We might investigate which examples work best for our students.

FIGURE 9.11   Region/surface models and side/edge models

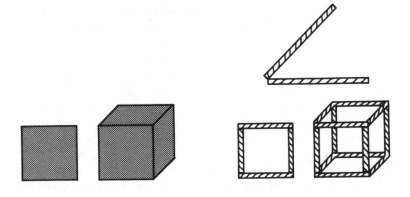

FIGURE 9.12   Concept card with examples and nonexamples

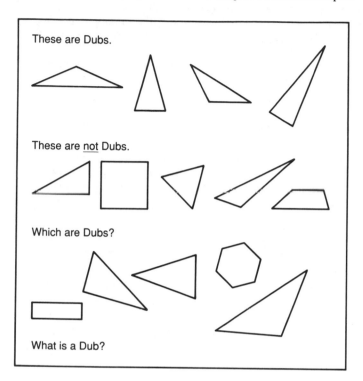

Children can identify examples of a concept by thinking in terms of prototypes, which has advantages (speed in recognizing familiar examples) and disadvantages (misidentification of unusual cases). Another way is to use a rule or definition for the concept, that is, to think in terms of key properties of the concept. Rule-based concepts are powerful in that they enable one to identify and generate examples and nonexamples and also to deduce conclusions from them (34).

One way to express a rule is by a verbal definition or list of properties called a "declarative specification" of the concept—that is, a statement of "what it is" in terms of its characterizing features (20, 34). Most textbook definitions are this type. Another way is through a "procedural specification," which enables you to construct or identify examples the concept. A child might give a procedural description for "square" by telling how to make it with manipulatives ("take four sticks the same size, put two like this for a square corner, and then . . .") or by a Logo procedure. Children can use one type of specification to understand another—for example, a third grader who came to understand her textbook's declarative definition for square by thinking about her procedural Logo-notion.

We can incorporate examples and nonexamples, best examples, and different representations of concepts into discovery and expository lessons for introducing geometric concepts.

Formulating a declarative definition from a procedural one
Confused by her text's definition for square (a quadrilateral with right angles and equal sides), Jenny reflects on her Logo experiences. "I need four FORWARD 100 and four RIGHT 90 . . . so oh . . . four sides . . . equal sides . . . right angles . . . yeah, I got it now." How might Jenny think about rectangles? Might she think of squares as special rectangles?

Discovery Lessons.   Present a concept card on the board and guide children to formulate and test a rule for the shape. One variation is to present the examples and nonexamples one at a time (on the board or via computer "guess-my-rule" software) and challenge children to predict where they go and why (Fig. 9.13). Another variation is to have children work individually or in small groups on concept cards in a learning center and later share their definitions.

Expository Lessons.   First present two "best examples" (leaving them out for viewing), next give the critical features of the concept as they relate to the examples, and then provide questions structured to have children check each critical property for several cases. This approach proved more effective for teaching third and fourth graders geometric concepts than did those not having "best examples" or not using examples and nonexamples (41), suggesting why the expository material in many textbooks may not suffice for developing concepts—namely, examples are seldom "best examples," nonexamples are rare, and exercises usually ask only for identification, not "why."

FIGURE 9.13   Guess-my-rule sort of examples and nonexamples

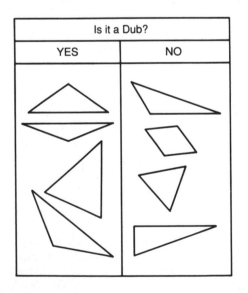

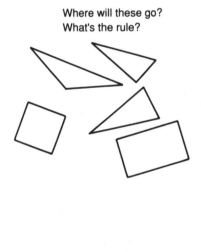

Checklist of critical properties

Answer these questions about shapes A, B, C, D.

Is it a polygon?	YES NO
Does it have all sides of equal length?	YES NO
Does it have all angles equal?	YES NO
Is it a regular polygon?	YES NO

Early Childhood Perspectives

Perspectives on teaching geometry in the primary grades can also be derived from general research, theory, and practice in early childhood education (16, 27). One guiding principle is that instruction should involve "the whole child" and his or her cognitive, affective, social, and physical needs and characteristics. Goals (16) fall into four areas: *knowledge, skills, dispositions,* and *feelings.* Too often pressures "to cover the curriculum" have a negative effect on these goals. A second principle is that instruction should be based on how children learn, namely: by doing, reflecting on their actions, and sharing their ideas with classmates and the teacher. Third, instruction should feature a variety of methods (play, learning center, projects, direct teaching). Teachers are cautioned that methods dominated by workpages can have a cumulative negative effect over a year or two, stultifying youngsters' disposition to learn. Finally, children need opportunities to engage in activities that call for extension, elaboration, and continuation of ideas and for sustained effort over time (days and weeks). A steady diet of tasks that children can finish quickly with little thought can have a delayed, detrimental effect on their desire to learn more and to explore (16).

Below are samples of geometry activities, projects, and environments that embody these kinds of principles. In reading them, think about which research perspectives on teaching and learning geometry they also reflect and how you might adapt them for your classroom.

Patterns Around Us. Children copy, extend, and create patterns with manipulatives such as pattern blocks, which leads to a hunt for geometric patterns around them (wallpaper, floor tiling) and patterns in their own lives (Fig. 9.14). Youngsters decide to create their own patterns with poster paints and geometric potato prints. Experiences with children's books on geometry (42) prompts some to make their own

FIGURE 9.14   Patterns and geometric designs

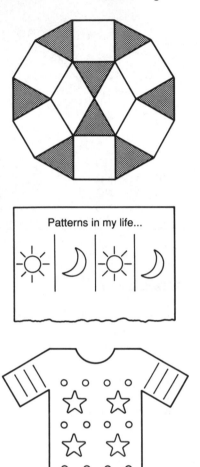

shape-books; others fashion colorful designs that become part of a class "patterns" wall mural. A culminating activity might be to make functional "pattern" objects such as designer T-shirts, bracelets, or soup can pencil holders.

Let's Build It.   Children design and build some large construction like a geodesic greenhouse, big-box learning center for their classroom, or model school bus (16), integrating skills in geometry, measurement, estimation, and construction. A discussion of the properties of shapes and their uses in constructions can lead to an exploration of relationships between "form" and "function."

The Block Corner.   Children enjoy building blocks. Their teacher capitalizes on this interest and creates block task cards (Fig. 9.15) that guide children to discover relationships between blocks (two ◓s make a "circle" wheel; four ▪s make a long block). As variations, the teacher creates similar task cards involving "found objects" such as woodscraps and cereal boxes and Water-blocs (soft 3-D shapes that adhere when wet) for use at the water table.

Triangle Investigations. Using the van Hiele phases to design a mini-unit on triangles, some teachers work together to prepare activities involving geoboards and straws and pipe-cleaner connectors. In their classrooms colorful displays show that children have explored triangle designs on geoboards and dot paper (*information*). Next children made triangles with straws cut in various lengths, sorted them (0, 2, 3 equal sides), learned names (scalene, isosceles, equilateral), and discussed why those names were appropriate (*orientation* and *explicitation*). Now they begin to work in groups on challenging geoboard problems (*free orientation*). Later, they will make mobiles of straw shapes to show the relationship between triangles and polygons that they had investigated previously (*intetgration*) (Fig. 9.16). Still later teachers plan a similar cycle of activities on quadrilaterals.

A Model City. Integrating geometry with children's study of their neighborhood or city, the class constructs a "model city." Working in committees (Bureau of Streets), they design and build a model city. Functional aspects of geometry (parallel and perpendicular lines, angles for streets; types of solids for buildings) are a natural part of this environmental geometry project. Children might also explore the "city" of American Indians or early settlers who lived in their area, noting geometric designs in their clothing, crafts, and living quarters (40).

FIGURE 9.15 Activity cards involving building blocks

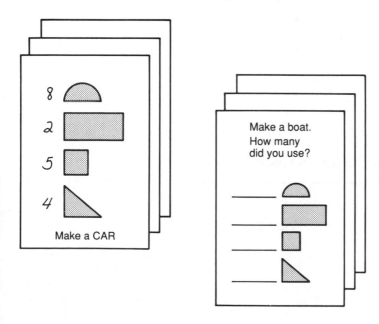

FIGURE 9.16   Mobile of shapes for families of triangles and polygons

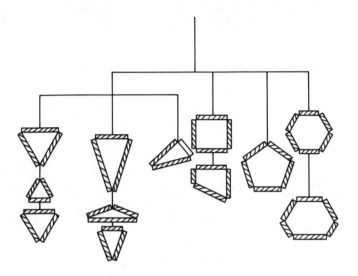

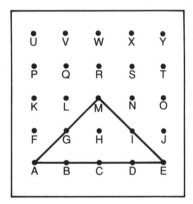

Free orientation activity about triangles on a geoboard

- How many isosceles triangles are there with side AE? with a corner at A? at M?
- Explore: What if we pick other points for a corner?

Conclusion

The research provides us with perspectives for reflecting on the geometry learning environment in our classroom today and also for planning for the future. It challenges us to provide a richer, more continuous activity-oriented program in geometry. It also offers principles and effective approaches for classroom practice. Finally, as we

FIGURE 9.17   Geometry explorer

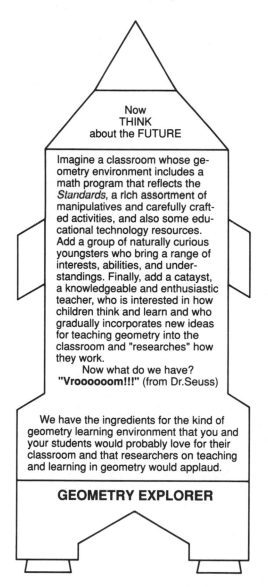

Now
THINK
about the FUTURE

Imagine a classroom whose geometry environment includes a
math program that reflects the
Standards, a rich assortment of
manipulatives and carefully crafted activities, and also some educational technology resources.
Add a group of naturally curious
youngsters who bring a range of
interests, abilities, and understandings. Finally, add a catayst,
a knowledgeable and enthusiastic
teacher, who is interested in how
children think and learn and who
gradually incorporates new ideas
for teaching geometry into the
classroom and "researches" how
they work.
     Now what do we have?
"Vroooooom!!!" (from Dr.Seuss)

We have the ingredients for the kind of
geometry learning environment that you and
your students would probably love for their
classroom and that researchers on teaching
and learning in geometry would applaud.

GEOMETRY EXPLORER

help youngsters become explorers of geometry, the research invites us to raise and
address questions about ways to improve the teaching and learning of geometry in
our classrooms.

Looking Ahead . . .

This chapter has messages for several audiences. Teachers need to think about the
geometry they *should* teach and how they can use research-based ideas in their

teaching. Those responsible for pre- and in-service training are challenged to provide experiences that develop teachers' geometric thinking, enthusiasm for geometry, and sensitivity to children's thinking about geometry. Researchers need to explore the nature of children's geometric thinking and ways to develop it in a variety of primary grade settings. Finally, we all need to share research findings and to work together to translate them into classroom practice.

David J. Fuys

Reflecting on the geometry learning environment in my classroom, I wonder about ways to create a more global and integrated geometry program. I am concerned about using time wisely and how to "fit in" all the important topics. I need to evaluate the activities my students currently use and identify additional resources for a more stimulating and enriched program. I wonder where I can find such resources, and how I can implement them using research-based approaches. Finally, I feel the need to interact with colleagues about our concerns, resources, and innovations involving the teaching and learning of geometry in our classes.

Amy K. Liebov

About the Authors

David J. Fuys teaches mathematics education courses at Brooklyn College, Brooklyn, New York. His interests include research on the van Hiele model, classroom instruction on basic facts, and instructional uses of video-technology.

Amy K. Liebov is a kindergarten teacher of the gifted at Hunter College Elementary School, New York, New York. She has also taught early-childhood mathematics education courses at Brooklyn College. Her interests include interdisciplinary instruction, learning centers, and education of the gifted.

References

1. BATTISTA, M. T., & CLEMENTS, D. H. (1988). A case for a Logo-based elementary school geometry curriculum. *Arithmetic Teacher, 2*(3), 11–17.
*2. BAUST, J. (1981). Spatial relations and young children. *Arithmetic Teacher, 29*(3), 13–14.
*3. BEZUK, N. S. (1988). Fractions in the early childhood mathematics curriculum. *Arithmetic Teacher, 35*(6), 56–60.
4. BISHOP, A. J. (1980). Spatial abilities and mathematics education—a review. *Educational Studies in Mathematics, 11*, 257–269.
*5. BRUNI, J. V., & SEIDENSTEIN, R. B. (1990). Geometric concepts and spatial sense. In J. Payne (Ed.), *Mathematics for the young child* (pp. 203–227). Reston, VA: National Council of Teachers of Mathematics.
6. BURGER, W. F., & SHAUGHNESSY, J. M. (1986). Characterizing the van Hiele levels of development in geometry. *Journal for Research in Mathematics Education, 17*(1), 31–48.
7. CLEMENTS, D. H., & BATTISTA, M. T. (1992). Geometry and spatial reasoning. In D. Grouws (Ed.). *Handbook of research on mathematics teaching and learning* (pp. 420–464). Reston, VA: National Council of Teachers of Mathematics.

8. CLEMENTS, D. H., & BATTISTA, M. T. (1989). Learning geometric concepts in a Logo environment. *Journal for Research in Mathematics Education, 20*(5), 450–467.

9. COPELAND, R. (1982). *How children learn mathematics: Teaching implications of Piaget's research.* New York: Macmillan.

10. CROWLEY, M. L. (1987). The van Hiele model of development of geometric thought. In M. M. Lindquist & A. P. Shulte (Eds.), *Learning and teaching geometry, K–12* (pp. 1–16). Reston, VA: National Council of Teachers of Mathematics.

*11. DEGUIRE, L. J. (1987). Geometry: An avenue for teaching problem solving in grades K–6. In M. M. Lindquist & A. J. Shulte (Eds.), *Learning and teaching geometry, K–12* (pp. 59–68). Reston, VA: National Council of Teachers of Mathematics.

*12. DEL GRANDE, J. J. (1990). Spatial sense. *Arithmetic Teacher. 37*(6), 14–20.

13. FUYS, D., GEDDES, D., & TISCHLER, R. (1988). The van Hiele model of thinking in geometry among adolescents. *Journal for Research in Mathematics Education* Monograph No. 3. Reston, VA: National Council of Teachers of Mathematics.

*14. HILL, J. M. (Ed.). (1987). *Geometry for the grades K–6: Readings from the Arithmetic Teacher.* Reston, VA: National Council of Teachers of Mathematics.

*15. HIRSH, E. (Ed.). (1984). *The block book.* Washington, DC: National Association for the Education of Young Children.

16. KATZ, L. (1988). *Early childhood: What the research tells us.* Bloomington, IN: Phi Delta Kappa Education Foundation.

17. KAY, C. (1986). Is a square a rectangle? The development of first grade students' understanding of quadrilaterals with implications for the van Hiele theory of the development of geometric thought. (Doctoral dissertation, University of Georgia) (Document Order No. 8628890)

18. KOUBA, V. L. , BROWN, C. A., CARPENTER, T. P., LINDQUIST, M. M., SILVER, E. A., & SWAFFORD, J. O. (1988). Results of the Fourth NAEP Assessment of Mathematics: Measurement, geometry, data interpretation, attitudes, and other topics. *Arithmetic Teacher, 35*(9),10–16.

19. LEHRER, R., RANDLE, L., SANCILIO, R. (1989). Learning preproof geometry with LOGO. *Cognition and Instruction, 6,* 159–184.

20. LEHRER, R., KNIGHT, W., SANCILIO, R, & LOVE, M. (1989, April). Software to link action and description in pre-proof geometry. Paper presented at the meeting of the American Educational Research Association, San Francisco, CA.

21. LINN, M. C., & HYDE, J. S. (1989). Gender, mathematics, and science. *Educational Researcher, 18,* 17–27.

*22. MANSFIELD, H. (1985). Projective geometry in elementary school. *Arithmetic Teacher, 32* (7), 15–19.

23. MARTIN, J. L. (1976). An analysis of some of Piaget's topological tasks from a mathematical point of view. *Journal for Research in Mathematics Education, 7*(1), 8–24.

*24. MITCHELL, C. F., & BURTON, G. M. (1984). Developing spatial ability in young children. *School Science and Mathematics, 84,* 395–405.

25. MITCHELMORE, M. C. (1982). *Final report of the Cooperative Geometry Research Project.* Kingston, Jamaica: UWI School of Education.

26. MOSES, B. (1982). Visualization: A different approach to problem solving. *School Science and Mathematics, 82,* 141–147.

27. NATIONAL ASSOCIATION FOR THE EDUCATION OF YOUNG CHILDREN. (1988). NAEYC statement on developmentally appropriate practice in the primary grades, serving 5- through 8-year-olds. *Young Children, 4*(2), 64–85.

28. NATIONAL COUNCIL OF TEACHERS OF MATHEMATICS. (1989). *Curriculum and evaluation standards for school mathematics.* Reston, VA: Author.

*29. PAPPAS, C. C., & BUSH, S. (1989). Facilitating understanding of geometry. *Arithmetic Teacher*, 36(8), 17–20.

30. PIAGET, J., & INHELDER, B. (1963). *The child's conception of space.* London: Routledge & Kegan Paul.

31. PORTER, A. (1989). A curriculum out of balance: A case study of elementary school mathematics. *Educational Researcher*, 18, 9–15.

*32. PRIGGE, G. R. (1978). The differential effects of the use of manipulative aids on the learning of geometric concepts by elementary school children. *Journal for Research in Mathematics Education*, 9 (5), 361–367.

33. PYSHKALO, A. M. (1981). *Geometry in grades 1–4 (Problems in the formation of geometric conceptions in pupils at the primary grades.)* (A. Hoffer, Ed., & I. Wirszup, Trans.). Chicago: University of Chicago. (Original document in Russian. Moscow: Prov-schchenie Publishing House, 1968)

34. REIF, F. (1987). Interpretation of scientific and mathematical concepts: Cognitive issues and instructional implications. *Cognitive Science*, 11, 395–416.

35. REIFEL, S. (1984). Block constructions: Children's developmental landmarks in representation of space. *Young Children*, 40(1), 61–67.

*36. ROBINSON, E. (1975). Geometry. In J. N. Payne (Ed.), *Mathematics learning in early childhood* (pp. 206–225). Reston, VA: National Council of Teachers of Mathematics.

37. SCHIPPER, W. (1983). The topological primacy thesis: Geometric and didactic aspects. *Educational Studies in Mathematics*, 14, 285–296.

38. SHIEKH, A., & SHIEKH, K. (Eds.). (1985). *Imagery in education.* Farmingdale, NY: Baywood.

*39. SMITH, R. (1986). Coordinate geometry for third graders. *Arithmetic Teacher*, 33(8), 6–11.

*40. TAYLER, L., STEVENS, E., PEREGOY, J. J., BATH, B. (1991). American Indians, mathematical attitudes, and the Standards. *Arithmetic Teacher*, 38(6), 14–21.

41. TENNYSON, R. D., YOUNGERS, J., & SUEBSONTHI, P. (1983). Concept learning of children using instructional presenting forms for prototype formation and classification-skill development. *Journal of Educational Psychology*, 75, 280–291.

*42. THIESSEN, D., & MATTHIAS, M. (1989). Selected children's books for geometry. *Arithmetic Teacher*, 37(4), 47–51.

*43. THOMPSON, C. S., & VAN DE WALLE, J. (1985). Patterns and geometry with LOGO. *Arithmetic Teacher*, 32(7), 6–13.

44. VAN HIELE, P. M. (1986). *Structure and insight.* Orlando, FL: Academic Press.

*45. YACKEL, E., & WHEATLEY, G. H. (1990). Promoting visual imagery in young people. *Arithmetic Teacher*, 37(6), 52–58.

CHAPTER 10

Introductory Common and Decimal Fraction Concepts

Karen Langford and Angela Sarullo

A 6-year-old who disliked peas was usually given a portion consisting of only six peas. Her mother would encourage the child to separate the portion into two "fair shares," or two shares with "the same number" of peas. Then she could choose to eat just one of the two shares. One night her mother asked, "Would you rather have one of two fair shares of the peas [putting the peas into two piles of three peas each], or [putting the peas into three piles of two peas each] would you rather have one of three fair shares of the peas? The child quickly moved the peas back into two piles of three peas each but took one pea out of each pile (Fig. 10.1).

The child's response to her mother mirrors the resourcefulness that all children bring to quantitative situations. As teachers, we probe and then capitalize on this resourceful thinking in order to help children create meaningful common and decimal fraction concepts. Children can then apply the meaningful concepts to practical situations in their daily lives and to related mathematical ideas.

The *Curriculum and Evaluation Standards* addresses the role that manipulatives, real-world situations, and language play in helping young children create numerical concepts. These features of instruction fit the needs of the child at this stage of mental maturation. Moreover, the document addresses the importance of giving children opportunities to make connections among mathematical ideas. Numerical ideas that successfully support procedural skills are, like detailed road maps, rich networks of interrelated ideas. Helping children connect mathematical ideas fits the nature of the discipline of mathematics.

FIGURE 10.1 Different meanings for the phrase "one of two fair shares"

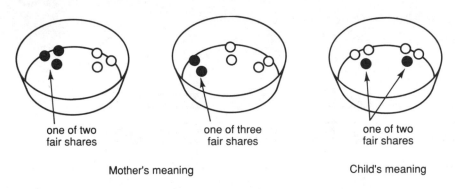

It is crucial that teachers use physical materials, diagrams, and real-world situations in conjunction with ongoing efforts to relate their learning experiences to oral language symbols. This K–4 emphasis on basic ideas will reduce the amount of time currently spent in the upper grades in correcting students' misconceptions and procedural difficulties. (19, p. 57)

The purpose of this chapter is to help teachers design instruction that fits children's developing mental needs and that fits the nature of the discipline. We will present research findings that describe children's views of common and decimal fraction concepts. Then we will discuss how teachers might apply the findings to their own research activities and to their teaching.

The actions of all teachers are guided, at least implicitly, by their understanding of their students' mathematical realities as well as by their own mathematical knowledge. . . . The teacher acts with an intended meaning, and the children interpret the actions within their mathematical realities, creating actual meanings. Obviously, to communicate successfully with children, there must be some fit between the intended and the actual meanings. The likelihood that a teaching communication will be successful is increased whenever the teacher's actions are guided by explicit models of the children's mathematical realities. (3, pp. 85–86)

The Nature of Common and Decimal
Fraction Concepts

Common and decimal fraction concepts fit physical situations that involve two actions: separating and identifying. A whole physical unit is separated into matching parts. Then some number of matching parts is identified.

In common fraction notation, a pair of numbers describes the sequence of actions (30). The second number of the pair denotes the number of parts into which the whole physical unit has been separated, while the first number denotes the number of parts identified. For example, if, as shown in Figure 10.2, a bag of candies is separated into three portions that have the same number of candies in each and one of the portions is identified, the common fraction notation that describes the sequence of actions is 1/3.

In decimal fraction notation, the placement of the decimal point denotes the number of parts into which the whole physical unit has been separated. The number signified by the digits denotes the number of parts identified. For example if, as shown in Figure 10.2, a cardboard region is separated into ten shares that are the same size and six of the shares are identified, the decimal fraction notation that describes the sequence of actions is 0.6. The decimal point placement assigns a

FIGURE 10.2   The separating and identifying actions that
fit common and decimal fraction concepts

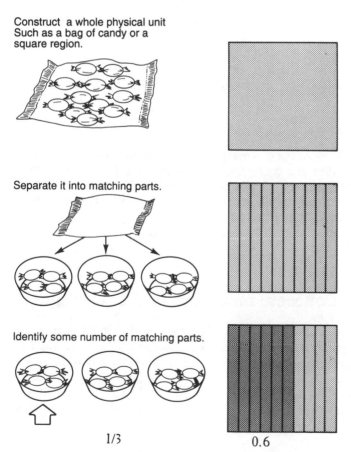

Construct a whole physical unit
Such as a bag of candy or a
square region.

Separate it into matching parts.

Identify some number of matching parts.

1/3

0.6

meaning of "tenths" to the digit 6, and it thereby denotes separating the whole physical unit into ten parts.

A "unit holder" approach:
A unit holder can be any container or drawing that is separated into a number of
equal sections. Each holder represents one unit, or one, or one whole. Counters
are placed in the sections to indicate fractional parts. Relate the familiar shaded
part-of-a-region concept to the "holder" approach.

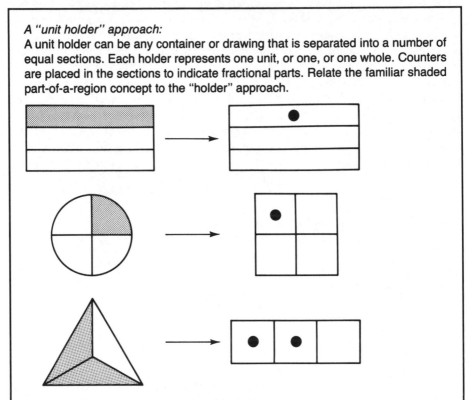

In common usage of fractions the denominator tells how many equal parts make
one whole. The numerator is a counter; it indicates the number of parts being
considered. The holder approach is quite useful in making the respective roles
of numerator and denominator clearly understood. The holder shows the denominator; the counters show the numerator. (31, pp. 6–7)

The Role of Concrete Materials and Language

In what ways does manipulating concrete materials and talking about quantitative
and spatial ideas help children build mathematical concepts? A theory for the language arts, adapted to mathematics, describes the interplay among action, language,
and thought (29). Children progress through four stages as they build mathematical
concepts. The first stage is nonverbal. The second stage involves listening and speak-
ing; the third, reading and writing words; and the fourth, reading and writing symbolic notation.

A Language Experience View of Mathematics Learning

In the beginning children play with concrete materials at a nonverbal level. They notice, for example, that when they fold a square piece of paper "corners to corners" along a line through the middle of the paper that the edges also meet. Opening the paper back up restores them to their starting situation—one square piece of paper. At this stage children mentally note and organize their observations about the properties of concrete objects and the results of their actions on these objects. They carry on conversations with *themselves* about these observations.

At the next stage children speak to *other* children about their observations and listen as their peers do the same. For example, children folding square pieces of paper might say things like, "My piece of paper goes corners to corners too, but it doesn't look like yours." The playmate's rejoinder might be, "That still makes halves." Another child may make two fold lines and say, "Here, we can all have a half of this paper!" as he doles out a piece to each of the three of them. The children may then talk about what "halves" means to them. Maybe one child thinks it means the pieces have to be the same size, regardless of the number of them. Another may not insist on same-size pieces. The children may use the words "a half" and "a piece" synonymously. The discussion involves listening and telling—one child as sender, the others as receivers—of messages that help all to refine and extend their ideas and to develop the language with which to express them.

Teachers learn a great deal about their students by listening to them explain their reasoning processes. The ability to make these explanations is an acquired skill. As with most language facility, it grows with use and practice. (18, p. 20)

At a third stage in the sequence of developing mathematical ideas, children share their understandings and access others' understandings in written form. For example, an adult might capture the discussion about folding and creating halves on paper as children talk. Children who were not a part of the group can read about the observations, thus "receiving" others' ideas and refining their own ideas.

So far, the language medium is the informal language of children's everyday world. Gradually children learn the conventional meanings of mathematical terms (2, 8, 12). Organized displays of the products of the children's manipulations and guided discussions can be used for this purpose. For example, the display shown in Figure 10.3 might come from the hypothetical discussion concerning halves. During the guided discussion children compare and contrast their meanings of "halves," and then the teacher identifies which of the meanings is accepted by "most people."

Expressing mathematical ideas in the symbolic "shorthand" of standard mathematical notation is a fourth stage in the theoretical sequence. It is viewed as another developmental leap.

The viewpoint underlying the theory is that mathematical ideas germinate in nonverbal interactions with concrete materials and grow in a language-rich environment. Next we discuss findings from the empirical research that describe the meanings

FIGURE 10.3   A hypothetical discussion
                        about halves

Jose: I made halves by folding my piece of paper

   this way,   and this way,   and this way.

Gwen: This way didn't make halves.

Jamar: This is how I made halves.

Angela: I gave halves to everybody.

children bring to concrete materials that are used to teach common and decimal fraction ideas. Then we discuss findings concerning the language, both informal and conventional, that children use to express these numerical ideas.

Concrete Models of Common and Decimal Fraction Ideas

Two types of concrete models of whole physical units are most frequently used in common and decimal fraction instruction. Examples are depicted in Figure 10.4. *Measurement models* are continuous material such as pies or various-shaped cardboard regions. *Unit set models* are collections of objects such as Mr. Parker's class or a set of matchbox cars.

FIGURE 10.4 Examples of measurement and unit set models of whole physical units

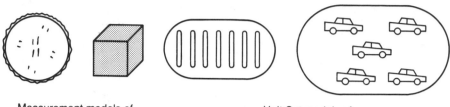

Measurement models of
whole physical units

Unit Set models of
whole physical units

In the first of the following studies children separated cardboard regions. In the subsequent group of studies children separated sets of blocks. In some of the studies they also identified a specified number of matching parts.

The children's words and actions give us insights into their thinking about the sequence of actions that fits common and decimal fraction concepts: How can you make fair shares? How can you be sure the shares are indeed "fair"? When is it impossible to make fair shares?

Measurement Models of Whole Physical Units

Two hundred children in kindergarten through grade 6 used straws to show how they would cut cardboard "cookies" of various shapes (25). They were told to "cut" the cookie so that specified numbers of children at a "party" would receive a "fair share," or "the same amount" of it. Then the children explained how they were sure each child at the party was getting a fair share of the cookie.

Children who were judged to have produced fair shares referred to features of the entire cookie. For example, they talked about measuring the lengths of opposite sides of a rectangular cookie in order to be sure separation lines would indeed halve the cookie. Or they showed fold lines that create shares that would have matching edges.

Children whose shares were judged to be *not* fair referred to features of shares of the cookie rather than to features of the entire cookie. Some of these children believed that the shares were the same size as long as they looked about the same size. Others overgeneralized; for example, if making a cross through the middle of a square cookie made four fair shares, then it would work for a heart-shaped cookie. Still others overcompensated; for example, if the shares of the cookie didn't *look* fair it was because the seemingly larger and smaller parts of each share would compensate for each other.

Children who focused on shares of the cookie rather than on the entire cookie had seen pictures of partitioned regions in textbooks. They had counted the number of shares in the region and the number of shares that were identified. But they had had few opportunities to manipulate concrete models of fraction ideas. *Counting* shares is not the same as *creating* the whole physical unit and *re-creating* it as the union of matching shares. When we use the verb "create," we mean that until a child actively molds the whole physical unit—either out of concrete materials or by organizing perceptual stimuli—it does not exist for that child as an example of the concept you intend to teach. For these reasons:

We asked children to share different shapes in two equal parts. One child responded with the usual solutions of a vertical, a horizontal, and a diagonal halving cut when partitioning a square into two equal parts. He then slanted a vertical halving cut (accidentally?) and declared the parts as equal. Suddenly he stated: "It can be done in many ways!" as he rotated the stick (halving cut) about the centre point. Children's discoveries are surprising indeed! (25, p. 36)

---

1. Ask children to create fair shares for regions that have not been partitioned (25).
2. Ask children how they figure out whether shares are fair. Ask them to show you as many ways as they can to partition a region into a certain number of fair shares (1, 6, 17, 32).
3. Present a partitioning that does *not* create fair shares. Ask children whether they think the whole unit is separated into fair shares. Ask them how they figure the shares are not fair.
4. Connect common and decimal fraction ideas to measurement ideas. For example, when separating a rectangular region into thirds, use straws as a nonstandard unit of length. Children can place copies of the straw along the perimeter of the region. Then count straw lengths to determine fold lines. With some fourth graders, it may be appropriate to use a clear plastic centimeter stick with arrows made of correction tape placed at the points that correspond to fold lines. Figure 10.5 illustrates materials that might be used for this activity.
5. Connect common and decimal fraction ideas to geometric ideas (26). For example, note the corners and edges of various shaped cutout regions. Note that some regions can be halved by folding along a line of symmetry so that the corners and edges of the halves match. Note that some other regions must be cut along a halving line and then flipped at least once in order to match the corners and edges of the halves, as Figure 10.6 shows.
6. In all of the activities, be sure to ask the children what they believe "the whole" or "one" is (6).

FIGURE 10.5   Connecting common fraction ideas to measurement ideas

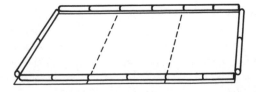
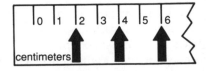

FIGURE 10.6   Connecting fraction ideas to geometric ideas

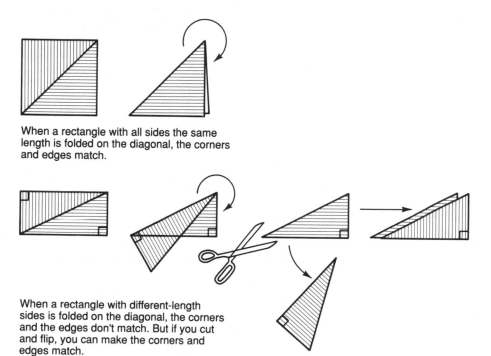

When a rectangle with all sides the same length is folded on the diagonal, the corners and edges match.

When a rectangle with different-length sides is folded on the diagonal, the corners and the edges don't match. But if you cut and flip, you can make the corners and edges match.

Measurement models of physical whole units tap spatial thinking. In contrast, we now examine the numerical thinking that takes place as children attempt to show given fractional parts of collections of objects.

Unit Set Models of Whole Physical Units

Nine children ages 5 to 8 shared candies among stuffed bears seated around a table (9). The children always started with four times as many candies as bears and they always used up all the candies. The number of bears seated around the table varied from two to five. Almost all the children successfully shared the candies among any number of bears by handing out the candies one by one until they were all gone. This behavior is a strength we can tap when we guide children to create fair shares of a collection of objects.

In a more complex set of tasks, third, fourth, and fifth graders showed one-fourth of a set of four blocks (20). Most of the children separated the blocks into two piles, with three blocks in one and a single block in the other. Explanations like this fourth grader's predominated: "You count four blocks. Then you shade this one [touching the single block pile]. This will be the top number and all the blocks together will be the bottom number." In this context the children's ideas about "fourths" appear to fit a conventional understanding—one of four fair shares.

Action research interview (adapted from 6)
Show this figure

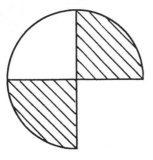

and ask the following—

1. What fraction could this figure represent?
    a. OK, if it shows ———————— (restate child's response), draw a picture of one whole unit.
    b. In the original figure, how many equal pieces has the whole unit been broken into?
       Draw a picture of one of these pieces.
    c. How many of the equal pieces are being considered as parts of the fraction?
    d. Do you still agree with your original answer?
2. Great. Now could the same original figure be used to show a different fraction? If so, what other fraction could it represent?
    If child gives a different fraction, ask parts a, b, c, and d again.

When the same children attempted to show one-fourth of a set of *eight* blocks different responses emerged. Some children maintained they couldn't do it because there were "too many blocks." Others put four of the blocks away and then showed one-fourth of the remaining four blocks. One child separated the eight blocks into two collections of four blocks and identified one set of four blocks as one-fourth. The children apparently equated "fourths" with "four;" whole-number meanings dominated their thinking.

To appreciate the mental maturity it takes to show one-fourth of a set of eight blocks, look back at the evolution of the underlying numerical concepts. Consider the whole number 1. In the beginning the whole number 1 refers to a collection that contains one object, such as one block. The numeral 1 tells "how many" blocks the child sees or feels. Then around second or third grade, the child uses a pair of whole numbers to refer to a sequence of actions on a set of blocks. For example, "1/4" is used in conjunction with a collection that contains four blocks. In this case the numeral 4 only coincidentally refers to "how many" blocks the child sees or feels. In a fraction sense it refers to "how many fair shares after separating." Likewise, the numeral 1 only coincidentally refers to "how many" in each share. In a fraction sense it refers to "how many fair shares identified." Does the child assign a "how many I see or feel" (whole number) meaning, or a "how many shares after separating or identifying" (fraction) meaning to the situation? The answer is more apparent when "1/4" is used with a collection of eight blocks. In this case, neither number in the pair tells "how many" blocks in the whole collection or "how many" blocks in a fair share. The notation "1/4" is meaningful to the child in this context only when he or she mentally acts on the blocks and assigns the number 1 to a *share* (two blocks) within a *separated* collection (four shares of two blocks).

> The critical instructional problem is not one of teaching additional information, but rather one of helping students see connections between pieces of information that they already possess. (8, p. 510)

Findings for children who are 9 years old or younger suggest that separating sets of objects into fair shares is often meaningful only in cases in which the number of objects in the set is equal to the specified number of shares. Findings for children who are 9 years old or older suggest that two aspects of instruction may help children move beyond whole number thinking. For these reasons:

1. Present novel, interesting problems. For example, Jeffrey, a fifth grader, believed it was impossible to show one-fourth of eight counting chips (14). Then he encountered the Parking Lot problem (see Fig. 10.7). Miming a helicopter pilot, he looked down at the parking lot and mused: "I'm trying to think of how many cars it

FIGURE 10.7   The parking lot problem

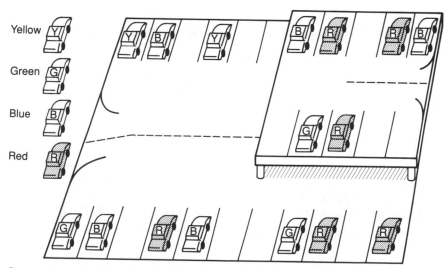

Suppose you are piloting a traffic helicopter and you are flying over this parking lot. This is the covered section of the parking lot (point to). There are some cars parked in there but you can't see them. You see these red cars. (Point to visible red cars; be sure child knows you're talking about <u>red</u> cars and counts them.) The red cars that you can see are three-fifths of all the red cars in the parking lot. How many red cars are there in the parking lot? (14, p. 208)

would be for, *per*, uhm, per third of the six. So if there's six of them, okay, six divided by three, two each. So there has to be four cars under here. Because if each fifth is worth two cars, then there has to be another two pairs under here to make five-fifths of, uhm, the red cars."

In this setting, Jeffrey applied his understanding of multiplication and division. In other studies we find that children demonstrate the ability to separate sets of objects into subsets of equal numbers of objects. Yet they do not apply the ability to fraction contexts (10). For example, Alan, a fourth grader, shared twelve cookies among four dolls. Yet, he did not successfully find "one-third of" twelve green eggs.

> Often it is assumed that students do not acquire a sufficient understanding of fraction and decimal concepts. This is probably true, but it also appears that many students possess unsuspected understandings that, for a variety of reasons, are not accessed by ordinary classroom tasks. (8, p. 504)

2.   Connect fraction language with directed set partitioning activities. For example, ten fifth graders saw a partially masked set of counting chips in the Eighteen Chips problem (14). Most of these children had not created fifths with a set of ten cars or fourths with a set of eight chips. But all of them did create ninths, sixths, and thirds of the set of eighteen chips in this activity.

Try this! *The Eighteen Chips problem*

Of the chips on this cardboard, how many can you see? There are 18 chips on the cardboard. Can you tell me how many chips are covered? How do you figure that out? Can you tell me what fraction of the chips is covered? How do you figure that out?
   When you count all of these chips by groups of two, how many groups of two are there? When I say, "twos," I'm referring to groups of two chips. You said there are nine twos. Can you tell me what fraction of the nine twos [trace finger around the cardboard containing the 18 chips] the *covered* chips are? How do you figure that out? [Ask the same sequence of questions after having child count the chips by groups of three . . . by groups of six . . . by groups of nine.] (14, pp. 207–208)

The importance of these findings for teachers of children at the K–4 level has to do with establishing readiness for making the leap from whole number to fractional number thinking. Children who can recall experiences like those we suggest will perhaps make the leap as soon as mental maturation will accommodate it.

Measurement versus Unit Set Models

Whether initial instruction on common and decimal fraction ideas should include unit set models of whole physical units is an unresolved issue in the research literature. A discussion of studies that incorporated both types of models, yet resulted in divergent conclusions, follows.

One study involved 9- and 10-year-old children (11). Half of the children manipulated popsicle sticks as unit set models of whole physical units. The other half manipulated paper strips as measurement models of whole physical units. Both groups of children solved a common set of fraction problems after five months of instruction. For some of the problems the children were required to use just one of the two models of whole physical units while in other problems the children chose either one of the two models. Differences in models prompted differences in separating strategies.

For paper strips, children used three different separating strategies. They are illustrated in Figure 10.8. A first strategy appeared when the number of matching parts was a power of two, such as fourths or eighths. Children created halves of a paper strip with one fold at the midline and then, without opening the strip, created fourths with another fold, eighths with yet another, and so on. The second and third separating strategies appeared when the number of matching parts was an odd number. Some children attempted to create thirds or fifths by repeatedly halving to approximate the requisite number of shares; they then made each of the shares a little bit bigger or smaller to decrease or increase the number of shares by one. Other children made a first fold that created an estimate of a third or a fifth; they then made additional folds to create either three thirds or five fifths. If there was still material left over in the paper strip, they went back and adjusted each of the fold lines.

For unit sets, children used two different separating strategies. Some children doled out one popsicle stick per share, then another per share, and so on, until they had used all the popsicle sticks. Others used multiplication or division facts to figure out how many popsicle sticks there should be in each share, and then counted out that number of popsicle sticks for each share.

The children who had been taught fraction meanings with unit set models were more successful in their attempts to solve problems cast in measurement model situations than were the children who had been taught with measurement models in their attempts to solve problems cast in unit set model situations. Knowledge of fractions based on unit set models was judged to be superior to fraction knowledge based on measurement models for two reasons. For the unit set model there were potentially two successful solution strategies for finding how much was needed to create one share of the set: doling out one at a time, or using multiplication or division facts. And the instances for which the strategies worked was independent of whether the number of shares was a power of two.

A very different conclusion emerged from another series of studies of children who had been taught fraction concepts with both models (21). Children were taught fraction concepts with measurement models and they successfuly completed measurement model tasks. Then the children were taught fraction concepts with unit set models. After the unit set model instruction, these children did not successfully com-

FIGURE 10.8   Strategies for folding paper strips

When the number of matching parts is a power of two children have little trouble:

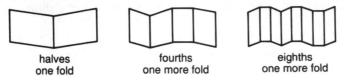

halves	fourths	eighths
one fold	one more fold	one more fold

When the number of matching parts is an odd number, for example, thirds, two other strategies appear.

Either work from halves,

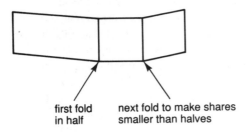

first fold   next fold to make shares
in half   smaller than halves

or approximate first fold, then refine

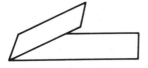

plete measurement model tasks. Instruction with unit set models was judged to interfere with previous learning of fraction concepts with measurement models.

Different researchers offer different responses to questions concerning when to introduce each type of model and how to sequence instructional models. The findings certainly show advantages and disadvantages associated with each type of model. We recommend that both types of models be included in instruction at the K–4 level. Let these questions guide your choice of models as you plan for instruction:

1.   Does the activity require the child to view the concrete material as a whole physical unit *before* the separating action begins? Doling out candies one at a time does not necessarily require such a view. Nor does folding paper strips one fold at a

time, if the desired number of matching pieces is a power of two. However, folding paper strips into an odd number of matching shares may require visualizing the separation action on a whole strip before executing the folds.

2. Does the activity require the child to assign a fraction meaning to the numerical information that is given? Showing one-fourth of a set of eight blocks necessarily requires this, as does showing one-fourth of a square region that has been folded into twelve matching shares.

Language

We now consider two language-related questions. First, what role might language labels serve for children while they are constructing their common and decimal fraction ideas? Second, to what extent are children familiar with the conventional language labels for these ideas?

Children may use words to "keep a handle" on ideas while they are considering the relationship between the ideas. For example, during a series of interviews, kindergarten and first grade children were given some red blocks and some blue blocks (5). They were told, "Here is a pile of blocks. There are blue blocks and there are red blocks and this is the pile. Who would have more toys to play with, someone who owned the blue blocks or someone who owned the pile?" (p. 112). The task requires the child to view the elements of a subset as simultaneously being members of the including set (the "pile") and members of the subset (the "blue blocks"). The use of the collective noun appeared to help children keep both aspects of the situation in their minds.

In the following example, a fourth grader used language to connect her understanding of whole number decimal places to her emerging understanding of decimal fraction place value. Julie had made up her own names for whole number decimal places, as is shown in Figure 10.9. Julie's names fit her spatial perceptions of the base-ten blocks with which she had worked. Later Julie extended the idea to decimal fraction places, with the small unit cube as "one." One-tenth of the small unit cube was an "ant," one-hundredth a "crumb," one-thousandth a "speck," and one ten-thousandth a "germ." Julie's language labels, coming out of her own experience, served as an anchor and a communicator.

To what extent are children familiar with the conventional language terms for common and decimal fractions? Apparently they are familiar with only a few of them (15, 16). And the few that are a part of their vocabulary are sometimes misused. For example, a third grader used the term "one-quarter" to describe one-third of a set of three cars as well as one car in a set of four cars, "Cause there's only one car" (16). In the same study, second and third graders produced only the fractional terms, "half," "quarter," "fourth," and "third" (Fig. 10.10).

Children encounter terms such as "third, fourth, fifth" in the context of ordinal counting, but they do not encounter them frequently in the context of common and decimal fraction ideas. Consider the many counting books for whole numbers that

FIGURE 10.9   Julie's names for base-ten blocks

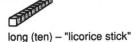

unit (one) – "ice cube"

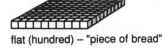

long (ten) – "licorice stick"

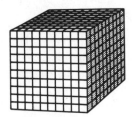

flat (hundred) – "piece of bread"

block (thousand) – "loaf of bread"
and, not pictured,
ten blocks (ten thousand) – "tree"
ten-by-ten blocks (one hundred thousand) – "side of a house"
ten-by-ten-by-ten blocks (one million) – "mansion"

are on library shelves; there is no counterpart in children's literature for fractional terms. With encouragement, children will use language labels that intuitively fit their understandings. And the collective nouns that teachers use in instruction may likewise support initial concept construction. For these reasons:

1.   Use collective nouns to refer to whole physical units and fair shares. Use children's literature as a resource, such as "A Cache of Jewels and Other Collective Nouns" (7).

2.   Encourage children to write counting books for fraction terms. For example, "A Book about Fourths" might devote one page each to each count from the number one-fourth through ten-fourths. Each page might develop a theme that is common to the book as do whole number counting books. Or each page may picture the models that the children construct with concrete materials.

3.   Address four aspects of language in instruction: informal language; nonverbal, manipulative language; mathematical language; symbolic language (12). Use children's invented language and symbols as a bridge between intuitive and conventional language and symbols.

4. Link models and language. First, model mathematical ideas for the children, using interesting pictures or stories. For example in the storybook, *The Little Mouse, the Red Ripe Strawberry, and the Big Hungry Bear* (34), a mouse is persuaded to share half his succulent strawberry. Using the story as a starting point, you could direct children to create concrete, pictoral, or written records of the modeling activity. And then encourage children to share their creations with each other.

> The most important mode for students' writing about mathematics is the simplest one: open-ended writing as a follow-up to a lesson. After students have been involved in some form of mathematical learning, they can be asked to write about what they have just done or learned. Writing is especially effective when it follows hands-on activities, since in those exercises the most active learning takes place. (33, p. 39)

FIGURE 10.10   Chart for fraction strips

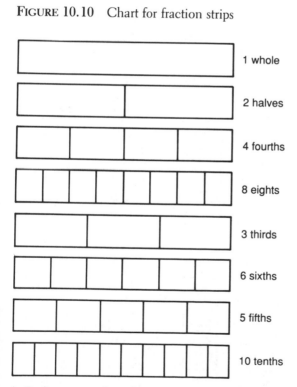

Let's play a game. I'm going to count with fractions like we have been doing, and as I count, you show it on your strips. But here's a trick. Suppose I count, 1, 2, 3, . . . without telling you what size piece I'm counting. Did you know that "1, 2, 3" automatically means wholes? You will have to show me 1, 2, 3 <u>whole</u> strips when I count 1, 2, 3. Otherwise, listen for the size. (23, p. 183)

5. Link models and language to the child's real world. For example, build a classroom bar graph of the ages of the children in the class as shown in Figure 10.11.

It's hard for young children to understand that, for example, Sean and Kate are the same age but they turned 5 during different months. The whole physical unit would be a bar that is twelve squares high (squared centimeter paper can be used). Each square represents one month in a child's life. Outlining and shading each year's twelve squares creates one bar that represents one year. At the beginning of the school day, during calendar time, note the birthdays that occur on that day of the month and direct those children to place another square on their part of the bar graph. For example, every child whose birthday falls on the 17th day of any month of the year will place a square on his or her part of the bar graph on the 17th day of every month. Refer to each month as "one-twelfth" of a year. For example, Kate puts one square on her bar on the graph on October 17 because she was born on February 17. She is "five and eight-twelfths" on October 17.

FIGURE 10.11   A bar graph showing the ages of children in a class

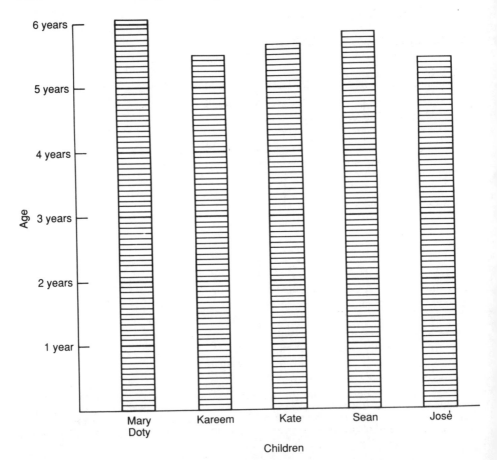

FIGURE 10.12   Sample entries in a mathematics pictionary

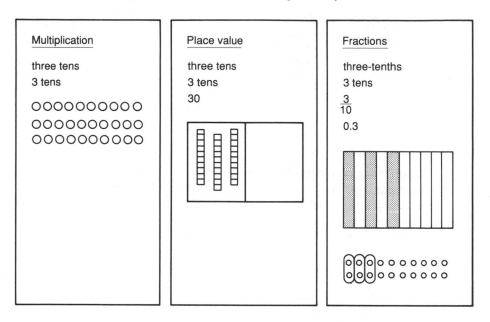

"I can't wait til I'm six and eleven-twelfths!" (Kate Langford at age six and zero-twelfths).

6.   Link models and language for common and decimal fractions to models and language for other mathematical topics. For example, create a "Mathematics Pictionary" throughout the school year. Composed of 6 × 8 file cards in a box, the pictionary incorporates the picture and story outcomes of modeling, creating, and sharing activities. Organize cards by the topic entry in the top left corner of the card. As a topic is developed, pull cards from the box that show related topics, such as those shown in Figure 10.12.

Possible connecting activities include cross-referencing cards by topic, and comparing and contrasting the pictures and associated language on sets of cards.

Comparison and Estimation

Meaningful common and decimal fraction ideas are like good mental maps. For example, if you have an accurate mental map of a neighborhood you can "feel" your way to an unknown place within it. It's "close to" or "far from" certain "landmarks." To find your way in an unfamiliar neighborhood you rely on printed maps or good directions. Or perhaps you draw upon prior knowledge about major thoroughfares

TABLE 10.1. Equivalence and estimation

Zero	Close to zero	One	Close to one	One-half
0 tenths	1 tenth	10 tenths	9 tenths	5 tenths
0 sixths	1 sixth	8 eighths	7 eighths	3 sixths
0 fifths	1 fifth	4 fourths	3 fourths	4 eighths

Arithmetic Teacher, 37 (8)

that pass through the neighborhood. Research findings tell us about the mental maps that children construct for common and decimal fraction "neighborhoods." Some children do think of common fractions as being "close to" certain familiar common fraction numbers. And some children draw upon prior knowledge to explore unfamiliar common and decimal fraction "neighborhoods" (Table 10.1).

Common Fractions

In one study, fourth graders manipulated models of common fractions for eighteen weeks (24). After every eighth lesson they were interviewed individually. In the interviews children were given two common fractions and were asked whether the first was greater than, less than, or equal to the second.

For pairs of fractions with the same numerators, children incorrectly applied whole number knowledge. For example, one-third was thought to be less than one-fourth because three is less than four. Although fewer children gave this type of reasoning late in the instructional sequence, some children never changed. Moreover, when children who had made apparent gains as a result of instruction were required to apply their understanding to novel problem settings, they returned to whole number thinking.

For pairs of fractions with different numerators and different denominators, many children incorrectly applied whole number knowledge. The children who successfully solved the problems relied on manipulating concrete material, or on mental images of prior manipulations. Still others used a third common fraction as a "landmark." One child, for example, said, " . . . three-elevenths is much less. Here we have eleven-thirds, and eleven-thirds is three and two-thirds. But three-elevenths isn't equal to one unit" (24, p. 331). Although this type of reasoning was not taught during the instructional sequence, it prevailed.

Decimal Fractions

In a study of 113 fourth through six graders, children referred to their "mental maps" for whole numbers or common fractions to compare pairs of decimal fractions (27). We briefly summarize the findings, using two pairs of decimal fractions, 4.7 and 4.08, and 4.7 and 4.78 to illustrate the children's thinking strategies.

Squares folded into equal or unequal parts

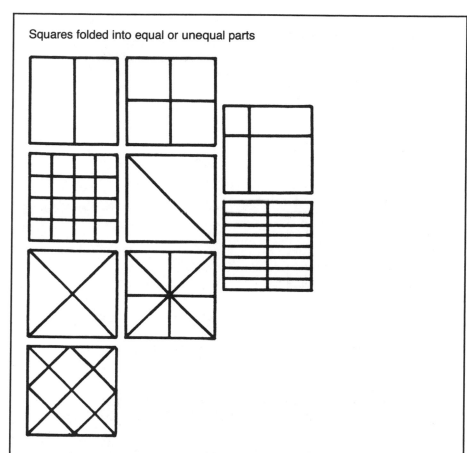

Look over all the squares you folded and tell me which has the biggest pieces. (The square folded in two.) Which has the smallest size pieces? (The square folded into sixteen pieces.) But sixteen is such a big number! Why are the pieces small? (Because you have to fit sixteen pieces into one square, and that makes each piece very small.)

The children who treated decimal fractions as they would treat whole numbers believed that the number with more decimal places is the greater number. For example, they judged 4.08 to be greater than 4.7. In some cases, such as for the number pair 4.7 and 4.78, the overgeneralized whole-number "rule" can generate a correct response.

The children who treated decimal fractions as they would treat common fractions believed that the number with more decimal places is the *lesser* number. These children focused on the place value of the rightmost digit of the decimal fraction. For example, in the number 4.7 the value of the rightmost place is one-tenth and in the number 4.08 it is one-hundredth. Because one-tenth is greater than one-hundredth, 4.7 is judged to be greater than 4.08. In this case, the overgeneralized common-

Comparing decimals to 0 and 1

Close to 0

1 tenth

2 tenths

Almost a whole

8 tenths

9 tenths

More than a whole

13 tenths

20 tenths

(23, p. 190)

fraction "rule" generates a correct response. For the number pair 4.7 and 4.78 it would generate an incorrect response.

The findings for comparisons between pairs of common and decimal fractions depict many good thinking strategies: referring to prior concrete experiences or to familiar numerical "landmarks," and attempting to link new learning to prior learning. Our role as teachers is to help children fine-tune the connections among whole number concepts, common and decimal fraction concepts, and numeration concepts. For these reasons:

1. Begin to develop comparisons at the concrete level. For example, compare the common fractions one-third and one-fourth by using objects such as paper strips or rods (1, 4, 17, 23, 32). Or compare decimal fractions by using base-ten blocks (23, 28).
2. Link concrete models to their pictoral representations by tracing copies of concrete models. As you trace, for example, paper strips or base-ten blocks, tell children that the picture stands for the strips or blocks (28).

3. Lead children to close their eyes and see pictures in their minds of the pictures you have made of the concrete materials.
4. Link concrete models, pictoral representations and mental images (26, 28).
5. Ask children how two given common fractions are alike and how they are different. For example, for one-third and one-fourth, lead children to observe that they have the same numerator and different denominators. Ask children what they know about fractions that are related this way. When they observe that the greater denominator denotes the lesser share, compare the generalization to rules for comparing whole numbers (32, 33).

Looking Ahead . . .

I hope that during the next ten years researchers will identify specific catalysts for the conceptual leaps children make among their common and decimal fraction understandings. How are these catalysts related to such issues as the quality of thought, language, motivation and interest, and timing? How do children integrate fraction understandings that derive from different models of physical whole units? I hope the overlap in researchers' and teachers' roles grows so that our united strengths will bring greater insight to the questions we pursue.

Karen Langford

For years, teachers have been concerned with the problem of teaching *understanding* of the concepts of common and decimal fractions. Computation seems much easier for students to master. Why are they having so much difficulty understanding fractions and decimals and their relationship to real-world situations? Have we not placed enough emphasis on the whole-language approach to mathematics, or on the use of manipulative materials, or on establishing a working conversation between teacher and pupil? Then there is the question of maturity. Are we expecting too much from them too soon?

Angela Sarullo

About the Authors

Karen Langford has taught mathematics at the primary and the middle school levels. She has taught preservice and in-service courses in methods and materials for teaching mathematics at the elementary school level. Her research interests include the nature of children's fraction concepts.

Angela Sarullo is a fourth grade teacher and mathematics staff developer at Christ the King School in Atlanta, Georgia. She has a special interest in developing new teaching ideas for problem solving and a whole language approach to learning and understanding mathematics.

References

*1. Bezuk, N. (1988). Fractions in the early childhood mathematics curriculum. *Arithmetic Teacher, 35*(6), 56–60.

*2. Callahan, L. G., & Hiebert, J. (1987). Decimal fractions. *Arithmetic Teacher, 34*(7), 22–23.

*3. Cobb, P., & Steffe, L. P. (1983). The constructivist researcher as teacher and model builder. *Journal for Research in Mathematics Education, 14*(2), 83–94.

*4. Coxford, A. F., & Ellerbruch, L. W. (1975). Fractional numbers. In J. Payne (Ed.), *Mathematics learning in early childhood* (1975 Yearbook) (pp. 191–203). Reston, VA: National Council of Teachers of Mathematics.

5. Fuson, K., Lyons, B., Pergament, G., Hall, J., & Youngshim, K. (1988). Effects of collection terms on class-inclusion and on number tasks. *Cognitive Psychology, 20,* 96–120.

*6. Greenwood, J. (1986). *Developing mathematical thinking.* Portland, OR: Multnomah Education Service District.

*7. Heller, R. (1987). *A cache of jewels and other collective nouns.* New York: Grosset & Dunlap.

*8. Hiebert, J. (1984). Children's mathematics learning: The struggle to link form and understanding. *Elementary School Journal, 84*(5), 497–513.

9. Hiebert, J., & Tonnessen, L. H. (1977). Development of the fraction concept in two physical contexts: An exploratory investigation. *Journal for Research in Mathematics Education, 9,* 374–378.

10. Hunting, R. P. (1983). Alan: A case study of knowledge of units and performance with fractions. *Journal for Research in Mathematics Education, 14,* 182–197.

11. Hunting, R. P., & Sharpley, C. F. (1988). Fraction knowledge in preschool children. *Journal for Research in Mathematics Education, 19,* 175–180.

*12. Irons, R. R., & Irons, C. J. (1989). Language experiences: A base for problem solving. In P. Trafton & A. Shulte (Eds.), *New Directions for Elementary School Mathematics* (pp. 85–98). Reston, VA: National Council of Teachers of Mathematics.

*13. Killion, K., & Steffe, L. P. (1989). Children's multiplication. *Arithmetic Teacher, 37*(1), 34–36.

14. Langford, K. S. (1989). Children's construction of unity for the fraction interpretation of rational number. *Dissertation Abstracts International, 50,* 1920A. (University Microfilms No. 8924691)

*15. Larson, C. N. (1986). The role of language in teaching beginning fraction concepts. *Journal of Language Experience, 3*(2), 25–29.

16. Larson, C. N. (1986). Primary grade students' ability to associate fractional terms and symbols with area and set models. In G. Lappan & R. Even (Eds.), *Proceedings of the Eighth Annual Meeting of the North American Chapter of the International Group for the Psychology of Mathematics Education* (72–77). East Lansing: Michigan State University.

*17. Leutzinger, L. P., & Nelson, G. (1980). Let's do it: Fractions with models. *Arithmetic Teacher, 27*(9), 6–11.

*18. Mumme, J., & Shepherd, N. (1990). Communication in mathematics. *Arithmetic Teacher, 38*(1), 18–22.

*19. National Council of Teachers of Mathematics (1989). *Curriculum and evaluation standards for school mathematics.* Reston, VA: National Council of Teachers of Mathematics.

20. Nik Pa, N. A. (1987). Children's fractional schemes. *Dissertation Abstracts International, 48,* 2827A. (University Microfilms No. 8800290)

21. PAYNE, J. N. (1976). Review of research on fractions. In R. A. Lesh (Ed.), *Number and measurement: Papers from a research workshop*. Columbus, OH: ERIC/SEMAC.

*22. PAYNE, J. N., & TOWSLEY, A. E. (1990). Implications of NCTM's standards for teaching fractions and decimals. *Arithmetic Teacher*, 37(8), 23–26.

*23. PAYNE, J. N., TOWSLEY, A. E., & HUINKER, D. M. (1990). Fractions and decimals. In J. Payne (Ed.), *Mathematics for the Young Child* (pp. 175–200). Reston, VA: National Council of Teachers of Mathematics.

24. POST, T. R., WACHSMUTH, I., LESH, R., & BEHR, M. J. (1985). Order and equivalence of rational numbers: A cognitive analysis. *Journal for Research in Mathematics Education*, 16, 18–36.

25. POTHIER, Y., & SAWADA, D. (1989). Children's interpretation of equality in early fraction activities. *Focus on Learning Problems in Mathematics*, 11, 27–38.

*26. POTHIER, Y., & SAWADA, D. (1990). Partitioning: An approach to fractions. *Arithmetic Teacher*, 38(4), 12–16.

27. RESNICK, L. B., NESHER, P., LEONARD, F., MAGONE, M., OMANSON, S., & PELED, I. (1989). Conceptual bases of arithmetic errors: The case of decimal fractions. *Journal for Research in Mathematics Education*, 20(1), 8–27.

*28. SCHMALZ, R. (1978). A visual approach to decimals. *Arithmetic Teacher*, 25(8), 22–25.

*29. SKYPEK, D. H. (1981). Teaching mathematics: Implications from a theory for teaching the language arts. *Arithmetic Teacher*, 28(7), 13–17.

*30. SKYPEK, D. H. (1984). Special characteristics of rational numbers. *Arithmetic Teacher*, 31(6), 10–12.

*31. VAN DE WALLE, J., & THOMPSON, C. (1980). Let's do it. Fractions with counters. *Arithmetic Teacher*, 28(2), 6–11.

*32. VAN DE WALLE, J., & THOMPSON, C. (1984). Let's do it. Fractions with fraction strips. *Arithmetic Teacher*, 32(4), 4–9.

*33. WILDE, S. (1991). Learning to write about mathematics. *Arithmetic Teacher*, 38(6), 38–43.

*34. WOOD, D., & WOOD, A. (1984). *The little mouse, the red ripe strawberry, and the big hungry bear*. Singapore: Child's Play.

PART III

Teaching

CHAPTER 11

Calculators and Computers

Patricia F. Campbell and Elsie L. Stewart

The major influence of technology in mathematics education is its potential to shift the focus of instruction from an emphasis on manipulative skills to an emphasis on developing concepts, relationships, structures, and problem-solving skills (12, p. 244).

During the mid-1980s, parents and teachers of young children struggled with the question of whether their children should interact with microcomputers and calculators. The critical issues were: Is technology developmentally appropriate? Why not wait until children are older before introducing them to technology? These questions reflected concerns regarding the relationship of technology to the cognitive development of the young child.

In less than a decade, perceptions of the use of technology in the classroom have changed. Parents and teachers continue to question the use of calculators in primary mathematics while they support inclusion of the microcomputer (31). A recent survey noted that 89 percent of the parents favored practice drill programs while only 40 percent of the teachers deemed drill software as appropriate (20). Thus the issue of whether *young* children should use calculators remains. For microcomputers, the issue now is *what* is appropriate use.

"People believe that calculators will prevent children from mastering arithmetic, an important burden which their parents remember bearing with courage and pride. Computers, on the other hand, are not perceived as shortcuts to undermine school traditions, but as new tools necessary to society that children who understand mathematics must learn to use. What the public fails to recognize is that both calculators and computers are equally essential to mathematics education and have equal potential for wise use or for abuse." *Everybody Counts* (31, p. 61).

Worth thinking about: Consider the parents of the children in your classroom. Do those parents think the calculator has a place in mathematics instruction? How can you educate parents as to the potential of the calculator? How can you keep your parents informed of why and how you wish to use calculators in your classroom?

As noted in the NCTM *Curriculum and Evaluation Standards* (30), an instructional model for teaching mathematics to young children should emphasize active learning and problem solving with concrete materials. Technology must support and enhance this model. The objective is not simply to use technology; the objective is to foster children's mathematical understanding. Research clearly indicates that technology only benefits children's learning of mathematics when a teacher understands how the activity in question supports curricular goals and connects that activity to other instructional outcomes (34).

Our perspective for using technology with young children is that these tools permit teachers and children to investigate the richness of mathematics. In this chapter we focus on research studies where technology has been used to assist and to support the learning of mathematics by young children. That is, when a calculator or a microcomputer has been used because it "(1) permits meaning to be the focus of attention; (2) creates problematic situations; (3) facilitates problem solving; (4) allows the learner to consider more complex tasks; and (5) lends motivation and boosts confidence" (45, p. 22). Although there are references in this chapter to the use of technology to reinforce and to motivate recall, our interpretations do not emphasize this research.

Technology offers the potential for change in the way that we teach mathematics. It also makes possible a change in the identification of the mathematics that we teach (12). Research is just beginning to reveal how young children may use microcomputer tools to explore and construct mathematics (16). The mathematics of the young child can be more than the recall of basic facts, the practice of computational algorithms, the identification of geometric forms, and the solution of one-step word problems. When presented within an environment that also supports the social, emotional, and active needs of young children, microcomputers and calculators may stimulate mathematical thinking and foster mathematical investigations. In this chapter, we offer our interpretations of existing research studies that have investigated the potential of technology for young children. We do so knowing that our interpretations are limited by current status. Technologies such as telecommunications, robotics, and speech synthesizers are only beginning to make their way into early-childhood classrooms. The current research base reflecting use of these technologies with young children is insufficient. Therefore, the future definition of what is an appropriately possible and desirable use of technology for the mathematics instruction of the young child will encompass aspects not even considered today.

"Two-thirds of all elementary school mathematics is taught in order to make calculators and microprocessors obsolete" (37).

Early Childhood and Technology

Questions have been raised as to whether preschool children who are just beginning to investigate the mathematics of their environment should be using presumably socially isolating, symbolic media such as the microcomputer or the calculator (3). The researchers who investigated these questions looked at children's behavior in the classroom from two different perspectives. One approach has been to examine whether the microcomputer holds such an attraction for young children that it thwarts social interaction. Other researchers have investigated the kinds of activities that preschool and kindergarten children initiate or participate in when microcomputers are available. This is because preschool programs are designed to encourage the young child's involvement in many different types of activities; if microcomputers are too engaging, perhaps they would upset the curricular balance. Research is clear: There are no harmful effects resulting from microcomputer presence in preschool classrooms, in terms of either social interaction or student involvement in other cognitive activities (14, 28). Children quickly decide that the microcomputer is just one more interest center, with no more inherent motivation than any other center in the classroom.

At first, the symbolic nature of the microcomputer may make its use with young children seem questionable. However, much of the activity that even preschool children engage in is symbolic. Their play, songs, and art are filled with symbols, and they constantly use gestures and language to communicate (41). The real issue is how is the technology used.

> Technology is "no more dangerous than books or pencils; all three types of devices can be used to push a child to read or to write or to learn mathematics facts too soon. However, each tool can also provide developmentally appropriate experiences." (7, p. 266)

Problem Solving

Problem solving has long been a goal in mathematics education, but problem solving should be more than a slogan. It should be an essential aspect of mathematics curriculum and instruction, providing a means to foster developing mathematical knowledge and a chance to apply and connect previously constructed mathematical understandings. When choosing microcomputer software or designing calculator challenges, teachers should consider whether each activity supports and complements existing goals for mathematics instruction. Microcomputer programs can lead to increased achievement *if* they are selected to match curricular goals (24). Otherwise, these adjunct devices will make no difference or actually decrease achievement (2).

The calculator and the microcomputer should be integrated with children's other problem-solving experiences with the teacher serving to foster children's construction of the inherent mathematical content (10). Problem-solving activities involving the microcomputer or the calculator may encourage children to understand a problem, to represent a problem, and to investigate approaches. Once students have identified a possible solution strategy, their task is to implement the strategy and evaluate the effectiveness of that strategy. These ideals also characterize problem-solving instruction without microcomputers or calculators. The difference is that technology permits the teacher to cultivate these ideals in a new and broader way. When computer-based investigations are integrated with other problem-solving activities in the classroom, the result can be complementary, and student learning can be enhanced (4).

Technology can provide a setting wherein students can build independence in problem solving. But the goal of independence will not be reached if the students seek assurance before every keypress ("Is this right? What do I do now?"). Teachers must prepare their students for the microcomputer or calculator activity, noting assumptions and providing connections to prior mathematical ideas. Much of the problem-solving software for young children can be enhanced if their use is coordinated with manipulative materials and concrete means of recording patterns and data (4).

> Worth thinking about: What happens if you always directly answer students' questions about operating computer software? What if, instead, you consciously tried to give the least amount of assistance possible? What if you responded to questions by expecting the students to first explain their strategies? What if this led to a discussion among the students with you serving mainly as a moderator or facilitator?

While young children generally work individually with calculators, they are often assigned to work with a microcomputer in pairs or small groups. This generally occurs for pragmatic reasons as the number of available microcomputers is generally less than the number of involved students. Theoretically, there are perspectives that suggest that peer interaction is beneficial to learning (49). Potentially, children who work together may assess their own knowledge and beliefs in light of the ideas, explanations, and experiences that derive from the group work. Whether children actually explore and adjust their understandings, fill in gaps in their knowledge, and acquire problem-solving skills seems to depend on the types of questions that children ask of themselves as they work together.

> Worth thinking about: Children will initially ask you to judge their work or to make a decision for their group. What kinds of responses could you offer to focus their attention on their own expectations or to foster their group interaction and negotiation?

Problem solving is promoted when group-generated questioning results in the description of a problem-solving strategy by some children and in the consideration of the validity of that reasoning by the other members of the group (22). Researchers are examining the types of questions that are most effective in these small-group settings.

Problem Solving with Microcomputer Software

Problem Solving Games.   Consider this example involving microcomputers and a second-grade class. The commercial software program *Blockers and Finders* (44) offers a series of games that require children to use inference skills and spatial reasoning. The setting for these games is a grid. Figure 11.1 portrays the simplest grid format. Some of the paths in the grid are more complex as they contain one or more hidden right-angle turns. The game begins when the child directs an engaging character, called the "Finder," to enter the grid at any point. The child then sees the Finder enter and emerge from the grid. Neither the Tilties, nor the actual path that the Finder takes, are visible. Children must reason whether the Finder met a Tiltie and, if so, in what direction the Tiltie was pointing. They are only told how many Tilties are hidden under the grid (Fig. 11.2). The children enter their prediction regarding the position and orientation of the Tilties; the microcomputer provides feedback. The goal is to locate the position and direction of all of the hidden Tilties.

Why did a second-grade teacher (the second author, Elsie Stewart) use this program? Her school district's second-grade curriculum guide stressed the problem-solving process. Further, logical reasoning and examination of data were content objectives in both the science and the mathematics curriculum. She decided that *Blockers*

FIGURE 11.1   *Blockers and Finders* grid

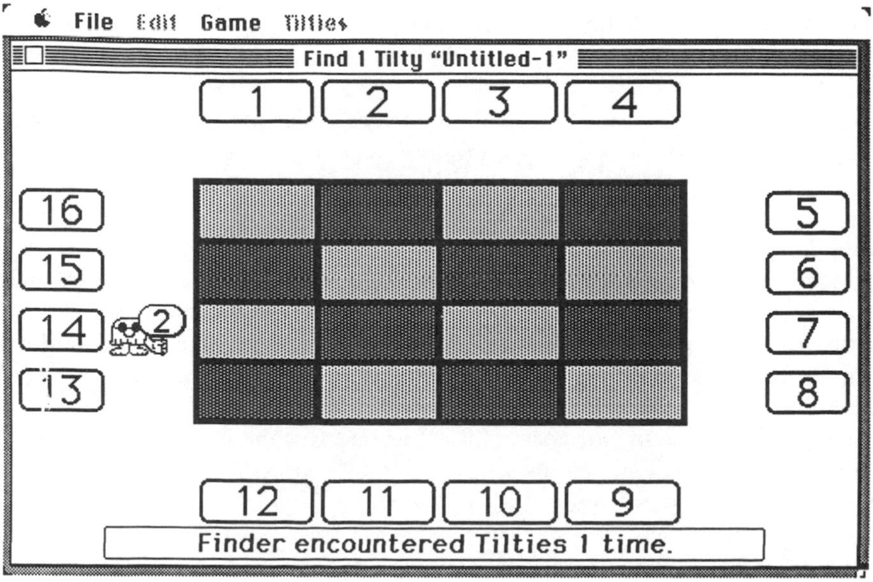

FIGURE 11.2   *Blockers and Finders* grid displaying hidden Tilties

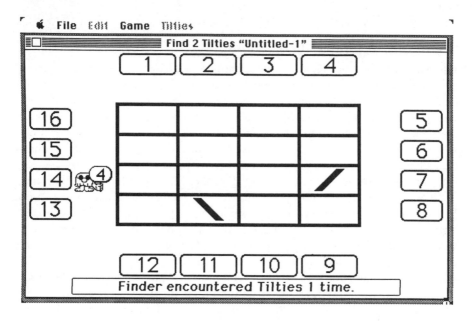

and Finders presented the potential for integrating and connecting a number of her instructional goals. However, as she began to work with the software in her classroom, she saw the need to modify how the software was used and to strengthen the mathematical connections being formed by her students. As she explored how to do this, she was engaged in "action research," that is, in reflecting on instructional practice and resulting events in order to inform her own teaching. Consider how this occurred.

Because the teacher frequently used commercial software programs with her class, she knew that the keystrokes to move the Finder and enter predictions were appropriate for her students. When she previewed the software she noted that the monitor display for *Blockers and Finders* was, for her second graders, dense with information. In prior discussion and reflection with her colleagues regarding students' ease in utilizing software, screen density was an important variable. Thus, she decided that introducing the software in the computer laboratory was insufficient. She preceded the visit to the computer laboratory with full-class discussion. Initially four-by-four grid transparencies for the overhead projector were prepared. She used the transparencies to discuss the operation of the game, characterize the keystrokes needed to operate the program, clarify the goal of the game, and raise questions for the children to consider when operating the software (e.g., "What does it mean if the Finder goes in here, but does not come out straight across from its entrance?"). Subsequently, a computer laboratory visit was arranged. However, once in the computer laboratory, the children were confused. As she reflected on their questions, the teacher realized that many of the children were not able to visualize the movement of the Finder when it encountered a Tiltie. They could predict a Tiltie's location, but they were at a loss as to the direction of the hidden Tiltie.

The teacher decided to pursue use of this game. She saw that her children were intrigued, albeit confused. She now viewed this software as a motivator for spatial investigations and as a setting where she could challenge her students to use and apply the geometric ideas they had learned previously. Back in the classroom, she laid wooden blocks end-to-end to define a large, square region on the floor. The children discussed the properties of a square and agreed that the region would only be entered through one of its sides, not through the corners. Paths through the region were created, and children were permitted to take turns following one of the paths. The children were seated around the square region, so this arrangement prompted much discussion of the perception of front, back, left, and right. Later, diagonal blockers were inserted into the paths, leading to a discussion of left and right turns. Soon the children were predicting which path would be used to exit the square region.

At this point she decided that the children were ready to use the *Blockers and Finders* grid, first on a static overhead transparency and then using a liquid crystal display screen to project the microcomputer display to the entire class. The teacher continually used and encouraged the children's use of the vocabulary of paths and turns and the descriptors of up, down, left, and right. Communication of the possible location of a Tiltie required use of a coordinate sytem as the children indicated position by noting how many squares left or right and up or down the predicted Tiltie lay from a reference point. Random guessing was limited as the teacher continually asked the children to explain their reasoning. Finally, the teacher showed the children a paper grid. This led to a discussion of how to represent motion on the paper grid and how predictions could be recorded.

Now that the teacher felt that the children were ready, the software was placed with the classroom microcomputer as a learning center, with accompanying paper grids that permitted the children to record and recall their observations as the game progressed. This program did promote problem solving as the children would initially randomly guess where to send the Finder, but then they quickly moved to recording observations or interpreting outcomes. They verbalized with one another and evaluated one another's predictions. Determining the direction of a hidden Tiltie demanded the intersection of both spatial reasoning and deduction. The microcomputer feedback was always available as their final judge, should they ask for it.

This piece of software was used to meet objectives of an existing mathematics and science curriculum as it presented problems that required use of logical reasoning, spatial perception, and data interpretation. Examination of this approach reveals that, in this context, existing curricular goals were enhanced. Initially the teacher prepared her class, establishing the problem and reiterating the need to plan and verify. When faced with misunderstandings, the teacher did not abandon the challenge. She reflected on her children's explanations, as offered in the computer lab. She hypothesized that their interpretations of a "turning" Finder were influenced by either their visual image of the hidden Tiltie or by their spatial perception. She also recognized that this software could encourage her children to communicate their interpretations of the geometry inherent in the grid and in the paths. To foster their imaging and spatial awareness, she used concrete materials to set the problem space. To foster their communication, she fully engaged the children as they investigated the constraints of the task. This discussion resulted in the posing of many problems to the children and a consideration of the mathematics of paths and turns. What does it mean to follow a straight path? How do you describe motion? Are these paths simple paths or closed paths? What kind of turns are being made? Are there other kinds of turns?

The problem presentation provided by this software was multisensory involving an active screen display, not just a written text. What made this software useful as a setting for problem solving were its provisions for clear feedback, for varying approaches to a solution, for multiple levels of difficulty, for repeated use with varying problems, and for intrinsic motivation, all the while supporting a meaningful objective (7, 47). But what stimulated problem solving in this classroom was not just the software. It was the structure and guidance provided by the teacher. She was not intimidated by her children's initial confusion. She reflected on their questions in an attempt to understand their interpretation of the Finder's movement. She hypothesized their conceptualizations and designed an instructional approach to facilitate their examination of the grid and paths. She was engaged in "action research" as she reflected on students' current understandings and reorganized her instruction to challenge their perceptions. The microcomputer was a tool that she used to define and support a problem-solving environment for her students.

It is unreasonable to use expensive microcomputers as an electronic textbook.

Problem Solving with Logo.   Logo is a computer programming language that can be utilized by children and adults. It offers another means of using technology to promote problem solving. The aspect of Logo typically used in the primary grades is Turtle Graphics (Fig. 11.3). In Turtle Graphics, a child directs a cursor called a turtle around the monitor screen by using the commands FORWARD, BACK, LEFT, and RIGHT. With these commands, drawings can be made and new commands can be defined. In the Logo context, children can hypothesize ideas, try out strategies, and validate guesses. It is a setting wherein even young children can pose and investigate mathematical problems.

"The intellectual environment offered to children by today's cultures are poor in opportunities to bring their thinking about thinking into the open, to learn to talk about it and to test their ideas by externalizing them. Access to computers can dramatically change this situation" (35).

But does Turtle Graphics really involve mathematics? What is the nature of Logo instruction? How effective is the integration of Logo into the curriculum (27)? A review of research on Logo learning offers conflicting views regarding its benefits. Some studies note the minimal level of programming competence that the students

FIGURE 11.3   Sample Logo procedure and resulting picture

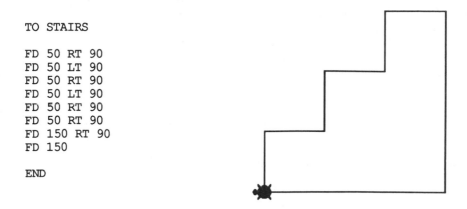

```
TO STAIRS

FD 50 RT 90
FD 50 LT 90
FD 50 RT 90
FD 50 LT 90
FD 50 RT 90
FD 50 RT 90
FD 150 RT 90
FD 150

END
```

attain, as well as the lack of transfer of problem-solving strategies to other settings (36, 46). Other reports suggest that there are cognitive benefits associated with the learning of Logo and that even young children may learn many concepts through it (9, 26). Mixed results such as these are confusing on the surface, but examination of the instruction presented within these Logo studies offers insight.

Generally those studies involving young children that reported increases in problem solving and cognitive development through Logo instruction were the studies where the curriculum fostered predetermined objectives (21). In these studies, the teachers encouraged the children to reflect on strategies and to generalize problem-solving language and approaches to other settings (23). The actual instruction often utilized off-computer activities that may have required students to experience motion as defined by direction and distance commands or to direct the movement of other children or objects (5, 25). Often concrete, physical models such as child-generated drawings were incorporated as plans, and the children were encouraged to think of the components within their drawings (9). The common element in these studies was instructional procedures that provided support, along with the expectation that the children's work would show growth.

> Originally many people "thought of programming as a kind of cognitive playground; mere engagement in the activity of itself would exercise the mind as real playgrounds exercise young bodies, without any need for instruction finely tuned to provoke such consequences" (39, p. 163). The reality of practice has convincingly argued against that view.

In the prior example, mathematical learning did not occur when the children interacted with the software game in the laboratory, although they could procedurally operate the software. Mathematical learning occurred when the teacher used the software as a tool to foster the children's understanding. This is also the case with Logo. Logo can be taught algorithmically as "an object of knowledge in itself" (16,

p. 8), or it can be used by teachers as a tool for learning. When considering inclusion of Logo in the primary curriculum, weigh also the following consistent research report: Logo mastery will require substantial time and effort on the part of the children and the teachers.

> "The importance of Logo is that it provides an unusually rich problem space within which children can confront important ideas; it does not guarantee that the confrontation will occur" (13).

Problem Solving with Calculators

Problem solving through technology is not limited to the computer. The calculator is the least expensive technological tool, and young children quickly master it (43). However, many parents and teachers are opposed to children's calculator use. The fear is that calculators will inhibit the children's mastery of basic facts and their proficiency in applying computational algorithms (50). Numerous research studies have examined the effects of calculators on mathematical achievement, and results are consistent. Calculators do not inhibit or debilitate children's computational skills. Also, children who are permitted to use calculators have a better attitude about mathematics (17).

> The position held by the National Council of Teachers of Mathematics is quite clear: "Appropriate calculators should be available to all students at all times." (*Curriculum and evaluation standards for school mathematics* [30], p. 9).

What, then, constitutes appropriate use of a calculator by young children? The recent National Research Council publication, *Everybody Counts* (31), characterizes mathematics as the search for order, as the activity of defining patterns and constructing relationships. This interpretation of mathematics coupled with a calculator opens a world of numeric patterns to the young child. For example, many primary teachers use the hundreds board with their students as a setting for investigating number patterns. These patterns may involve skip counting, factors of 2, 3, 5, or 10, or place–value multiples. These tasks often involve counting strategies that either encourage the child to count in a particular fashion or to keep track of the number of counts. The calculator is a useful supporting device with these tasks. If a calculator has an automatic constant for addition, then the calculator can also be used to generate skip counting with any number.

> Worth thinking about: Upon being presented his own calculator, a fourth grader asked his mother, "If we always had these in school, then what would math be?"

With the calculator and the hundreds board, even young children can collect data, record data, make a prediction, examine their prediction in further cases, and then offer a rationale for their hypothesis. The natural by-product is communication of ideas, representation of patterns, and connections between mathematical concepts. As envisioned in the *Curriculum and Evaluation Standards* (30), the result is problem solving and mathematical learning. Research indicates that this type of calculator use promotes enthusiasm and confidence while fostering greater persistence in problem solving (38). Indeed, students' problem-solving facility is increased as their focus is on the problem-solving process rather than on computational recall and algorithmic routines (17).

Mathematical Concepts

Teachers can use technology to broaden the contexts wherein children experience mathematical concepts. It is the teacher who must decide what problems to pose and what questions to ask in order to stimulate children's investigation of mathematical concepts, to catalyze the formation of relationships. Calculators and microcomputers can serve as tools in this setting, tools that may facilitate those investigations and widen the range of feasible problems. Conceptual understanding and problem solving are intertwined. Many of the researchers investigating children's construction of mathematical concepts within calculator or microcomputer settings are attempting to determine "what is possible." They ask questions such as: "What approaches do children implement and construct as they solve problems using technology?" and "What understandings about mathematical concepts are fostered when children use technological tools to solve problems?" To illustrate this, consider results from research studies that investigated children's understanding of geometric concepts within a Logo environment.

Although geometry is included in the primary curriculum, it is often relegated to symmetry and shape recognition. But children do not learn about shape and form from their perception of objects. They learn from the actions they perform on the objects, from searching for common characteristics in the objects they analyze, and from abstracting geometric notions from those actions (48).

Recent work indicates that a powerful way for children to think about geometric objects is as records of movement (11). Children's intuitive knowledge about paths and turns may be highlighted by walking and drawing. When coordinated with Logo activities, the mathematical aspects of paths and their components seem to become more conspicuous to children. Further, the need to define distance and direction commands strengthens the connection between geometry and measurement (17, 33). Logo challenges students to learn by defining actions to produce examples or representations of a concept. In this way, children are constructing their procedural knowledge (18).

Calculators are beneficial tools to help children learn ideas about number, counting, and the meaning of the arithmetic operations. Research studies of limited duration have consistently supported the value of the calculator in stimulating problem solving, in widening children's number sense, and in strengthening understanding of arithmetic operations (17, 38, 51). But there has not been research on the effects of a curriculum that totally integrates the calculator nor has there been research on how children construct mathematical understandings within such a curriculum.

There are commercial software packages aimed at supporting mathematical concepts such as number, estimation, and arithmetic operations. This software is probably best described as an instructional game because the intent is more than simply drill and practice. Mathematical concepts are embedded within the structure and design of these games. As children complete these games, the developers propose that children must apply concepts (9). Generally this type of software presents specific task-oriented goals to the student, as well as rules for playing the game, some elements of competition, and a motivating, interactive setting. Research on instructional mathematics games for young children is limited, but one conclusion seems warranted. These types of educational games may be beneficial, but only if they are carefully selected to match curricular goals. Without an introduction that connects the game to its mathematical intent, the game's instructional benefit may be lost as the children may not recognize or focus on the inherent mathematical concepts. Rather, the activity will degenerate into "playing with the computer" (2).

Microcomputers and calculators offer much potential for concept development as they serve as a link between real-world manipulative experiences and mathematical ideas. When fostered by instruction that ensures connections between the technology and the mathematics, children may be motivated to seek questions, investigate relationships, and use these tools to undertake the study of mathematics.

Mathematical Facts and Skills

The most striking gains related to the use of microcomputers in instruction have been found in arithmetic skills for primary-grade children (e.g., 32). In one study, for example, second graders who spent an average of one hour in computerized drill and practice over a two-week period responded correctly to twice as many items on an addition facts speed test as did students in a control group (24). Similar results were noted with fourth graders who regularly practiced multiplication facts with microcomputer drill-and-practice software (8). However, carefully controlled flash card drill, designed to promote speed and to present problems tailored to the needs of the student as defined by prior flash card drill, is just as effective as microcomputer programs (15). Thus, the advantage of computerized drill is probably its potential as a motivating manager. Drill-and-practice software may present computational items in a variety of contexts to stimulate interest and maintain motivation. At the same time they can provide rapid feedback, error correction, and error tracking—permitting selection of items based on prior individual student performance.

However, drill alone is not sufficient, and computerized drill may be misleading. The implications of two studies are important to keep in mind. While computer-assisted instruction programs are very effective in promoting computational skills and basic facts, classroom instruction with the traditional curriculum is more effective in improving students' concept application skills (29). On a basic facts test, children who use a drill-and-practice microcomputer program may outperform children who do not use the microcomputer. However, research that examined these types of test results revealed that the children in both groups were making the same type of errors. The difference was that the children in the computerized setting simply were able to answer more items; they were more efficient in responding to the problems without possessing any stronger grasp of the concepts (1). Computerized drill programs may be one aspect of classroom instruction, but the focus of the instruction must be on fostering understanding and meaningful application of mathematics. These drill programs must be carefully integrated with other instruction.

> "Mathematics drill-and-practice programs can foster recall, but recall without understanding is worthless." (7, p. 278).

There are some software packages for computational drill that include options relating mathematical content to meaning, including concrete models of arithmetic operations. Other software packages have practice within situations that encourage exploration and investigation of concepts. These commercial programs extend computation beyond basic fact drill to contexts that require estimating solutions, constructing problems to produce given answers, or investigating numeric relationships. With this software, the microcomputer can be an adjunct to complement not just skill practice, but also arithmetic exploration.

Managing Microcomputers with Young Children

How might children's microcomputer experiences be organized? While not definitive, several guidelines have been suggested (19, 45). Through personal or collegial investigation and reflection, teachers must determine what steps offer the most beneficial approach for organizing and managing microcomputers for their classroom and students. The following suggestions are the product of the second author's "action research" with her colleagues.

A Classroom Center

Particularly for very young children, the easiest way to access the microcomputer is through a classroom learning center. This center might include a microcomputer and a printer on a cart or table with a supporting bulletin board highlighting guidelines for microcomputer use. To encourage interaction, place two chairs in front of the microcomputer. Eliminate the potential of the microcomputer distracting the rest of the class by keeping the computer's monitor turned from the other students' line of vision. The advantage of a cart is that it permits the teacher to roll the microcomputer around to permit whole-class viewing for demonstrations or to roll the microcomputer to the classroom overhead projector if a connecting liquid crystal display screen is available. Although there are special keyboards for young children on the market, they are not necessary.

Even preschoolers can work cooperatively with minimal supervision, if they initially have adult support. In the preschool, children are more attentive, more interested, and less frustrated when using the microcomputer if an adult is nearby (40). Therefore, in the preschool, place the center adjacent to an area that already requires some adult supervision. In that way the teacher can assist in the activity as needed.

Young children may need to be taught what constitutes a "turn" in a particular game. Kindergarten children may respond best if they do not have to share a microcomputer when constructing computerized projects (5).

Another useful management device involves keeping track of which students should be next cycled into the center. The simplest device works as follows: Write each child's name on a separate note card. Punch a hole through the stack of note cards; the hole should be large enough to permit easy insertion of a medium-size key ring. Also punch a hole through a blank note card that is a different color from the other cards. Order the cards so that the names of the children that are to be paired at the center are on consecutive cards with the colored card on the bottom of the pile. Simply insert the stacked cards through the key ring and hang it near the microcomputer center. The center should also have a small timer that does not beep too loudly. The first pair of children will go to the center, as called by the teacher. When their time has expired, they will flip their name cards about the key ring and tell the next two children named on the ring that it is their turn to use the center. The colored card identifies where the rotation started so that, if necessary, the rotation can be completed the next day by keeping those unused name cards on the top of the next day's ordering.

A Computer Laboratory

When scheduling a microcomputer laboratory, consideration must be given to the order in which the laboratory will be used. If all of the first-grade classes are going to use the same program, much time can be saved by scheduling those classes back-to-back. If consecutive classes are not going to use the same software, intervening time must be scheduled. Also, if the laboratory only has one entrance, additional time must be scheduled to permit one class to leave before the next class arrives.

Effective organization is necessary. A laboratory assistant is critical, particularly if that person has training regarding procedures to monitor computer problems. In that way, minor problems may be solved or accurate information may be relayed when service personnel are called.

The software should be ordered alphabetically within content-specific locations. The assistant must know which programs are networked and which are not. The assistant should let faculty members know what types of new software are available in the laboratory, but teachers will still need time to preview programs. Open laboratory time should be scheduled each week. The most effective way to maximize use of new software is to schedule brief teacher inservice sessions.

Teaching with Technology

Teachers who use technology effectively with primary children take a positive approach, emphasizing cooperation and exploration rather than correct answers and competition. Do not quiz children too much and do not offer help before the students request it. Rather, prompt the children to explain their actions or reasoning and use indirect, open-ended questions. Preparation and follow-up are just as necessary when a microcomputer or calculator is in use as they are for other forms of instruction. Expect and encourage questions. Permit sufficient time and varied opportunities for students to work with the technology. Conduct whole-group discussions about the work. Consider using a microcomputer or calculator modified for the overhead projector during these discussions. Technology often places many additional demands on the teacher. Plan carefully and use technology when it will benefit your students and support your objectives.

> "On the one hand, some researchers are heralding the microcomputer as a revolution in the classroom about to happen. On the other hand, we have yet to see software that is creative enough or effective enough or persuasive enough to get teachers to use microcomputers to anywhere near the degree that would be required to fuel a revolution. The impact of technology is bound to be extensive, probably in ways we cannot yet even imagine." (42, p. 29)

There are some principles that may guide teachers as they begin to use calculators and microcomputers with young children (7, 51).

- Use technology to enhance your curriculum goals, not for their own sake.
- Use technology to supplement manipulative activities, not to replace them.
- Use microcomputer software that is developmentally appropriate.
- Demand interactive software that capitalizes on the potential of the microcomputer.
- Encourage the students to question and help one another.
- Help students to determine when technology is appropriate and when other approaches are more appropriate or efficient.

Looking Ahead . . .

Microcomputers and calculators now permit mathematical investigations that were not accessible to children ten years ago. The challenge is to be more visionary in developing instruction with technology and, at the same time, to better understand what mathematical understandings can be fostered through instructional settings that implement technology. It is not a question of using an electronic tool to teach traditional primary mathematics; the question is "What can primary mathematics be, now that these tools are available?"

Patricia F. Campbell

As teachers, we must help students see the relevance of mathematics to their lives. When teaching problem solving, we must involve the students in applying mathematics to real-life situations. In this way, mathematics will have meaning for our students. Calculators and computers can help students understand the mathematics and solve problems while having fun. They are positive motivators. Children must be taught both how and when to use them. Knowing how to use technology will assist our students and will make mathematics fun at the same time.

Elsie L. Stewart

About the Authors

Patricia Campbell is associate professor at the University of Maryland at College Park where she teaches graduate and undergraduate mathematics education courses.

Elsie Stewart is a second-grade teacher at Paint Branch Elementary School, a mathematics/science/technology magnet school in Prince George's County, Maryland.

References

1. ALDERMAN, D. L., SWINTON, S. S., & BRASWELL, J. S. (1979). Assessing basic arithmetic skills and understanding across curricula: Computer-assisted instruction and compensatory education. *Journal of Children's Mathematical Behavior, 2,* 3–28.
2. BAKER, E. L., HERMAN, J. L., & YEH, J. P. (1981). Fun and games: Their contribution to basic skills instruction in elementary school. *American Educational Research Journal, 18,* 83–92.
3. BARNES, B. J., & HILL, S. (1983). Should young children work with microcomputers— Logo before Lego™? *The Computing Teacher, 10*(9), 11–14.
*4. BROWN, S. (1990). Integrating manipulatives and computers in problem-solving experiences. *Arithmetic Teacher, 38*(2), 8–10.
*5. CAMPBELL, P. F. (1988). Microcomputers in the primary mathematics classroom. *Arithmetic Teacher, 35*(6), 22–30.
6. CAMPBELL, P. F. (1990) Young children's concept of measure. In L. P. Steffe and T. Wood (Eds.), *Transforming early childhood mathematics education.* Hillsdale, NJ: Erlbaum.
*7. CAMPBELL, P. F., & CLEMENTS, D. H. (1990). Using microcomputers for mathematics learning. In J. Payne. (Ed.), *Teaching and learning mathematics for the young child* (pp. 265–283). Reston, VA: National Council of Teachers of Mathematics.
8. CARRIER, C., POST, T. R., & HECK, W. (1985). Using microcomputers with fourth-grade students to reinforce arithmetic skills. *Journal for Research in Mathematics Education, 16,* 45–51.
*9. CLEMENTS, D. H. (1989). *Computers in elementary mathematics instruction.* Englewood Cliffs, NJ: Prentice-Hall.
10. CLEMENTS, D. H. (1985). Research on Logo in education: Is the turtle slow but steady, or not even in the race? *Computers in the Schools, 2*(2–3), 55–71.
11. CLEMENTS, D. H., & BATTISTA, M. T. (1989). Learning of geometric concepts in a Logo environment. *Journal for Research in Mathematics Education, 20,* 450–467.
12. CORBITT, M. K. (1985). The impact of computing technology on school mathematics: Report of an NCTM Conference. *Mathematics Teacher, 78,* 243–250.

13. FEIN, G. G. (1985, April). Logo instruction: A constructivist view. Paper presented at the annual meeting of the American Educational Research Association, Chicago.

14. FEIN, G. G., CAMPBELL, P. F., & SCHWARTZ, S. S. (1987). Microcomputers in the preschool: Effects on social participation and cognitive play. *Journal of Applied Developmental Psychology, 8,* 197–208.

15. FUSON, K. C., & BRINKO, K. T. (1985). The comparative effectiveness of microcomputers and flash cards in drill and practice of basic mathematics facts. *Journal for Research in Mathematics Education, 16,* 225–232.

16. HAREL, I. (1990). Children as software designers: A constructionist approach for learning mathematics. *The Journal of Mathematical Behavior, 9,* 3–40.

17. HEMBREE, R., & DESSART, D. J. (1986). Effects of hand-held calculators in precollege mathematics education: A meta-analysis. *Journal for Research in Mathematics Education, 17,* 83–99.

18. HIEBERT, J., & LEFEVRE, P. (1986). Conceptual and procedural knowledge in mathematics: An introductory analysis. In J. Hiebert (Ed.), *Conceptual and procedural knowledge: The case of mathematics* (pp. 1–27). Hillsdale, NJ: Erlbaum.

*19. HOPKINS, J. (1985–1986). The learning center classroom. *The Computing Teacher, 13*(4), 8–12.

20. HUMPHRIES, J. H., & SILLIMAN, B. (1989–1990). Computer use in preschools: Views of parents, teachers, inservice teachers and 3- to 5-year-olds. *Journal of Computing in Childhood Education, 1*(2), 31–36.

21. JOHANSON, R. P. (1988). Computers, cognition and curriculum: Retrospect and prospect. *Journal of Educational Computing Research, 4,* 1–30.

22. KING, A. (1989). Verbal interaction and problem-solving within computer-assisted cooperative learning groups. *Journal of Educational Computing Research, 5,* 1–15.

23. KINZER, C., LITTLEFIELD, J., DELCLOS, V. R., & BRANSFORD, J. D. (1985). Different Logo learning environment and mastery: Relationships between engagement and learning. *Computers in the Schools, 2*(2–3), 33–43.

24. KRAUS, W. H. (1981). Using a computer game to reinforce skills in addition basic facts in second grade. *Journal for Research in Mathematics Education, 12,* 152–155.

*25. KULL, J. A., & COHEN, B. (1989). Pre-Logo games. *The Computing Teacher, 17*(1), 37–43.

26. LEHRER, R., & RANDLE, L. (1987). Problem solving, metacognition and composition: The effects of interactive software for first-grade children. *Journal of Educational Computing Research, 3,* 409–427.

27. LERON, U. (1985). Logo today: Vision and reality. *The Computing Teacher, 12*(5), 26–32.

28. LIPINSKI, J. M., NIDA, R. E., SHADE, D. D., & WATSON, J. A (1986). The effects of microcomputers on young children: An examination of free-play choices, sex differences and social interactions. *Journal of Educational Computing Research, 2,* 147–168.

29. McCONNELL, B. B. (1983). *Evaluation of computer instruction in math. Pasco School District* (Final Report). Pasco, WA: Pasco School District 1. (ERIC Document Reproduction Service No. ED 235 959)

30. NATIONAL COUNCIL OF TEACHERS OF MATHEMATICS. (1989). *Curriculum and evaluation standards for school mathematics.* Reston, VA: Author.

31. NATIONAL RESEARCH COUNCIL. (1989). *Everybody counts: A report to the nation on the future of mathematics education.* Washington, DC: National Academy Press.

32. NIEMIEC, R. P., & WALBERG, H. J. (1984). Computers and achievement in the elementary schools. *Journal of Educational Computing Research, 1,* 435–440.

33. Noss, R. (1987). Children's learning of geometrical concepts through Logo. *Journal for Research in Mathematics Education, 18,* 343–362.
34. Office of Technology Assessment. (1988). *Power on! New tools for teaching and learning.* Washington, DC: U. S. Government Printing Office.
35. Papert, S. (1980). *Mindstorms.* New York: Basic Books.
36. Pea, R. D., Kurland, D. M., & Hawkins, J. (1985). Logo and the development of thinking skills. In M. Chen & W. Paisley (Eds.), Children and microcomputers: Research on the newest medium (pp. 193–212). Beverly Hills, CA: Sage.
37. Pollak, H.O. (1984). Mathematics in American schools. In T. A. Romberg, & D.M. Stewart (Eds.), *School mathematics: Options for the 1990's. Volume 2: Proceedings of the conference.* Reston, VA: National Council of Teachers of Mathematics.
*38. Reys, R. E., Bestgen, B. J., Rybolt, J. F., & Wyatt, J. W. (1980). Hand calculators—What's happening in schools today? *Arithmetic Teacher, 27*(6), 38–43.
39. Salomon, G., & Perkins, D. N. (1987). Transfer of cognitive skills from programming: When and how? *Journal of Educational Computing Research, 3,* 149–169.
40. Shade, D. D., Nida, R. E., Lipinski, J. M., & Watson, J. A. (1986). Microcomputers and preschoolers: Working together in a classroom setting. *Computers in the Schools, 3,* 53–61.
41. Sheingold, K. (1986). The microcomputer as a symbolic medium. In P. F. Campbell & G. G. Fein, (Eds.), *Young children and microcomputers* (pp. 25–34). Englewood Cliffs, NJ: Prentice-Hall.
42. Sowder, J. T. (1989). *Setting a research agenda.* Reston, VA and Hillsdale, NJ: National Council of Teachers of Mathematics and Lawrence Erlbaum Associates.
*43. Spiker, J., & Kurtz, R. (1987). Teaching primary-grade mathematics skills with calculators. *Arithmetic Teacher, 34*(6), 24–27.
44. Sunburst Communications. *Blockers and finders* [Microcomputer Program]. Pleasantville, NY: Author.
*45. Torgerson, S. (1983–1984). Classroom management for Logo. *The Computing Teacher, 11*(5), 12–14.
46. Vaidya, S. R. (1985). Individual differences among young children in Logo environments. *Computers and Education, 9,* 221–226.
47. van Deusen, R. M., & Donham, J. (1986–1987). The teacher's role in using the computer to teach thinking skills. *The Computing Teacher, 14*(4), 32–34.
48. Van Hiele, P. M. (1986). *Structure and insight.* Orlando, FL: Academic Press.
49. Vygotsky, L. S. (1962). *Thought and language.* Cambridge, MA: MIT Press.
*50. Wheatley, G. H. (1990). Calculators and constructivism. *Arithmetic Teacher, 38*(2), 22–23.
*51. Yvon, B. R. (1987). A compelling case for calculators. *Arithmetic Teacher, 34*(6), 16–19.

CHAPTER 12

Classroom Organization and Models of Instruction

Carol A. Thornton and Sandra J. Wilson

> *The learning of mathematics must be an active process. . . . Teachers need to create an environment that encourages children to explore, develop, test, discuss, and apply ideas (32, p. 17).*

$\mathbf{E}$arly childhood mathematics classrooms should be places where interesting problems are explored—introducing children to important mathematical ideas. Research on classroom organization and models of instruction has been directed to questions of how a constructive environment can be established and how instruction can be planned to enhance teaching and active learning of mathematics.

> "Ages 5 through 8 are wonder years. That's when children begin learning to study, to reason, to cooperate. We can put them in desks and drill them all day. Or we can keep them moving, touching, exploring." (27, p. 50)

The way in which instruction is planned and supported by the classroom environment is crucial to what students learn. The instructional approach and the classroom setting with its math centers, active learning bulletin boards, and manipulative materials forms a hidden agenda about what counts in learning and doing mathematics (33).

Although many questions still remain unanswered, recent research is helpful in pointing out approaches and ideas that teachers have successfully used to meet the wide range of abilities and achievements of their students in the mathematics classroom. This chapter will summarize research findings related to the effective implementation of various instructional models for the teaching and learning of mathematics at the primary level.

Proactive Planning for the Mathematics Classroom

A synthesis of the research on effective instruction suggests that, to enhance learning, the classroom mathematics teacher should take a direct and active role as planner and manager. It is the teacher's charge to create an intellectual environment in which serious engagement in mathematical thinking is the norm.

> "Good classroom management is a way to increase academic time." (44, p. 23)

Planning ahead to organize the mathematics classroom can lead to higher level thinking and greater learning in mathematics (16, 17, 37, 44). By managing time wisely and designing effective classroom arrangement schemes, teachers can more successfully stimulate student thinking, guide activities, and monitor progress. These aspects of instruction are critical for helping young students clearly understand and execute classroom activities that provide the experiential basis for the growth of knowledge and positive feelings toward mathematics.

Classroom Arrangement

A major difference between more effective and less effective teachers is found in planning. One of the first decisions to consider when planning mathematics instruction is choosing a classroom design that facilitates effective learning. In order for design planning to maximize appropriate student interaction and minimize distractions, several important factors might be considered (44). Effective design planning:

- ensures that all students are visible from the teacher's desk,
- arranges student work areas, including materials in the computer or math center, for easy access by both teacher and students,
- keeps frequently used materials and supplies readily accessible, and
- establishes major traffic patterns away from students' desks.

> The arrangement of desks and tables in a classroom is an important part of pre-planning. The ability to see all students at all times and the traffic patterns that are established contribute to an effective use of instructional time. (44, p. 24)

When students are given more choices and greater mobility, the complexity of the classroom social scene increases and a greater demand for monitoring student actions is placed on the teacher. When independent "think" or study time is desired, on-task behavior improves when students all turn the same way rather than face one another in group clusters. By utilizing this arrangement, the quantity of work increases while the quality of work remains the same (16).

Toward this end some primary teachers simply say "front" when they want children to turn their desks to face the front of the room; and "groups" when they want children to move their desks into clusters of three or four. Figure 12.1 illustrates the value of creating a flexible room arrangement that can be easily modified to suit instructional purposes.

Allocated and Engaged Time

Allocated time is the amount of time scheduled for teaching a subject. Engaged time is that portion of allocated time in which students are "on task," focused on the lesson's objectives. Classes in which less time is allocated to mathematics instruction are likely to have relatively poorer mathematics achievement (37). When mathematics classes are consistently scheduled for only 20 or 30 minutes a day, student achievement is less in comparison to classes having 40, 50, or more minutes each day.

Academic learning time is a high correlate of achievement. It occurs when

- adequate time is allocated for instruction on valued topics/objectives
- students are actively engaged in learning tasks
- students are succeeding on learning tasks. (44, p. 19)

Aware of young children's relatively short attention span but recognizing the value of allocated time, some primary teachers routinely schedule a ten- to fifteen-minute mathematics period for activities like problem solving, mental math, mathematics enrichment, or review. These sessions are in addition to their regular class period of twenty-five to thirty-five minutes.

Many teachers avoid scheduling mathematics classes in the afternoon when students tend to be less attentive. This scheme assures that, on days of early dismissal, mathematics class will not be cancelled. Students tend to learn more when more time is allocated for mathematics (44).

To an even greater extent, mathematics learning improves when teachers increase the amount of time students spend actually engaged in learning activities. In mathematics classrooms with higher achievement, more time typically is spent "on task" and less on passing papers, correcting misbehavior, and pursuing activities irrelevant to the mathematics lesson at hand (9). Throughout the school year, a great amount of time can be lost on nonacademic activities. What seems to be only five minutes wasted due to poor organization or idle chatter per hour accumulates into fifteen wasted days per year!

FIGURE 12.1 Flexible room arrangements on cue

> "Teacher practices that support high rates of student engagement include efficient classroom management procedures, pacing and sequencing of instruction, and much "active teaching." (44, p. 23)

To decrease the time spent on nonacademic matters, it is important to take time at the beginning of each school year to establish and assure that students clearly understand classroom rules and routine procedures for commonly occuring learning activities in mathematics (17). It is helpful, during the first weeks of school, to provide opportunities for students to practice basic routines and to restate expectations as needed (44). Students who finish early, for example, should never be without something to do. Otherwise, time will be wasted due to confusion and lack of understanding the classroom organization.

Effective teachers are *proactive* in that they plan ahead in issues related to classroom organization, time management, and the approach to be taken when teaching mathematics. In their long-range planning, most teachers select from a variety of instructional approaches as they attempt to develop the wide range of mathematical abilities among their students.

Because no single teaching method in itself is sufficient to support increased student involvement and foster the development of mathematical power (30, 39), both teacher-centered and student-centered alternatives to teaching and learning are considered below. Whatever the model of choice, it should support the long-range instructional goals, be well structured, and be aligned with the content and process goals that underlie the mathematics learning objectives of each lesson (39).

Teacher Centered Models of Mathematics Instruction

Teachers are the key figures in changing how mathematics is learned and understood by young children. The kind of teaching envisioned by the NCTM *Professional Standards for Teaching Mathematics* (33) is significantly different from what many teachers themselves have personally experienced. Because learning occurs as students *construct* knowledge based on new information and experiences, mathematics instruction should foster active student involvement.

> The learning time that is most powerfully linked with achievement gains is not mere "time on task," but the *way in which* time is actively utilized for teaching.

An active learning interpretation of direct teacher instruction (17, 18, 19) involves an interactive approach to learning, usually associated with whole groups, and emphasizes a structured teaching environment. Control of the learning environment is in the hands of the teacher, who performs the function of discussion leader and class supervisor. The teacher actively engages students in classroom activities and discussions, stopping only to explain or introduce topics, to summarize key points, and to provide closure to a learning activity.

> "The teacher of mathematics should orchestrate discourse by . . . deciding when to provide information, when to clarify an issue, when to model, when to lead, and when to let students struggle with a difficulty." (33, p. 35)

This *active learning* approach to direct instruction goes beyond the typical profile of a teacher-directed mathematics lesson in which the teacher begins by reviewing or checking the previous day's assignment, develops the new content, and assigns seatwork. Good, Grouws, & Ebmeier (19) mesh active learning with active mathematics teaching. The following guidelines highlight their suggestions and those of others to present a broader view of teacher-directed instruction (7, 9, 19, 23, 38, 44):

- Be proactive by constructing detailed long- and short-range plans; by checking prerequisite concepts or skills.
- Make students aware of the major objective(s) of the lesson.
- Spend at least half the period developing material in a way that *actively engages* all students and emphasizes understanding.
- Involve students in important problem solving, estimation, mental math, and mathematical extensions related to the lesson.
- Communicate the expectation that if students attend they will be able to master the material.
- Be clear; provide relevant examples as well as nonexamples.
- Ask many "why," "how," and other high-level questions.
- Be organized; maintain a brisk pace to foster time on task.
- Allow time for guided seatwork before independent seatwork.
- Regularly assign a small amount of homework to develop fluency with knowledge or skills previously mastered, to stimulate thinking about the next day's lesson or to provide open-ended challenges.

> "The teacher of mathematics should promote classroom discourse in which students . . . use a variety of tools to reason, make connections, solve problems, and communicate." (33, p. 45)

Direct, whole-class instruction is helpful at the beginning of the year to establish classroom structure and procedures (44). It also has proved particularly useful for teaching basic skills to younger, low level, and "educationally at risk" students. For the latter two groups, particularly, learning improves when teachers provide students with structured activities, close supervision, and active, teacher-led instruction (17, 18).

Depending on topic and need, most effective teachers combine whole-class, direct instruction with cooperative learning or other models of student-centered instruction, discussed below (Fig. 12.2). For example, a teacher might develop new material with the whole class and allow children to break up for individual or small-group work during part of the period for one or more activities. The class is then brought together for a teacher-mediated discussion so children can hear ideas from students in other groups. The teacher ends the discussion by providing closure on the lesson for the day. This method of integrating whole- and small-group work has been more effective than direct instruction alone for developing higher-level thinking skills (15, 17, 18, 34).

FIGURE 12.2   Orchestrating teacher-centered and student-centered instruction

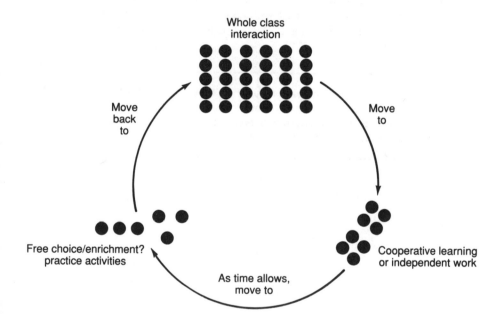

Student-Centered Models of Mathematics Instruction

A key factor in student-centered learning is actively involving children in their own learning. Teachers can facilitate this by allowing children to discover information for themselves, relating topics to specific examples which apply in the children's lives, and enhancing their presentations with enthusiasm and imagination (Fig. 12.3). In doing so, teachers create an atmosphere where children's curiosity is aroused, and where the learning process can become intrinsically rewarding (1). Student participation in the learning process improves the effectiveness of teaching and can be undertaken in an organized environment with a high degree of time-on-task and smooth transitions between learning activities (17).

Traditional instruction in classrooms has been described in terms of teacher-led discussions followed by written seatwork. Unlike traditional instruction that has focused on the teacher's role, constructivist and cooperative learning models focus on the role of the child in the learning process. A discussion of these models follows.

> "Students learn mathematics well only when they construct their own mathematical understanding. . . . This happens most readily when students work in groups, engage in discussion, make presentations, and in other ways take charge of their own learning." (30, pp. 58–59)

FIGURE 12.3   Classroom noise

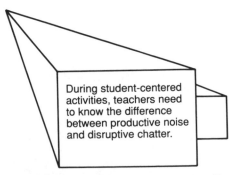

During student-centered activities, teachers need to know the difference between productive noise and disruptive chatter.

Kristina Burlage, middle grades teacher, San Francisco, CA

Constructivist Models of Mathematics Instruction

Recent research efforts emphasize constructivist approaches to teaching and learning mathematics. A chief feature of an instructional model that is based on the constructivist view of learning is that instructional activities should give rise to problems for students to resolve (46). Self-discovery is central to this model. The construction of knowledge by the learner is regarded as the process of making connections between new pieces of information and the learner's existing network of knowledge.

In a conducive setting, primary-aged children have been shown to use what they already know to develop personally meaningful solutions in mathematics (46). A research program called Cognitively Guided Instruction (CGI) has demonstrated these results in relation to the early addition and subtraction program in a large number of classrooms. Current efforts are being made to broaden this study to the entire mathematics curriculum.

> "Teachers informed about research on children's learning can modify their instruction to help students construct knowledge." (35, p. 42)

As one example of a constructivist approach, CGI begins with an emphasis on teachers being in tune with their students' existing knowledge as well the students' thinking and learning during instruction. Nonstandard problems in addition and subtraction, as well as more standard problems, have been given to first grade students. For example,

> Tim had 8 butterflies in his collection. After he gave some to Bill, he still had 5 in his collection. How many butterflies did he give to Bill?

In early instruction CGI students tended to use counters to model and solve the problems. In later stages many of the children used known facts to solve the problems. CGI teachers found what several other researchers discovered (46), that children at differing conceptual levels use different solution methods.

Constructivist teachers tend to establish a baseline relative to the understandings, types of problems, and solution strategies with which individual children initially are successful. They then combine their own understanding of the curriculum to help children internalize important concepts and skills and extend their problem-solving abilities. The teacher becomes a mediator who guides children toward their own learning and understanding of mathematics, individually or in cooperative groups (46).

Learning begins from within the child's own knowledge base, rather than from the teachers' construction. Inherently, the approach emphasizes:

• an on-going assessment of students' thinking as discussed in Chapter 15 and
• an encouragement of diverse ways of thinking.

> Teachers need to use the knowledge they derive from assessment and diagnosis of children to design appropriate instruction.

This process nurtures flexible thought patterns and encourages students to communicate their mathematical thinking with others, in keeping with recommendations of the NCTM *Curriculum and Evaluation Standards* (32). The thrust of constructivist models is on active questioning, observation, and on-going assessment as children work to solve problems, and thus is well adapted to cooperative learning options (46).

Cooperative Learning

Cooperative learning involves setting a group goal and inviting student collaboration in groups on the task with the purpose of promoting each member's learning. There is ample evidence that cooperative methods are instructionally effective in the primary grades, particularly from grade 2 on (8, 24, 25, 41, 42, 46).

Cooperative learning approaches are ideally suited to problem exploration in virtually any topic in mathematics. The atmosphere typically is one of mutual collaboration in which individual students help rather than compete against one another. Team goals are set and met. When competition is used in cooperative learning settings, groups, rather than individuals, compete. The role of the teacher in structuring group work and creating productive mindsets toward cooperative learning is critical. (13, 25, 41, 46).

> "Cooperative learning can benefit all students, even those who are low-achieving, gifted, or mainstreamed." (43, p. 4)

For cooperative learning to be effective in increasing student achievement, *group goals* and *individual accountability* must be incorporated (42). When this is done, minority students who have not traditionally performed well in school, like their peers, benefit from cooperative learning situations (Fig. 12.4).

Other less obvious benefits emerge, particularly for special education students and for those of different racial or ethnic backgrounds. Students engaging in the cooperative learning process have been observed to:

- hold stronger beliefs that one is liked and accepted by peers,
- believe that other students care about how much they learn and want to help them learn,
- have a lowered fear of failure and higher self-confidence, and
- adopt more frequently the perspective of others.

These and similar results continue to validate the effectiveness of cooperative learning efforts in teaching (8, 25, 41, 42).

FIGURE 12.4 Grouping for cooperative learning

"As students communicate their ideas, they learn to clarify, refine, and consolidate their thinking." (32, p. 6)

The positive effects of cooperative learning combined with research on "wait time" culminates in a viable teaching/learning device called the Think-Pair-Share model (31). Research over the past twenty years has confirmed the value of allowing three or more seconds of silent thinking time both before and after a student's response. The Think-Pair-Share method is organized into a multimode discussion cycle as follows:

- **Think.** Students listen to a question or presentation and are allowed time to think individually.
- **Pair.** Students share their ideas and solutions with a partner.
- **Share.** Students are encouraged to share their responses with the larger group.

Throughout these steps, the teacher acts as a manager of the activity by signaling students when to switch from one mode to the next (Fig. 12.5). This allows teachers to combat the effects of competitiveness, impulsivity, and passivity often present in recitation models.

The Think-Pair-Share paradigm is a simple but powerful technique for increasing child talk during a mathematics lesson. Instead of posing a problem or asking a question and calling on one child to respond, *all* children think and then discuss the situation with a partner before the teacher invites someone to explain their thinking to the whole class. Compared to learning groups of three or four students, the Think-Pair-Share model also is a very manageable form of cooperative learning that has been introduced successfully early in a school year with young primary-aged children.

FIGURE 12.5   Think-Pair-Share

Think   Pair   Share

A unique feature is the THINK step, which actively encourages all students to evolve their own response before hearing other students. Both the Pair and Share steps encourage students' communication of mathematical ideas with others, and thereby are consonant with the communication thrust of the NCTM *Standards* (32).

Working together, we can do what many of us can not do alone.

The PAIR step provides an opportunity for the less verbally assertive members of a class or group to relate their thoughts to a single partner before being invited to SHARE with a larger group. Increasing student communication relative to mathematical problem solving, a concept or important procedure is crucial because, for many children, "to verbalize is to internalize."

Modifications of the Think-Pair-Share model encourage students to reach a consensus with a partner or engage in problem solving. Another useful modification is:

represent—show and tell—share

In this version of the model, students are encouraged to use blocks or counters to REPRESENT a mathematics problem they are given. Then they are instructed to pair up with a partner to show and tell how they represented or solved the problem. Students check their results with one another before the teacher calls on students to SHARE their ideas with the entire class. The sharing step involves teacher feedback on the mathematical understandings or processes utilized by children in the situation.

Teachers can use a variety of team structures to engage their students and invite individual accountability. One example is "Numbered heads together."

- Children number off within groups: 1, 2, 3, 4.
- The teacher then asks a question, and tells students to "put their heads together" to make sure that everyone on the team knows the answer.
- The teacher calls a number (1, 2, 3, or 4), and children with that number can raise their hand to respond. (26, p. 13)

Johnson and Johnson (24, 25) introduce options specifically relevant to small group cooperative learning sessions. To clarify group goals and foster individual accountability of students, teachers assign specific roles for students in the group setting (Fig. 12.6). Possible roles include the following:

- **Problem restater***: Uses own words to describe the information provided as well as the information sought.
- **Elaborator**: Relates the problem to a concept or problem that has already been learned.
- **Recorder***: Keeps track of the group's problems, strategies, and actions.
- **Strategy suggester/seeker**: Suggests possible alternative strategies and attempts to elicit strategies from others (all students can engage in this role).

FIGURE 12.6 Assigning student roles in a group

Reader

Recorder

Reporter

- **Approximator**: Estimates and approximates the answer before solving it exactly (the key is to determine a range of answers that are reasonable).
- **Review/mistake manager**: Asks how the group can learn from mistakes or arrive at the answer in a different manner.
- **Reporter***: Presents group results/conclusions to the class.

Starred roles (*) typically are part of most group work. Depending on group size, other roles might be assigned.

Throughout cooperative learning activities, all children should encourage the efforts and attitudes of others in order to solve the problem by working together. Essential principles in any cooperative learning task include:

- the concept of positive interdependence (the perception that one is linked to and cannot succeed without the help of others)
- face-to-face interaction of students
- individual accountability
- use of collaborative and evaluative skills for the entire group's function
- heterogeneous grouping, including students of different genders, social backgrounds, skill levels, and physical attributes

---

"When you create heterogeneous teams and make them heterogeneous not only by achievement but by race, you get strong improvement in race relations." (5, p. 10)

Groups of three or four students work well for many tasks. It is particularly important to inform students of the rules for small group work. The following appear to be most useful (8, 10, 13):

- Do your fair share of the work.
- Disagree with ideas, not people (put-downs not allowed).
- Take turns; listen to what others have to say.
- Help one another.
- Ask the teacher for help only when everyone in your group has the same question.

Some teachers add: "Use a twelve-inch voice so that only those in your group hear what you have to say."

Effective use of cooperative learning procedures in the classroom is not an easy task. As with other models, this one takes time, effort, and organizational support. Professional workshops on implementation and collegial support are important factors in assuring the success of cooperative learning methods (25).

Another model of cooperative learning is Student Team Learning (41, 42). This model emphasizes group success in which students not only experience successes in learning but help others to do so as well. Since group success and team recognition are vital features of this model, students are held individually accountable but become involved in a unified group effort.

> "The teacher of mathematics should create a learning environment that fosters the development of students' mathematical power by respecting and valuing students' ideas and ways of thinking . . . and by consistently expecting and encouraging students to work independently and collaboratively as members of a learning community making sense of mathematics." (32, p. 13)

Peer Tutoring

Peer tutoring has received increased attention as a valuable tool for instruction. Meta-analysis findings from sixty-five independent evaluations of school tutoring programs (12) report positive effects of peer tutoring on academic performance, while attitudes of both the tutor and tutee toward the subject matter were found to increase. Peer or cross-age tutoring has been used most successfully with disadvantaged, bilingual, and handicapped students. The special-needs students may play the role either of tutor or client. The most notable gains in mathematics appeared when the tutoring program was structured for the participants.

Peer or cross-age tutors usually work one-on-one using specific procedures planned by a teacher, modeling expected behaviors, and providing feedback and reinforcements. As with other approaches in mathematics education, tutoring programs with the highest efficiency or greatest gains share common characteristics. Since peer tutoring is inherently a social experience, social learning theorists advise choosing a tutor who has:

- a somewhat higher ability
- a similar or slightly higher social acceptance
- good interpersonal communication abilities
- positive view of the role of tutor

The perceptions of a peer tutoring program as a game, homework, or class requirement will influence the nature of the interaction and its overall effectiveness (11).

Tutees receiving more tutoring a week were found to show greater gains. Supervision of the tutoring interaction is necessary, but not to the extent of stifling open communication and ideas between the tutor and tutee. Some training in listening skills, monitoring, corrective feedback, effective communication, and patience will provide greater likelihood of a successful tutoring relationship.

> Peer and cross-age tutoring has been used successfully with disadvantaged, bilingual, and handicapped students. The special needs students may play the role either of tutor or client. (36)

In general, peer tutoring appears to be a solid teaching technique that provides a learning structure that is highly individualized and allows for the positive effects of modeling to occur. Preparation and care given to the selection and training of tutors, as well as supervising and evaluating the tutoring relationship, greatly determine the effectiveness of a peer-tutoring relationship.

Ability Grouping Strategies

While ability grouping has traditionally dominated the classroom setting as one of the most popular alternatives for instruction, there is little research available to support its continued use. At best, homogeneous ability grouping provides teachers with an easier way of presenting materials to their students. At worst, it reduces the achievement levels of average- and low-ability groups, encourages lowered expectations, and narrows vocational options for lower-track students. In general, it hinders more than it engenders learning.

Advocates of ability grouping assume that:

- low-ability students develop a more positive image of themselves when not forced to compete with students of much higher ability
- grouping decisions can be made fairly and accurately on the basis of previous performance or ability
- teachers are better able to accommodate individual differences in homogeneous ability groupings
- students, including the more gifted, will learn better when grouped with those of similar academic ability

(14)

> The research evidence is consistent: Ability grouping exaggerates the initial differences among students rather than providing a means to better accommodate them.

Although these assumptions have a widespread "common sense" acceptance, the research available to substantiate these assumptions is sparse. In fact, the arguments for homogeneous ability grouping based on benefits for lower-ability learners is an invalid assumption (14, 40). There is little chance for vicarious learning, and lower-ability students who are placed in a self-contained class with other low-ability students do not experience the stimulation that takes place when exposed to higher-level thinking. This approach tends to maintain if not worsen the status quo, separating low from higher level achievement patterns.

> Myth: Ability grouping increases achievement levels in mathematics.
> Reality: For most students ability grouping produces slower rates of learning and, in the long run, smaller chances of succeeding. . . . The cumulative losses are greatest when tracking starts in the *early* elementary grades. . . . Lower-level students tend to be hurt the most. (4)

When low- and high-ability groups are established within a class, instructional time for each group is lessened in proportion to the number of groups into which the class is divided. Either plan often concentrates problem children in the same group, making teaching more difficult.

Further, educators are in disagreement as to the best and fairest method of dividing groups. Too often, the evaluation for movement between groups is done infrequently and in a haphazard manner. There is a potential for bias in placing those of racial and cultural minorities in the lower-ability groups and a likelihood of those children remaining in lower-track groups.

This is not to say that tracking has no place in gifted programs for which there is adequate follow-up *through high school,* but recent research suggests that heterogeneous and flexible grouping solutions better stimulate achievement gains for all students. The needs of higher-level students can continue to be met in mixed-ability groups through horizontal, as opposed to vertical acceleration (Fig. 12.7). Pull-out enrichment programs for gifted and talented students also have been used satisfactorily.

Horizontal acceleration for bright students provides enrichment experiences that build upon and expand a student's understanding of mathematical concepts and relate topics in other areas of study. This is in contrast to vertical acceleration that allows the brightest students to move at a more rapid pace through content material typically designated for the current or subsequent grade level(s).

FIGURE 12.7   Flexible grouping

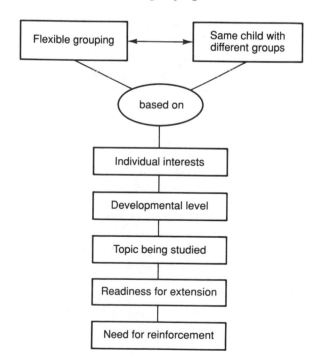

Slavin's (40) meta-analysis of ability grouping research provides support for these restricted uses of ability grouping:

- Students are assigned to heterogeneous classes but are regrouped homogeneously for one or two topics.
- Grouping assignments are flexible and frequently reassessed.
- Teachers actually alter instruction to accommodate students' needs.

A low proportion of current ability grouping programs fulfill these criteria. When all of the criteria *are* met, positive gains have been found in mathematics learning.

Mastery Learning

Mastery of subject matter has for years been the predominant focus of mathematics education research. Mastery learning is based on the premise that different children learn material at different rates and in different ways. As an outcome-based instructional model in mathematics, mastery learning involves providing quality instruction that best suits children's needs *and* the amount of time needed by each individual for mastering important concepts and skills. It also implies that children are willing to spend the time needed to insure learning.

> "Since thinking is a knowledge-based activity, the coordination of . . . mastery learning with thinking processes is truly a way of teaching for thinking." (3)

Many school districts formally adopting a mastery learning model establish competency levels (usually 85–90 percent) for mastery of certain concepts or skills at each grade level, and teachers reteach those students who do not achieve minimum competency. A strong point of this approach is that it highlights the need to devote the necessary time and effort to help slower learners. As a result, the percent of students who are successful at subsequent learning tasks is greater, making for overall higher achievement and self-concept gains (2).

However, few teachers can successfully manage the great diversity introduced by letting some individuals advance while others are retaught or given more time to reach mastery. Many teachers prefer a group-based mastery learning approach in which children learn, for the most part, cooperatively with their classmates. The instructional time is relatively fixed, and teachers focus activity on a topic until "most" children in the class have mastered the more important and relevant understandings or skills. Students who learn faster might be given enrichment opportunities but do not advance far beyond their peers in the basic plan of study. The "slowest"-learning students in the class are provided extra help to the greatest extent possible, both from the teacher and peers in cooperative groups.

The honest effort to promote mastery on an earlier topic will be renewed through review and reteaching, as time allows, even though strict competency levels may not have been set or reached by all children. As an instructional leader and learning facilitator, the teacher has helped children advance as far as possible for the time being from their individual starting points (20).

"The teacher of mathematics should create a learning environment that fosters the development of students' mathematics power by . . . providing and structuring the time necessary to explore sound mathematics and grapple with significant ideas and problems." (33, p. 57)

Math Centers and Learning Stations

Although there is little recent research on the effectiveness of math centers or learning stations, there is renewed interest in these instructional models—often in the context of some form of cooperative learning. The general atmosphere promoted by stations, centers, and other lab-oriented approaches is child-centered rather than teacher-dominated. A primary goal has been to stimulate the learning of mathematics with understanding and retention. In many early childhood programs, activity centers characterize the major scheme for mathematics learning.

Math centers and learning stations provide an inquiry-based environment that promotes children's involvement with materials, other children, and adults. To be most effective, the range of tasks, problems, or activities presented should allow for differences in children's abilities, learning styles, interests, needs, and previous experiences and be mathematically interesting.

"I hear, I forget.
I see, I remember.
I do, I understand."
(Chinese proverb)

A shelf, table, cabinet, or corner in the classroom where mathematics activities as well as books and manipulatives are housed—this is the beginning of a mathematics learning *center*. In contrast to a learning center that houses a variety of resources and activities, a mathematics learning *station* typically invites students to focus on just one specific task or idea. A desk, table, shelf, or bulletin board might be used for station set-up.

While working independently or in cooperative groups with others at a station, students usually complete one activity of their choice from a set of given activities related to the same topic. Instructions are frequently taken from assignment cards or sheets.

During the regular mathematics period, several related stations might be set up about the room. Children either complete as many activities as they can in the allotted time, or work on each station's activity until a signal is given to shift to the next station. Frequently, stations are left up for a period of several days so children can work through them on their own time, either as an option or as part of an ongoing assignment (Fig. 12.8).

The overriding structure and organization of station and center activity in relation to curricular goals is critical. Adequate introduction to the tasks or activities, time

FIGURE 12.8 Learning stations

for student interaction and problem solving related to the tasks, quality discussion to establish critical connections and closure, and workable assessment schemes are elements central to the success of these approaches.

Even though lab-oriented approaches were generally found to be used practically and effectively in the 1970s, it was found that on cognitive-related tasks other meaningful instruction worked as well or better (45). Given the current ways in which math centers or station activity is conceptualized, and in which students are held individually accountable, has this situation improved? The general enthusiasm of students and of teachers currently using these techniques, among other approaches in their repertoire, invites further study.

Lab-oriented approaches provide an opportunity for:

- free exploration of materials, ideas, and relationships
- fostering social, emotional, and intellectual growth
- child initiation as well as teacher initiation of activities
- the exploration, reinforcement, and extension of ideas related to a mathematics topic
- building on the mathematical potential of a child's interests, questions, or discoveries (21, p. 9)

Mathematics Games

When teachers use appropriate mathematics games, both student learning and motivation are strengthened. Bright, Harvey, and Wheeler (6) suggest that the current practice of using games only for drill and practice of low-level skills is limiting. Mathematics games can and should be used before, during, and after instruction to help students develop higher-level thinking skills. (6, 22)

> De-emphasize competition in mathematics games. Winning should not be related to teacher praise. Winning, like losing should both be treated casually.

Kamii (28, 29) encourages group games not only as an avenue for structured play, but specifically to inspire children to communicate and to construct critical, logical thinking patterns. To be useful, games must be carefully selected to match curricular goals, be introduced, played, and talked about. A group game should:

- have a clear, specific predetermined end result
- suggest something mathematically interesting and challenging
- provide a setting in which children can build upon their knowledge base to construct new understandings or skills
- permit all players actively to participate and communicate
- make it possible for children themselves to judge their success
- be discussed to highlight the mathematical concepts, relationships or skills learned

Properly designed, mathematical games promote autonomous thinking in young children. They provide an alternative to the teacher as the source of right answers. As children interact with their peers to determine which answers are correct, they develop confidence in their ability to figure things out, an important goal in mathematics. Games can stimulate children to be alert, curious, and critical, and to see themselves as problem solvers. They can nurture initiative in creating game strategies. Games help very young children develop their ability to decenter and coordinate different points of view.

> Game play is a particularly powerful form of activity that can promote higher-level thinking, social achievement, and constructive activity. . . . Games can help students think creatively about mathematics.

A place–value trading game in which children twirl a spinner, take cubes or sticks to match the number of the spin, trade for a ten whenever possible, and try to reach a target number (e.g., 50) is an example of a game that can be used during instruction to develop conceptual understanding. Games can nurture other sorts of learning, such as problem solving, pattern finding, analyzing data, decision making, reinforcing learned material, and enhancing student participation and enthusiasm.

Concluding Comments

Teaching presents challenging questions. In relation to classroom organization, recent research has stressed the need for teachers to make wise decisions in relation to classroom design and time management. The most critical decision is the creation of a mathematically stimulating environment through active teaching.

Research findings highlight the role of active learning methods in direct instruction, present information on new models like Cognitively Guided Instruction, and indicate effective ways of utilizing cooperative learning and other student-centered models of instruction. Collectively, these findings from research provide teachers with a repertoire of ideas and information about the effectiveness of instructional options that can be used flexibly to enhance the teaching and learning of primary school mathematics.

> Teachers who are well versed in a variety of approaches can create effective lessons that engage their students' physically and mentally. . . . The complementary nature of many instructional models must be emphasized if teachers are to understand how to integrate them and translate that synthesis into classroom practice.

Looking Ahead . . .

Many factors influence the choice of organizational patterns and models of instruction for mathematics. The most critical decisions, deserving of continued reflection and further research, are those that relate to maintaining *balance* and *flexibility* in planning and instruction. There is as much a place for teacher structuring and guidance as for constructive activity by students so that important mathematical concepts and connections are developed, understood, and used. The research agenda for the future might well focus on identifying effective, flexible schemes that provide a balanced setting for the teaching and active learning of K–4 mathematics.

Carol A. Thornton

We believe that *children* think mathematically as they actively construct, modify, and integrate ideas by interacting with their physical world and other children. Their communication of mathematics provides confrontation of points of view— and learning takes place. Among educators, there is a diversity of theories on how to organize for instruction and teach mathematics, but we are rarely in a position where there is opportunity to interact meaningfully. How can we *adults* (classroom teachers, administrators, researchers) actively construct, modify, and integrate our thinking as we communicate and confront different points of view so that we can learn to be better teachers of mathematics?

Sandra J. Wilson

About the Authors

Carol Thornton is distinguished professor of mathematics at Illinois State University, Normal, Illinois. She teaches undergraduate and graduate mathematics education courses, co-directs staff development projects for teachers, is involved in research related to curriculum development, and has written mathematics materials for teachers and children.

Sandra Wilson is an experienced elementary teacher in District #27, Lincoln, Illinois. She has a master's degree in mathematics education and conducts staff development sessions for teachers. She also teaches adult education courses in mathematics.

References

1. ABRAMI, P. C., LEVENTHAL, L., & PERRY, R. P. (1982). Educational selection. *Review of Educational Research, 52,* 446–452.
2. ANDERSON, L. W., & BURNS, R. B. (1987). Values, evidence, and mastery learning. *Review of Educational Research, 57,* 215–223.
3. ARREDONDO, D. E., & BLOCK, J. H. (1990). Recognizing the connections between thinking skills and mastery learning. *Educational Leadership, 47*(5), 8.
4. BRADDOCK, J. H., & McPARTLAND. (1990). Alternatives to tracking. *Educational Leadership, 47*(7), 77.
5. BRANDT, R. (1989). On cooperative learning: A conversation with Spencer Kagan. *Educational Leadership, 47*(4), 10.
6. BRIGHT, G. W., HARVEY, J. G., & WHEELER, M. M. (1985). Learning and mathematics games. *Journal for Research in Mathematics Education, Monograph 1.*
7. BROPHY, J. (1986) Teaching and learning mathematics: Where research should be going. *Journal for Research in Mathematics Education, 17,* 323–346.
*8. BURNS, MARILYN. (1989). The math solution: Using groups of four. In N. Davidson (Ed.), *Cooperative learning in mathematics: A handbook for teachers* (pp. 21–46). Menlo Park, CA: Addison-Wesley.
9. BURTON, G. M. (1986). The focal point: Whole-group instruction. *Focus on Learning Problems in Mathematics, 8,* 1–4.
*10. CHARLES, R., & LESTER, F. (1986). *Mathematical problem solving.* Springhouse, PA: Learning Institute.
11. COHEN, J. (1986). Theoretical considerations of peer tutoring. *Psychology in the Schools, 23,* 175–185.
12. COHEN, P. J., KULIK, J. A., & KULIK, C. C. (1982). Educational outcomes of tutoring: A meta-analysis of findings. *American Educational Research Journal, 19,* 237–248.
*13. DAVIDSON, N. (1990). Small-group cooperative learning in mathematics. In T. J. Cooney and C. R. Hirsch (Eds.), *Teaching and learning mathematics in the 1990s* (1990 Yearbook, pp. 52–61). Reston, VA: National Council of Teachers of Mathematics.
14. DAWSON, M. M. (1987). Beyond ability grouping: A review of the effectiveness of ability grouping and its alternatives. *School Psychology Review, 16,* 348–369.
15. DOYLE, W. (1983). Academic work. *Review of Educational Research, 53,* 159–199.
16. DOYLE, W. (1986). Classroom organization and management. In M. C. Wittrock (Ed.), *Handbook of research on teaching* (3rd ed.) (pp. 392–431). New York: Macmillan.
17. EVERTSON, C. M., EMMER, E., CLEMMENTS, B., STANFORD, J., & WORSHAM, M. (1989). *Classroom management for elementary teachers.* Englewood Cliffs, NJ: Prentice-Hall.
18. GERTSEN, R., & KEATING, T. (1987). Long-term benefits from direct instruction. *Educational Leadership, 44,* 28–31.
19. GOOD, T. L., GROUWS, D. A., & EBMEIER, H. (1983). *Active mathematics teaching.* New York: Longman.
20. GUSKEY, T. R. (1985). *Implementing mastery learning.* Belmont, CA: Wadsworth.
21. HARCOURT, L. (1988). *Explorations for early childhood.* Reading, MA: Addison-Wesley.

22. HARVEY, J. G., & BRIGHT, G. W. (1985). Mathematical games: Antithesis or assistance? *Arithmetic Teacher, 32*(6), 23–26.

23. HUNTER, M. (1984). Knowing, teaching, and supervising. In P. L. Hosford (Ed.), *Using what we know about teaching* (pp. 169–192). Alexandria, VA: Association for Supervision and Curriculum Development.

*24. JOHNSON, D. W., & JOHNSON, R. T. (1989). Cooperative learning in mathematics education. In P. R. Trafton & A. P. Shulte (Eds.), *New directions for elementary school mathematics* (1989 Yearbook, pp. 234–245). Reston, VA: National Council of Teachers of Mathematics.

*25. JOHNSON, D. W., & JOHNSON, R. T. (1989). Using cooperative learning in math. In N. Davidson (Ed.), *Cooperative learning in mathematics: A handbook for teachers* (pp.103–125). Menlo Park, CA: Addison-Wesley.

26. KAGAN, S. (1989). A structured approach to cooperative learning. *Educational Leadership, 47*(4), 13.

27. KANTROWITZ, B., & WINGERT, P. (1989, April 17). How kids learn. *Newsweek,* pp. 50–54.

28. KAMII, C. (1990). Constructivism and beginning arithmetic (K–2). In T. J. Cooney & C. R. Hirsch (Eds.), *Teaching and learning mathematics in the 1990s* (1990 Yearbook, pp. 22–30). Reston, VA: National Council of Teachers of Mathematics.

29. KAMII, C., & DEVRIES, R. (1981). *Group games in early education: Implications of Piaget's theory.* Washington, DC: The National Association for the Education of Young Children.

30. MATHEMATICAL SCIENCES EDUCATION BOARD, NATIONAL RESEARCH COUNCIL. (1987). *The teacher of mathematics: Issues for today and tomorrow.* Washington DC: National Academy Press.

31. MCTIGHE, J., & LYMAN, F. T., JR. (1988). Cueing thinking in the classroom: The promise of theory-embedded tools. *Educational Leadership, 45* (7), 18–24.

*32. NATIONAL COUNCIL OF TEACHERS OF MATHEMATICS (1989). *Curriculum and evaluation standards for school mathematics.* Reston, VA: Author.

*33. NATIONAL COUNCIL OF TEACHERS OF MATHEMATICS (1991). *Professional standards for teaching mathematics.* Reston, VA: Author.

34. PETERSON, P. L. (1988). Teaching for higher order thinking in mathematics: The challenge for the next decade. In D. Grouws, T. Cooney, & D. Jones (Eds.), *Perspectives on research on effective mathematics teaching* (pp. 2–26). Reston, VA: National Council of Teachers of Mathematics.

35. PETERSON, P. L., FENNEMA, E., & CARPENTER, T. (1988). Using knowledge of how students think about mathematics. *Educational Leadership, 46* (4), 42–46.

36. REYNOLDS, M. C. (Ed.) (1989). *Knowledge base for the beginning teacher.* NY: Pergamon Press.

37. ROMBERG, T. A., & CARPENTER, T. P. (1986). Research on teaching and learning mathematics: Two disciplines of scientific inquiry. In M. C. Wittrock (Ed.), *Handbook of research on teaching* (3rd ed.) (pp. 850–873). New York: Macmillan.

38. ROSENSHINE, B. V. (1986). Synthesis of research on explicit teaching. *Educational Leadership, 43* (7), 60–69.

*39. ROWEN, T. E., & CETORELLI, N. D. (1990). A model for teaching elementary school mathematics. In T. J. Cooney & C. R. Hirsch (Eds.), *Teaching and learning mathematics in the 1990s* (1990 Yearbook, pp. 62–68). Reston, VA: National Council of Teachers of Mathematics.

40. SLAVIN, R. E. (1987). Ability grouping and student achievement in elementary schools: A best evidence synthesis. *Review of Educational Research, 57,* 293–336.

*41. SLAVIN, R. E. (1987). Cooperative learning and individualized instruction. *Arithmetic Teacher, 35,* 14–16.

*42. SLAVIN, R. E. (1989). Student team learning in mathematics. In N. Davidson (Ed.), *Cooperative learning in mathematics: A handbook for teachers* (pp. 69–102). Menlo Park, CA: Addison-Wesley.

43. SLAVIN, R. E. (1989). Here to stay—or gone tomorrow? *Educational Leadership, 47*(4), 4.

44. SPARKS, D., & SPARKS, G. M. (1984). *Effective teaching for higher achievement.* Alexandria, VA: Association for Supervision and Curriculum Development.

45. VANCE, J. H., & KIEREN, T. E. (1971). Laboratory settings in mathematics: What does research say to the teacher? *Arithmetic Teacher, 18,* 585–589.

*46. YACKEL, E., COBB, P., WOOD, T., GRAYSON, W., & MERKEL, G. (1990). The importance of social interaction in children's construction of mathematical knowledge. In T. J. Cooney & C. R. Hirsch (Eds.), *Teaching and learning mathematics in the 1990s* (1990 Yearbook pp. 12–21). Reston, VA: National Council of Teachers of Mathematics.

CHAPTER 13

Curriculum: A Vision for Early Childhood Mathematics

Barbara J. Dougherty and Loretta Scott

A curriculum is something to be felt rather than something to be seen. The transplanting of the structural aspects of a promising program tends to overlook the fact that the true blueprint is in the minds and hearts of the teacher (29, p. 27).

In August, Terry Long began to outline what she would teach her fourth-grade students in mathematics during the coming school year. Terry had always used the textbook as the primary source for her planning. But this year she decided to use some of the ideas from an in-service session sponsored by her district that she had attended.

During this in-service, Terry and other teachers were grouped in fours. Tasks were presented for teacher/learners to explore and solutions were found cooperatively. The in-service presenter served as a guide while the groups worked through solutions using materials such as base-ten blocks, Cuisenaire rods, tangrams, and pentominoes. As they participated in the activities, teachers were asked to think about how they solved problems. Additionally, teachers were asked to create an implementation plan for using small groups and activities within their own classrooms. Terry and her colleagues had come away from the session feeling very positive about the mathematics they had experienced, and wanted to provide a similar learning environment for their students.

Like many teachers, Terry had felt powerless, prior to the in-service, concerning alternative choices to her mathematics text. She had read research that confirmed her suspicions that curriculum developers, school boards, administrators, test authors, and textbook publishers were making curriculum decisions that affected what she was teaching (26). But now she had alternative sources (such as 6, 8, and 19) to her textbook manual's approach to achieving the goals of the district's curriculum guide. Armed with these tools and her in-service experiences, she set out to incorporate new explorations into the fourth-grade mathematics curriculum.

> " . . . mathematics teachers must alter the ways in which they perceive the field of mathematics and the processes of teaching and learning: it is an open-ended field, enriched by exploration and experimentation, and is not a static body of facts." (9, p. 238)

Terry's experience is similar to that of many of us who attempt to shape and direct meaningful mathematics curriculum in our classrooms. We struggle with what curriculum is because the word conjures up many definitions in the minds of teachers and administrators alike. But for our purposes "curriculum" is a statement of what we believe mathematics and its instruction to be. It is our interpretations of curriculum that give rise to the mathematical content included and pedagogical methods used.

> "Many [teachers] believe that their main task is to teach rapid computation, that good problem solving is done quickly, that problems always have one right answer, and so on. With such a narrow view of mathematics, with little knowledge of the way children learn mathematics, and with a limited sense of the importance of mathematical thinking and reasoning, it is likely that they would emphasize the rote, the algorithmic, and the procedural. It is hardly the fault of these teachers—as students themselves they experienced little else." (34, p. 225)

Mathematics and its instruction can be interpreted in at least three ways. Mathematics is sometimes thought of as a game that requires memorization, but students are never given the strategies for winning the game (2). Or mathematics may be considered a static body of knowledge that is passed from teacher (active) to student (passive), likened to filling an empty pitcher. Finally, mathematics may consist of experiences that each individual fits into his or her own existing ideas, and instruction is similar to the teaching of natural sciences where students formulate conjectures, test hypotheses, and establish generalizations.

Ultimately, each teacher's interpretations of mathematics affect the mathematics curriculum. Other influences, however, also play a part in determining what is taught. This chapter will summarize research descriptions of these influences and their effects on planning and organizing the elementary mathematics curriculum.

Other Influences on Curriculum Decisions

What teachers teach in elementary school mathematics is influenced by several factors. These include, but may not be limited to, the following: (1) national, state, and local curriculum documents, (2) standardized tests and state assessments, (3) textbooks, (4) principals/administrators as curriculum designers, and (5) teachers. The amount of influence each contributes to curricular decisions may vary from school to school, classroom to classroom, but, nevertheless, their influence is evident.

> " . . . what is taught in schools requires deliberate choice. . . ." (26, p. 132)

Curriculum Documents: Guide or Prescription?

National, state, and local agencies may provide curriculum documents intended to affect school curricula, but their influence varies within each school setting. Some documents such as the *Mathematics Framework for California Public Schools* and the *Missouri Key Skill and Core Competencies* may be in the form of prescribed objectives or goals that teachers are required to follow in some manner.

Unfortunately, documents that are too specific in their prescriptions lack sensitivity toward individual students. Using the same standardized objectives from year to year assumes all fourth graders will (need to) learn exactly the same information, but student needs are often far removed from these objectives, academically and intellectually. Thus, while giving direction to mathematics instruction, these documents may also be constraining, narrow, and fragmented in their presentation of mathematics for both students and teacher.

> "A curriculum is more for teachers than it is for pupils." (5, p. xv)

In an effort to allow more latitude in the mathematics curriculum, other documents are less prescriptive and merely suggest what should be included in the curriculum. The effect of these documents can be minimal in some instances. For example, given the suggestion that probability concepts should be included in primary grade curriculum may not affect their inclusion. Some teachers may have difficulty deciding how to teach or what to teach of probability concepts for third graders without explicit instructional directions. They are not comfortable with unfamiliar content nor loosely stated objectives so they resort to teaching as they have in the past by neglecting content or using traditional approaches.

In other schools, curriculum objectives or suggestions may be stifling and not in alignment with current reform movements. For example, some school districts still structure their curriculum around basic skills that are defined as only computational, requiring memorization of basic facts and fostering instruction that focuses on algorithms designed to promote skill proficiency. There obviously has been little restructuring of what mathematics consists and a disregard for important ideas related to areas outside of computation such as probability and statistics, spatial relations or geometry, number theory, and technology.

New ideas for curriculum change can be found in the *Curriculum and Evaluation Standards for School Mathematics* (19). The *Standards* (19) has made suggestions for curriculum veering from the traditional in grade levels K–4, 5–8, and 9–12. At the K–4 level, the once skill-driven curriculum is moving toward a conceptually oriented one with emphasis on the development of children's mathematical thinking and reasoning abilities. Children are envisioned as active participants in the learning process who will explore mathematical applications and a broader range of topics than before. These ideas are enhanced with the addition of technology such as computers and calculators and through interactions among students and between students and teacher.

Recommendations like these support a different sort of curriculum than the traditional one, suggesting changes in teacher roles, content inclusion, and instructional strategies. Consequently, as teachers, we must be more than just aware of new recommendations. We must read them with a critical eye, constantly assessing our views of mathematics and its instruction and how they fit with what is recommended and our actual classroom instruction.

Standardized Tests: Curriculum Driven or Curriculum Driver?

During the school year, standardized tests or state assessments are administered to determine student achievement. Some school administrators judge individual teacher effectiveness by student performance on such tests. As a result, teachers want their students to perform well and may leave an established curriculum to review and/or teach concepts or skills that may be covered on these tests. While many teachers would deny this to be true, surveys and observations of teachers can substantiate this claim (28).

How standardized tests or state assessments influence the curriculum is an important area that needs further examination in both practical and research situations. On the practical side, teacher involvement in selecting appropriate tests should increase with initial work in comparing tests (both ones available to the school and those used by the school) with the curriculum. If mismatches are uncovered, alternatives should be considered. For example, if the curriculum focus is on problem solving, little information about the effectiveness of the curriculum and student achievement within that curriculum can be gained from tests composed of predominantly computational items. These types of misalignments only perpetuate straying from the curriculum to accommodate test objectives, suggesting that either the curriculum needs revamping or the test is inappropriate.

Since tests should be chosen *after* the curriculum is in place, teachers can begin to design other evaluation methods including authentic performance assessments. These may be in the form of individual student interviews, other problem contexts different from the test (supplemental items), or activities in a realistic setting where students demonstrate proficiency. (See Chapter 15 for specific details.) Opportunities abound in investigating the use of alternative evaluation techniques.

> "In the design of an effective new curriculum, one important component is an understanding of the new viewpoints that are developing at the frontiers of research. Yet the curriculum must be suitable for all children, not just for those who will become research scientists." (30, p. 188)

Textbooks: The Total Curriculum?

Research provides different perspectives about the role of the textbook in curriculum. On the one hand, textbooks may define what we choose to teach in our classrooms (11) as well as how we teach it. In the most extreme case, the textbook dictates the lesson of the day as students and teacher methodically plod through each successive page. When we use textbooks in this manner, teaching suggestions provided in the teacher's guide—including examples and algorithmic techniques—become the lesson. Hence, the philosophy of the textbook is the driving force of the classroom curriculum in both content and instructional aspects.

In a more appropriate manner, textbooks are considered only as resources that teachers use in terms of what topics (and possibly their sequence) are taught. The degree of attention given to each topic is increased or decreased as perceived appropriate (24). Over time, the emphasis we give to the topics and teaching techniques suggested in our textbook should change to reflect our maturing visions of mathematics education.

To encourage this growth, caution must be exerted when selecting the textbook. Many of them continue to overload our curriculum with computation, leaving little time for development of conceptual foundations. Thus, we must reflectively consider what is inherently important in a school mathematics program, based upon reform calls, student needs, and our professional knowledge, and select a textbook(s) accordingly. We must also be cognizant of, and sensitive to, the role we allow textbooks to play in our instruction. If instruction has become dependent upon "what the book does," we need to make a concerted effort to consider new alternatives to an otherwise constrained instructional program.

As teachers, we can directly affect what textbooks are chosen by volunteering for curriculum committees so that our opinions about what we expect in terms of content topics, particularly as we move from skill-oriented topics to more conceptual ones, are heard. On a larger scale, we can encourage other teachers and/or schools to purchase only those texts that subscribe to a conceptual approach to mathematics.

Administration: Curriculum Leadership?

Because administrators control much of what occurs in schools, it is reasonable to acknowledge their role in at least two areas of elementary school mathematics curriculum: (1) organizational atmosphere created by school policies and (2) selection of curriculum planning committees or of the curriculum itself (3). The structure of global school policies may be under administrators' direct control to the extent that certain philosophical threads are often common throughout school policy. Entire schools frequently are organized around school policies that influence and/or structure subject matter content (23). If school policy reflects a goal of having students be proficient in restricted "basic" skills, instructional materials selected may reflect a heavy emphasis on computational algorithms and, consequently, influence topics introduced in the classroom.

> "The key issue for mathematics education is not *whether* to teach fundamentals but *which* fundamentals to teach and *how* to teach them." (30, p. 2)

Curriculum committees may also influence what is placed in school curricula since each committeeperson has particular views on what topics and teaching approaches should be included. Membership of these committees may be determined by principals/administrators and is an important piece of establishing curriculum. Selection could result from the recognition of philosophical matches between administrators and teachers in terms of instruction and content issues or from the recognition of qualified teachers capable of making appropriate curricular decisions. On the other hand, administrators may allow committee membership to include only those who volunteer. In any case, this membership gives teachers the opportunity to take a stand on curricular issues and influence school policy.

If the administration does take an active role in curriculum planning, they must be up-to-date on issues important to providing appropriate content and instruction. Some principals may have a narrow knowledge base about mathematics content and instructional strategies. They may not be aware of alternatives to what is currently being done in their school. Consequently, teachers must assume some of the responsibility in educating administrators and providing them with information, such as sharing a copy of the *Curriculum and Evaluation Standards* (19) and the *Professional Teaching Standards* (20). Some school districts encourage teachers to speak about reform issues at faculty or local school board meetings. Other districts promote professional development by sending teachers *and* administrators to specific subject matter meetings such as NCTM state, regional, and/or annual conventions. Whatever means is appropriate for the district, teachers have to be vocal in, first of all, expressing to the administration what curriculum content should be, and second, in providing current information to the administration with rationales as to why it is important and relevant to a particular school situation.

Teachers: The Final Say

Even though school policies may dictate some aspects of instruction, teachers ultimately can make the final decision about what and how elementary school mathematics is taught in their own classroom (24). Teachers decide how to teach a topic, what topic(s) will be covered in a day or a school year, how much time to spend on a topic, what supplementary materials to use, what the daily lesson objectives will be, and so on.

This control we have in the classroom places responsibility on teachers and emphasizes professionalism needed in making decisions. Appropriate curricular decisions cannot be based on what and how we have taught in the past (24). Instead, we must make decisions resulting from our serious reflections on what research has described as mathematics important for students to explore and also how students come to understand that mathematical knowledge. Additionally, we must consider what appropriate instructional strategies and classroom management techniques are necessary to implement the content (27). In any school, this requires some level of teacher autonomy where teachers can use the textbook, tests, NCTM *Standards* (19, 20), and school policy to determine what is to be taught in the classroom as they consider the needs of the students.

> "The mathematics teacher is responsible for creating an intellectual environment in which serious engagement in mathematical thinking is the norm." *Professional Teaching Standards* (20, p. 12)

Furthermore, teachers need opportunities to talk with other teachers about what and how mathematics is taught in their own classroom. Research (25) has found that teachers interpret even rigid curricular policies and issues quite differently. These different interpretations indicate that teachers, in fact, have more curricular flexibility than they may think. Hence, it is important to find time to discuss content and teaching strategies with other teachers to gain insight into others' interpretations of policy.

The teacher is responsible for shaping and directing activities so that students have opportunities to engage meaningfully in mathematics. Textbooks can be useful resources for teachers, but we must also be free to adapt or depart from texts if student ideas and conjectures are to help shape the content framework. Consequently, tasks in which students engage must encourage them to reason about mathematical ideas, to make connections, and to formulate, grapple with, and solve problems.

Curriculum Issues

As we acknowledge the influence of several factors on global curriculum decisions, we must also consider what issues are important in curriculum implementation. These may include the scope of the curriculum and the integration of topics, concepts, skills, and activities incorporating problem solving, thinking, and reasoning. Each of these will be discussed in turn.

Scope of the Curriculum: But I Can't Teach Everything!

Given the vast number of mathematical topics for elementary school, it is difficult deciding what should be taught and when. Some schools may decide to define the breadth of an elementary school mathematics program very narrowly so that it focuses on mathematical strands that are computational in nature and skill oriented. Thus, there is an emphasis on algorithms with few connections made among topics or strands.

> "It makes little difference what we teach if we do not change how we teach." (34, p. 8)

In a traditional sense, these topics are often limited to whole numbers, fractions, and decimals, and are usually repeated grade after grade so that students do not get exposure to areas beyond computation (arithmetic). The *Curriculum and Evaluation Standards* (19) advocates a broader curriculum to help students become more mathematically literate. This recommendation is based on the need for knowledge of geometry, probability, statistics, and algebra, required in many occupational fields.

The inclusion of different and broader content would drastically affect the structure of the subject matter. First, making connections among topics would be facilitated due to a broader foundation. For instance, as students investigated measurement, they would see the need for a number system (fractions or decimals) that could help them describe measurements of continuous data. When measurement and fractions or decimals are treated in a narrow sense, little relevance between them is detected, and fraction or decimal operations become simply another set of rules that must be memorized.

> "As mathematics teachers, we have to grow up and say goodbye to old friends. Mathematical topics cannot be retained just because we like them or because we've finally learned how to teach them." (16, p. 2)

Second, the inclusion of new topics may help to decrease review time. The amount of time spent reviewing at the beginning of the school year is quite large, often the first 2–3 months. Since it is review, drill-and-practice is usually the instructional focus, with worksheet after worksheet. This extensive review period, often necessitated by students previously memorizing procedures with little meaning attached, needs to be reconsidered (34).

The review portion of a school year, or a lesson for that matter, definitely influences the scope of a curriculum. Some believe that if review time were decreased, then fewer strands would be covered but in greater depth (23). This approach would seem to be more difficult to implement with appropriate mathematical connections since there appears to be a greater risk of placing topics within strands into grade "slots" that are compartmentalized and distinct. On the other hand, increasing the number of strands or topics in place of the review appears to be a more feasible situation. This can be accomplished by reviewing "old" content in new content areas of geometry, probability, statistics, algebra, and so on. Students not only get exposure to new content but are able to connect new ideas with old knowledge (13).

> "The best time to learn mathematics is when it is first taught; the best way to teach mathematics is to teach it well the first time." (21, p. 13)

The spiral curriculum approach also seems out of place if we are attempting to expose students to a broader range of topics. To move from a spiral approach, coverage of some topics would end sooner and others be introduced later, creating more time for new areas. This movement is already detectable in some state plans (32).

Connections among Topics, Concepts, Skills, and Tasks: Pieces of the Mathematics Puzzle

The *Professional Teaching Standards* (20) encourages teachers to "stimulate students to make connections and develop a coherent framework for mathematical ideas" (p. 25). These recommendations can be accomplished through several means that may be as broad as increasing the number of topics to as specific as the development of appropriate tasks and related instructional aspects.

> "Some experiences are miseducative. Any experience is miseducative that has the effect of arresting or distorting the growth of further experience." John Dewey (10, p. 25)

Tasks. Tasks can be defined as problems and activities that teachers use to present mathematics. Paper-and-pencil tasks have often dominated our lessons and most frequently consist of worksheets and textbook pages. There are, however, other contexts that can provide for appropriate mathematical explorations. These may incorporate the use of manipulatives, computer software, and calculators.

Some commercial sources that teachers of levels K–4 can use as resources for mathematical tasks include *A Collection of Math Lessons* (6), *Ideas from the Arithmetic Teacher* (15), and *Mathematics Their Way* (1). Another source of tasks comes directly from student-prompted questions or their suggestions for problems to explore. A class could investigate questions ranging from favorite baseball teams to which lunches served by the school cafeteria are most popular with other students at school. Experiences in collecting data, graphing, and interpreting graphs may come immediately from these questions generated by students. As they explore one task, additional questions or hypotheses worthy of investigation are raised.

> " . . . [one's] function as educator is to make [oneself] dispensable." (14, p. 21)

As tasks are designed or selected, they should not be picked indiscriminately. There are certain characteristics of "good" tasks that can be described (20). It is important that tasks seize student inquisitiveness so that they will accept the invitation to explore further. Many teachers would say that this is best accomplished by relating problems

Standard 1:
WORTHWHILE MATHEMATICAL TASKS

The teacher of mathematics should pose tasks that are based on—

* sound and significant mathematics;
* knowledge of students' understandings, interests, and experiences;
* knowledge of the range of ways that diverse students learn mathematics;

and that

* engage students' intellect;
* develop students' mathematical understandings and skills;
* stimulate students to make connections and develop a coherent framework for mathematical ideas;
* call for problem formulation, problem solving, and mathematical reasoning;
* promote communication about mathematics;
* represent mathematics as an ongoing human activity;
* display sensitivity to, and draw on, students' diverse background experiences and dispositions;
* promote the development of all students' dispositions to do mathematics. *Professional Teaching Standards* (20, p. 25)

to real-life experiences of students. Real-life experiences can motivate investigations of space travel, geometry in nature, probability related to lotteries, and so on.

"Mathematics itself is now significantly more diverse than it was several decades ago when today's leaders and educators went to school." (21, p. 4)

Students find it interesting to pursue open-ended tasks, those that have more than one solution or even no one correct solution. These allow students freedom in both their thinking and solution processes and also help to accommodate different ability levels. If, for instance, students are asked to find two numbers that sum to 12, all students will be able to identify at least one solution, usually whole numbers, say 1 and 11. Others may be able to consider different numbers such as − 3 and 15, .75 and 11.25, or 1 1/3 and 10 2/3, thus, adapting in a natural way to individual ability levels while challenging all to reach higher.

"Standard school practice, rooted in traditions that are several centuries old, simply cannot prepare students adequately for the mathematical needs of the twenty-first century." (30, p. 2)

Tasks like these provide a rich environment that encourages classroom communication. As one student shares ideas about a task, other students are exposed to mathematical thinking from their peer group, and these comments carry a different connotation from those of the teacher. Reasoning with other students and the teacher through interactive communication provides a collaborative setting that enhances mathematical learning and creates a context for constructing mathematical ideas.

Tasks must also set the stage for higher mathematical thinking. Providing problem contexts that stimulate higher-order thinking usually necessitates the consideration of other sources besides textbooks since between 72 and 100 percent of the problems in all series at all grades require students only to practice or emulate a set of procedures (22). As teachers, we must recognize that applying an algorithm, even though students are indeed thinking about mathematics, certainly does not move past the low end of the cognitive continuum.

Task selection also involves teacher knowledge about student learning. Teachers have to be certain that we are not making erroneous assumptions about the way our students learn. For example, the Cognitively Guided Instruction Project (7) involves teachers in working with tasks that use word contexts for addition and subtraction before students know basic facts of addition and subtraction or have worked with symbolic representations. We often assume that students cannot work with word contexts before they have mastered symbolic ideas; this is not necessarily the case. Students can use physical objects to solve many complex tasks if encouraged to do so.

> "To help students see clearly into their own mathematical futures, we need to construct curricula with greater vertical continuity, to connect the roots of mathematics to the branches of mathematics in the educational experience of children." (30, p. 4)

Manipulatives. An important part of all tasks is the use of manipulatives and the many roles they can assume in instruction. Manipulatives have an integral role in student learning when their inclusion in a lesson is carefully considered and planned. Used appropriately, they help students form a stronger foundation of mathematical concepts and decrease the need for later remediation (14). However, to gain optimal benefits from their use, several considerations must be made.

A manipulative's representation of the mathematical concept is very important (17, 35). Use of a manipulative just because it is available—but not appropriate for the concept—is as detrimental to student understanding as not using a manipulative at all. Consider the situation of teaching regrouping concepts in a subtraction lesson. Use of the base-ten blocks would be less abstract than use of an abacus or colored chips since students are better able to see the relationships among place–values with the blocks. But bundled sticks may be more appropriate for a child's current level of understanding or as a match with your lesson objectives. Thus, there is a marriage between student needs and lesson objectives to appropriate representation of mathematics by the manipulative.

A characteristic of a good manipulative is its applicability in modeling a wide range of mathematical ideas. Cuisenaire rods, for example, can be used to investigate number, represent fractions, model the four basic operations, and so on. This increases their appeal in terms of buying power and it also provides contexts where students can make connections among concepts.

Budget constraints should not rule out the use of physical materials or become an excuse for bypassing a hands-on approach (12). Teachers can substitute inexpensive or teacher-made alternatives when commercial ones are not available (see Table 13.1).

How should we use manipulatives in our curriculum? First, we need to provide students with ample time to work with physical materials (17) not only over more grade levels but also within each grade. Instead of allowing only one mathematics period for manipulative work on a new concept, several periods may be used so that students become accustomed to the mathematical ideas involved. Additionally, manipulatives should be readily available with every lesson for students needing or desiring to use them in their explorations (17, 31).

Adequate time is important not only for concept development using manipulatives, but also for transition to the symbolic or abstract level. The jump cannot be made too quickly or too radically. We need to understand student needs and differences and allow for that within tasks. Some students will be ready for pictorial representations very quickly while others need more time. Still others may only need to see teacher-demonstrated materials and move directly into the abstract level. To accommodate these differences we must be sensitive to our individual students and monitor their progress accordingly through their participation in tasks, contributions to class discussions, and substance of their mathematical writings.

It is not, however, merely a question of how often or how long manipulatives are used. Some teachers feel that if they are used in a task, then that is sufficient; this is not necessarily the case. As students investigate mathematical ideas with manipulatives, they need the opportunity to discuss and reflect on their findings. To accomplish that, we must devote time to allow students to explain and possibly demonstrate

TABLE 13.1. Substitutes for Commercial Products

Commercial Product	Substitute Product(s)
Base-ten blocks, Dienes blocks	Popsicle sticks in bundles, tagboard "flats," "strips," and "units"
Plastic counters	Buttons, beans
Metric rulers	Strips of tagboard or adding machine tape, string
Dice/spinners	Cubes of foam rubber/tagboard spinners with cardboard, tagboard or paper clip spinners
Geoboards	Wood with nails or sheets of acetate with the outline of the nails
Sorting materials	ANYTHING—buttons, old toys, jar and bottle lids, whatever students or parents can donate from home
Tangrams	Tagboard or cardboard sets, sets cut from acetate sheets
Attribute blocks	Decks of playing cards
Plastic tiles	Tagboard squares, acetate squares

for peer groups what they were thinking as they worked through the task. We may also need to interact explicitly with students if they seem to be "missing the point."

To increase student reflection about their work with manipulatives, some teachers have their students keep written records of the manipulative activities wherein they explain how they used the manipulatives to solve problems. Students keep mathematical journals where they record these ideas about their investigations. As they write about manipulative use, it is natural for them to resort to pictorial representations of the manipulative (see Fig. 13.1).

Homework. Tasks are not restricted to those that are included in mathematical lessons but extend to out-of-class time or homework. Frequently, drill-and-practice sheets constitute the majority of homework activities. Obviously, there are other tasks that are appropriate for homework.

Given that homework tasks should be assigned only if they are worthwhile (4), we need then to consider our own purpose(s) for assigning homework. Reasons include offering students the opportunity to (1) synthesize concepts, (2) analyze new situations, (3) apply existing knowledge, and (4) evaluate ideas (4). Clearly, the types of thinking skills involved in tasks suggested by these reasons would be quite different from those used in drill-and-practice type assignments.

FIGURE 13.1   Journal excerpt from Jeremy, a fourth grader

Today my group did rectangles on a (geo) board. We tried to find some that had permeter (perimeter) of 6. At first we couldn't find any and then Josh found 1 that looked like this

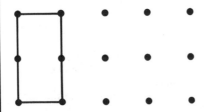

Grace thought their (there) was only one but I found 1 to (too).

Keri said they were the same thing because we could turn the (geo) board to look the same. I'm not sure. I know that there are the same (number of) squares inside both of them. But I don't know if that makes them the same.

Note: Jeremy has raised new questions involving congruency and area while exploring perimeter with manipulatives.

With these considerations beyond drill and practice, what kinds of homework tasks might be assigned? Students could be asked to write their own problems based on the day's work. At the fourth-grade level where they had been investigating area and perimeter of quadrilaterals, they might be given the following statement to prove or disprove: "As perimeter of a quadrilateral increases, so does area." In the instance of a first-grade classroom where they had been working with subtraction, students could be asked to write a problem using something that happened at home that evening and show how subtraction could solve it.

The number of problems assigned cannot be large when critical or creative thinking is a primary consideration. The perimeter problem from above requires students to set conditions and build a case for affirmation or disproval of the conjecture. Creativity of thought is needed to approach this task and may necessitate that students spend more time than if they were doing an assignment of twenty skill problems.

> "Mathematics, the science of patterns, is itself changing. For the sake of our future we must harness mathematics to the patterns of change. And to do that we must change the way that mathematics is taught, to create a new generation able to perceive and manipulate new patterns." (30, p. 216)

Homework Evaluation.   Before a homework task is assigned, we must consider how it will be evaluated. There are many options available besides merely collecting papers and grading each problem for its correct answer. Papers may be collected and only selected problems graded. Students may trade papers and grade all or some of the problems. Solutions may be placed on the board or overhead by students or the teacher as mathematics class begins. Homework quizzes where students are allowed to use their homework papers may also be given. Teachers have several options from which to choose, depending on how each fits into their classroom structure. But the more important aspect is *what* should be considered as we evaluate.

If we are to evaluate only the final answer, it is often misleading. For example, in one particular case (33), students were presented with the problem "Four of five dentists interviewed recommended Yukkey Gum. What percentage of the dentists interviewed did not recommend it?" One student responded with 20 percent but when asked to explain how she arrived at the answer, she said she multiplied four times five because "of" meant to multiply. Merely assessing the answer would have given us false information about this student's mathematical knowledge.

To uncover student thinking, teachers may choose to have students present their homework solutions to the class at the board or on the overhead as they justify their answers through sound mathematical arguments and respond to peer questions. If a one-to-one setting between student and teacher is desired, an interview format may be used to delve deeper into student thought processes by discussing a specific task from their homework. Another method is to have students discuss their homework within groups and then pull the class together to share their group discussions with the whole class. Or students may write about some piece of the assignment in a journal. Each of these methods gives more information about student understanding than grading only the final answer on their paper.

How homework is evaluated is somewhat dependent upon the teacher's purpose for assigning it. If homework is considered an augmentation of what was done in class, a time to reflect on ideas encountered there, or a settling in of new knowledge, then grading for correct answers only defeats such a purpose. Evaluation is more appropriate in the form of student discussion or another means by which consideration is given to thought processes. If, however, homework was meant to provide practice on skills, then other evaluation techniques may be more useful.

As homework assignments are planned, we must consider, first of all, why we are assigning it, what is important to evaluate, and, finally, the best technique for that evaluation. These considerations lead to variety in handling and assigning homework and makes us as teachers more aware of its role in instruction.

> "Newton credited his extraordinary foresight in the development of calculus to the accumulated work of his predecessors: 'If I have seen farther than others, it is because I have stood on the shoulders of giants.' Those who develop mathematics curricula for the twenty-first century will need similar foresight." (30, p. 7)

In our own classrooms, it is ultimately our decision as to what is taught and the instructional techniques used in the lessons. Our goal is to provide a stimulating environment that encourages students to construct mathematical ideas, make predictions, and model situations as they become powerful problem solvers through their interactions with mathematics. In fulfilling this goal, students, along with their teacher, discover that mathematics can provide an exciting journey of explorations in a rich and creative discipline.

Looking Ahead . . .

The mathematical empowerment of students must be the central goal of our curriculum. This cannot be accomplished by increasing the scope or number of topics, but rather by lowering barriers between students and the mathematics they explore and in so doing construct meaning about. Teachers and researchers must work together in the challenge of creating a curricular framework that encourages student involvement and interaction, and yet is both mathematically sound and implementable in practice.

Barbara Dougherty

Whether I use a cooperative grouping approach or a combination of whole group, small group, and individual instruction, questions remain. Will I help my students understand the power of mathematics in both physical and social contexts through the use of manipulatives? Can I emphasize how solutions are obtained in a problem-solving approach and foster a supportive classroom atmosphere where students are willing to risk sharing ideas and answers? How do I create an activity-based assessment to use instead of, or in connection with, written tests? What alternative assessment data can I find in student journals and folders that include work samples and teacher observations?

Loretta Scott

About the Authors

Barbara Dougherty is assistant professor of mathematics education at the University of Hawaii—Manoa, Honolulu. She is a member of the NCTM Task Force on Monitoring the Effects of the Standards. Her research interests are in the areas of teacher change and curricular implementation practices.

Loretta Scott teaches fourth grade at Columbia Catholic School, Columbia, Missouri. She is interested in improving mathematics instruction in the elementary grades and has been a lead teacher in the Missouri KSAM Project. The Missouri Council for American Private Education recognized her as an Educator of Achievement in 1990.

References

*1. Baratta-Lorton, M. (1976). *Mathematics their way.* Menlo Park, CA: Addison Wesley.

2. Blaire, E. (1981). Philosophies of mathematics and perspectives of mathematics teaching. *International Journal of Mathematics in Education, Science, and Technology, 12*(2), 147–153.

3. Brady, L. (1987). Explaining school-based curriculum satisfaction: A case study. *Journal of Curriculum Studies, 19*, 375–378.

4. Braswell, J. (1985). One point of view: Improving performance. *Arithmetic Teacher, 32*(9), 1, 38.

5. Bruner, J. S. (1977). *The process of education.* Cambridge, MA: Harvard University Press.

*6. Burns, M. (1987). *A collection of math lessons from grade 1 to 3.* New Rochelle, NY: Cuisenaire.

7. Carpenter, T. P., & Fennema, E. (1988). Research and cognitively guided instruction. In E. Fennema, T. P. Carpenter, & S. J. Lamon (Eds.), *Integrating research on teaching and learning mathematics* (pp. 2–19). Madison: Wisconsin Center for Education Research.

*8. Charles, R., & Lester, F. (1982). *Teaching problem solving: What, why & how.* Palo Alto, CA: Dale Seymour.

9. Cooney, T. J. (Ed.). (1990). *Teaching and learning mathematics in the 1990s.* Reston, VA: National Council of Teachers of Mathematics.

10. Dewey, J. (1938). *Experience and education.* New York: Collier.

11. Flanders, J. R. (1987). How much of the content in mathematics textbooks is new? *Arithmetic Teacher, 35*(1), 18–23.

12. Gilbert, R. K., & Bush, W. S. (1988). Familiarity, availability, and use of manipulative devices in mathematics at the primary level. *School Science & Mathematics, 88*(6), 459–469.

13. Hiebert, J. (Ed.). (1986). *Conceptual and procedural knowledge: The case of mathematics.* Hillsdale, NJ: Erlbaum.

14. Howson, A. G. (Ed.). (1983). *Curricular development and curricular research.* Windsor, Berks, England: NFER-Nelson.

*15. IMMERZEEL, G., & THOMAS, M. (1982). *Ideas from the arithmetic teacher, grades 1–4.* Reston, VA: National Council of Teachers of Mathematics.

16. KANSKY, B. (1985). Looking back, I think I see the future. *Arithmetic Teacher, 32,* 2–3.

17. LEWIS, K. E. (1985). From manipulatives to computation: Making the mathematical connection. *Childhood Education, 61*(5), 371–374.

18. MOSER, J. M. (1986). Curricular issues. *Arithmetic Teacher, 33*(6), 8–10.

*19. NATIONAL COUNCIL OF TEACHERS OF MATHEMATICS. (1989). *Curriculum and evaluation standards for school mathematics.* Reston, VA: Author.

*20. NATIONAL COUNCIL OF TEACHERS OF MATHEMATICS. (1991). *Professional standards for teaching mathematics.* Reston, VA: Author.

21. NATIONAL RESEARCH COUNCIL. (1989). *Everybody counts: A report to the nation on the future of mathematics education.* Washington, DC: National Academy Press.

22. NICELY, R. F., FIBER, H. R., & BOBANGO, J. C. (1986). Research report: The cognitive content of elementary school mathematics textbooks. *Arithmetic Teacher, 34*(2), 60–61.

23. PORTER, A. (1989). A curriculum out of balance: The case of elementary school mathematics. *Educational Researcher, 18*(5), 9–15.

24. PORTER, A., FLODEN, R., FREEMAN, D., SCHMIDT, W., & SCHWILLE, J. (1988). Content determinants in elementary school mathematics. In D. A. Grouws, T. Cooney, & D. Jones (Eds.), *Perspective on research on effective mathematics teaching* (pp. 96–113). Hillsdale, NJ: Erlbaum; Reston, VA: National Council of Teachers of Mathematics.

25. PORTER, A. C., & KUHS, T. (1982, April). *A district management-by-objectives system: Its messages and effects.* Paper presented at the annual meeting of the American Educational Research Association, New York.

26. ROMBERG, T. (1983). A common curriculum for mathematics. In G. D. Fenstermacher & J. I. Goodlad (Eds.), *Individual differences and the common curriculum* (pp. 121–159). Chicago, IL: National Society for the Study of Education.

27. ROMBERG, T. (1988). Can teachers be professionals? In D. A. Grouws, T. A. Cooney, & D. Jones (Eds.), *Perspectives on research on effective mathematics teaching* (pp. 224–244). Hillsdale, NJ: Erlbaum; Reston, VA: National Council of Teachers of Mathematics.

28. ROMBERG, T., ZARINNIA, E. A., & WILLIAMS, S. R. (1989). *The influence of mandated testing on mathematics instruction: Grade 8 teachers' perceptions.* Madison, WI: National Center for Research in Mathematical Sciences Education.

29. SPEARS, H. (1950). *The high school for today.* New York: American Book.

30. STEEN, L. (Ed.). (1990). *On the shoulders of giants: New approaches to numeracy.* Washington, DC: National Academy Press.

31. SUYDAM, M. N. (1984). Research report: Manipulative materials. *Arithmetic Teacher, 31*(5), 27.

32. Texas Education Agency. (1989). *Revised content for textbooks: Mathematics 1–8.* Austin, TX: Author.

33. THOMPSON, A. G., & BRIARS, D. J. (1989). Assessing students' learning to inform teaching: The message in NCTM's evaluation standards. *Arithmetic Teacher, 37*(4), 22–26.

34. TRAFTON, P. R. (Ed.). (1989). *New directions for elementary school mathematics.* Reston, VA: National Council of Teachers of Mathematics.

35. TRUEBLOOD, C. R. (1986). Hands on: Help for teachers. *Arithmetic Teacher, 33*(6), 49–51.

CHAPTER 14

The Teacher's Influence on the Classroom Learning Environment

William S. Bush and Lisa A. Kincer

> *I am firm in my belief that a teacher lives on and on through his [one's] students. Good teaching is forever and the teacher is immortal.*
> —*Jesse Stuart, renowned Kentucky author*

The *Professional Teaching Standards* (46) offers an interesting analogy for the teacher's role in the classroom—that of teacher as orchestrator. The early childhood classroom is filled with a complex array of interactions, goals, emotions, needs, and personalities (21), and we, as teachers, are at the center of this multifaceted environment. We consciously and subconsciously set the stage for the types of interactions established. We determine whether the environment will be conducive to learning mathematics, fostering positive attitudes, and establishing healthy social interactions. Daily, we make countless decisions (19, 54, 55) and maintain routines (39) that affect classroom environments. The nature of these decisions and routines determine, for the most part, if and how students learn mathematics and whether students enjoy mathematics, perceive mathematics as useful, and become confident in mathematics. Decisions and routines also effect the kinds of classroom interactions that are established.

> Like a piece of music, the classroom discourse has themes that pull together to create a whole that has meaning. The teacher has a central role in orchestrating the oral and written discourse in ways that contribute to students' understanding of mathematics. *Professional Teaching Standards* (46, p. 35)

Although factors such as student performance and attitudes, curriculum, re-sources, school policies, parents, and administrators affect our ability to implement goals effectively, the way we behave in the classroom is driven by our own personal instructional goals. These goals might include enhancing mathematics learning, developing positive attitudes toward and confidence in mathematics, communicating and reasoning with mathematics, or establishing healthy classroom interactions. The priorities of these goals are based largely on teachers' knowledge of, beliefs about, and attitudes toward mathematics, students, and learning.

The *Professional Standards for Teaching Mathematics* rests on the following two assumptions:

- Teachers are key figures in changing the ways in which mathematics is taught and learned in schools.
- Such changes require that teachers have long-term support and adequate resources. (46, p. 2)

Change in classroom discourse, or teaching behavior, affects and is affected by many factors. Any consideration of changing our behavior must begin with an analysis of our own knowledge, beliefs, and attitudes in relation to our goals, students, curriculum, and societal influences. We hope that the research-related findings discussed in this chapter will provide information and insight that can serve as a basis for self-reflection. The chapter is divided into five sections: (1) reconceptualizing goals and roles, (2) knowledge of mathematics, (3) attitudes toward mathematics, (4) expectations and biases, and (5) changing classroom discourse. The first section describes the learning outcomes and teaching practices recommended by mathematics educators and NCTM through its *Curriculum and Evaluation Standards* (45) and *Professional Standards for Teaching Mathematics (Standards)* (46). The second and third sections describe teachers' knowledge of and attitudes toward mathematics; they explain how these constructs affect teaching practices and student learning; and they offer suggestions for implementing change. The fourth section describes some classroom processes that result from teacher expectations and biases based on student achievement, gender, race, and socioeconomic status. The final section offers suggestions in making ongoing changes in classroom discourse in order to meet appropriate instructional goals.

Reconceptualizing Goals and Roles

The *Professional Teaching Standards* offers a dynamic vision of teaching mathematics in the early childhood grades. The approach is oriented to fostering students' abilities to construct their own mathematics (15, 21). It focuses on the developmental capabilities of learners, what they require to understand mathematics, and what teaching strategies are necessary to facilitate learning. Learning outcomes in early childhood mathematics are more than the attainment of a collection of discrete facts. Teachers in this context will spend more time in the role of facilitator of learning than in the more traditional role of transmitter of information (21).

The foremost premise of the *Curriculum and Evaluation Standards* is that mathematics instruction should help children become mathematical problem solvers. In addition, instruction should enhance their ability to communicate and reason mathematically. It should build their confidence in doing mathematics and help them learn to value mathematics (45). Clearly, we must effectively model these behaviors if we are to expect as much from our students. Then learning environments can be established which (1) are conceptually oriented, (2) actively involve children in doing mathematics, (3) emphasize the development of children's mathematical thinking and reasoning abilities, (4) emphasize applications of mathematics, (5) include a broad range of topics, and (6) make appropriate and ongoing use of calculators and computers (46).

Phi Delta Kappan, Volume 71, Number 1 (September 1989), p. 38. Used by permission.

Important decisions that a teacher makes in teaching—

- Setting goals and selecting or creating mathematical *tasks* to help students achieve these goals;
- Stimulating and managing classroom *discourse* so that both the students and the teacher are clearer about what is being learned;
- Creating a classroom *environment* to support teaching and learning mathematics;
- *Analyzing* student learning, the mathematical tasks, and the environment in order to make ongoing instructional decisions. *Professional Teaching Standards.* (46, p. 5)

Teachers' roles should include those of consultant, moderator, and interlocutor, not just presenter and authority. Classroom activities must encourage students to express *their* approaches, both orally and in writing. *Everybody Counts* (48, p. 61)

Knowledge of Mathematics

Research on early-childhood teachers' general knowledge and achievement in mathematics presents a good news/bad news scenario. The bad news is that early-childhood teachers typically have not scored well on mathematics achievement tests, nor have they taken many high school or college mathematics courses. However, the good news is that there is no evidence to indicate that low mathematics achievement or few mathematics courses adversely affect teaching behavior or student achievement in early childhood mathematics (7).

It is widely believed that the more a teacher knows about his subject matter, the more effective he will be as a teacher. The empirical literature suggests that this belief needs modification and in fact suggests that once a teacher reaches a certain level of understanding of the subject matter, then further understanding contributes nothing to student achievement. (7)

Teacher educators have long believed that more mathematics knowledge enhances mathematics teaching ability and student achievement. The Commission on the Education of Teachers of Mathematics (CETM) clearly identifies what mathematics content should be learned by elementary teachers (22). The Commission recommends three years of high school mathematics including two years of algebra and one year of geometry, a course on number systems through the rational numbers, a course on informal geometry, and a course on methods of teaching mathematics.

Prospective teachers of mathematics at any level should know and understand mathematics substantially beyond that which they may be expected to teach. They should be able to relate that mathematics to the world of their pupils, to the natural sciences, and to the social sciences. Teachers should be able to provide illustrations of the role of mathematics in our culture and should have sufficient understanding of its nature and philosophy to interpret the various strands of the curriculum beyond a superficial level. They should have a knowledge of the historical development of mathematics in the different cultures of the world so that they can illustrate its cross-cultural nature using examples that will appeal to students from the diverse cultures represented in our society. (22, pp. 1–2).

A survey sent to all teacher education programs approved by the National Council on the Accreditation of Teacher Education found that 92 percent of the schools required at least one mathematics course of their elementary majors, but only 34 percent required a second course. Ninety percent of the institutions required at least one mathematics methods course (24).

Standard 2:
KNOWING MATHEMATICS AND SCHOOL MATHEMATICS

The education of teachers of mathematics should develop their knowledge of the content and discourse of mathematics, including—

- mathematical concepts and procedures and the connections among them;
- multiple representations of mathematical concepts and procedures;
- ways to reason mathematically, solve problems, and communicate mathematics effectively at different levels of formality;

and, in addition, develop their perspectives on—

- the nature of mathematics, the contributions of different cultures toward the development of mathematics, and the role of mathematics in culture and society;
- the changes in the nature of mathematics and the way we teach, learn, and do mathematics resulting from the availability of technology;
- school mathematics within the discipline of mathematics;
- the changing nature of school mathematics, its relationships to other school subjects, and its applications in society. (46, p. 132)

The contention that more mathematical knowledge means better mathematics teaching in the early childhood grades is not supported by research. Granted, several studies have shown that early childhood teachers have serious misconceptions about many elementary mathematical concepts and processes, such as multiplication and division (3, 28, 58), fractions (38), zero (60), geometric concepts (44), and proof (41). Although one would expect that misconceptions, say of multiplication, would seriously affect teachers' ability to teach multiplication and students' ability to learn multiplication, none of these studies investigated the effects of the misconceptions on teaching performance or student achievement. Although one study found that first-year teachers' level of achievement in mathematics was related to student mathematics achievement (53), other studies have found little or no relationship between teacher achievement in mathematics and teaching performance (4) or student achievement (14, 15). Certainly more research is needed on the relationship between teachers' knowledge of specific mathematics content and the teaching of that content.

The critical question raised by these results and that must be addressed is "What mathematical knowledge is necessary to be an effective early childhood mathematics teacher?" A critical limitation with research on the effects of teacher knowledge on student achievement has been the types of mathematical knowledge measured. With the exception of one study (15), research has focused on general achievement in mathematics or the number of college mathematics courses taken.

> In the process of developing learning environments for children, we became aware that the classroom had simultaneously and unintentionally become a learning environment for the teacher. As the teacher implemented the instructional activities and interacted with her students, her beliefs about her own role, the students' role, and the nature of mathematics changed dramatically. (62)

These criteria, however, are clearly inappropriate. A teacher may be highly competent in teaching first-grade mathematics without an overall, comprehensive understanding of mathematics, high achievement in mathematics, or an extended list of mathematics coursework. What is important is a highly specific, detailed knowledge of the mathematics taught through the fourth grade.

For instance one group of researchers investigated first-grade teachers' knowledge of strategies, perceived difficulty of the strategies, and perceived success of their students for simple addition and subtraction problems. They found no significant relationships between teacher knowledge of strategies and student performance. However, they found that teacher knowledge of student success and student performance were related (15). Certainly more research along these lines would provide greater insight into the relationship between teacher knowledge and student achievement. An improved mathematics knowledge base for teaching early childhood mathematics is needed, and college mathematics courses for early childhood teachers should provide experiences to help them acquire this knowledge.

> Here is an activity to test your own knowledge of early childhood mathematics. Select a mathematics textbook from grades kindergarten through four. Randomly select several topics from the table of contents and answer the following questions for each:
>
> - How do I define this concept or explain why this procedure works?
> - What other ways can I define or explain it?
> - What physical models, manipulatives, or diagrams illustrate this topic?
> - What must children know beforehand in order to learn this topic?
> - Why should children at this grade level learn this topic?

Attitudes toward Mathematics

As with knowledge, the effect our attitudes have on classroom discourse, student achievement, and student attitudes is unknown. Basically, measures of attitudes toward mathematics in general are not accurate predictors of success as an early childhood mathematics teacher.

> A teacher who is fascinated by mathematics in all of its forms, who understands and appreciates the elegance with which mathematical concepts fit together, who is intrigued by the inevitability of mathematical results, who takes pleasure in exploiting the flexibility of mathematical forms in the world around him, who feels a constant urge to learn more and more about mathematics—such a teacher is certain to inspire at least some of his students to a deep intellectual curiosity. Enthusiasm is contagious. (34, p. 22)

For example, teacher mathematics anxiety did not significantly affect the teaching practices of experienced teachers (14) or lesson planning and presentation of preservice teachers (4). Conversely, however, first-year teacher attitudes were related to student achievement, but not to teacher or student attitudes (53). Early childhood majors and teachers, as a group, tend to be anxious about mathematics. They tend to avoid mathematics courses and hold negative attitudes toward mathematics (6, 12, 32). It is a common belief that these negative attitudes and anxieties are transmitted from teachers to students (12, 32, 33, 61). However, early childhood teachers in other studies enjoyed learning and teaching mathematics (6, 17).

> In general, the kind of person who is drawn to elementary school teaching is not necessarily the kind who enjoys mathematics in the broad sense—from its logical beauty to its real-world applications. (12, p. 55)

One problem with the research that investigated effects of teacher attitudes on teaching performance and student attitudes was the way in which attitudes were measured. Most of the studies focused on teachers' mathematics anxiety and attitudes toward mathematics at the high school or college level. Two studies, however, found that teachers possessed negative attitudes and anxiety toward high school or college mathematics, but enjoyed and were enthusiastic about early childhood mathematics (6, 17). In fact, some teachers, because of their negative personal experiences in school mathematics, sought to establish a positive environment for their students' mathematics learning.

> Care should be taken not to blame all the problems in the learning of mathematics by children on their teachers' anxieties about the subject. (6, p. 51)

As with research on the effects of mathematics knowledge, research on the effects of teacher attitudes toward mathematics should focus more on teacher attitudes toward early childhood mathematics. Instruments measuring teacher attitudes toward early childhood mathematics and mathematics teaching would seem more appropriate than general measures of attitude and anxiety.

The key issue regarding teacher attitudes toward mathematics is how these attitudes are conveyed in teaching. If the existence of negative attitudes or anxiety has a negative impact on classroom discourse or student attitudes, then a problem exists. The first step in solving the problem is awareness. Research seems to indicate that teachers who are aware of their negative attitudes or anxieties tend to compensate for them in positive ways. The second, and certainly the most difficult, step is to reduce personal negative attitudes or anxieties toward mathematics. Because attitudes and anxieties typically develop over a long period of time, this activity will be very difficult and time-consuming for some persons. One way this can be accomplished is by understanding the sources of our attitudes or anxieties concerning mathematics. Were they caused by a specific teacher or mathematics class? Are they related to some negative experience? Talking to others about attitudes and anxieties will help provide some relief. The fact that others hold similar feelings is often reassuring. Finally, learning new, or perhaps relearning old, mathematics at a comfortable and appropriate level often provides new revelations and confidence.

The following activity will allow you to examine your own attitudes toward mathematics and determine how your attitudes or anxieties toward mathematics are conveyed in your teaching. Appoint a student in your class to audio-record one of your mathematics lessons arbitrarily. (It is imperative that you do not know what lesson is being recorded.) At a later time, listen to the recording and listen for comments that reflect your attitude toward mathematics. Comments reflecting a negative attitude might include, "Get out your textbooks; you *have* to do some more long division problems today." "Today's math lesson will be cut short to give you time to complete your reading assignment." "I was never very good at math either." Comments reflecting a positive attitude might include, "Today we are going to learn a new, exciting way to multiply." "I love to solve this kind of mathematics problem." "You can learn a lot from your mistakes in mathematics." Next, survey your students regarding their attitudes and anxieties toward mathematics. Include questions about specific mathematics topics. Compare your signals with students' attitudes and anxieties.

The following teaching suggestions for enhancing student attitudes and reducing student anxiety are helpful (51):

- Relax and enjoy mathematics teaching.
- Curb excessive competitiveness.
- Eliminate or reduce speed tests.
- Praise a student's efforts.
- Never humiliate students.
- Develop a sense of humor about mathematics.
- Be a positive role model.
- Do not use mathematics as punishment.
- Teach students how to read mathematics.
- Treat girls and boys equally.

- Provide opportunities for students to develop spatial relations.
- Have students make up problems.
- "Humanize" mathematics.

Teacher Expectations and Biases

Early-childhood teachers know their students very well and can accurately predict student success or failure (10, 11). With experience, many teachers seem to improve their ability to interpret and predict student behavior. Experienced, expert teachers who are more thoughtful and aware of student needs prefer to rely more on their own instincts in drawing conclusions about students. These teachers amass more information about students than do novice counterparts (16).

> Public attitudes, which are reflected and magnified by the entertainment industry, encourage low expectation in mathematics. Only in mathematics is poor school performance socially acceptable. *Everybody Counts* (49, p. 74)

Teachers' differential treatment of students with varied attributes has been studied extensively since the publication of *Pygmalion in the Classroom* (52). Research on early childhood teacher expectations has focused on differential treatment of high- and low-achieving children, of males and females, and of racial and socioeconomic groups.

Ability and Achievement

Comprehensive reviews of the research on teacher expectations for high- and low-achieving students indicate that although teachers treat the two groups differently, the effects in actual classrooms are probably quite small and highly dependent upon individual teachers, grade level, group size, time of year, and subject matter (10, 23, 27) (Fig. 14.1).

> Students felt that achievement status was more important than gender in the teachers' behavior toward children in the class. Actual expectation effects are probably minimal in most classrooms, although they do exist and are probably substantial in classrooms taught by teachers with certain personal characteristics. (10, p. 631)

The effects were small because (1) teachers' perceptions of their students are generally accurate, (2) teachers readily change their views based on new information, and (3) the effect of student achievement on teacher behavior is probably far stronger than the effect of teacher behavior on student achievement (10). Although effects seem to

FIGURE 14.1   A model to explain differences in mathematics achievement based
on the race, sex, and socioeconomic status (SES) of students

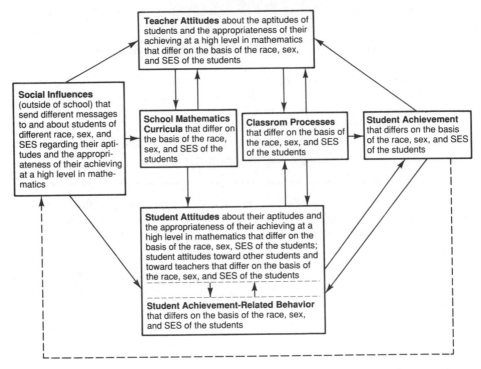

Reyes, L. H., & Stanic, G. M. A. (1988). Race, sex, socioeconomic status, and mathematics. *Journal for Research in Mathematics Education*, *19*(1), 26–43.

be small, differential treatment can seriously affect some students and should be eliminated. In general, high achievers are (1) given both more positive and negative attention, (2) given the benefit of the doubt in grading more often, and (3) sent more positive nonverbal cues than were low achievers (10).

Gender

Several studies have shown that males achieve higher in mathematics at the secondary level and beyond than females (18, 26). Furthermore, females seem to lose interest in mathematics and avoid mathematics courses and careers more than males do (2, 56, 57).

A logical place to look for reasons for these tendencies is in the classroom and in research. Recent studies have shown that boys and girls participate differently in mathematics classrooms (5, 29, 50). The research on differential treatment of girls and boys in mathematics classes provides some insight into reasons for the findings above. The list below summarizes many of the findings from both nonmathematics and mathematics classes:

- Boys were scolded and corrected for minor misbehavior more frequently than were girls (8).
- Girls received less teacher praise, hugging, and instructional assistance than boys (5, 8).
- Boys were praised more often for intellectual competence while girls were provided more negative feedback on the quality of their performance (8).
- Boys received more open questions (5).
- Boys received more overall attention and more explanations than girls (5, 8).
- Girls were given more attention in mathematics on product questions while boys were given more attention on process questions (5, 35).

Boys, in general, seem to receive much more attention from teachers than girls in the early childhood classroom. Teachers simply socialize with boys more often. In mathematics classes, teacher interactions with boys were more intellectual. The teachers studied clearly had higher academic expectations in mathematics for boys than for girls.

Race and Socioeconomic Status

Race-minority children do not achieve in mathematics at a level comparable to white children (1, 13, 31, 43), although Hispanics and blacks made significant gains on the Fourth Mathematics Assessment of the National Assessment of Educational Progress (31). Race minorities are severely underrepresented in mathematics-related courses, fields, and jobs (47, 49, 57). (It is encouraging to note, however, that Hispanics have made substantial gains and blacks have made modest gains in enrollments in advanced classes since 1978 [31].) On the basis of these results, one would expect some differential treatment toward students based on race or socioeconomic status. However, the few research studies conducted in this area found that preschool black children were more likely to be asked questions not related to mathematics by their teachers (40) and that teachers gave white students the benefit of the doubt when grading, but did not do so for Native American students (9). The lack of research in this area has prompted calls for more analysis and study of teacher–student interactions in early childhood classrooms (30, 42). More action research by teachers will provide useful information regarding the effects of teacher expectations on minority students and students of low socioeconomic status.

Among the reasons commonly given for black students' lack of interest in taking mathematics are (a) an absence of role models, (b) a lack of significant others, such as parents, who have an interest in mathematical achievement, (c) a failure to receive positive career counseling, (d) a view of mathematics as a subject appropriate for white males, (e) an inability to see the usefulness and relevance of mathematics to their lives, both present and future; and, of course, (f) a lack of success in previous mathematics courses. (30, p. 149)

While the exact consequences are unknown, teacher expectations appear to have some effect on student mathematical performance and student attitudes toward mathematics. Differential treatment of students is natural and inevitable (10). To like some students more than others and to judge students based on their experience and background is part of human nature. However, problems arise in the classroom when treatment is based on feelings and such extraneous factors as gender, race, or socioeconomic status. The key to overcoming differential treatment seems to be awareness. Most treatment is unintentional and often unconscious. Damaging unintentional verbal and nonverbal behavior can only be eliminated through analysis and reflection. The following suggestions can help teachers avoid behaviors that unintentionally reflect inappropriate expectations or biases (10):

- Keep expectations for students current by monitoring their progress closely; stress present performance over past history.
- Stress continuous progress relative to previous levels of mastery rather than normative comparisons or comparisons between individuals.
- When giving students feedback, provide useful information rather than evaluate their performance.
- When students do not understand an explanation, diagnose their difficulty and re-explain in a different way rather than repeating.
- Think about challenging, stimulating, and encouraging students to achieve as much as they can rather than protecting them from failure or embarrassment.

The following suggestions were offered to eliminate gender stereotyping in teaching (8). We believe that they are appropriate practices to eliminate stereotyping of any type.

- Tape record portions of lessons and analyze the tapes for discrimination.
- Keep a daily log of how you assign students to classroom and school tasks or roles.
- Support children when they engage in new roles in the classroom.

Changing Teaching Practices

Why is it that some teachers seem to grow, or change, in teaching while others do not? Experience seems to be one critical factor. Recent studies comparing the thoughts and practices of expert and novice teachers (36, 37, 38) have been quite revealing. Expert teachers who consistently obtained gains in their students' mathematics achievement:

- had more consistent behavior over time
- had smoother transitions
- combined presentation, review, and practice more often
- constructed lessons around a core of activities
- had shorter and more efficient presentations
- included more guided practice
- had a large repertoire of flexible routines
- gave more elaborate and flexible lessons

- knew a greater variety of ways to explain topics
- had cohesive and tightly connected explanations
- used cleaner language with more precise meanings
- were better at juggling multiple goals

Basically, the expert teachers were more efficient, analytical, flexible, and knowledgeable in their teaching. The Berliner studies, in particular, suggest that, over time, expert teachers developed specific skills for classroom teaching. The studies also indicate that growth in teaching is developmental and that appropriate experiences aid in developing these skills. What teachers do with and how they react to their experiences is critical for change or growth. Continuous reflection is necessary to grow and change in teaching (25). "Besides a belief in the teacher as an active agent in his own learning, there is an underlying assumption that the more aware a teacher is of his own actions, the greater the likelihood that he can control or change them" (25, p. 139). Addressing "problematic classroom situations" followed by reflection and an attempt at new ideas has proved to be a successful means to change teaching practices (20). Successful resolution of the situation will increase the likelihood of change in teaching practices. In essence, growth and change are possible only within the confines of the classroom and only when knowledge, beliefs, attitudes, and goals are in alignment.

To make the changes necessary to become a more effective early childhood teacher of mathematics, one must possess (1) a positive attitude toward mathematics, teaching mathematics, and children, (2) a view that mathematics is a cohesive, dynamic body of knowledge, (3) an understanding that students learn primarily through exploration and discovery, (4) a comprehensive understanding of the mathematics to be introduced in grades K–4, and (5) a willingness to make changes and to grow in teaching. Changes in teaching must occur in the context of the classroom (21, 62), and development of beliefs, knowledge, and attitudes in teachers must form in conjunction with teaching behaviors.

> Our current work with teachers is based on the alternative assumption that beliefs and practice are dialectically related. Beliefs are expressed in practice, and problems or surprises encountered in practice give rise to opportunities to reorganize beliefs. (62)

> Teachers' own experiences have a profound impact on their knowledge of, beliefs about, and attitudes toward mathematics, students, and teaching. Teachers' thirteen years as learners of K–12 mathematics provide them with images and models—conscious or unconscious—of what it means to teach and learn mathematics. (46, p. 124)

Changes cannot occur unless teachers perceive that the changes will result in better outcomes, such as enhanced student mathematics learning, more positive attitudes toward mathematics, or healthier social interactions. The following suggestions are offered for self-reflection:

- Reflect upon and identify your own attitudes toward, beliefs about, and knowledge of mathematics, students, and teaching. You might wish to read the *Curriculum and Evaluation Standards* (45) or *New Directions for Elementary School Mathematics* (59) for insight.
- Reflect upon and analyze your teaching practices. Are they consistent with your beliefs and attitudes? Are they realistic and attainable? Are they relevant and appropriate?
- Develop a comprehensive understanding of the mathematics you teach and how your students learn that content. Excellent sources include the *Arithmetic Teacher* and numerous methods books for teaching elementary mathematics.
- Try new ideas and activities in your teaching. Constantly look for ways to integrate new activities, problems, or technology in your lessons. As you do so, observe your students and reflect upon the outcomes. Talk to your students; seek their input.
- Expect difficulty. Change often involves a reconceptualization of student roles and goals. Be patient with yourself and your students.
- Be flexible. Observe and listen to your students and adjust to their needs.

Changing teaching practices is not easy, but many early childhood mathematics teachers have successfully done so. The key to growth in teaching is constant, ongoing reflection—about personal beliefs and attitudes, about personal instructional goals, about teaching practices, and about student learning and attitudes.

As a subject with an extensive and substantial history, mathematics more than any other science has been taught as an ancient discipline. A nation that persists in this view of mathematics is destined to fall behind scientifically and economically. Parents who persist in this view deny their children the opportunity to develop and prosper in the information age. *Everybody Counts* (49, p. 75)

Looking Ahead . . .

Undoubtedly, we, as teachers, influence our students in many ways. We try to establish mathematical learning environments where our students grow intellectually, emotionally, psychologically, socially, and culturally. This difficult task requires that we not only hold appropriate beliefs, attitudes, and understanding, but that we have support from other teachers, administrators, parents, and students themselves. To be successful, we must reflect upon and analyze our own actions, as well as the actions of others. Future research on early childhood teachers should explore, develop, and test teacher preparation and enhancement programs. This research should encourage teachers to reflect, analyze, and grow. Our children and our future depend upon this effort.

William S. Bush

This is certainly an exciting time to be a teacher of mathematics, especially in the early childhood grades. The NCTM *Professional Standards for Teaching Mathematics* and *Curriculum and Evaluation Standards* emphasize the importance of laying a strong mathematical foundation and creating a positive learning environment at this level. It will take the cooperative effort of many people—colleagues, principals, superintendents, parents, school board members, community members, and, most importantly, the children. I wonder how best to gain and maintain the support of these persons.

Lisa A. Kincer

About the Authors

William S. Bush is associate professor of mathematics education at the University of Kentucky. His teaching responsibilities include graduate and undergraduate methods courses in early childhood, middle school, and secondary mathematics. He is currently the director of a statewide program to establish a network of K–4 mathematics specialists.

Lisa A. Kincer was a third-grade teacher at Southern Elementary School in Lexington, Kentucky, during earlier drafts of this chapter. She is currently employed by Jostens Learning Materials as a regional sales representative. Her new position permits her to visit many schools and classrooms.

References

1. ANICK, C. M., CARPENTER, T. P., & SMITH, C. (1981). Minorities and mathematics: Results from the National Assessment of Educational Progress. *Mathematics Teacher, 74,* 560–566.
2. ARMSTRONG, J. M. (1981). Achievement and participation of women in mathematics: Results of two national surveys. *Journal for Research in Mathematics Education, 12,* 356–372.
3. BALL, D. L. (1990). Prospective elementary and secondary teachers' understanding of division. *Journal for Research in Mathematics Education, 21*(2), 132–144.
4. BATTISTA, M. T. (1986). The relationship of mathematics anxiety and mathematical knowledge to the learning of mathematical pedagogy by preservice elementary teachers. *School Science and Mathematics, 86,* 10–19.
5. BECKER, J. R. (1981). Differential treatment of females and males in mathematics classes. *Journal for Research in Mathematics Education, 12,* 40–53.
6. BECKER, J. R. (1986). Mathematics attitudes of elementary education majors. *Arithmetic Teacher, 33*(5), 50–51.
7. BEGLE, E. G. (1979). *Critical variables in mathematics education: Findings from a survey of the empirical literature.* Washington, DC: Mathematics Association of America.
8. BOSSERT, S. T. (1981). Understanding sex differences in children's classroom experiences. *Elementary School Journal, 81,* 255–266.
9. BROD, R. L. (1976, June). *Major sources of Native American academic underachievement: Evidence against current sociological assessments.* Paper presented at the meeting of the American Association for the Advancement of Science, Missoula, MT.
10. BROPHY, J. (1983). Research on the self-fulfilling prophesy and teacher expectations. *Journal of Educational Psychology, 75,* 631–661.

11. BROPHY, J., & GOOD, T. (1974). *Teacher–student relationships: Causes and consequences.* New York: Holt.

12. BULMAHN, B. J., & YOUNG, D. M. (1982). On the transmission of mathematics anxiety. *Arithmetic Teacher, 30*(3), 55–56.

13. BURTON, N. W., & JONES, L. V. (1982). Recent trends in achievement levels of black and white youth. *Educational Researcher, 11*(4), 10–14.

14. BUSH, W. S. (1989). Mathematics anxiety in upper elementary school teachers. *School Science and Mathematics, 89*(6), 499–509.

15. CARPENTER, T. P., FENNEMA, E., PETERSON, P. L., & CAREY, D. (1988). Teachers' pedagogical content knowledge of students' problem solving in elementary arithmetic. *Journal for Research in Mathematics Education, 19,* 385–401.

16. CARTER, K., SABERS, D., CUSHING, K., PINNEGAR, S., & BERLINER, D. (1987). Processing and using information about students: A study of expert, novice, and postulant teachers. *Teaching and Teacher Education, 3,* 147–157.

17. CHAVEZ, A., & WIDMER, C. C. (1982). Math anxiety: Elementary teachers speak for themselves. *Educational Leadership, 39,* 387–388.

18. CHIPMAN, S. F., BRUSH, L. R., & WILSON, D. M. (Eds.). (1985). *Women and mathematics: Balancing the equation.* Hillsdale, NJ: Erlbaum.

19. CLARK, C. M., & PETERSON, P. L. (1986). Teachers' thought processes. In M. C. Wittrock (Ed.), *Handbook of research on teaching* (3rd ed.) (pp. 255–296). New York: Macmillan.

20. COBB, P., WOOD, E., & YACKEL, E. (1988). Curriculum and teacher development: Psychological and anthropological perspectives. In E. Fennema, T. P. Carpenter, & S. J. Lamon (Eds.), *Integrating research on teaching and learning in mathematics* (pp. 92–131). Madison: Wisconsin Center for Education Research.

21. COBB, P., WOOD, T., & YACKEL, E. (in press). Classrooms as learning environments for teachers and researchers. *Journal for Research in Mathematics Education Monographs.* Reston, VA: National Council of Teachers of Mathematics.

22. COMMISSION ON THE EDUCATION OF TEACHERS OF MATHEMATICS. (1981). *Guidelines for the preparation of teachers of mathematics.* Reston, VA: National Council of Teachers of Mathematics.

23. COOPER, H., & GOOD, T. (1983). *Pygmalion grows up: Studies in the expectation communication process.* New York: Longman.

24. DOSSEY, J. A. (1981). The current status of preservice elementary teacher-education programs. *Arithmetic Teacher, 29*(1), 24–26.

25. FEIMAN-NEMSER, S. (1979). Growth and reflection as aims for teacher education: Directions for research. In G. E. Hall, S. M. Hord, & G. Brown (Eds.), *Exploring issues in teacher education: Questions for future research* (pp. 133–152). Austin, TX: Research and Development Center for Teacher Education.

26. FENNEMA, E. (1984). Girls, women, and mathematics. In E. Fennema & M. J. Ayer (Eds.), *Women and education: Equity or equality?* (pp. 137–164). Berkeley, CA: McCutchan.

27. GOOD, T. (1981). A decade of research on teacher expectations. *Educational Leadership, 38,* 415–423.

28. GRAEBER, A. O., TIROSH, D., & GLOVER, R. (1989). Preservice teachers' misconceptions in solving verbal problems in multiplication and division. *Journal for Research in Mathematics Education, 20,* 95–102.

29. HART, L. E. (1989). Classroom processes, sex of student, and confidence in learning mathematics. *Journal for Research in Mathematics Education, 20,* 242–260.

30. JOHNSON, M. L. (1984). Blacks in mathematics: A status report. *Journal for Research in Mathematics Education 15*(2), 145–153.
31. JOHNSON, M. L. (1989). Minority differences in mathematics. In M. L. Lindquist (Ed.), *Results from the Fourth Mathematics Assessment of the National Assessment of Educational Progress*, (pp. 135–148). Reston, VA: National Council of Teachers of Mathematics.
32. KELLY, W. P., & TOMHAVE, W. K. (1985). A study of mathematics anxiety/avoidance in preservice elementary teachers. *Arithmetic Teacher, 32*(5), 51–53.
33. LARSON, C. N. (1983). Techniques for developing positive attitudes in preservice teachers. *Arithmetic Teacher, 31*(2), 8–9.
34. LAZARUS, M. (1974). Mathophobia: Some personal speculations. *The National Elementary Principal, 53*(2), 16–22.
35. LEDER, G. C. (1987). Teacher student interaction: A case study. *Educational Studies in Mathematics, 18*, 255–271.
36. LEINHARDT, G. (1989). Math lessons: A contrast of novice and expert competence. *Journal for Research in Mathematics Education, 20*, 52–75.
37. LEINHARDT, G., & PUTNAM, R. R. (1986). Profile of expertise in elementary school mathematics teaching. *Arithmetic Teacher, 34*(4), 28–29.
38. LEINHARDT, G., & SMITH, D. A. (1985). Expertise in mathematics instruction: Subject matter knowledge. *Journal of Educational Psychology, 77*, 247–271.
39. LEINHARDT, G., WEIDMAN, C., & HAMMOND, K. M. (1987). Introduction and integration of classroom routines by expert teachers. *Curriculum Inquiry, 17*, 135–176.
40. MACNAMEE, G. D., KATZ, L. L., & BOWMAN, B. T. (1981, April). *Mathematical development in low income black preschool children.* Paper presented at the meeting of the Society for Research in Child Development, Boston.
41. MARTIN, W. G., & HAREL, G. (1989). Proof frames of preservice elementary teachers. *Journal for Research in Mathematics Education, 20*, 41–51.
42. MATTHEWS, W. (1984). Influences on the learning and participation of minorities in mathematics. *Journal for Research in Mathematics Education, 15*(2), 84–95.
43. MATTHEWS, W., CARPENTER, T. P., LINDQUIST, M. M., & SILVER, E. A. (1984). The Third National Assessment: Minorities and mathematics. *Journal for Research in Mathematics Education, 15*(2), 165–171.
44. MAYBERRY, J. (1983). The van Hiele levels of geometric thought in undergraduate preservice teachers. *Journal for Research in Mathematics Education, 14*, 58–69.
45. NATIONAL COUNCIL OF TEACHERS OF MATHEMATICS. (1989). *Curriculum and evaluation standards for school mathematics.* Reston, VA: Author.
46. NATIONAL COUNCIL OF TEACHERS OF MATHEMATICS. (1991). *Professional standards for teaching mathematics.* Reston, VA: Author.
47. NATIONAL SCIENCE FOUNDATION. (1980). *Science education databook* (SE 80–3). Washington, DC: U. S. Government Printing Office.
48. NATIONAL RESEARCH COUNCIL. *Everybody counts: A report to the nation on the future of mathematics education.* Washington, DC: National Academy Press.
49. PENG, S. S., FETTERS, W. B., & KOLSTAD, A. J. (1981). *High school and beyond: A national longitudinal study for the 1980's.* Washington, DC: National Center for Educational Statistics.
50. PETERSON, P. L., & FENNEMA, E. (1985). Effective teaching, student engagement in classroom activities, and sex-related differences in learning mathematics. *American Educational Research Journal, 22*, 309–335.

*51. POSAMENTIER, A. S., & STEPELMAN, J. (1986). *Teaching secondary school mathematics: Techniques and enrichment units*. Columbus, OH: Charles E. Merrill.

52. ROSENTHAL, R., & JACOBSON, L. (1968). *Pygmalion in the classroom: Teacher expectation and pupils' intellectual development*. New York: Holt.

53. SCHOFIELD, H. L. (1981). Teacher effects on cognitive and affective pupil outcomes in elementary school mathematics. *Journal of Educational Psychology, 73*, 462–471.

54. SHAVELSON, R. J. (1976). Teachers' decision making. In N. L. Gage (Ed.), *The psychology of teaching methods (The seventy-fifth yearbook of the National Society for the Study of Education)* (pp. 372–414). Chicago: University of Chicago Press.

55. SHAVELSON, R. J., & STERN, P. (1981). Research on teachers' pedagogical thoughts, judgements, decisions, and behavior. *Review of Educational Research, 51*, 455–498.

56. SHERMAN, J., & FENNEMA, E. (1977). The study of mathematics by high-school girls and boys: Related variables. *American Educational Research Journal, 14*, 159–168.

57. THE TASK FORCE ON WOMEN, MINORITIES, AND THE HANDICAPPED IN SCIENCE AND TECHNOLOGY. (1988). *Changing America: The new face of science and technology* (Interim report). Washington, DC: Author.

58. TIROSH, D., & GRAEBER, A. O. (1990). Evoking cognitive conflict to explore preservice teachers' thinking about division. *Journal for Research in Mathematics Education, 21*(2), 98–108.

59. TRAFTON, P. R., & SHULTE, A. P. (Eds.). (1989). *New directions for elementary school mathematics: 1989 yearbook*. Reston, VA: National Council of Teachers of Mathematics.

60. WHEELER, M. M., & FEGHALI, I. (1983). Much ado about nothing: Preservice elementary school teachers' concept of zero. *Journal for Research in Mathematics Education, 14*, 147–155.

61. WILLIAMS, W. V. (1988). Answers to questions about math anxiety. *School Science and Mathematics, 88*, 95–104.

*62. WOOD, T., COBB, P., & YACKEL, E. (in press). The contextual nature of teaching: Change in mathematics but stability in reading. *Elementary School Journal*.

CHAPTER 15

Assessment and the Evaluation of Learning

G. Edith Robinson and Karen T. Bartlett

> *What I Learned This Year in Math*
> *I learned that math is not just numbers. It is Life. The reason I say that is because math can be made from anything, art, music, clothes, ice cream, even the ceiling. I could go on forever.*
> *Math is also thinking things out that confuse you. . . .*
> *—Grace Padienstan, grade 3 (41)*

$\mathbf{T}$he preceding chapters illustrate an expanded interpretation of school mathematics as described in the new NCTM *Curriculum and Evaluation Standards* (27). Student goals include the development of number sense and spatial sense. And affective goals such as the acquisition of a positive attitude. Moreover, students are expected to operate at a higher cognitive level—one that is above recall, recognition, and iteration. How is progress toward these goals to be measured?

In addition to different goals, a different view of the way in which mathematics is learned is apparent: Children are considered to be constructors, rather than receivers, of mathematical knowledge. Teachers are urged to provide opportunity for the active involvement of students in the learning process, giving them latitude to explore, collaborate, reflect, communicate, question, and sometimes to be wrong without risk. Clearly, counting the number of correct answers to questions such as "8 + 3 = ?" will not be sufficient to evaluate the learning that takes place in the kind of classroom now envisioned.

An Expanded View of Assessment

Dissatisfaction with pencil-and-paper tests as the sole means of assessing student learning has characterized much of the literature of the last ten years or so, and the *Curriculum and Evaluation Standards* recommends multiple sources of information, noting that, "Although written tests structured around a single correct answer can be reliable measure of performance, they offer little evidence of the kinds of thinking and understanding advocated in the Curriculum Standards." (27, p.196)

> Generally, the easier a test is to score, the less it tells you about what a student understands.
>
> —Joan Akers

The expanded view of mathematics and how it is learned leads to an expanded view of both the purposes of assessment and the selection or design of the method of assessment.

Expanding the Purposes of Assessment

Assessment information is collected for a variety of purposes—assignment of grades, decisions about promotion, diagnosis and remediation, evaluation of the instructional program or curriculum, or because it is mandated at some administrative level. Increasingly, however, attention is being directed to the importance of assessment for guiding instruction. There are several implications to this point of view:

- Assessment should be continuous, and integrated with instruction rather than an activity separate from instruction.
- Informal assessment becomes more important; a written test is not necessary.
- Good questions are needed—teachers need to devise questions to probe students' thinking.
- A score is not necessary; qualitative evaluation can be very informative.

Teachers have always asked questions in class and made judgments on the basis of the answers, but not always with instructional planning in mind. Questions that require only the recall of facts or the recognition of a geometric shape, for example, do not give evidence of children's thinking or their problem-solving ability.

> Presentation and repetition help students do well on standardized tests and lower-order skills, but they are generally ineffective as teaching strategies for long-term learning, for higher-order thinking, and for versatile problem-solving. *Everybody Counts* (28)

The challenge to assessment of the new goals arises from the fact that no "mastery" level can be set. When a mathematics program is built around the acquisition of facts and computational skills, it is easy to measure the degree of mastery of these goals. But what is "mastery" of number sense? Or estimation? At what point might a student be said to have "mastered" problem solving? Planning appropriate experiences requires information about where students are now, today; hence the point of view that assessment must be an integral, ongoing part of instruction.

Factors to Consider in Selecting/Designing Means of Assessment

That any method of assessment should be aligned with instructional objectives has always been a truism. One criticism of published tests, for example, has been that they may not measure local objectives. When the instructional goals take a differenct direction, as is the case with the new *Curriculum and Evaluation Standards*, different methods of assessment are needed. Assessment of number sense, or estimation, or problem solving requires different techniques than, say, assessment of computational skill.

Alignment of assessment with the method of instruction is also important. For younger children, it is recommended that conceptual knowledge be assessed with manipulatives (13) since manipulatives are such an integral part of instruction at that level. Do students know the difference between 15 and 51? Between 105 and 150? Having the students bundle sticks or lay out numeration blocks to show the differences gives the teacher more information than having them write the numeral for either a printed picture or some manipulatives already prepared. The former gauges their understanding; the latter measures recognition only.

It has recently been pointed out (10) that the new standards refer to *qualities*, not quantities. This is an important distinction for it means that assessment data may not always be attainable in the form of a score. But if assessment is to guide instructional planning, then evidence of student progress (or lack of it!) must be obtained, but not necessarily from a formal "assessment instrument." As described in current literature, assessment data can be obtained by such informal means as good questions asked in class, observation, individual interviews, and student portfolios. These methods are described in more detail in this chapter.

> Assessment is more than testing. It is continuous and is often an informal view of children's understanding of processes, interrelationships, and applications.

Informal Means of Assessment

Asking Good Questions

A number of examples are cited in the literature of "right answers" that successfully mask serious misconceptions. In one such situation (39, p.25), a student correctly responded "20" to the following exercise:

> Four of five dentists interviewed recommended Yukkey Gum. What percentage of the dentists interviewed did not recommend it?

When asked to explain her solution, the student responded, " 'Of' means multiply, so I multiplied four times five and got 20 percent!"

As a second example (31, p.15) a student correctly carried out a computation as follows:

$$3\frac{1}{3} - 2\frac{5}{6} = \frac{10}{3} - \frac{17}{6} = \frac{20}{6} - \frac{17}{6} = \frac{3}{6} = \frac{1}{2}$$

When the student was subsequently asked which was larger, 3/6 or 1/2, he responded that 1/2 was larger since, "the denominator is smaller, so the pieces are larger and one of the great big pieces is more than three of the tiny pieces."

It is always tempting, when a student supplies "the correct answer," to offer praise to that student and move along. As the examples above illustrate, however, there is frequently opportunity for getting a right answer for the wrong reason. Follow-up questions that probe the method, or call for some other evidence of understanding, can provide the kind of assessment information that is needed to guide instructional planning.

Some questions are better suited for eliciting information than others. Consider the two displays below, in which the task is to identify triangles (39, p.26):

FIGURE 15.1   Trivial recognition task

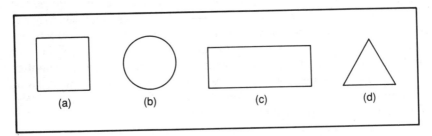

(a)   (b)   (c)   (d)

FIGURE 15.2   Nontrivial recognition task

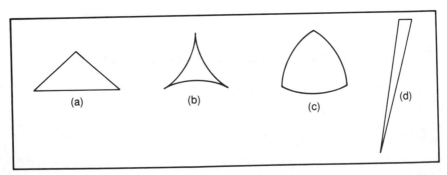

(a)   (b)   (c)   (d)

A student correctly identified the triangle in Figure 15.1, but when presented the choices shown in Figure 15.2, responded that (a), (b), and (c) were all triangles, since they had three sides, but (d) was not a triangle because it was "too sharp to be a triangle." An evaluation based on Figure 15.1 would be that the student "knew" what a triangle was; the response to Figure 15.2 shows that the concept was poorly developed. What we see in this example is that devising good questions requires not only a clear understanding of the mathematics involved, but also a knowledge of likely misconceptions. In this respect conversations with children are invaluable, and good suggestions for such conversations are to be found in previous chapters of this book as well as in some of the references.

Careful sequencing of questions can yield better information. The box below shows three subtraction problems with different structure:

Examples of three problem types for subtraction (20):
A. Separate, result unknown
   Connie has 8 marbles. She gives 3 marbles to Jim. How many marbles does she have left?
B. Join, change unknown
   Connie has 3 marbles. How many more marbles does she need to collect to have 8 marbles all together?
C. Compare
   Connie has 8 marbles. Jim has 3 marbles. How many more marbles does Connie have than Jim?

As reported (20, p. 53), a teacher selected the second type, made up a problem with similar structure, distributed counters, and asked her class to solve the problem. She reasoned that if the students could solve this problem, they probably could solve one with the same structure as A. She found that several strategies were used by different members of the class; those who could not solve the problem were noted, and the teacher planned to check them on the (easier) problem-type A. Thoughtful advance planning of the assessment enabled her to plan the instruction to follow.

Routine word problems lend themselves to follow-up questions that check understanding. Some students, for example, rely on verbal cues to tell them what to do—"If the word 'left' is in the problem, you subtract." Questions such as "Suppose this number were larger (smaller), would your answer be larger or smaller?" and then, "Why do you think so?" direct attention to the mathematical, rather than the verbal, characteristics of the problem. Student responses to such questions also supply evidence of their understanding of number. Another suggestion given (13) is a display such as the one shown in Figure 15.3, in which the numerals are equally spaced:

FIGURE 15.3   6 is closer to which of the
                   other two numbers?

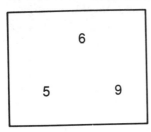

The question for the students is "six is closer to which of the other two numbers?"
This could be followed up by asking, in turn, about the five and nine. Another
example of a question to prompt some thinking is "Given that 46 + 59 = 105,
what is 47 + 58?" (13). Then ask, "Why?" As these examples illustrate, source material for good questions is easy to come by; the questions themselves provide opportunity for assessing students' understanding of mathematics and their ability to
communicate.

> Just as knowledge is not a collection of separate facts, so learning competence
> is not a collection of separate skills.
>
> —Lauren Resnick

The Individual Interview

In contrast to the informal questioning that takes place in class, an interview involves a series of questions in a one-on-one situation. The procedure can be time-
consuming, but need not be—one team of researchers describes interviews in which
only an hour was needed to question an entire class of thirty-two (31). Brief interviews
were conducted following the administration of a paper-and-pencil placement test.
The results of the interviews led the team to conclude that had they relied on the
results of the written test alone, more than half of the class would have been mis-
judged. The discrepancy arose from the difference between conceptual understanding
and computational proficiency: Some students could carry out the mechanics of
computation without any understanding of the underlying concept, whereas others
had good conceptual understanding but made errors in computation. Subsequent
instruction was then tailored to the special needs of the two groups.

> Assessment is the process of trying to understand what meaning students give
> to activities.

Good questions are necessary for a successful interview—questions well thought
out in advance. But flexibility on the part of the interviewer is also necessary, for the

responses of the student being interviewed must be taken into consideration. Thinking of the interview as a conversation, or dialogue, rather than an assessment can go a long way toward establishing the right sort of atmosphere. Questions may need to be rephrased in the child's vocabulary, and the teacher should be prepared to prompt when the child's first response is "I don't know." Giving the child ample time to respond, and resisting the urge to evaluate responses on the spot, can elicit a more productive interchange. Children, especially young children, are prone to give answers they think are expected of them. In order to gain information about the child's own thinking, there should be a neutral, accepting atmosphere in which the interviewer is not looking for a particular answer or a particular wording for the answer.

> What you learn from children in a few interviews can have a dramatic effect on what you teach, when you teach it, how you teach, and how you evaluate children's progress.
>
> —E. Labinowicz

Observations/Checklists/Portfolios

Some goals of mathematics learning can, in the case of young children, only be assessed by observation: perseverance, for example, or communication, or the habit of checking answers. Checklists can be prepared for recording observations of individual students at work. Checklists focus attention on the particular behavior or attitude to be observed, and also serve as an aid to memory for the busy teacher. A checklist can be organized so as to provide a place to note whether the attitude or behavior is frequently, sometimes, or never observed. Or it can be prepared so as to record what was observed on a particular day (Fig. 15.4). A schedule of observations ensures that each child receives attention while freeing the teacher for other instructional tasks.

> The teacher needs to be a trained observer.
>
> —Skip Fennell

Individual portfolios of students' work, whether maintained by the teacher or the child, serve as a record of progress and a basis for evaluating that progress. For some suggestions about other material to be included, see the next section, which includes information on assessment of problem solving, and also 21, 24, and 39.

Two Special Assessments

Two of the goals of school mathematics—the development of competence in estimation and problem-solving processes—are troublesome to assess with pencil-and-paper tests. Although the informal methods of assessment discussed above provide

FIGURE 15.4   Observation notes

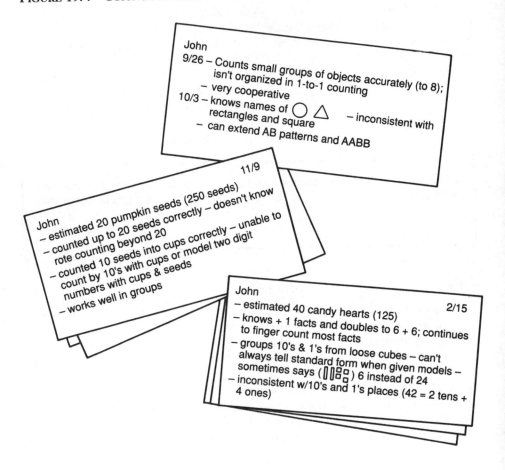

opportunity for charting student progress toward these goals, various writers have given attention to more formal means of data gathering.

Assessing Estimation

When faced with a question on a written test asking for an estimate, many students carry out the computation and then round off their answer to get their "estimate." This of course gives no information about their skill at estimating answers before the fact! Some suggestions for administering a written test so as to get a more valid measure are (33):

- Control time by using the overhead projector. If the children do not have time to compute, they will have to make an estimate.

- Choose numbers that encourage estimation; that is, large numbers as opposed to small numbers, and "messy" fractions as opposed to simple ones.
- Use small answer sheets that do not allow room for computation.

Test questions can be devised to encourage estimation on written tests, even those in multiple choice format. In the following example, the use of the masked digit gives no opportunity for computation.

$$
\begin{array}{r}
2\ \square \\
+\ 1\ 6 \\
\hline
\end{array}
$$

The answer is closest to which of these?

20   30   40   50

Having surveyed a number of examples, one author comments that coverage of estimation varies among commercial achievement tests " . . . but is, at best, sketchy and inadequate" (33, p.28). Thus the burden of assessing students' estimation skills falls largely on the classroom teacher.

Another research team (35) tested children in grades 5–8 on questions requiring different strategies for estimation. They found that the students tended to estimate by first rounding the given numbers to the nearest power of ten even when this was inappropriate for responding to the question. This suggests that rounding is the estimation strategy most familiar to students, which in turn suggests that it may be the sole strategy included in the instructional program. This seems particularly likely in view of the small number of textbook lessons devoted to estimation—less than 5 percent according to one survey (32, p.4). Yet it is generally agreed that estimation is important not only as a real-life skill, but also as a factor in the development of number sense, in mathematical thinking, and in problem solving.

Even when computational estimation is not formally taught, there are exercises that can assess concepts underlying estimation. With a different choice of numbers, the exercise suggested with Figure 15.3 can pave the way toward the idea of rounding: The numbers 15, 18, and 20 might be chosen, or the numbers 10, 18, and 20. And it has also been suggested that students could be asked to predict the number of digits in a sum, difference, or product (24, p.40), as, say $105 - 9$. In any case, students should be asked for their explanations so as to give information about their thinking.

Surveys show that mental computation and estimation are used in more than 80 percent of all real-world problem-solving situations outside the classroom. (32)

Assessing Problem-Solving Processes

A great deal has been written about the teaching, learning, and evaluation of problem solving since the publication in 1980 of *An Agenda for Action* (26). For example, between September, 1984, and May, 1988, each issue of the *Arithmetic Teacher* contained a two-page spread entitled "Problem Solving: Tips for Teachers." Many of these contain suggestions for assessment; some of the other starred entries in the References contain practical advice for the assessment of problem solving.

If the processes of problem solving are to be given the recommended weight, then evaluation of students' problem-solving ability cannot rest on the correctness of the answer alone. It has been noted (5, pp. 160–161) that there are three aspects to problem solving about which evaluation information is desirable:

- whether the student has enough facts
- whether the student has the requisite and appropriate skills
- whether the student can "call upon the knowledge and skills in a nonpredetermined order to make sense of a new experience"

The first two of these are easy to assess and are the usual objectives of written tests; the third is the one that poses difficulty. The analysis above underscores the nonalgorithmic nature of problem solving as it is currently conceived, and a number of writers have addressed the issue, with suggestions for both formal and informal assessments. Space permits only a summary of some of these efforts, and readers are urged to consult the sources for more detailed information.

The problem-solving ability of young children has been well documented. Even preschool children can solve one-step problems by modeling the action with objects or counters, and some use still other strategies. For young children, then, assessment can involve the use of objects in an interview situation. As mentioned earlier, considering the interview as a conversation allows the child to talk about his or her own thinking, using his or her own words.

Older children are more likely to be asked to show their solutions in written form. One method of assessing the process (as opposed to the product, or answer) is an analytic scoring guide. The authors of the one shown below (4, p. 30) identified three aspects of problem solving: understanding the problem, planning a solution, and getting an answer. For each of these phases they selected a score of 0, 1, or 2 to correspond to predetermined levels as follows:

Understanding the problem	0:	Complete misunderstanding of the problem
	1:	Part of the problem misunderstood or misinterpreted
	2:	Complete understanding of the problem
Planning a solution	0:	No attempt, or totally inappropriate plan
	1:	Partially correct plan based on part of the problem being interpreted correctly
	2:	Plan could have led to a correct solution if implemented properly

Getting an
answer

0: No answer, or wrong answer based
on an inappropriate plan

1: Copying error; computational
error; partial answer for a problem
with multiple answers

2: Correct answer and correct label
for answer

Teachers can easily adapt this scheme to their class and the types of problems being used. With the plan above, each student's work would receive a score of 0 through 6 for each problem, and the score takes into consideration the process as well as the "answer."

An alternative plan is to set up in advance a scoring system of, say, 0 through 5, and describe, for each score, the characteristics of the work that would earn that score. For example, a score of 4 might be given for an appropriate strategy, with the work showing understanding of the problem, but including a computational error. On the other hand, if the strategy shown was appropriate, but the student either ignored some condition of the problem, gave an incorrect answer for no apparent reason, or if the thinking processes were unclear, a score of 3 might be given (4, p. 49). For consistency in measuring students' work, the plan should be devised ahead of time. There are several good references that give more detail about these methods of assessment. Both methods give information about distinct phases of the problem-solving process, suggesting specific directions for instructional planning.

Objective tests have also received attention with the idea of focusing on the process of problem solving. One plan (6) is to present a situation and then a series of questions, each of which represents a different cognitive level. The first of the series of questions, for example, might ask about information given in the description of the situation; another might call for an inference; the last question in the list would require the examinee to work at an abstract level using relationships he or she established.

**WHAT IS TESTED IS
WHAT GETS TAUGHT.**
(And how it is tested is how it is taught.)

Everybody Counts

Multiple-choice questions can also be devised to probe students' thinking. A problem can be posed and a mythical student's "solution" shown. The examinee is to answer the question "Is this solution correct?," choosing from a list such as this:

1. Yes
2. No, they should have multiplied instead of adding
3. No, they used the wrong numbers
4. No, they made a mistake in arithmetic

The choice of a reason in case the examinee thinks the solution is wrong gives information about how he or she thinks the problem should be solved.

Recognition of the mathematical structure of a word problem seems important to success in problem solving (20). Many students apparently have difficulty because they pay too much attention to the surface characteristics. One way to assess their ability to recognize the mathematical structure is to present a series of contexts involving the same numbers:

1. Joe bought 4 books and each book cost 3 dollars
2. Marc is 4 years old and 3 feet tall
3. Ann has 4 hamsters and 3 goldfish

The question for the students is "In which of the above does it make sense to add 4 and 3 to find how many in all?" A variation on this type of question is to give a problem, then ask which of a series of other problems is like the given one.

Other Assessment Issues

Some of the research on assessment has centered around broad issues—not specifically aimed at mathematics, but having implications for assessment in mathematics. Following are two that are of particular interest.

Are Tests Fair?

This question is usually leveled at so-called "standardized" tests. Such tests grew in popularity largely on the basis of their objectivity—each question on the test has a single best answer to be recorded on a special answer sheet and machine scored. Thus every student taking the test is evaluated on exactly the same criteria. It is not the case, for example, that different students giving 3/6 as an answer might receive half credit, full credit, or no credit depending on different teachers' philosophies about the importance of standard names for numbers. On a standardized test, all examinees giving the same answer receive the same amount of credit for that answer.

In the past decade, serious challenges have been aimed at standardized tests. In the case of young children, the opportunity for clerical errors in the use of separate answer sheets has been pointed out. And as the use of standardized tests has proliferated, the phenomenon of "test-wiseness" has arisen. On the one hand, the misplaced mark on an answer sheet is considered to be detrimental to a student's overall test score (although conceivably it could have the opposite effect!); test-wiseness, on the other hand, is often assumed to give an inflated test score. Both, of course, impinge on the validity of the measure.

Another concern that has been voiced and that calls into question the validity of standardized tests is the possibility of test bias. A test question is said to be biased if differential performance on that question by different subgroups of examinees is attributable solely to factors such as gender, ethnicity, or socioeconomic status. It is doubtful that any test question is completely biased—that is, it is unlikely that there exists a test question that is answered correctly by *every* girl (boy) and incorrectly by *every* boy (girl). Nevertheless, assessment instruments used in a mathematics class should measure mathematical objectives and not clerical skills, test-wiseness, gender, ethnicity, or socioeconomic status.

A number of studies address issues related to the fairness of standardized tests. Are bilingual students, for example, penalized by tests written in English? Not according to a study reported in 1983 (19). The students in this study—408 fourth- and fifth-graders from five schools—did better when tested in English than on the Spanish version of the same test. (Half of the students took the Spanish version first; half took the English version first.) The results were the same whether the students' reading comprehension in English was classified as low, medium, or high. The authors suggest that bilingual students will do better when tested in the language of instruction.

Another study (44) compared test results of third-graders using (a) separate answer sheets with practice, (b) separate answer sheets without practice, and (c) space in the test booklet for their answers. Significantly lower scores were made by children using separate answer sheets in the case of computation, but not in the case of questions on concepts or problem solving.

Clearly, a standardized test is not fair if its content is not in alignment with the curriculum of the school. Recommendations of the NCTM's *An Agenda For Action* and *Curriculum and Evaluation Standards* emphasize problem solving, estimation, communication, and other aspects of mathematics that are not measured on standardized tests currently available. Therefore, attention is now being given to alternate means of assessment. In particular, the use of multiple means of assessment is strongly advocated since multiple sources give a more complete picture of students' progress toward goals currently considered important. Better means of assessment are clearly called for. One report noted "striking differences" in the content covered by four commonly used standardized tests and concluded:

> For this and other reasons, it is likely that there will be significant discrepancies between the content a teacher presents to students and the content which is being tested on the standardized test administered. These mismatches between content taught and content tested have negative effects on the utility of standardized tests for facilitating instruction. They may also result in underestimates of student achievement. (11, p. 54)

If, as many believe, the most important purpose of assessment is to guide instruction, then the recommendation to use multiple means of assessment cannot be too strongly supported.

Mathematics
understandings
are not mastered,
but are developed,
elaborated, deepened, and
made more complete
over time.
—Joan Akers

The Role of Technology in Assessment

Two aspects of technology are seen to have relevance for assessment: the issue of the use of hand held calculators in formal testing situations, and the anticipated use of computers for the delivery of tests. Although these matters may have greater import for older students, there are some implications for students in grades K–4.

The use of calculators in formal testing situations has been urged for years. The most obvious difficulty with implementing this recommendation is the weight given to computation on most standardized tests. If examinees were to be allowed the use of calculators, the tests would no longer measure the kind of achievement for which they were constructed. Different kinds of tests and tasks should evolve if calculator use is to be permitted. Another difficulty, however, is less obvious. In practice, when students have been allowed to use calculators on a test, it has been found that they try to use the calculator on every question, whether or not it is appropriate. This may be due to lack of familiarity with calculator use in general, or it may be a case of a sort of test un-wiseness. By beginning calculator use earlier, on tests as well as in class, students might become familiar with the appropriate use of this tool. Work is already in progress on tests containing questions that are not "calculator sensitive"; and some are being organized into separately timed parts, one "calculator allowed," and one "calculator not allowed."

Some of the advantages seen for computer-delivered tests are the capacity to give the examinee immediate feedback, the potential for simulation, and the capability for individualizing the test—that is, delivering sets of questions based on the response pattern of the examinee. Individualized test delivery not only avoids boredom—examinees are not faced with a series of similar exercises if they are successful with one key example—but there is the potential for some instruction along with the testing situation. Tests are seldom designed to teach, but the potential is there, and the computer is a likely medium for the development of just such tests.

Evaluation

To evaluate is to assign a value to something. Put another way, assessment may be thought of as data gathering, evaluation as data interpretation (18). If assessment is to guide instruction, then teachers must evaluate test results and other means of assessment. Simply recording scores in a grade book is not sufficient. As mentioned before, a score is not needed for evaluation (21, p. 37). What is needed is a collation from a number of sources—observation, interview, informal questioning in class, and students' written work. Teachers can also make use of the item analyses supplied with standardized tests, paying particular attention to the individual questions, and studying in detail those that give useful information (40).

It has been emphasized (21) that a test, or any other single means of assessment, provides only a sample of what a child knows and can do; none can cover all that a child is expected to do. By considering results from a variety of sources, a more complete evaluation of each student's progress becomes possible. It has also been pointed out (18) that for each goal set for students, it is possible to find more than one assessment strategy.

Basing evaluation on multiple sources of information required that meaning be attached to each indicator, and this is what constitutes evaluation (21, p.37).

What's Going On

> By confusing means and ends, by making testing more important than learning, present practice holds today's students hostage to yesterday's mistakes. *Everybody Counts* (28)

A number of states are taking steps to revise their testing programs. Georgia and North Carolina, for example, are replacing norm-referenced tests with interviews and other means of assessing while teaching. North Carolina supplies each first- and second-grade teacher with a grade-level notebook of assessment strategies. The strategies are written so that they can be used as instructional activities as well as evaluation tasks with total classes, small groups, or individual students. Profiles are provided for teachers to record their observations twice during the year, and seven content areas are evaluated (Fig. 15.5). Teachers base their judgments on conversations with children, observation of how students arrive at answers, and samples of students' work.

Connecticut began allowing the use of calculators on certain parts of their eighth grade test in the fall of 1986 (24, pp. 55–56). And California has been revising its achievement tests (CAP) to assess problem solving with a multiple-choice format.

> "There is widespread agreement that CAP is able to test some of the most important aspects of problem solving with the multiple-choice format . . ." (5, p. 180)

NCTM, through its ADDENDA Project, is producing a series of books for the elementary grades that incorporate classroom activities for major content strands. Since there will be a strong focus on language and connections in these books, teachers should find in them good ideas for ongoing assessment.

Looking Ahead . . .

Assessment has been called the key to change in the K–4 curriculum (18), and the amount of interest in the topic is most encouraging. But more work is needed.

More good questions are needed—questions that probe, that may have more than one answer, yet permit evaluation of the responses. Computer capability needs further exploration. Current work offers promise of a revised definition of "test" as an individualized set of questions, tailored to a student's present status, rather than an instrument constructed for group use.

Recent work has been good and innovative; we look forward to its continuation.

Edith Robinson

FIGURE 15.5 North Carolina Assessment Profile

MATHEMATICS: Grade 1   Student _____

Teacher _____   School _____ 19__ - __

Goal 1: The learner will identify and use numbers 0 to 100.

1.1 Count using 1 to 1 correspondence				
1.2 Make sets; match numerals				
1.3 Compare and order sets				
1.4 Identify ordinal position				
1.5 Conserve numbers				
1.6 Read and write numerals; read number words 0 to10				
1.7 Count on				
1.8 Recognize one more/ less/ before/ after/ between				
1.9 Compare/sequence numerals				
1.10 Rote count by 1's, 10's, 5's, and 2's; Group objects to count by 10's, 5's, and 2's				
1.11 Count by using tallying				
1.12 Make reasonable estimates of "how many"				
1.13 Group objects into tens and ones; record				
1.14 Recognize models; build 2 digit numbers; write numerals				
1.15 Represent numbers in a variety of ways				

Code: M = Most of the time   S = Sometimes   N = Not yet

FIGURE 15.5 *(Continued)*

Goal 2: The learner will identify and use geometric ideas.

2.1 Identify open and closed figures					
2.2 Identify, describe, and model plane figures; recognize in environment					
2.3 Use directional/ positional words					
2.4 Describe likenesses and differences					
2.5 Identify and describe solid figures; recognize In the envIronment					

Goal 3: The learner will demonstrate an understanding of classification, patterns, and seriation.

3.1 Describe objects by their attributes; Compare and order					
3.2 Sort by given attribute; by more than one attribute; explain sorting rules					
3.3 Sort objects by own rule; explain sorting rule					
3.4 Copy/ continue patterns; translate into different forms					
3.5 Create patterns with actions/words/objects					
3.6 Find and correct errors in patterns					
3.7 Identify patterns in the environment					

Code: M = Most of the time   S = Sometimes   N = Not yet

From a practitioner's point of view, many questions still linger: Can a single test identify both the strengths and weaknesses of a child's understanding? Can tests give students an opportunity to learn and to evaluate their own progress? Should test time be limited when *thinking* is being evaluated? Is there a balance to be achieved between problem-solving process and product, and how should any such balance be weighed? Can testing keep up with the use of technology in classroom instruction? Addressing these questions will spark interest from individuals, classrooms, counties, regions, and states.

Assessment is an ongoing enterprise, and the current concern for assessment issues is a beginning, not an end, for improved student learning.

Karen T. Bartlett

About the Authors

Edith Robinson is a former mathematics teacher in both public and private schools and a teacher educator at the university level. More recently she was a designer of tests, many of which were experimental in purpose or delivery mode. Although officially retired, she still "moonlights" for NCTM and others.

Karen T. Bartlett is in her twenty-third year of teaching third grade at Black Mountain Primary School in Black Mountain, North Carolina. She was selected 1988 NCCTM Outstanding Elementary Math Teacher and received the 1990 State Presidential Award for Excellence in Mathematics.

References

*1. BEATTIE, J., & ALGOZZINE, B. (1982). Testing for teaching. *Arithmetic Teacher*, 30(1), 47–51.

*2. California Mathematics Council (1989). *Assessment alternatives in mathematics: An overview*. Berkeley, CA: EQUALS.

*3. CHAMBERS, D. L. (1989). One point of view: Calculating the influence of tests on instruction. *Arithmetic Teacher*, 36(9), 10–11.

4. CHARLES, R., LESTER, F., & O'DAFFER, P. (1987). *How to evaluate progress in problem solving*. Reston, VA: The National Council of Teachers of Mathematics.

5. CHARLES, R. I., & SILVER, E. A. (Eds.). (1988). *The teaching and assessing of mathematical problem solving*. Reston, VA: National Council of Teachers of Mathematics.

6. COLLIS, K. F., ROMBERG, T. A., & JURDAK, M. E. (1986). A technique for assessing mathematical problem-solving ability. *Journal for Research in Mathmatics Education*, 17(3), 206–221.

*7. COSTA, A. L. (1989). Re-assessing assessment. *Educational Leadership*, 46 (7).

8. CROSSWHITE, F. J., DOSSEY, J. A., & FRYE, S. M. (1989). NCTM standards for school mathematics: visions for implementation. *Journal for Research in Mathematics Education*, 1989, 20(5), 513–522.

*9. Essential mathematics for the twenty-first century: The position of the National Council of Supervisors of Mathematics. *Arithmetic Teacher*, 37(1), 44–46.

10. FENNELL, F. *Assessment is a must! Strategies to help you assess math readiness, achieve-*

ment, and attitude. Paper presented at the annual meeting of the National Council of Teachers of Mathematics, Salt Lake City, Utah, 1990.

*11. FREEMAN, D. J., KUHS, T. M., KNAPPEN, L. B., & PORTER, A. C. (1982). A closer look at standardized tests. Arithmetic Teacher, 29(7), 50–54.

12. HANEY, W., & MADAUS, G. (1989). Searching for alternatives to standardized Tests: Whys, whats, and whithers. Phi Delta Kappan, 70(9), 683–687.

13. HATFIELD, M. Assessing the primary child—Issues and techniques related to NCTM's Standards. Paper presented at the annual meeting of the National Council of Teachers of Mathematics, Salt Lake City, Utah, 1990.

14. HEMBREE, R. (1987). Effects of noncontent variables on mathematics test performance. Journal for Research in Mathematics Education, 18(3), 197–214.

*15. KRULIK, S., & REYS, R. E. (Eds.) (1980). Problem solving in school mathematics. Reston, VA: National Council of Teachers of Mathematics.

*16. LABINOWICZ, E. (1987). Assessing for learning: The interview method. Arithmetic Teacher, 35(3), 22–25.

*17. LABINOWICZ, E. (1985). Learning from children. Menlo Park, CA: Addison-Wesley.

18. LINDQUIST, M. M. Assessment: The key to change in the K–1 curriculum. Paper presented at the annual meeting of the National Council of Teachers of Mathematics, Salt Lake City, Utah, 1990.

19. LLABRE, M. M., & CUEVAS, G. (1983). The effects of test language and mathematical skills assessed on the scores of bilingual Hispanic students. Journal for Research in Mathematics Education, 14(5), 318–324.

20. LOEF, M. M. CAREY, D. A., CARPTENTER, T. P., & FENNEMA, E. (1988). Research into practice: Integrating assessment and instruction. Arithmetic Teacher, 36(3), 53–55.

*21. McKILLIP, W. D., & STANIC, G. M. A. (1988). Assessing for learning: Putting the value back into evaluation. Arithmetic Teacher, 35(6), 37–38.

22. McKNIGHT, C. C., CROSSWHITE, F. J., DOSSEY, J. A., KIFER, E., SWAFFORD, J. O., TRAVERS, K. J., & COONEY, T. J. (1987). The underachieving curriculum: Assessing U.S. school mathematics from an international perspective. Champaign, IL. Stipes.

23. MARTINEZ, M. E., & LIPSON, J. I. (1989). Assessment for learning. Educational Leadership, 46(7), 73–75.

*24. NATIONAL COUNCIL OF TEACHERS OF MATHEMATICS (1985). Arithmetic Teacher, Focus Issue: Mathematical Thinking, 32 (6).

*25. NATIONAL COUNCIL OF TEACHERS OF MATHEMATICS (1986–87). Arithmetic Teacher, 34.

26. NATIONAL COUNCIL OF TEACHERS OF MATHEMATICS (1980). An agenda for action. Reston, VA: National Council of Teachers of Mathematics.

*27. NATIONAL COUNCIL OF TEACHERS OF MATHEMATICS. (1989). Curriculum and evaluation standards for school mathematics. Reston, VA: Author.

28. NATIONAL RESEARCH COUNCIL. (1989). Everybody counts. A report to the nation on the future of mathematics education. Washington, DC: National Academy Press.

*29. NORTH CAROLINA DEPARTMENT OF PUBLIC INSTRUCTION. (1989). Grades 1 and 2 mathematics assessment. Raleigh, NC: The Department.

*30. OTIS, M. J., & OFFERMAN, T. R. (1988). Assessing for learning: How do you evaluate problem solving? Arithmetic Teacher, 35(8), 49–51.

*31. PECK, D. M., JENCKS, S. M., & CONNELL, M. L. (1989). Improving instruction through brief interviews. Arithmetic Teacher, 37(3), 15–17.

*32. REYS, B. J., & REYS, R. E. (1986). One point of view: Mental computation and computational estimation—their time has come. Arithmetic Teacher, 33(7), 4–5.

33. REYS, R. E. (1988). Assessing for learning: Testing computational estimation—some things to consider. Arithmetic Teacher, 35(7), 28–30.

*34. REYS, R. E. (1985). Testing mental computation skills. *Arithmetic Teacher*, 33(3), 14–16.

35. SCHOEN, H. L., BLUME, G., & HOOVER, H. D. (1990). Outcomes and processes on estimation. *Journal for Research in Mathematics Education*, 21(1), 61–73.

36. SHEPHERD, L. A. (1989). Why we need better assessments. *Educational Leadership*, 46(7), 4–9.

*37. SILVER, E. A., & SMITH, M. S. (1990). Research into practice: teaching mathematics and thinking. *Arithmetic Teacher*, 37(8), 34–37.

*38. STARKEY, M. A. (1989). Calculating first graders. *Arithmetic Teacher*, 37(2), 6–7.

*39. THOMPSON, A. G., & BRIARS, D. J. (1989). Implementing the standards: Assessing students' learning to inform teaching: The message in NCTM's evaluation standards. *Arithmetic Teacher*, 37(4), 22–26.

*40. TRAFTON, P. (1987). Assessing for learning: Tests—a tool for improving instruction. *Arithmetic Teacher*, 35(4), 17–18.

41. TRAFTON, R. P. (Ed.). (1989). *New directions for elementary school mathematics: 1989 yearbook*. Reston, VA. National Council of Teachers of Mathematics.

42. WIGGINS, G. (1989). Teaching to the (authentic) test. *Educational Leadership*, 46(7), 41–47.

43. WILSON, J. W., & KILPATRICK, J. (1989). Theoretical Issues in the development of calculator-based mathematics tests. In J. W. Kenelly (Ed.), *The use of calculators in the standardized testing of mathematics*. New York: College Entrance Examination Board.

44. WISE, S. L., DUNCAN, A. L., & PLAKE, B. S. (1985). The effect of introducing third graders to the use of separate answer sheets on the ITBS. *Journal of Educational Research*, 78, 306–309.

PART IV

Classroom Research

CHAPTER 16

Teacher as Reflective Practitioner

Margaret Ackerman

What is a reflective practitioner? How do we become one? How do we take the research findings and implications presented in this volume and implement them in our classrooms? Reading the previous chapters, I find myself thinking about the separation that sometimes exists between theory and practice. Teachers ultimately make the final decision about which methods they will use to facilitate the development of their students' knowledge of and feelings toward mathematics. Teachers often make these decisions instinctively or out of habit. A "reflective practitioner" is merely one who consistently attempts to make each decision part of a continual learning and growth process by consciously looking back on its consequences. Designing and conducting research becomes a new way of reflecting on children, change, and ourselves.

If we are to see ourselves as reflective practitioners, we must be willing to learn and change. Through attending workshops, listening to and questioning our students, reading current research on mathematics education, and sharing ideas with colleagues, we can work toward improving our instruction. By monitoring our short- and long-term plans for our classrooms, we can better determine what is best for our students. Reflective practitioners constantly question their goals and aims, and therefore are more open to change. This volume can only provide us with insights and directions from other educators' research. It is now our challenge to transform this knowledge into effective classroom strategies in our individual classrooms.

Cognition and Evaluation (Chapters 1 and 15)

In Chapter 1, Ginsburg and Baron emphasize the connection between formal and informal mathematics. As elementary teachers, we have many opportunities to encourage children's use of their own methods. Since informal mathematics is hands-on, our instruction should be as well. To facilitate children's construction of personally meaningful mathematics, I ask them to write and talk about their mathematical ideas amd problem-solving processes.

In my classroom, I carefully plan experiences with manipulatives. Helping a child explore a concept through a manipulative can provide a link to formal mathematics. Whether we are taking the lunch count, graphing ice cream choices, tallying votes for class governor, or finding the probability of being chosen as the helper of the day, my students are "talking" about mathematics and experiencing it firsthand.

I have found that talking with small groups of students has improved my instruction. Not only do I have the chance to learn what reasoning they have "invented," as Ginsburg suggests, but I also learn the direction in which my instruction should proceed. Through listening to my students and questioning them, I feel that they become responsive to mathematics. They begin to think mathematically without my assistance. Mathematics is more than a worksheet to them.

Using student presentations as a means of assessment has given me the opportunity to gain insight into my students' understanding of mathematical concepts. From their explanations, I have found which children have made connections between their informal knowledge and formal mathematics. As a classroom teacher, I would like to see more emphasis given to understanding the processes in mathematics versus memorization of facts. Ginsburg and Baron provide us with research to support this focus on process; however, typical evaluation procedures in mathematics education are still mostly product oriented. Alternative types of assessments should provide classroom teachers with different perspectives on their students' thought processes. Observations of groups, listening to and interviewing individuals, and questioning are all practical ways to gain the depth of information needed to make successful teaching decisions.

In Chapter 15, Robinson and Bartlett point out the discrepancies that can exist between conceptual understanding and computational proficiency. One simple approach is to give children credit for the process as well as the product of their work. When I began teaching, I assigned credit too frequently to correct solutions without exploring the origin of the solution. Since the answer was correct, I assumed the children understood. I now realize that often this is not the case.

It would be interesting to compare the results of a concrete/hands-on approach to learning with the results of a computationally based program. If our goal is to find out what children understand about mathematics, we should not assume that a standardized test would be the only or even the best measure. We could find out more during an interview with children from both types of classrooms than by reviewing the results of a standardized test. Research on cognition and evaluation challenges us as educators to use a variety of assessments in our data collection and evaluation to improve our instruction and children's understanding.

The Teacher Influence and Affect
(Chapters 2 and 14)

Early-childhood teachers certainly influence the direction of children's learning and attitude toward mathematics. As I read the chapters on affect and teacher influence,

I tried to remember my own childhood experiences with mathematics. Mathematics has always been challenging to me. How did my teachers motivate me to learn and be persistent, especially when I was frustrated or unsure of myself? How do I motivate my students? My goal is to provide every child with opportunities to expand his or her thinking and meet challenges at his or her level.

In my classroom, we work with partners or in groups to accomplish our mathematics goals. At first, it was difficult for me to become more a learning facilitator and less a dispenser of knowledge. This role has become easier for me to accept as I have viewed the positive attitudes my students develop when they take charge of their learning.

After working sessions, we often share our thoughts using the overhead projector. I have found the overhead projector to be motivational for young children. They learn to accept different approaches to solving problems by listening and watching their peers present their results. Through this process, my students have become better risk-takers. When a child's solution approach is incorrect, his or her classmates' questions can often redirect the child's problem-solving efforts.

I have also found the use of individual slates with the children effective in assessing individual performance as well as providing them with a break from paper-and-pencil modes. From time to time, I have my students fill out an interest inventory. These results help me plan mathematics instruction based on their interests.

Research discussed by Renga and Dalla suggests that mathematics anxiety is not as prevalent in the early elementary years as it is in middle school and high school. Nevertheless, I wonder how I can teach children to be persistent in their problem solving without increasing their levels of math anxiety?

Another area of research I would like to know more about is the relationship between the attitudes of teachers and their ability to teach higher levels of thinking and reasoning. Some teachers typically teach higher levels of thinking in mathematics. Do these teachers themselves feel more comfortable with mathematics? How do we create confidence in providing challenging and abstract activities that enhance learning?

Early Number and Numeration and Number Sense (Chapters 3 and 6)

The thought of teaching mathematics through a number awareness approach as described by Van de Walle and Watkins in Chapter 6 and by Payne and Huinker in Chapter 3 is very exciting to me. I do feel that as early childhood educators we are still too often letting textbook pages drive the mathematics curriculum. We need to get beyond the pencil- and-paper aspect of mathematics and create opportunities for mental computation, estimation, and the development of number sense. Children analyze more critically and on higher levels of learning when they are allowed to explore numbers on their own.

One area of research that needs to be examined in elementary education is mental computation. Van de Walle and Watkins state that mental computation is a building block for so many concepts. If we begin to focus on this aspect of mathematics, then the question of assessment arises again. I might begin my exploration by asking children to talk into tape recorders while explaining their mathematical solutions.

The research on place–value in these chapters does concern me. If mentally adding the tens column and then the ones column is a natural progression for adults as well as for children, then why do we approach the addition algorithm from the ones column? I would like to explore the concept of "long addition." Let children add the tens column first, record, add the ones, and then record under the tens. Would this not be more natural for children? We need to look for methods that allow children to focus on whole numbers, not just single digits where the meaning of the number is lost.

Payne and Huinker suggest that very young children should learn to count based on groups of ten. I would like to see more research conducted on the transfer that is made between place–value and counting by tens with young children. If we begin to teach recognition of the tens place at an earlier age, regrouping of numbers should be easier for older children. In my classroom, we constantly use base-ten blocks to explore numbers. The children work with partners using place–value mats while other students demonstrate using overhead base-ten blocks. While playing a banker addition game with the base-ten set, I recently observed a student who had a score of 35 roll "7." He immediately gave the banker five units and asked for a long and two units. He was able to imagine the regrouping of the ten units mentally. Later, when his partner rolled "8," she asked for eight units. She added the eight units to her original number, 27, and then traded ten units for a long declaring she now had three longs and five units or thirty-five. Both students were correct in their addition; however, they each had their own approach. Next time, I will encourage more discussion between the players about the reasoning behind their strategies. Students learn from interacting with one another as well as from manipulatives they use. The manipulatives provide the necessary link between the process and the product that allows each student to have a greater understanding of place–value.

Providing numerous opportunities for children to talk about numbers will help them make "sense" of numbers. We, as educators, need to enlighten the public that children can gain understanding of numbers by studying one problem in depth instead of page after page of problems.

Addition/Subtraction, Multiplication/Division, and Technology (Chapters 4, 5, and 11)

In Chapters 4 and 5, Baroody, Standifer, Kouba, and Franklin also remind us of the importance of providing a connection between a child's informal base of knowledge and the formal instruction we present in our classrooms. Children need the opportunity to develop connections between symbolic mathematics and story problems. Opportunities to think critically are often replaced with factual worksheets. As a teacher, I sometimes feel caught between trying to provide the necessary time to create meaningful connections and knowing what curriculum lies ahead. How do we make the necessary links between process and fact in addition and subtraction, as well as in multiplication and division? In my classroom, children use concrete materials to explain these processes to their peers and me. This method of teaching requires a great deal of time. I find myself constantly behind my colleagues in the text; however, my children have gained an understanding by visualizing the processes.

If we are to enhance a child's ability to solve story problems in addition, subtraction, multiplication, and division without teaching key words, children need to be given the opportunity to devise their own strategies. If you entered my room while my children were working on story problems, you might feel that there was a lack of management. It is not uncommon to hear objections or acclamations of agreement. Children are busy justifying that their solutions are correct. Their knowledge is extended beyond the drill and practice of worksheets because they have created solutions, successfully explained solutions, or modified their solutions based on their own discovery.

As we consider instruction in these processes, we must also consider the role of technological advances in mathematical education. Campbell and Stewart justify the use of technology in the classroom because of the link that is provided between the real world and abstract thinking. In my classroom, children eagerly anticipate their turn at the computer and willingly interact with the program. My most difficult task is to ensure that the software supports, enhances, and supplements the curriculum. Selection of appropriate software is as important as the selection of manipulatives.

When computers and calculators are viewed as tools, we can enrich our students' mathematical thinking and reasoning abilities. Recently, my students were solving word problems that required addition and subtraction. In groups of four, they decided which operation was appropriate and proceeded to use the calculator to find the answer. The use of the calculator would not have been beneficial if they had not known which operation to use. We do our students a disservice when we do not provide opportunities for them to learn how to use these tools.

Problem Solving (Chapter 7)

After reading Chapter 7, I am wondering about ways to promote problem solving in my classroom. The research shows us that there is a correlation between free exploration of problems and successful problem solving. Are we providing our children with opportunities to "invent" their own problems to solve? Are there ways that I can teach second-graders to become more successful problem solvers?

Reflecting on my teaching, I find that I ask my children lots of verbal problems. For example, as we listened to the announcement that Atlanta would host the 1996 Olympics, I posed these questions to them: How old will you be in 1996? How old are the people now who will be in second grade in 1996? The first problem was fairly simplistic for my children. The second created some discussion among them. Some children were "counting on" and convinced that "14" was the answer. Although others knew it was six years away, they were having difficulty in deciding what to do with the six.

As primary teachers, we need to provide children with opportunities to develop reasoning abilities and to become reflective thinkers. We must all experiment to find out what methods will best accomplish this goal for our children. As we interact with children, we need to take into account that their different levels of cognitive development will greatly influence their problem-solving strategies. The challenge is to learn ways of effectively helping children at each of the different developmental levels.

I have had to learn to accept different styles of answers. Some children in my room are more comfortable with manipulative illustrations while others can explain in writing what they have found. Several of my students tape record their answers because their writing abilities are weak. I now believe that a child's understanding is more important than the way he or she conveys that understanding.

As primary teachers, we have an exciting task ahead of us. We are preparing children to become abstract problem solvers. I would like to hear from other teachers and researchers about successful methods for reaching children of different ability levels.

Measurement and Geometry (Chapters 8 and 9)

In Chapters 8 and 9, we are presented with powerful research implications for our classrooms. After reading these chapters, I began to reflect on the sequence of measurement and geometry topics within my curriculum. I hope to create a firm foundation for understanding measurement and geometry through the use of real-world applications.

As a teacher of young children, measurement has been a concept that I incorporate on a daily basis. Within the last two years, I have begun to allow more free exploration of measurement. I have provided opportunities for my students to measure objects without choosing their tools of measurement for them. The child who records the width of the classroom in inches using a ruler will more likely value a yard after observing his or her peers quickly measure the width with a yardstick. After completing a measurement task, my children frequently write about their findings. Their math journals provide me with an opportunity to address individual questions and allow me to assess the knowledge they have gained from the task.

As I assimilate the research from Chapter 9 into my philosophy of mathematics instruction, I am wondering how I can integrate geometry throughout the disciplines to create a sense of real-world application. My experiences with textbooks informs me that geometry, as well as measurement, tends to be taught in isolation. The text cannot provide the experience in manipulating physical materials that children need to develop their spatial abilities.

Fractions and Decimals (Chapter 10)

Langford and Sarullo challenge us to help young children develop a firm foundation for relationships between whole numbers, fractional numbers, and decimals. As early-childhood educators, we need to provide the foundation for these concepts that will facilitate our students' leap into abstract thinking at a later point.

Through the use of number lines, overhead transparencies, fraction bars, and various other manipulatives, my children begin their exploration of fractions. In this chapter, several suggestions are made that I will incorporate into my lessons, such as providing children with more opportunities to compare and contrast fractions as well as opportunities to decide whether a fraction is close to 0 or to 1.

As a second-grade teacher, I would like to explore decimals with my children as I teach fractions. What manipulatives will be beneficial in helping these children understand the concept of decimal value? I find the instruction of this concept to be very exciting. Sometimes we underestimate what children can accomplish. I will be interested to see what they are capable of mastering. What role will working with concrete materials play in helping my children build decimal awareness? What role will talking about decimals play in developing their understanding?

Models of Instruction (Chapter 12)

As teachers, we are constantly searching for ways to foster positive attitudes toward mathematics. In the classroom, our own attitudes are reflected in our instruction. Are we excited about mathematics instruction? Would an outside observer sense eager anticipation during our mathematics lesson? In Chapter 12 Thornton and Wilson impress upon us the importance of our learning environment. We must vary our instruction to encourage children to be active participants in their learning.

After reading this chapter, I am wondering what models of instruction I use more frequently. Some analysis through videotaping my lessons might provide helpful insight into my mathematics instruction. Are my children actively engaged in a variety of activities designed to enhance their learning? Through an on-task analysis of my lessons, I could target the strengths and weaknesses of my lessons. Comparing my analysis of the videotaping with my lesson plans would allow me to see where my plans were effective and what styles of instruction worked well. Since planning time in elementary schools is very limited, I might be overlooking ways to incorporate different styles of teaching. This experience would provide some valuable information for planning future instruction.

Planning and Organizing Curriculum (Chapter 13)

Has our mathematics curriculum become so skill oriented that we have lost sight of the processes? Has our teaching become too product oriented in an effort to accommodate standardized testing? By choosing to use textbooks and curriculum guides as resources instead of the only means to an end, we can satisfy our desire to reach above and beyond the basic skills while also accomplishing our state and local mandates.

Dougherty and Scott concur that curriculum is what we believe mathematics and instruction to be. If we believe that a mathematics curriculum should be an active, process-centered plan that provides for higher levels of mathematical instruction, then how do we accomplish this goal? The NCTM *Curriculum and Evaluation Standards* calls for a refocus of our curriculum. The second-grade teachers at my school made positive changes in our mathematics instruction last year. We realized that memorization of basic facts and mathematical rules does not mean that our students understand mathematics. We now look for ways to make our curriculum more effective by considering alternatives to the textbook. We have found that alternative approaches such as problem solving in cooperative learning groups, manipulatives, games, and computer programs often provide more critical thinking and concrete experiences than are possible in a textbook lesson.

Reflective Practitioner

At this point, you have read about many components of mathematics instruction for young children. Within each chapter, ideas have been supported by research, questions have been raised, and challenges have been issued. You may be somewhat overwhelmed as you think back over what you have reviewed; however, some central thoughts were carried throughout each chapter.

As reflective practioners, our goals should allow us to change, to be willing to try new avenues. To search constantly for methods to make connections between formal and informal mathematics. To have our students verbalize their findings as well as write about them. To listen to student discussions as a means of informal assessment. To try different methods and manipulatives for developing conceptual understanding. To challenge our students to become reflective thinkers.

About the Author

Margaret Ackerman teaches fourth grade at Gwin Oaks Elementary in Lawrenceville, Georgia. Through her graduate work at Emory University, she became interested in helping children become problem posers.

Research Ideas for the Classroom: Middle Grades Mathematics

Contents

Research Ideas for the Classroom: High School Mathematics

Contents

PART III   Teaching

PART IV   Research

Index

Index

A

Ability grouping strategies, 284–86
Ability of student, 319–20
Acceleration, 285
Achievement, 27–28, 319–20
Achievement tests, 16, 53
Active learning approach, 114–16, 175, 273–76
Addition. *See also* Multidigit addition and subtraction; Single-digit addition and subtraction
  Change-Add-To view of, 75, 79, 82, 84, 85
  concepts, 85
  cross-cultural research on, 8
  evolution of calculations in, 7–8
  focus on, 72
  as informal mathematics, 6–7, 75
  part-whole approach to, 51
  reflective practitioner and, 354–55
  teaching, 14–15, 72–74
Administration, 298–99
Affect
  attitudes of students, 23–24
  beliefs of students
    confidence in learning, 25–28
    learned helplessness, 32–33
    mathematics anxiety, 28–30
    self-perceptions, 30–32
  case studies of, 22
  motivation, 33–36
  reflective practitioner and, 352–53
Algorithms, 91–92, 114–16
Allocated time, 271–73
Angles, 182–84, 187
Approximate results, accepting different, 144–45

Area, 180–81
Arithmetic instruction. *See* Teaching
Assessment
  cognition and, 15–17
  by discourse, 17
  of estimation, 336–37
  evaluation and, 342–43
  expanded view of, 330–31
  fairness of tests and, 340–41
  of formal mathematics, 15–17
  of geometry skills, 207–8
  of homework, 307–8
  of informal mathematics, 15–17
  informal means of, 331–35
  measurement of progress and, 329
  of more than numerical answer, 116–17
  of problem solving, 337–40
  purposes of, 330–31
  selecting/designing means of, 331
  technology in, 342
  test fairness, 340–42
  by written work, 16–17
Asymmetrical situations of multiplication and division, 106–10
Attitudes, 23–24, 317–19

B

Base name, 54, 64
Basic fact mastery, 141–42
Beliefs of students
  confidence in learning, 25–28
  learned helplessness, 32–33
  mathematics anxiety, 28–30
  self-perceptions, 30–32
Biases of teachers, 319–22

C